HANDBOOK OF
NATIVE AMERICAN
MYTHOLOGY

Handbook of Native American Mythology

*Dawn E. Bastian
and Judy K. Mitchell*

OXFORD
UNIVERSITY PRESS

OXFORD

UNIVERSITY PRESS

Oxford University Press, Inc., publishes works that further
Oxford University's objective of excellence
in research, scholarship, and education.

Oxford   New York
Auckland   Cape Town   Dar es Salaam   Hong Kong   Karachi
Kuala Lumpur   Madrid   Melbourne   Mexico City   Nairobi
New Delhi   Shanghai   Taipei   Toronto

With offices in
Argentina   Austria   Brazil   Chile   Czech Republic   France   Greece
Guatemala   Hungary   Italy   Japan   Poland   Portugal   Singapore
South Korea   Switzerland   Thailand   Turkey   Ukraine   Vietnam

First published by ABC-Clio, Inc., 2004
130 Cremona Drive, Santa Barbara, CA 93116-1911

First issued as an Oxford University Press paperback, 2008
198 Madison Avenue, New York, NY 10016

www.oup.com

Oxford is a registered trademark of Oxford University Press

Library of Congress Cataloging-in-Publication Data
Bastian, Dawn E. (Dawn Elaine), 1961–
Handbook of Native American mythology /
Dawn E. Bastian and Judy K. Mitchell.
—Oxford University Press Pbk.
p. cm.
Originally published: Santa Barbara, Calif. : ABC-CLIO, 2004,
in series: Handbooks of world mythology.
Includes bibliographical references and index.
ISBN 978-0-19-534232-1 (pbk.)
1. Indian mythology—North America–Handbooks, manuals, etc.
I. Mitchell, Judy K. II. Title.
E98.R3B26 2008
398.2089'97—dc22
2007032137

1 3 5 7 9 8 6 4 2
Printed in the United States of America
on acid-free paper

CONTENTS

PREFACE

Most North Americans possess some knowledge of the entertaining and illuminating world of mythology. This knowledge was typically gained by reading translations of various stories, including those found in biblical literature, or through formal study of art history or the classical texts that have long been a traditional cornerstone of Western literary education. Indeed, North Americans are most familiar with the myths of the ancient Greeks, or their Roman adaptations. It is likely that they have some literary or visual knowledge of the Greek god Zeus as the supreme ruler or lord of the sky, and that his daughter Aphrodite is the goddess of love and beauty. To many, these two are better known by their Roman names, Jupiter and Venus. These same readers would likely know that Hera, or Juno, is Zeus's wife and sister, and that she is a jealous goddess prone to causing trouble. Many know that the story of Persephone and Demeter explains the change of seasons and are aware that there is a Norse god of thunder, war, and strength called Thor. Those with a more in-depth education in the field might also possess the knowledge and ability to converse with some authority about the great epics of Homer and myths of the ancient Egyptians.

Sadly, however, few North Americans have developed much awareness or appreciation of the rich and diverse mythic traditions and heritage of the hundreds of cultures of Native peoples who inhabited the continent before them. Most cannot speak with any knowledge of the culture hero Glooskap, the tricksters Coyote and Raven, the sea woman Sedna, or the many tales of creation that feature animal characters like Beaver, Duck, Mink, Muskrat, Turtle, or Loon. However, the fascinating and lively panorama of imaginary beasts, human heroes, powers of nature, and nurturing spirits that comprise one of the world's most varied and abundant bodies of mythology was already firmly established when the first European explorers came to the Americas around 1500. Certainly, a familiarity and understanding of the mythology of the continent on which we live is just as important as a knowledge of the mythology of the ancient Greeks and Egyptians and northern Europeans.

This *Handbook of Native American Mythology* is designed to introduce the reader to the mythology of cultures found in native North America, including the region from north of Mexico to the Arctic Circle.[1] Users will include those interested in researching, browsing, or identifying material on the topic—teachers and students, and those reading for pleasure and exploring the subject out of self-interest. Although the myths of Native Americans have been recorded since the first European contacts, research shows that it is difficult to place them within specific time periods because they are a part of oral traditions that have often changed and evolved through history as they were told, re-told, and intentionally polished to fit the needs or suit the literary tastes of a specific audience. They are placed in historical context in the introduction and the chapter on time.

Because this is a reference work for a general audience, with the intent of guiding the user to information in studies that are more narrow, detailed, and focused, its own content and coverage is broader. It would be impossible, given the scope of this study, to be comprehensive or deeply analytical. As a result, for example, we did not analyze differences in mythological traditions between regions, explore links between the historical record and the development of those traditions, trace the diffusion of mythic elements across Native cultures, or distinguish between mythical ideas that are exclusively Native and those that originated with Europeans. Such discussions are best treated in smaller, more limited studies that are usually scholarly in nature.

An examination of our focus reveals that, in selecting entries, we aimed to achieve broad cultural and regional representation across North America. We also chose themes or stories that are important because they distinguish a particular culture or cut across cultures. We also identified myths that are less well-known but thought to be as interesting or entertaining to others as they were to us. While we realize that Native American mythology, ritual, and religion are often intertwined and difficult to separate, we have deliberately chosen not to expound on the theological aspects, where they exist, of the stories, legends, and mythological characters. Other reference resources delve into those issues, and we have cited some of them in the bibliography.

In this volume's introductory chapter, we explore the topic of myth in general and explain the definition, selected from among the many that exist, that we used to focus this work. We also explore the geography and climate of the North American continent and briefly discuss the history of Native peoples in North America. In addition, we consider the ten culture areas American anthropologists use to organize the study of topics related to Native Americans, including mythology, and the sources and development of the study of Native American myths. In the second chapter, we explore history and time from a mythic viewpoint. The third chapter is comprised entirely of selected entries, arranged alphabetically, of characters, themes, and stories from Native American mythology. An annotated bibliography of selected print and nonprint resources follows. A glossary, list of references, and subject index are also included. The bibliography and references will be helpful to those wishing to pursue further information and study.

This volume reflects the state of published research on Native American mythology. This means that some or all of the information in many entries is derived from the work of non-Native historians, anthropologists, and ethnographers, many of whom were active in the nineteenth and early twentieth centuries. In addition, some of their publications are found in the list of references and the bibliography, publications that are a record of the past and reflect the attitudes, beliefs, and perspectives of different times. As librarians, we thought it important to consult and present a variety of works that support study of the topic, including those that may contain material that is offensive to some readers. We do not in any way endorse the views found in these resources. We thought it of paramount importance to use, whenever possible, works by Native Americans as the basis for this study, and we have also selected print and electronic resources by Native Americans for inclusion in the bibliography, plus videos and DVDs made by Native American–owned firms or in consultation with Native American advisors, organizations, or institutions.

A NOTE ABOUT VARIANT AND PREFERRED NAMES AND SPELLINGS

Tribal names and spellings of those names have varied considerably over the centuries, and still do. For example, the Navajo have declared a preference for that spelling over *Navaho*. In addition, many Navajo routinely call themselves *Dineh (Diné)*, their traditional name in their native language, though the group as a whole continues to refer to itself as *the Navajo Nation. Ojibwa, Ojibway,* and *Chippewa* are all variant names for the same people who have always referred to themselves by their traditional name of *Anishinabe*. The former Winnebago of Wisconsin have officially renamed themselves the *Ho-Chunk*, but the Winnebago of Nebraska still retain this name. *Sioux* is the popular name for the Dakota, Lakota, and Nakota peoples. For consistency within this work, and ease of information retrieval in library catalogs, we have chosen to use the standard form of tribal name found in the twenty-sixth edition (2003) of the controlled vocabulary known as the *Library of Congress Subject Headings (LCSH)*. Almost all tribal names used in this work happen to reflect common usage; in those rare cases when they do not, the commonly used term has been supplied in the text in parentheses. It should be noted that the standard form of a tribal name found in *LCSH* and the commonly used term are not necessarily the terms preferred by Native American peoples.

In the United States, the terms *Native Americans* and *American Indians* tend to be used interchangeably. The preferred collective name for Native peoples in Canada is *First Nations*.

A NOTE ABOUT INUIT AND ESKIMO

The aboriginal peoples of the Arctic have long been known by the popular term *Eskimo*. Those who inhabit the region from northern Alaska to western Greenland prefer to call themselves *Inuit*, which means "the people" in the Inuit language. Many Inuit regard the word *Eskimo* as pejorative, in part because it was long thought, erroneously, to mean literally "eater of raw meat." In Canada, use of the word *Eskimo* has practically vanished, and *Inuit* is used officially by the Canadian government. In Alaska, however, there are two language and culture groups, the Inupiat and the Yupik. While the word *Inuit* exists in the Inupiat language, it does not exist in Yupik, Alaska's most widely spoken Native language. The indigenous people of southwestern Alaska prefer to be called *Yupik* or *Yupik Eskimo*, and those from northwestern Alaska prefer the term *Inupiat*.

Regardless of the local self-designations mentioned above, *Inuit* has also come to be used in a wider sense, in reference to all Native people traditionally called *Eskimo*. Nevertheless, the term *Eskimo* continues to be used worldwide, especially in historical and archaeological contexts, and in reference to the indigenous Arctic peoples as a cultural and linguistic entity.

ACKNOWLEDGMENTS

As with any project of this magnitude, there are many whom we must thank for their invaluable assistance in completing it. They include Joan Beam and Barbara Branstad of the Morgan Library Reference Department of Colorado State University, and Dr. Irene Vernon of the Center for Applied Studies in American Ethnicity, all of whom provided advice and opinions. In addition, Allison Cowgill, also from the Reference Department of Morgan Library, offered her editorial services and located information. Finally, the staff of the Access Services and Interlibrary Loan departments assisted us in obtaining materials not held by the Library.

1

INTRODUCTION

What, exactly, is a myth? This question elicits a variety of responses, since many definitions exist and long-term scholarly debates about the meaning of the word continue. Most would probably reply that myths are the traditional stories, stories that are not true, of a particular culture. A religious historian might say that a myth is an expression in words of sacred rites or beliefs. An anthropologist would likely refer to a myth as a narrative that justifies a behavior, practice, or social institution. Myths are commonly defined as stories that attempt to explain something, such as a natural phenomenon or the origin of the world; myths are stories about gods and goddesses, or heroes and heroines; myths are stories used to educate or to provide guidance by sharing collective knowledge or experience. All of these definitions are valid, and, in fact, myths are true—true because they are based on reality and address issues of the tangible world in which we live, even if the characters and events themselves are imaginary.

One of the reasons it is difficult to define the term *myth* is because of similarities and analogies between myths and other traditional literary or narrative forms. Examples include legends, fables, fairy tales, folktales, sagas, epics, and parables. As with myth, there is no consensus among scholars regarding definitions, and boundaries for these terms tend to be fluid. Scholars also disagree about how the various genres relate to both myths and each other. Myth, folktale, and legend often merge in a particular narrative; this is particularly true if the story is lengthy and elaborate, or if it has been retold many times over a long period. Nevertheless, some useful lines of distinction can be drawn between myths and all of the aforementioned, with the possible exception of folktales.

Folktales are sometimes considered a subdivision of myth, and myths are sometimes thought to be a branch of folktale. Eminent American folklorist Stith Thompson declares that "attempts at exact definition of 'myth' as distinguished from 'tale' seem futile" (Thompson 1971, xvii). He believes the one particular characteristic of myth that differentiates it from folktale is the nature of its narratives. They feature the world as it was in the past, and explain the origin and creation of its current condition. Some scholars, such as British classicist Geoffrey S. Kirk, regard the two categories as distinct but overlapping. In his *Myth: Its Meaning and Functions in Ancient and Other Cultures*, he declares that myths serve a purpose other than to simply tell a story, whereas folktales "tend to reflect simple social situations; they play on ordinary fears and desires as well as on men's appreciation of neat and ingenious solutions . . ." (1970, 41). Examples of themes that occur in folktales include adversarial encounters between humans and supernatural beings such as witches, ogres, or giants; contests to win a bride; or triumphs by trickster heroes over an opponent using wit and cunning. Since these motifs often appear in stories that are classified as myths as well, it is readily apparent that distinguishing myths from folktales is a complex and perhaps impossible task.

In this *Handbook of Native American Mythology*, we have not attempted to make any distinction between myth and folktale, legend, or other forms of story. We have considered as myth any story that bears the imprint of a specific Native American culture, or of Native American cultures in general, whether it explains the existence of some belief or natural phenomenon, tells about tribal customs, describes the origin and establishment of rituals, instructs in proper behavior, or simply entertains.

FUNCTIONS OF MYTH

Myth has two primary functions. The first is to provide an explanation of facts, whether natural or cultural. Mythology evolved as peoples sought to answer questions about their world: Who was the first man? How was fire acquired? Where did the salt we use every day come from? A myth of the Wyandot (Huron) of the Great Lakes region, for example, tells of the origin of tobacco: a dead girl's father discovers an injured hawk that bursts into flames as he approaches it. All that remains is a flaming coal, in which he sees his daughter's face. She tells her father of a precious gift she has for her people, a gift of tobacco seed, and stays to show him how to raise and harvest this new crop. In addition to providing an explanation, the narrative form and imaginative qualities of a myth such as this lend credibility to the explanation and transforms it into something memorable and lasting.

The second primary function of myth is to justify, validate, or explain the existence of a social system and traditional rites and customs. In Potawatomi origin stories from the Northeast, for example, the culture hero Wiske creates the Potawatomi clans and gives them medicine bundles. Each clan has a bundle that is associated with specific rights and obligations. The Man clan has rules for ritual use of its bundle before going to war. Members of the Fish clan renew their medicine four times a year. The Siksika (Blackfeet) hold a sacred Sun Dance each summer, a ceremony of thanks for the Creator's blessing, to commemorate and honor a gesture of the Sun told in a story about Star Boy. Star Boy and his mother are cast down from the Sky World because of her disobedience. He is marked with a mysterious scar and becomes known as Scarface. In order to marry, he makes a journey to the Sun and gains the Sun's forgiveness for his mother's transgression. The Sun removes the scar and Star Boy returns to earth, his bride, and his people with the sacred knowledge of the Sun Dance. After death, he is taken back to the Sky World.

Myth also has secondary functions. Myths are important as a vehicle for instruction. Those that portray, for example, the origin or end of the world, the land of the dead, or paradise, describe what people are unable to understand and experience for themselves. Myths often comprise the most important model for teaching and learning in traditional, preindustrial societies, since a formal and separate system of law or philosophical inquiry does not exist. They illustrate noble conduct by example and demonstrate bad conduct by showcasing its ill consequences.

Myths also function as sources of healing, renewal, and inspiration. Recitation of creation myths plays a significant role in healing the sick among the Navajo. Icelandic poets are said to be celebrating the origins of their art and therefore renewing it when they sing of the Norse god Odin winning the "mead of song" (a drink containing the power of poetic inspiration) for both gods and men. Myths have inspired and influenced self-expression in archaic and modern societies alike. Mythical themes and images from classical Greek and Roman mythology are widely prevalent, for example, in Western art and literature.

Ruling families and elites of ancient civilizations and societies worldwide frequently based their claims to position, power, and privilege on mythological origins. Known examples come from Ancient Greece, pharaonic Egypt, Imperial China, West Africa, India, Polynesia, and the empires of the Hittites and Incas. Justification of marriage and funerary customs from every known cultural tradition, including those of Native Americans, is grounded in mythology.

TYPES OF MYTH

Myths come in a wide variety of categories. There are creation or origin myths, myths of death and destruction, and myths about culture heroes. Some myths focus on nature, time and eternity, providence and destiny, memory and forgetfulness, or birth and renewal. Some feature high beings or celestial gods, founders of religion or religious figures, or kings and ascetics. Myths can hold special meaning for just one person or for many. Families have their own myths, as do schools, organizations, associations, institutions, neighborhoods, cities, regions, and countries. Myths often reflect the worldviews of various social classes.

Kirk proposes three main categories of myths (1970, 252–261). His first category includes mythical narratives told solely for entertainment. Some may challenge the validity of this category, as myths that fall into it are rare—or these stories might more plausibly be classified as folktales or legends. His second category includes operative, iterative, or validatory myths that are thought to have the power to change the world, and "tend to be repeated regularly on ritual or ceremonial occasions . . . to bring about a desirable continuity in nature or society" (1970, 254–255). The stories are meant to *do* something as much as *say* something—to cure illness, to ensure that a king's power continues, to prepare for hunts, to bring rain, to move one along through the cycle of life. Within this second category falls the model or charter myths that validate, record, and provide authority for a people's customs and institutions. Kirk's third category includes explanatory or speculative myths. These may simply explain the origin of a natural feature, animal, or object (etiological myths), or they may be complex stories that attempt to provide answers to questions that perplex humanity, such as why natural disasters occur or people die. Some myths appear to recognize that some of these difficult questions may not have answers. Instead, they provide the strength, ability, and will to face the mysteries, contradictions, and sorrows of life. All of these categories of myths are represented in the mythology of Native Americans. Before exploring this mythology, it is useful to consider the geography and climate of North America, excluding the area south of northern Mexico, because associations between geography, climate, and Native American myths are strong.

GEOGRAPHY AND CLIMATE OF NORTH AMERICA

The vast North American continent, shaped roughly like an inverted triangle, extends from the permanent Arctic ice cap to the subtropical areas of Florida and California. A highland zone in the east includes the ancient Appalachian Mountains and a low, rocky plateau of Precambrian rock known as the Canadian Shield. Also in Canada are the Laurentian Highlands in Quebec, and the Torngat Mountains in northern Labrador. This entire zone is called the Eastern Highlands. In the west, much younger, more rugged mountain chains run north to south in a complex zone interspersed with plateaus and hills. Known as the Western Highlands, this area includes a double range of mountains along the coast, the Sierra Nevada and the Cascades farther inland, and the Rocky Mountains farther east. Within this area is a huge dry valley in Utah and the surrounding region. Between these two major mountainous areas of the east and west lies the high plains, a vast region of prairie, and a tremendous area of low plains running almost continuously from the Arctic Ocean to the Gulf of Mexico, including the river basins of the Mississippi and Missouri. This is the Interior Plain. During the last ice age, the plains of the north were scoured out, producing a region where low sandy hills have dammed up the waterways to produce the Hudson Bay and the Great Lakes. Within this immense area, few natural barriers existed that would impede migration.

The climates of North America are as extraordinarily diverse as its geography. Ranging from tropical in the southernmost part of Florida to polar in the Canadian Archipelago and Greenland, certain well-defined climactic types are recognizable, except in the high mountain areas, where climactic distribution is spotty and conditions vary by site and exposure to sun and wind. Some climactic belts run east and west but are not continuous from coast to coast because they are broken by variations in elevation, particularly in the western and southwestern United States. Moving northward and northeastward from the southwestern United States, temperatures are lower in both summer and winter. Along the entire West Coast, the ocean has a moderating effect on temperature and winters are mild. The East Coast is less affected by ocean currents.

Adjacent to the mountains in the west is a vast interior area of arid and semi-arid climate. Starting on the west coast just south of Los Angeles, it can be followed inland and northward along the eastern face of the Sierra Nevada and Cascade mountain ranges. It continues around the central Rockies and north into southern Alberta in Canada. It then leaves the Rockies and swings east and south in an arc across the Great Plains into southern Texas. Within this dry belt, temperatures fluctuate markedly, both daily and seasonally.

East of the Rockies, climactic belts stretch farther without interruption. The southern tip of Florida has a truly tropical climate, with ample rainfall, hot, humid weather, and virtually no true winter. Moving northward from Florida to approximately the line of the Ohio and Missouri rivers, running from the Atlantic coast to the Great Plains, is a subtropical climate with mild, humid winters and hot, humid summers. Even farther north, extending almost to the shores of the Arctic, lies a belt of extreme climate where summers are hot and humid and winters are cold, humid, and severe. The severity of the winters gradually increases and summers are less warm and less humid as one moves farther and farther to the north. Through central Alaska and Canada north of the St. Lawrence–Great Lakes line, summers are short and winters long and excessively cold. Offsetting the shorter summers are long daylight hours, while extensive hours of darkness compound the severity of winter. Along the Arctic Coast and over to the Canadian Archipelago and Greenland, there is no true summer season. Average temperatures during the warmest months barely rise above freezing over a majority of the area, and snow and ice cover is permanent over most of Ellesmere Island and the interior of Greenland.

Precipitation on the continent varies tremendously, from a high of 96 to 128 inches on the northwest coast to a low of 0 to 16 inches in the desert areas of the southwestern United States and northern Mexico. Throughout the dry belt of the interior, rains are infrequent and unreliable. Moving eastward on the Great Plains, moisture becomes gradually more plentiful and reliable. Generally, moving inland away from the coastal areas, rainfall decreases and becomes less frequent. As with rain, snowfall within the northernmost climactic belts is heavier on the coasts and tends to be lighter in the interior.

THE FIRST NATIVE AMERICANS

According to scholars, archaeological evidence suggests that the earliest ancestors of the Native Americans, referred to as "Paleo-Indians," were nomadic hunters from Asia who migrated to the continent probably during the last glacial period (Wisconsin) some 20,000 to 35,000 years ago.[2] Some have asserted that the first arrivals came even earlier, perhaps as early as 60,000 years ago. It is believed that they crossed the Bering Strait land bridge between Siberia and what is now Alaska, which was then exposed by a drop in sea level, in pursuit of the large game animals on which their livelihood depended.[3] Latter arrivals, including the Aleut, Athabascan, and Inuit peoples, no doubt followed the same route, probably crossing by boat or on winter ice after the land bridge sank once again under water, about 8000 B.C.E. These newcomers shared certain ancient cultural traits with their Eurasian and African contemporaries, including the use of fire, the domesticated dog, various types of stone implements, cordage, netting, and basketry, and particular rites and healing beliefs.

Early Paleo-Indians were hunters and gatherers whose cultures predate the adoption of horticulture and the bow and arrow. In response to climactic changes and population pressures that impacted their plant and animal food sources, these wandering hunters and their descendants eventually settled throughout the Americas, adapting to new ecological conditions and developing a variety of indigenous cultures over a period of seven or eight thousand years. Groups that lived in areas where a variety of game was plentiful became hunters almost exclusively. Those who lived near rivers, lakes, and the ocean learned to fish. Still others, who lived in areas where rainfall was sparse and animals and fish were relatively scarce, largely became gatherers and foragers, living off whatever plants and animals the land provided. And some survived chiefly by acting as middlemen in the trade that flourished over distances short and long between people exchanging surplus raw materials and handicrafts for necessary items that were lacking or in short supply in their own areas. New weapons were invented and new hunting techniques evolved, and people devised new tools, dwellings, clothing, and craft for water travel. Sometime around 1500 B.C.E., some native groups expanded their food supply by adopting horticulture in places where there was good soil and ample water resources, leading to a more sedentary life in villages that were larger and more permanent.

Scholars refer to the later native peoples who led a life that was more complex and locally focused as "Archaic Indians" to distinguish them from their "Paleo-Indian" ancestors. As they proliferated and learned to exploit their environment, they became more distinctive culturally, developing specific languages, oral traditions, rituals, customs, and strategies for survival. This process of cultural differentiation occurred most rapidly and profoundly among the native peoples of the Pacific Northwest and northern California, an area rich in both resources and micro-environments.

By the time of first contact with the Europeans at the end of the fifteenth century, a mosaic of Native American cultures had existed in all parts of the North American continent for thousands of years, and native population patterns were well established. Though archaeological evidence suggests that much of the Americas was densely settled by 1492, it is difficult for scholars to arrive at accurate estimates of the aboriginal population then. Information is scant, as natives lacked statistical records and their first conquerors rarely kept any. Data on which estimates are based were gathered by traders, missionaries, explorers, and others, and that information is only as valuable as their observations were reliable. A significant complication is that by the time this data was collected, some of the native populations had already been sharply reduced by European diseases. Estimates for the pre-Columbian populations of the Americas have ranged from a low of about 10 million to a high of 100 million or more.[4] Following European contact it is certain, however, that Native American populations suffered rapid and steady decline. Only in the twentieth century did their numbers begin to increase, partly in response to a decrease in infant mortality.

Native Americans once spoke a variety of languages. It is difficult to determine an exact number, since many became extinct following contact between Natives and Europeans.[5] Native American languages as a whole do not comprise a group of languages that are linked historically (as Indo-European languages are, for example). Furthermore, while different theories have been advanced, none has acceptably demonstrated a relationship between Native American languages and any language group in the Old World. The only possible exception is a proposed link between the Eskimo-Aleut family and some languages of nearby Siberia (Champagne 2001, 448–449). Therefore, it appears that the ancestors of Native Americans migrated so long ago that any relationship that did exist was lost via linguistic change.

European conquest and colonization ultimately led to the extinction of many Native American language groups and greatly impacted those that did survive. Though more than 100 native languages may still be spoken in North America, one-third of the aboriginal languages north of Mexico have disappeared entirely, and most of the surviving languages are slowly dying out. Those that continue to flourish include Cherokee, spoken in Oklahoma and North Carolina; the Assiniboine dialect of the Dakota language in the northern portions of the Midwest; Navajo in New Mexico and Arizona; and Ojibwa in the northern United States and southern Canada. Among these groups, however, a high proportion of speakers are bilingual.

MAJOR CULTURE AREAS OF NATIVE AMERICA

For the purposes of organizing just about any subject related to Native Americans, American anthropologists have grouped tribes into about ten culture areas based on locations that largely reflect geographic or environmental differences. The exact number depends on what system is used; the Smithsonian Institution's *Handbook of North American Indians*, a comprehensive, multivolume work that began publication in 1978, recognizes the following: Arctic, Subarctic, Northwest Coast, California, Southwest, Great Basin, Plateau, Plains, Southeast, and Northeast.[6] Each area is thought to have its own distinctive style or styles of culture. To provide a context for appreciating the wide variety of myths and stories told in the various regions of the North American continent, we will consider each culture area in turn.

Arctic

In North America, the Arctic culture area extends from southern Alaska and around the northern rim of the continent to eastern Greenland. In the west, it extends into northeast Siberia, making it the longest continuous stretch of terrain occupied by a single common culture and language group anywhere in the world. Bordered by crashing seas and quiet bays, the Arctic is a vast desert of

The "wolf dance" of the Kaviagamutes Eskimo of Alaska, ca. 1914. (Library of Congress)

cold ice, treeless tundra, and rocky islands and beaches. The population of the Arctic has always been relatively small, as this land is a difficult one, though with a stark and fantastic beauty of its own. One of two primary native groups found here is the Inuit ("The People"), long a source of fascination to explorers and scholars; the other is the Aleuts of the nearly 100 islands of the Aleutian archipelago off the southwest coast of Alaska. Both groups developed a remarkable culture that enabled them to survive the conditions of the earth's cruelest environment.

Inuits are commonly thought to embody the characteristics of that group living the farthest north, on Canada's Arctic islands and along northwestern Greenland. They retained their traditional customs longer than Inuit from other areas, because they remained relatively uninfluenced by European culture until the early part of the twentieth century. Here the Inuit dressed in heavy fur clothing for most of the year, lived in snow igloos, hunted seals and walrus, and, aided by their dogs, pursued polar bears across the vast ice fields. The reality, however, is that the culture of the Inuit exhibited variations by region. In other areas, the economy was based on hunting and fishing of various other wildlife, including salmon, whitefish, trout, capelin, the narwhal, beluga or bowhead whales, seals, walrus, or caribou. Of primary importance to most Inuit was the seal.

Because of the harsh and demanding world they inhabited, life for the Inuit was always difficult, and survival a never-ending struggle. Fearing starvation, the Inuit led a nomadic existence following the available supply of game. Because they moved regularly, they did not evolve political structures or lead a highly developed village life. Today, many Inuit continue to subsist by hunting and fishing the same species they harvested in aboriginal times. But various forms of wage labor have become increasingly common, and many Inuit have been drawn into government service, the military or communications, or work in trading stores, the oil fields, mines, or tourism-related occupations.

Like the Inuit, the Aleuts became experts at deriving maximum benefit from the meager resources their forbidding environment had to offer. Their villages were always located on the shore because they subsisted by gathering the resources of the sea. Sea lions, seals, whales, sea otters, fish, shellfish, and ocean birds were important sources of food. Inland areas were important for eggs, roots and berries, stone for weapons, grass for weaving, and heath for fuel. Many dwellings were partially underground to protect against the cold, damp, foggy weather. Clothing worn by men included skirts of feathered bird skins, while women used sea otter and fur seal skins. Aleut women were skilled sewers, weavers, and basket makers. The Aleuts had a system of social classes, a system that included slaves. Because they were an island people, the Aleuts tended to be more settled than most Inuit.

Today, the Aleuts' traditional way of life has been almost completely abandoned. More than a century of oppression and slavery followed the Russian exploration and occupation of the Aleutian Islands in the 1700s. Brutalized and exposed to diseases of the white man, thousands of Aleuts perished. By 1867, when the United States purchased Alaska and assumed control of the islands, the native population had dropped from more than 15,000 to 2,500. Today, the small numbers of remaining Aleuts are primarily commercial fishermen.

Myths of the Arctic culture area commonly feature tricksters, shamans and shamanic journeys, and a mistress of sea animals.

Subarctic

The Subarctic culture area covers most of Canada, except for the Northwest Coast and the Arctic margin, and includes the interior of Alaska. It reaches south to where the Great Plains and cultivable lands begin. Given the vast land area included in the Subarctic, the population was always relatively small. The Indians who lived here faced a constant foe in the weather and harsh climate, as this was a cold, wet region of tundra, forests, mountains, rivers, lakes, swamps, and other waterlogged land. During the few weeks of summer, it rained heavily, while winters were long and marked by deep snows and savage temperatures. All conspired to make travel extremely difficult except by canoe, toboggan, or snowshoes. The Subarctic was home to various Native American peoples that can be divided into two great language groups: the Athabascan speakers of western Canada and the Alaskan interior (such as the Ahtena, Chipewyan, Dena'ina (Tanaina), Dogrib, Kawchottine (Hare), Kaska, and Tsattine (Beaver), and the Algonquian speakers of eastern Canada (including the Cree, Ojibwa, Montagnais, Naskapi, and others).

Most Native Americans who lived in the Subarctic were nomadic peoples who hunted the vast migrating herds of caribou, from which they derived virtually all necessities of life. Fish were important too, especially when game was scarce. Dwellings of bent poles and tanned caribou skins were not permanent and were designed to be easily moved. The family was the basic social unit. Subarctic tribes lived off the land, on a bare subsistence level, which discouraged the formation of large, interdependent groups that were not as likely to survive in a time of crisis as small, self-sufficient ones. Others were a much less mobile forest hunting and fishing people, tracking smaller groups of migrating caribou and deer, moose, bear, beaver, and other small game. Hunting and fishing were supplemented with plant gathering. Villages were small and had no political or tribal character, as they were typically comprised of autonomous family groups. Birchbark was a staple, used for everything from canoes to wigwams to cooking vessels.

The decline and dissolution of the Subarctic culture was a response to a disruption of the area by the fur trade in the sixteenth and seventeenth centuries. Like other Indians of the continent, those living in the Subarctic had been self-sufficient, hunting and gathering food, making their own tools, and bartering with one another. Following the establishment of the Hudson's Bay Company, whose primary objective was to acquire furs for the European market, trading posts were set up in the Canadian wilderness. Here, goods such as wool blankets, copper pots, bolts of fabric, and muskets were offered to the Indians in exchange for pelts. The Indians became dependent on this readymade merchandise and abandoned their traditional handicraft products. Hunting evolved from a subsistence activity to a commercial one as they focused on supplying the white traders with pelts, mostly beaver. Since beaver were most easily caught by trapping, hunting became an individual endeavor rather than the communal activity it was when caribou were the main target. Competition and conflict developed among and even within tribal groups, and traditional domains were no longer respected. Instead of migrating in pursuit of animals, the Indians settled near the trading posts, where women and children lived in permanent villages while the men went away for extended periods to trap. Indians prospered as never before—as long as the supply of beaver held out. When the beaver became nearly extinct in the Subarctic by the beginning of the nineteenth century, poverty was all that remained. Disease, alcoholism, and other Western influences also took their toll.

The Earth Diver creation myth and myths that feature transformers and tricksters are found in the Subarctic.

Northwest Coast

The natives who inhabited the rugged coastal terrain stretching from southern Alaska through British Columbia and as far south as northern California belonged to numerous cultures. Collectively called the Northwest Coast Indians, they enjoyed a temperate but damp climate and a relatively comfortable life amidst the bounty of the ocean and the countless rivers of the region. Important groups were, from north to south, the Haida, Hupa, Karok, Kwakiutl, Nootka, Salish, Tlingit, Tsimshian, and Yurok.

While these Indians depended almost entirely upon the rich supply of salmon for their livelihood, there were also candlefish, cod, halibut, herring, and smelts. Whales, porpoises, sea otters, sea lions, and hair seals abounded. Clams, mussels, sea urchins, and the eggs of seabirds were theirs for the taking. The land, too, offered riches: caribou, moose, mountain sheep and goats, deer, and a wealth of small animals as well as roots and berries. Agriculture was not practiced. The wood of the forest were used for constructing homes and canoes; bark fibers and mountain-goat wool were used to make clothing and blankets. So numerous were the available resources, and so thoroughly were they exploited using highly specialized technology, that these peoples were able to achieve a complex, sophisticated, and affluent culture with a highly stratified social structure that was unrivaled by any other people north of Mexico.

Villages were built on the mainland shores and on the mountainous offshore islands near the mouths of rapidly flowing rivers. While housing varied in design from tribe to tribe, all were built of heavy wooden posts and beams in a square or rectangular shape, with cedar planking for walls and roofs. Village populations traditionally consisted of 100 or more related people; each person in every village was ranked according to his or her closeness to the head leader or chief. This strict hierarchical system only excluded an outcast or slave category that was comprised of war captives and debtors.

Individual and group wealth was highly valued and measured by a count of possessions such as cedar-bark blankets, dried fish and fish oil, dentalium shells, dugout canoes, slaves, and carved pieces of metal known as *coppers*. The interwoven themes of rank and wealth, so prevalent in Northwest cultures, were dramatically expressed in an elaborate ceremonial display of giving and receiving known as the *potlatch*. The host of a potlatch acquired rights of rank and status by giving gifts that were evidence of wealth, while the guests' acceptance of these gifts meant they acknowledged the validity of the host's claims. While the potlatch served this same purpose among tribal groups all along the Northwest Coast, procedures varied from one group to another.

Kaw-Claa. Tlingit native woman in full potlatch dancing costume. (Library of Congress)

Danish explorer Vitus Bering first discovered the Northwest Coast Indians in 1741 while sailing under the auspices of the Russian crown and seeking the possible existence of a land bridge between the southern tip of Siberia and the American mainland. Although fleeting, this contact resulted in discovery of the rich, lustrous fur pelt of the sea otter in this area. The fur trade and territorial ambitions brought at least 100 ships to the Northwest Coast between 1774 and 1794. Conflict, disease, guns, and alcohol took their rapid toll, and the traditional culture and economy of the people was severely undermined.

Stories about clans and lineage, the transformer, the trickster, and the relationship between hunters and animals are all part of Northwest Coast mythology.

California

The Indians of California were fortunate to live in a rich and spacious environment that covered approximately the current area of the state, minus the southeast section along the Colorado River. The climate was favorable, without extremes, and rain fell generously on the western slopes of the mountains. Food was varied and abundant, and raw materials for shelter, clothing, tools, and weapons were plentiful and easily obtained.

Conditions here allowed the native peoples to flourish, and the aboriginal population was estimated at more than 300,000 people at the time of first contact in 1540. California was marked by a great complexity of tribal groups and languages; some 100 tribes and bands spoke more than 200 independent dialects. This mix suggests that the immigrant peoples who populated California were unrelated by language, and their separation by mountain, valley, and coastland within this vast territory fostered divergence in dialects. Prominent groups included the Chumash, Maidu, Miwok, Modoc, Ohlone (Costano), Patwin, Pomo, Salinan, Wintun, Yokuts, and Yuki.

Despite the great diversity among the native populations and their languages, cultural patterns that developed among them exhibited more similarities than differences. All native Californians were primarily foragers and practiced no agriculture except along the Colorado River. They relied heavily on plant foods, including acorns, grass seeds, cattails, and others. Fish were also a staple for almost all groups, and deer, elk, smaller game, and birds were hunted. Clothing was typically made of hides, and dwellings were simple and made to house a single family, the basic social unit. Basket weaving was the main form of artistic expression. Villages were typically comprised of a small group of families related through the male line. These villages were self-contained and not allied with any tribal organization; common rights were extended to all within their living space, which was defined by custom and tradition.

Juan Rodriguez Cabrillo explored California and made contact first with the coastal natives in 1542. His ship was followed by hundreds of others whose impact on the native inhabitants is still unclear. In the mid-eighteenth century, Spain decided to tighten the claim it had made on California, fearing it would be contested by the British or Russians and would therefore threaten its more valuable empire to the south.

To achieve this objective, the Spanish established a string of missions along the coast, the first in 1769, that would give Spain a physical presence, establish a buttress against Protestantism and Orthodoxy by converting the Native Americans to Roman Catholicism, and create a native labor force for future development by gradually moving the native peoples away from gathering and hunting and convincing them to adopt a life of peasantry. The Mission Period lasted only 65 years, but this proved to be plenty of time to effect the almost complete demise of Indian culture in California. The diet of the native people changed; they became susceptible to alcohol; and they surrendered their own religion, language, and independent village life. Because the Spanish failed to colonize north of San Francisco, some escaped the mission experience but later fell prey to the effects of the gold rush that began in 1848. The tide of expansionism that followed ensured that the native peoples were dispossessed of their land. By 1900 fewer than 15,000 survived, their cultural traditions largely destroyed.

Origin myths, animal myths, and stories of tricksters and transformers are common in the California culture area.

Great Basin

The Great Basin, a vast expanse of desert and salt flats intersected by mountains, centers on the modern states of Nevada and Utah and extends into portions of California, Oregon, Idaho, Wyoming, and Colorado. Here the dry climate was marked by extremes of seasonal heat and cold, with a widely scattered population that for centuries had managed to wrest a living from a rigorous and inhospitable environment. Major groups, nearly all of whom spoke Shoshonean languages, included the Bannock, Paiute, Ute, Washo, and others.

Prior to European contact, these nomadic peoples lived primarily as foragers and gatherers, in small bands often comprised of just a single family. Because rainfall in the Basin was minimal, agriculture was not practiced. Since large game animals were scarce, scattered, and difficult to stalk, hunting was not a primary mean of acquiring food or clothing. During the summer, the native peoples subsisted on wild seeds, roots, berries, pine nuts, and cactus fruits; insects, snakes, lizards, fish, and small mammals were also eaten, along with the occasional antelope and deer. In the winter, fish and game were scarce, and they were forced to rely on foods that had been gathered and stored during the summer. As the people were constantly moving in search of food, water, and firewood, only rudimentary shelters were constructed. Made of willow poles covered with reeds or brush, they were built whenever and wherever the people happened to camp, and freely abandoned to the weather or the next group who found them.

Because the independent, self-sufficient family was the principal unit of the Basin people, social and political organization was casual. Families came together with others only to form large communal bands for special events such as certain hunts or dancing, typically during brief periods of plenty or the lean winter months. Leadership was informal and usually exerted by respected elders, usually males.

During the eighteenth and early nineteenth centuries, some of the Great Basin peoples acquired horses, formed bands of mounted hunters and warriors,

Paiute Indian group posed in front of adobe house. (Library of Congress)

and adopted some of the cultural characteristics of the Plains Indians. The real catalysts for change, however, were the discovery of California gold in 1848 and the subsequent discovery of both gold and silver in Nevada. Because native cultures were based on the cycles of nature and the barest margin of survival, they quickly collapsed and disappeared as prospectors and settlers freely dispossessed the peoples of their lives and land.

Many trickster and heroine myths are found in the mythologies of the Great Basin.

Plateau

The Interior-Plateau culture area of the Columbia and Fraser River basins was home to numerous small tribes of peaceful, foraging village dwellers that included such well-known groups as the Kootenai, Nez Perce, Ntlakyapamuk (Thompson), Okanagan, Salish (Flathead), Shuswap, Skitswish (Coeur d'Alene), Spokane, and Yakama. Culturally, they were similar to their neighbors from the Northwest Coast, Great Basin, and California areas, and, like most other Native Americans, structured their lives around the seasons and the availability of lo-

Group of Salish men gathered around a drum, with tipis in background, 1937. (Library of Congress)

cal foods. Languages spoken included numerous dialects of the Algonquian, Athabascan, Salish, and Shahaptian linguistic families.

The boundaries of this high, varied land of well-watered grasslands, dense forests, and snow-covered mountains were the Rocky Mountains on the east and the Cascade Range on the west, the upper Fraser River on the north, and a line running through modern-day Oregon and Idaho on the south. Also included in this region was part of British Columbia, a section of western Montana, a wedge of Wyoming, and central and eastern Washington.

The Columbia, the Fraser, and their tributaries were the lifeblood of this landlocked region. Numerous small villages were located on their hospitable banks; travel and trade flourished, and were inevitably accompanied by cultural interchanges. In the early eighteenth century, some 200 years after its introduction by the Spanish, the horse came to the Plateau from the Plains and Great Basin. Its economic value was soon recognized, and the Plateau peoples, acting as middlemen, facilitated a thriving exchange of slaves and horses that emerged between slaveholding tribes of the Northwest Coast and the Plains. The Plateau tribes also became participants in the great bison hunts.

Most Plateau peoples spent the winters in circular log homes built partly underground. Summer dwellings were made of bullrush mats layered over frames of cottonwood. They relied on the salmon, sturgeon, and trout caught from the many fast-running rivers and streams as a major source of food. Since the climate was cold enough to inhibit the development of agriculture, wild roots, berries, and nuts were gathered. Another very important food was the starchy bulb of the camas, a type of lily. Wild game hunted included rabbits, deer, elk, and mountain sheep. Like their Great Basin and California neighbors, the Plateau tribes had a decentralized political structure and casual sense of community. Exceptions were the Nez Perces and Skitswish (Coeur d'Alene), who adopted a more structured tribal organization from the Siksika (Blackfeet) of the Plains.

White expansion eventually destroyed the traditional way of life on the Plateau as it did for tribes living in other culture areas. American seafarer Robert Gray sailed up the Columbia River in 1792, and members of the Lewis and Clark Expedition spent time with all the major tribes of the Plateau, breaking ground for fur traders and trappers who came to the area later. Although trade between the whites and native peoples in the years immediately following Lewis and Clark's landmark journey fostered a mutually beneficial relationship, it also brought exposure to disease. Later, the arrival of missionaries and tens of thousands of pioneers introduced bloody, intermittent conflict and loss of life and land. By 1878, the last of the Plateau tribes had been forced to relocate to reservations.

Many transformer and trickster myths are found in the Great Basin.

The Plains

The vast, almost unbroken swath of grassland known as the Great Plains, once sparsely or intermittently inhabited except for great herds of buffalo, extends from northern Alberta and Saskatchewan south to the Gulf of Mexico. East to west, it runs from the foothills of the Rocky Mountains to the Mississippi River. The Plains was once home to about three dozen or more tribes, many of whom became the hard-riding warriors and hunters of legend after they acquired horses in the seventeenth and eighteenth centuries. They included the Arapaho, Cheyenne, Comanche, Crow, Dakota (Sioux), Hidatsa, Kiowa, Mandan, Osage, Pawnee, Siksika (Blackfeet), and Wichita.

Few, if any, of these peoples could trace their ancestry within the region back more than several hundred years. The original inhabitants of the Plains were small numbers of nomadic peoples who eked out a living forging its river bottoms and hunting buffalo on foot. By about 1000 c.e., some of the peoples were acquainted with the rudiments of farming and were able to raise crops to

Dakota Indians, Pine Ridge, South Dakota, 1910. (Library of Congress)

supplement their diet of buffalo meat and wild plants. But many of them were forced into other territories because of successive drought, and the population did not show a marked increase until a great drift onto the Plains began around 1300 C.E. The region became a melting pot as drought elsewhere and increasing population pressure in the Woodlands caused tribes to converge from all four directions. Later, the coming of European settlers to the east forced native peoples westward as their lands were taken.

Most tribes who came to the Plains had been semi-sedentary villagers who lived as farmers and gatherers. By 1700, however, the horse was available throughout the Plains, and the native people rapidly became peerless riders, trainers, and breeders, enabling them to adopt a nomadic lifestyle organized around the buffalo hunt. In fact, the buffalo became the focus of Plains Indian culture, the center of their social life and daily routine. Its flesh provided them with food, its hides with clothing and shelter. Bones and horns were used to make tools; sinews, thread and string. Many Plains myths and legends naturally related to the buffalo.

Tribes spent the winter in conical earth lodges near the rivers; during the summer, encampments consisting of portable teepees were established for intensive, large-scale bison hunting. Here, people united in supplication to the Great Spirit through celebration of public ceremonials and rituals such as the Sun Dance, which, in some tribes, were accompanied by acts of self-mutilation and feats of deprivation or endurance.

Government among the Plains tribes was not hereditary, elected, or structured. Related bands were organized into tribes, each governed by a chief upon whom the title was often bestowed as an honorific because of the individual's wisdom or bravery. The chief was assisted by a council of elders. Social systems among the Plains Indians were highly developed; some tribes had clans, but most had warrior societies. Rank was derived through ownership of large numbers of horses, success in raids, war honors against enemies, or spiritual power obtained through visions sought as part of rituals and ceremonies.

Plains culture in its full flower was spectacular, made possible by the European's horse. However, after little more than a century, Europeans sealed the fate of both the Plains culture and the bison. English and French trappers, traders, and the Lewis and Clark Expedition generated a flood of interest in the economic potential of the West. The trappings of white civilization that soon arrived had insidious effects on Indian culture, as convenience goods like knives, blankets, and kettles undermined self-sufficiency and led to dependence. The availability of guns upset the balance of power among tribes. Worst of all, the traders brought diseases such as measles, diphtheria, and smallpox, to which the Indians had no resistance.

By 1840, the demand for beaver pelts, the beavers themselves, and the trappers and traders were gone. Next came the forty-niners on their way to California, and settlers moving to Oregon territory. Many chose to remain on the Plains when they discovered the area's rich black soil and gold was discovered in Colorado. Following the Civil War, the transcontinental railroads brought the potential for millions to settle the region. After 1850, the history of relations between whites and Indians on the Plains was marked by an endless succession of broken treaties and fierce, bloody conflicts. By 1880, the gradual but steady depletion of buffalo herds by white sport and commercial hunters reduced the Indians to penury, and they were forced to settle on reservations established by the federal government.

Many types of creation stories are part of Plains mythology. Culture hero tales, trickster stories, and myths that feature mediators between gods and humans are also common.

Southwest

The Southwest culture area comprises present-day Arizona and New Mexico, parts of Utah, Colorado, Texas, and northwest Mexico. While rivers, rain, and oases make life possible in this hot, arid region of desert and mountains, the availability of water fluctuates and is always a concern. At different times, the territory has been home to a variety of both hunter gatherers and agricultural peoples. Included among the former are the Apache, Havasupai, Hualapai (Walapai), Seri, and Yavapai. The Mohave, Navajo, Pima, Pueblo peoples (including the Hopi and Zuni), Tohono O'Odham (Papago), Yaqui, and Yuma are some of the latter. The Southwest is home to some of the best-preserved archaeological remains in the United States, evidence that suggests this area has been inhabited for at least 6,000 years.

The early occupiers of the region, the hunter-gatherers, depended on wild food, both plant and animal, such as saguaro cactus fruit, yucca, prickly pear, mesquite pods, antelope, rodents, fish, rabbits, and deer. To supplement their diet, they began to cultivate some varieties of maize and squash by about 1500 B.C.E., a practice likely introduced from Mesoamerica. Eventually, they developed strains of maize better suited to growing in a more northern climate, and cultivation of maize and other crops started to spread. Because farming in the Southwest was labor-intensive, requiring irrigation and flood control, the peoples gradually transformed into increasingly sophisticated, sedentary village-dwelling farmers with a diet centered on maize, beans, and squash.

Two similar, complex cultures that emerged in the Southwest between about C.E. 300 and 1100 were the Hohokam and the Anasazi, comprised of various linguistic groups and many independent communities. Both groups constructed large stone and adobe towns (later called *pueblos* by the Spanish) directed by a hierarchy of men with combined roles of chief and priest. Both also built and maintained elaborate irrigation systems to water their crops.

The Hohokam, probable ancestors of the Pima and Tohono O'Odham, and the Anasazi, ancestors of the Acoma, Hopi, and Zuni, were both influenced by the culture of central Mexico. Both groups traded with peoples in the region and learned from them how to cultivate food crops and cotton and weave cloth. Ball courts and platform temple mounds could be found within the largest Hohokam villages.

During the twelfth and thirteenth centuries, the Hohokam and Anasazi experienced a decline that was likely triggered by a series of severe crises. An excessive reliance on corn resulted in depletion of the soil. As yields declined, overpopulation also became a problem. A prolonged period of drought exacerbated the problem, eventually leading to crop failure, malnutrition, and violent clashes.

The Hohokam abandoned their villages and reverted to a nomadic lifestyle of hunting and gathering; most of the Anasazi moved south and east into impressive new pueblos in locales where more water and new soil were available. The oral traditions of the Acoma, Hopi, Pueblo, and Zuni all reflect the fact they left their earlier homes because of disease, drought, famine, and violence.

Archaeologists believe the Apache and Navajo migrated to their present Southwest homeland later, possibly around the thirteenth century. Speakers of Athabascan languages closely related to those found in the Subarctic, from where they probably came, they initially roamed the mountains in search of food, occasionally raiding their Pueblo neighbors. While the Apache largely remained hunter-gatherers, the Navajo eventually borrowed heavily from the Pueblo Indians, particularly in the areas of agriculture, arts, and weaving.

The first Spanish explorers arrived in the Southwest in the early sixteenth century, lured by rumors of the existence of rich cities and the potential to save new souls. Though they found no treasure, they did make contact with the native peoples, inspiring successive ventures favored by missionaries seeking new converts and a government in search of land, labor, subjects, and taxpayers.

From the moment the missionaries arrived, conflict was inevitable, since the people were not prepared to abandon their religion. The Spaniards treated the people with contempt, hostility, and brutality. While individual pueblos did rebel, uprisings were always crushed. In 1680, the year of the Pueblo Revolution, the pueblos united in a well-coordinated rebellion and routed the Spanish, who retreated southward to El Paso, only to return to the pueblos of the Zuni and the Rio Grande twelve years later. Following another Pueblo rebellion, the peoples of the Southwest and the Spaniards eventually compromised and were able to coexist.

Following the outbreak of the war with Mexico and the annexation of present-day New Mexico and Arizona to the United States in 1846, other white settlers eventually flocked to the area. Like the native peoples of other culture areas, those of the Southwest were eventually forced to live on reservations.

The emergence myth is the most prominent myth of cultures in the Southwest. Migration legends and the monster-ridding cycle are also important.

Southeast

The Southeast, a land of relatively mild winters and abundant rainfall, stretches eastward from the lower Mississippi River to the Atlantic, northward to the colder regions of the Mississippi and Ohio Valleys, and southward from Virginia and Kentucky to the Gulf of Mexico. Its modern political divisions include

Seminole Indian children and adults posed near thatched building, Monroe Station Indian village, Florida. (Library of Congress)

southern and eastern Arkansas, part of eastern Texas, Louisiana, Mississippi, Alabama, Georgia, Florida, South Carolina, western North Carolina, Tennessee, and those areas of Missouri, Illinois, and Kentucky that border the Mississippi River. In this area of diverse topography and fertile soil, plant and animal life were abundant before the arrival of Europeans; forests were filled with game, fruits, grasses, and wild nuts, and the rivers teemed with fish. Prominent Native American groups included the Alabama, Caddo, Cherokee, Chickasaw, Choctaw, Creek, Natchez, Seminole, and Tunica.

Early explorers who penetrated the Southeast found a Native society that was one of the most advanced north of Mesoamerica, by which it was strongly influenced. The Southeastern Indians were accomplished builders and skilled craftsmen, farmers, fishermen, and hunters who were knowledgeable in the use of herbs and medicines as well as conservation of natural resources. Some of the peoples were emerging from the long decline of the once prosperous and sophisticated Mississippian culture (ca. 700 to 1200 C.E.), known for its large and complex ceremonial mounds, which served as homes, tombs and temples, and for its cultivated fields of maize, beans, and squash. Though the earthen mounds were gradually passing into disuse, life was still village-based.

Most villages were governed by a council of warriors and elders, presided over by a chief. They were generally laid out around a central plaza of beaten earth, with separate buildings, public and private, on different sides. On the margin of the plaza sat a conical winter council house where tribal leaders held their discussions. Winter houses were constructed of cane withes and clay, with thatched roofs. During the warmer months, families moved to adjoining rectangular summer houses raised on posts for better ventilation. Because they were often at war and raids were frequent, many larger settlements were enclosed by palisades as high as sixteen feet.

The surrounding forest was used for hunting and gathering. Women cultivated maize, beans, squash, and pumpkins, while the men ventured dozens and sometimes hundreds of miles in pursuit of game. When crop yields were small, the villages dispersed and subsisted by gathering roots, berries, and nuts to supplement their game harvest.

Although they were divided into a large number of groups and spoke a wide variety of languages, the Indians of the Southeast shared a complex set of beliefs about both themselves and the natural and supernatural worlds, beliefs interconnected with farming and hunting. Their most important ritual was the Green Corn Ceremony, an elaborate festival of thanksgiving and renewal that coincided with the ripening of the autumn crop. They also followed a matrilineal clan system in which all blood relationships were determined by descent from the mother. All forbade marriage between a man and woman of the same clan.

Early contact with Europeans resulted in disaster for the Native peoples, as their lives began to shatter almost immediately. Many who were not killed or enslaved fell victim to various diseases. The exchange of furs and skins for manufactured goods had a destructive impact on both Native cultural patterns and the environment. As Spain, France, and Britain struggled for control of the region, the Indians became enmeshed in their battles, and eventually their land was coveted by white settlers. Nearly all who survived the period of exploration and colonization were forcibly removed from the Southeast by the United States government and sent west to present-day Oklahoma.

Mythology of the Southeast culture area includes many hero and trickster tales, and stories that feature a council of animals.

Northeast

The Northeast, a region of varied climate and environments, is a vast expanse of land stretching east to west from the Atlantic coast to the Mississippi River, bordered on the north by southern Canada and on the south by present-day

Iroquois Indians. (Library of Congress)

Tennessee. Here, diverse Indian cultures flourished in the fertile woodlands and prairies and sustained themselves through hunting, gathering, fishing, and agriculture. These cultures are classified into two principal divisions: Iroquoian speakers, including the Cayuga, Erie, Mohawk, Oneida, Onondaga, Seneca, Tuscarora, and Wyandot (Huron); and Algonquian speakers, including the Delaware, Fox, Kickapoo, Menominee, Miami, Ottawa, Pequot, Sauk, Shawnee, and Wampanoag.

The Native peoples of the Northeast, like some of their neighbors to the south, were descended from ancient mound-building cultures. These cultures, the Hopewell (ca. 100 B.C.E. to C.E. 350) and Adena (ca. 500 B.C.E. to C.E. 200), both left behind vast earthworks that enclosed domed or cone-shaped burial mounds. Both peoples lived in villages, and corn was a staple of their diet. The Hopewells were skilled craftsmen and artists, and had a well-organized society led by an elite upper class.

By the early 1500s, cultures of the Northeastern peoples were based largely on hunting, because cold weather limited horticulture to the region's more temperate areas. The Iroquoian-speaking tribes resided in fortified villages organized by matrilineal clans and lineage groups, each governed by a council. Politically sophisticated, the Iroquois were intensely committed to warfare and raids and terrified the Algonquians and dissident Iroquois who remained outside of the powerful Iroquois League that formed during the sixteenth century. The Iroquois resided along the Saint Lawrence River in present-day upstate New York and along the lower Great Lakes and were subject to territorial disputes with their Algonquian neighbors.

The Algonquian-speaking peoples, who predominated in both number and territorial domination, occupied coastal regions in present-day New England and south to the mid-Atlantic. Most lived in small, semi-sedentary villages and subsisted by hunting, fishing, and cultivating corn, beans, pumpkins, and other vegetables. Because foraging along coastal areas was usually excellent, horticulture there was not as developed.

From about 1497 onward, the tribal peoples of the Northeast were in almost constant contact with Europeans. Native land struggles were intensified by European colonization, and by the 1700s, the pressure forced many Algonquian nations to migrate farther west to the Great Lakes, where they competed with other Natives for resources and eventually displaced some of them. Indian nations of the Northeast resisted European domination and employed various political and military strategies to impede their encroachment, such as organized alliances. Step by step, however, their lands were taken away. Some groups were removed to Oklahoma and other areas west; others were sent to reservations within their traditional homelands, where their descendants live today.

Trickster stories, clan myths, and the culture hero cycle are important in the Northeast.

EMERGING PATTERNS

When these ten culture areas are considered as a whole, a pattern of distribution of myths emerges, and what distinguishes them from place to place is the combination of motifs and elements.[7] For example, trickster stories are common to both the Northwest coast and the Northeast. A trickster mink known for his sexual escapades and multiple marriages is found in cultures of the former. In those of the latter, the trickster is a rabbit who prolongs the life of various animals by teaching them how to deceive and fool their enemies. In emergence myths of the Southwest, the existence of the present population is explained by the emergence of inhabitants of one or more worlds from below the surface of the earth; in the Choctaw emergence myth of the Southeast, peoples emerged from the underworld at Nanih Waiya, a well-known mound near Philadelphia, Mississippi. Myths from across the continent tell of various contests between the local fauna.

SOURCES OF NATIVE AMERICAN MYTHOLOGY

Judging from the volume of available documents, Stith Thompson's statement that "outside of Western civilization, few ethnic groups have been studied as much as the Indians of North America" (1979, 297) was absolutely valid. Stories of native mythmakers have been recorded since the first European contacts, collected and published extensively during the late nineteenth to early twentieth century, and reissued at an accelerated rate during recent years as interest in multiculturalism has emerged. New versions of myths narrated by today's storytellers have become available, and various tribal governments are collecting and publishing their own oral traditions, primarily for use in their classrooms.

The study of Native American mythology is an extremely ambitious project, not only in light of the accessible material, but also because its themes are numerous and extremely diverse. The myths and stories belong to the many indigenous peoples, peoples whose language, culture, and history are different and in some cases totally unrelated. Those myths and stories, which reflect their various cultures and experiences, developed and evolved over time and as the Native peoples were impacted by the cultures of newcomers to the North American continent, particularly Europeans. Despite language differences, oral traditions passed freely from one culture to another; facilitated by trade and proximity, this exchange helped further shape both mythologies. Even today, versions of traditional myths are retold and re-worked to reflect current conditions.

In any study of mythology, we must remember that a myth reflects the culture, values, experience, and perspective of the person who tells it, so we are automatically distanced from the myth itself and its meaning. The anthologies in which myths and stories appear often lack sufficient background material to place them in cultural context for the reader. Native American myths were recorded by non-Natives and translated into English; because the translation process involves some interpretation, it does not result in a perfect replica of the original source. It is therefore difficult, if not impossible, for a non-Native to gain a full and complete understanding of Native American mythology. Even so, all humans create myths and stories from our need to interpret and explain our world, our history, and who we are. We should want to develop an awareness of and appreciation for Native American mythology, no matter how difficult the process, no matter how limited our understanding, as part of our North American and human experience.

Our sources for published Native American myths are the mythmakers themselves, whose stories have been collected largely by various scholars, including anthropologists, historians, and linguists. Interested lay people and Native Americans themselves have also assembled collections. The first Europeans to record these myths were the Jesuit missionaries of New France, many of whom were accomplished linguists who studied and wrote down tribal languages. They collected some myths east of the Great Lakes and documented them beginning in 1633 in *The Jesuit Relations,* annual reports and narratives sent to their superiors in France.[8] Henry Rowe Schoolcraft, explorer, Indian agent, and spouse of a half-Ojibwa daughter of a fur trader, is credited with initiating the modern appreciation for the study of Indian myth and the documentation of entire bodies of

The snow-shoe dance to thank the great spirit for the first appearance of snow. (Library of Congress)

Native American mythology.[9] Other important collectors who followed include artist George Caitlin, who studied the myths and rituals of the Woodland tribes in the 1830s, including the now vanished Mandan; noted anthropologist James Mooney, who studied myths of the Cherokee at the turn of the century; and his contemporary Franz Boas, one of the pioneers of modern cultural anthropology. It was Boas who categorized Native American myths and noted common traditions they revealed, laying the foundation for Stith Thompson's development of the complex motif index of traditional narratives found in his *Tales of the North American Indians* (1929). Others of the many important contributors to our knowledge of Native American mythologies include Ruth Benedict, Natalie Curtis, Frank Hamilton Cushing, George Dorsey, Richard Erdoes, George Bird Grinnell, Claude Lévi-Strauss, Alice Marriott, Alfonso Ortiz, Elsie Clews Parsons, Paul Radin, Lewis Spence, and Ruth Underhill. Some noted Native myth collectors include William Beynon and Henry Tate for the Tsimshian, George Hunt for the Kwakiutl, Mourning Dove for the Okanagan, Clara Pearson for the Tillamook, and Ella Deloria for the Dakota (Sioux).

The collection and translation of Native American texts reached its height between 1887 and 1934, as scholars scrambled to record these texts before the people and their mythological heritage vanished. As Bierhorst (2002, 2) noted, this time period, when Indian mythology was at its most vulnerable, is framed by the passage of General Allotment Act and the Indian Reorganization Act, the former a means of dismantling Indian communities, the latter an attempt to restore them, in many cases belatedly. While much was preserved, we can only guess at the number of stories that were lost forever with the demise of languages and cultures following European contact, conquest, and colonization.

Early significant publications of Native American oral literatures, some in their native languages, appeared in government documents and volumes issued by professional societies. After anthropology was organized as a discipline and became part of the curricula in higher education, they were published in academic journals and monographic series of colleges and universities, in whose library collections they reside.[10] Native American mythology that was preserved was, initially, at least, largely inaccessible to the reading public. Fortunately, both Native Americans and scholars have been calling attention to Native oral literatures in recent years, and much is now available from mainstream presses.

*Mourning Dove (1888–1936), also known as Humishuma. Novelist, activist, and collector of Okanagan myths and stories. (*Mourning Dove, A Salishan Autobiography/*Collection of Jay Miller/University of Nebraska Press)*

THE IMPORTANCE OF NATIVE AMERICAN MYTHOLOGY

The traditions and history of Native Americans are embodied in their myths and rituals. A familiarity with Native American mythology therefore contributes greatly to respecting and understanding their cultures, as it provides insight into daily life and society and the collective experience of a tribe, past and present.

Information on the organization of families, gender roles, the operation of various political structures, the importance of certain foods, the reenactment of ceremonies, the glorification of honor in war, funerary practices, natural disasters, migrations, encounters with Europeans, and displacement can all be found in Native American myths. Sometimes myths are the only remnants of a particular native culture, and scholars rely on them to supplement the historical record.

The current interest in multiculturalism at the primary, secondary, and college levels has brought written literature of Native Americans to the attention of students as never before. Because Native written literature is greatly indebted to the long-standing oral literature, a familiarity with the mythology that lies at the heart of every aspect of Native tradition and culture is advantageous to understanding the written literature.

Native American myths and legends may also promote scholarly and scientific theories and beliefs and contribute constructively to their debate. The Iroquois have possessed a viable material culture for several thousand years; both the archaeological record and a rich body of surviving folklore provide supporting evidence (Erdoes 1984, xii). Oral traditions about geologic and climactic events may be a significant source of information; various peoples of the Plains speak of the Great Flaming Rock tradition. Some scientists have theorized that Paleo-Indians caused the extinction of megafauna through over hunting, while Indians attribute their demise, in almost every instance, to an act of the Great Spirit, an implication that some kind of natural event was behind their disappearance (Deloria 1997).

The role and importance of mythology in Native affairs has expanded in recent times, becoming a charter for cultural revival and a mechanism Native Americans have used to justify their rights to traditional lands, achieve economic parity, and repossess human remains and certain cultural items held by non-native cultural institutions and government agencies. In 1997, as the result of a suit pressed by the Gitksan, the Supreme Court of Canada recognized the Northwest Coast Bear Mother myth as evidence in support of their claim to roughly 22,000 square miles of land in British Columbia. Although the Gitksan did not actually secure rights to the land they sought, this case established that oral traditions must be taken into consideration in such cases. In 1988, the United States passed the Indian Gaming and Regulatory Act, which created the jurisdictional framework that governs the numerous Indian gaming enterprises that have emerged in recent decades on traditional Indian lands, the rights to some of which have been affirmed in court using oral traditions. Some proceeds have been used to finance museums and cultural centers where Indian history has been dramatized. The Native American Graves Protection and Repatriation Act, passed in 1990, explicitly states that oral traditions may be used in support of repatriation of grave goods and human remains (Bierhorst 2002, 234–237).

NOTES

1. Though we have used the term *mythology* in this book, we would like to emphasize that there is no *one* Native American mythology, just as there is no single group of people called Native Americans. It is more accurate and sensitive to recognize the distinctions between the *mythologies* of the various tribal groups, just as it is more accurate and sensitive to recognize distinctions between other aspects of their cultures.

2. We would like to stress that much of the information about native origins in this introduction is based on theory and speculation, and dates are approximations. The archaeological record suggests multiple possibilities, so much remains controversial.

3. It is important to note that many Native Americans have vigorously challenged the Bering Strait migration theory in part because it cannot be reconciled with any of their traditions or memories that have been transmitted from generation to generation by their ancestors. See Deloria (1997).

4. Taylor (2001, 40, 45) refers to the "low counters," scholars of the early twentieth century, and the more recent "high counters." Low counters estimated the native population of the Americas to be about 10 million in 1492 (including about 1 million in the present United States and Canada). At minimum, the high counters estimate this population to be 20 million; some go as high as 100 million. Most now estimate around 50 million, including about 5 million living north of Mexico. By 1800, only about 600,000 Indians remained in present-day Canada and the United States.

5. According to Taylor (2001, 10), native peoples spoke at least 375 distinct languages in 1492.

6. Champagne's *The Native North American Almanac* (2001, 267–375) prefers to define a series of culture areas that more closely reflects contemporary Indian life: Native Peoples of the Northeast; Southeastern Indians; Southwestern Indians; Northern Plains Indians; Northwest Coast Indians; Alaska Natives; Oklahoma Indians; Indians of the Plateau, Great Basin, and Rocky Mountains; California Indians; Aboriginal Peoples in Canada.

7. Bierhorst (2001, 17–19) identifies the Native American mythological pattern and proposes mythological regions that closely follow the traditional culture areas used by anthropologists. See also Leeming and Page (1998, 4–14) for a discussion of this mythological pattern and the traditional culture areas.

8. *The Jesuit Relations*, vital to recreating the history of the French in North America, contains a wealth of information about the aboriginal peoples with whom the French made contact, and the economic, social, political, demographic, and religious consequences of that contact.

9. Schoolcraft, a contemporary of Henry Wadsworth Longfellow (*The Song of Hiawatha*), was the source of Longfellow's information about Native American myths.

10. See Miller (1992, 159–162) for a summary of publication of the classic sources of Native American mythology.

2

TIME

I n order to understand and appreciate the events, themes, and people in non-Western mythology or legend, it may be helpful to look briefly at concepts of time, since many cultures around the world have conceived of time in a manner that differs with that of the European tradition.

According to Viola F. Cordova, Western cultures have a tendency to assign a linear dimension to time, which allows it to be quantified and measured. Non-Westerners, on the other hand, view time as an immeasurable abstraction—time exists, but there is little notion of measured segments that may be highly anticipated and then are gone forever (Cordova in Weaver 1998, 29).

LINEAR TIME

One who has been raised with the Western/European concept of time understands time in a linear fashion. Events occur on a continuum—a timeline. Students in social studies and history classes are taught to construct timelines to help them understand the relationship of events in time. Next to hash marks on a line that represents time, students pencil in important events, such as battles of the American Civil War or major world events. In Western thought, time has a specific beginning. In the Judeo-Christian tradition, time began with the creation of the universe. By the volition of the Creator, the heavens, earth, night and day, the plants, animals, and finally human beings came into existence. Although the Creator himself transcended time, the creation had a beginning and will have an end at the final judgment.

Western science agrees that the universe had a sudden beginning. Various theories have been proposed over the centuries, with the "Big Bang," or variations of it, currently the most widely accepted. This theory states that the universe, and time, began billions of years ago with a great explosion. Experts in disciplines such as physics and astronomy support their theories with results from extensive studies. One of the most exciting outcomes of recent technological advances in astronomy is the ability of the Hubble Space Telescope and several earth-based telescopes to peer deep into the primordial past. Due to the great distances light or radio waves must travel, the farther from earth the telescopes look the older the galaxies are, thus enabling scientists to look back across time. Evidence of galaxies that are mind-boggling distances from earth is now being discovered, and scientists hope that they will soon be close to seeing the universe shortly after the Big Bang event.

A human life, too, can be depicted along a timeline, with the moment of conception at the beginning of the line and death at its terminus. We each find ourselves somewhere along the line between those two points, steadily progressing toward the end.

CYCLICAL ASPECTS OF TIME

Not all cultures, however, have seen time as being one directional. The ancient Greeks observed natural phenomena and described the cyclical nature of time. Nature, they believed, consisted of opposing forces, such as night and day, winter and summer. One of the opposing forces would prevail briefly and then fade while the other force became dominant, and the opposing forces alternated their dominance in repeatable cycles. The Greeks and other ancient cultures learned to observe the movement of the sun, moon, and stars to define a "year"—the period of time it took for these celestial bodies to move through the heavens and align themselves again at the same location. The Lakota's complex mythology describes the "four times." The first was daylight and the second nighttime. The third time consisted of the phases of the moon. The fourth time was not created until Tate's sons (see the entry entitled **Wind**) had returned from their mission to establish the four corners of the earth and the four seasons. They had been away from home twelve moon times; thus it was established that twelve months would make a year.

Time's cyclical aspects can also be seen in the passage of generations: living beings are born, give life, die, and then the next generation repeats the process, and in cultures around the world sacred rites are associated with these significant cyclical events. Agriculture, too, is cyclical. The cycles of the seeding or sowing, watering (especially where people depend on seasonal rains), growing, and then harvesting domestic plants are seen as sacred processes. Some cultures developed fertility rites to assure a plentiful supply of food; others offered special prayers of thanksgiving for the plants, the rain, and the sun that produced a good crop. When the harvest was completed and preparations were made to store some of the harvested grain for the next year's cycle, thanksgiving ceremonies took place. Due to the cyclical nature of agriculture, many Native American groups held thanksgiving ceremonies throughout the year as each

Native American Navajos creating sand painting. (Paul Chesley/Getty Images)

crop was harvested. The late winter when the maple sap flows, the spring when berries are gathered, and the late summer when the three sisters—beans, corn, and squash—are harvested are all times of thanksgiving. Prayers offered at these and other important times acknowledge the Creator and give thanks for all that has been provided (Bruchac 1993, 79–80).

Not only does time operate in a cyclical manner, Bruchac points out, but so does all of nature. This can be seen in the pattern of the seasons, the movement of the moon and sun, and even in the way birds build their nests. He explains that just as all points on the perimeter of a circle are equidistant from the center, so all of creation is equally significant. This extends to the entirety of nature; all living and nonliving things, as well as natural phenomena such as the wind and rain, have not only great importance, but also a vital connection with the rest of creation (Bruchac 2003, 10–11). Truly being part of the whole of nature, and not merely the master of it, has permeated the worldview of Native people across North America and guided their relationship to the land, to natural resources, and to each other.

SACRED SPACE

Long before Newton, Kant, Einstein, or Minkowski, ancient cultures around the world understood that there was a relationship between time and space. They understood that an event happening right here, right now could be imbued with a sacredness that not only set the event apart from the mundane, but also set apart the time and the place where it occurred. In the remembering of the event, whether by telling and hearing oral narratives, or by participating in or viewing various ceremonies, people were able to transcend the present and become part of the sacred. Oftentimes this process included going back to that holy spot. It's not unusual for people around the globe to save their money for years in order to visit what they believe to be a holy place. Indeed, some religious traditions require that one undertake certain pilgrimages during one's lifetime.

Another example of the melding of sacred time and space is described by anthropologist Trudy Griffin-Pierce in her study of Navajo sandpainting. The power of Navajo sandpainting is in the merging of time and space into a place where the present and the mythic past coexist, Griffin-Pierce writes. The Navajo consider sandpaintings to be "sacred, living entities" with the power to "compress time and space." It is through the power of sandpainting and the associated rituals that an individual can be transported to a place where the present and the mythic world are one, a place where supernatural assistance and healing can be found (Griffin-Pierce 1992, 98–99).

Native American people believe that time is cyclical and dynamic, and that this cyclical time functions not only in the spiritual realm, but in the day-to-day existence of all living things. One Hopi scholar has called this relationship "mythic reality." In other words, the truth of this present, physical world exists simultaneously with that of the mythic, spiritual world. This is a difficult concept to accept for many people with Western philosophical and scientific backgrounds. It necessitates the suspension of former beliefs in order to fully comprehend the Native view of the land, the environment, family, and the past, present, and future (Griffin-Pierce 1992, 6–7).

Many myths tell of sacred places. These are locations where specific events took place in the distant past that have spiritual meaning for today or are remembered because the event changed the way humans live or interact with this world. One such story relates how Raven created Nunivak Island from a piece of soil he had taken from a certain cape on the mainland. He carried the soil on his back until he found the spot where he wanted the island. After dropping the soil in the ocean, he tied it down with a rope he had fashioned from roots. But that didn't seem right, so he unleashed the clump of soil and sent it swimming away. Later on, the clump of soil found a large block of ice floating along and joined up with it to become Nunivak Island. Then Raven looked it over and decided the island needed a mountain, so he flew off to find a suitable mountain. When he returned, he hauled the mountain onto the island. Raven still thought it didn't look right, so he caused the wind to blow, which caused mountains to form on the end of the island.

In the Pacific Northwest, several mountains, lakes, and rivers are identified in local myths. Stories of the Great Flood tell of people in canoes or rafts landing on the high mountains when the water started to subside. Mt. Rainier, the highest mountain in the area, is a frequently named location in these myths. The great rivers of the Northwest are also featured in numerous myths. The rivers not only provided a means of transportation, but they were also the source of salmon, one of the main dietary staples of people in that region.

Sweet Medicine, the Cheyenne hero, after being banished from his village, traveled to a sacred mountain. There he received instruction from a group of elders (actually spirits) who taught him about the Four Sacred Arrows and numerous other rules and ceremonies. He spent four years there learning all of these things, and then the Old Ones sent him home with the sacred arrow bundle. He was welcomed back at his village and the people gladly accepted the new teachings. Sweet Medicine continued to live a very long life, but when the time drew near for him to die, the people carried him to the sacred mountain. They built a shelter for him at the base of the mountain and then withdrew a few miles away. The Cheyenne continued to observe all that Sweet Medicine had taught them and to this day consider Devil's Tower in Wyoming to be a sacred mountain (Stands In Timber 1998, 27–41).

A MYTHOLOGICAL CHRONOLOGY

The task of putting the myths and legends included in this volume into a concise chronology is beset by several obstacles. These include the fact that until around the time of European contact, the written word was virtually unknown in North America. Many groups used visual representations, painted or carved on rock, wood, or leather, that depicted series of events—wars or battles, meteorological occurrences, and other extraordinary happenings. These were cues to help remind a storyteller (or history teller) of key points in a narrative. The real story, however, was held in the memory of the one to whom it was entrusted.

Events related through oral history are difficult to pin to a timeline without the associated context. Many oral histories can be tied to events that have happened within the memory of several generations. For example, a person might have known a great-grandparent who knew a soldier from the American Civil

War. A connection, albeit distant, could be felt to those events because of the stories the great-grandparent had heard and then repeated to him or her. But many mythological tales are so old that no one during historical (recorded) time remembers knowing anyone who was involved in or witnessed the events described.

A second difficulty related to assigning a chronology or temporal framework to the mythologies of Native North America is that of the diversity of people represented. There is not one body of mythology to consider, but many. However, there are common threads. Though we don't want to overgeneralize, we will attempt to relate several important beliefs that appear to be widely held across the North American continent. We would caution our readers that while we have tended to use past tense in many of our descriptions and explanations, it is merely an editorial choice. We by no means feel that the belief systems or religions of North America's first people are invalid or dead.

MYTHIC TIME

One of the basic distinctions between mythology, legend, or folklore can be viewed as the issue of placing these narratives in a time frame. However, just saying the phrase "placing these narratives in a time frame" exposes our Eurocentric backgrounds. Western cultures give time a dimension not considered by many non-western people. We want to pin down an event and put it into "context" with other events—did it happen before, simultaneously, or after another event? The focus of the relationship of an instance in time is in regard to other instances.

A question we must ask is: how do Native North Americans view time and especially mythological time?

Free of the cultural constraints of western thought and not bound to a timeline, native people across North America have considered time, and the passing of it, as being part of a much larger concept. Time is also viewed in relationship to space giving sacredness to locations where specific events took place. Through the cycles of nature, and indeed of human existence, the world and all that is in it are brought back to a spiritual center. Religious ceremonies and rites of passage are repeated, some with the passage of the seasons, and some with an individual's movement through the phases of life. The rhythmic cycles of these observances keep the people in touch with nature and with each other. Passing on the knowledge of ceremonies, songs, dances, beliefs and values, and their language to the next generation is an important responsibility that many parents and elders take seriously.

Mythological time is seen as being in the long, long ago, a time when the world was different than it is now. The myth narratives that tell about that era often begin, "It was a very long time ago," or "This happened a long time ago." Very few myths describe the world as created from nothingness as does the Judeo-Christian tradition or even the Big Bang theory. Most Native American myths that speak of the beginning of the world start with either an emergence theme or an earth diver. In the emergence, people (often pre-humans or animal people) depart from an original world that is often located at a lower level. The beings must climb up to subsequent levels and eventually reach the level that is the present earth. Another widespread beginning-of-time myth features an earth diver. A common element in this one is that a few animal people are floating or swimming in the waters that cover the earth. They eventually wish for land to live on and after a series of attempts to bring mud up from the bottom of the water, one of the earth divers is successful. From that small bit of mud, a tiny island is formed. The island grows and grows, until it stretches farther than anyone can see. Plants are distributed across the land (sometimes from seeds mixed in with the mud), and thus the land is prepared for the coming of humans. In the Northeast Woodlands, a common variation is that the mud is spread on the back of a turtle and thus the earth is seen as an island on turtle's back.

Hopi tradition states that there have been four worlds. The first world existed harmoniously for a very long time, but some of the people began doing evil and the Creator chose to destroy nearly everyone. The survivors went to the second world. In time, this world also became exceedingly evil and was destroyed by the Creator. He let the few remaining faithful people continue to the third world, described as being in the "womb of the earth," or an ant kiva. Here the survivors from the second world remained while it was destroyed by ice. The people lived happily in the third world for a time. But then they became evil and caused trouble. The Creator sent a flood to rid the land of the evil doers. However, a few faithful people were able to escape in hollow reeds. They floated around until the waters eventually subsided and the reeds landed on a high mountain. Spider Woman led them down the mountain to the fourth world. (Versluis 1992, 24–25). This is the one in which we live now. The four worlds comprise four separate but related time cycles, each ending with the destruction of the previous cycle.

The Navajo also believe that there have been previous worlds, this being the fifth. The earlier worlds were abandoned by the First People because of dissent among the inhabitants. It was in this fifth world that the birds and animals became as they are today.

IN THE TIME OF TRANSFORMERS
AND ANIMAL PEOPLE

According to Jane McGary (in Swann 1994, 93), Raven was the Transformer whose changes brought the world from myth time to historical time. Myths that feature Raven abound across the far north and the northwest coast regions. He was a crafty, greedy, and frequently self-centered fellow whose adventures, or more often misadventures, centered on his pursuit of lustful desires. Frequently, Raven's cons backfired on him, but some of Raven's actions benefited mankind, whether he meant them to or not. It was Raven who desired light and devised an elaborate plan that eventually netted him the prize. But in the process, he unleashed the stars, moon, and the sun, and they are now in the heavens for all to enjoy. The people who lived at that time were not used to the sun's blazing light, so they ran off into the forests and became the animals we know today.

In the most distant past, the first people were not actually humans or animals. These beings were more like spirits or minor gods. Over time, however, Animal People eventually came to be. Later, after the earth was formed (or reformed after a great flood or other cataclysmic event), many of the Animal People were changed into either real humans or real animals. They are still related, and the bond that formed when animals and humans were one is still important today.

A Miwok myth tells of a time long ago in which animals were like people. In this narrative, Falcon and Coyote decided to make humans, and Coyote pretended to be dead. Soon buzzards and crows came and began pecking away at Coyote's buttock. The birds kept pecking deeper into his buttock until Coyote suddenly closed the opening and trapped the scavengers inside. With Falcon's help, the birds were extracted and their feathers plucked. Then Coyote and Falcon planted the feathers in the four directions. Soon the crow feathers turned into people and the buzzard feathers transformed into chiefs. Coyote then pointed out to Falcon that the new people looked just like them, so they would have to become animals. Then all of the First People became the animals and birds that we have today. (Erdoes 1998, 12).

Ethnographers and anthropologists have attempted to collect, analyze, and categorize the mythologies of numerous Native peoples. In late-nineteenth-century California, over a five year period, Jeremiah Curtin recorded myths told by an elderly Wintu man. When the collection was published in 1898, Curtin stated in his introduction that the myths outlined three epochs. The first consisted of a time when nonhuman and nonanimal spirits (which he referred to as the "first people") existed in harmony. Second came a time of catastrophic upheaval in which the natural order was overturned. During this age, the first people were turned into the animals found in the world today. Humans appeared in the third age. By that time, plants, animals, and the earth's landscape was as it is now. The mythological narratives served as a history of how the world began and informed the people about how their society should function (Nabokov 2002, 87).

Writing about the Creeks, Bill Grantham identified two concepts of time: temporal (linear) and cyclical (seen as myth or sacred) time. In an ancient time, animals and people weren't all that different. Animals spoke the same language and behaved in similar ways to humans. All life was connected in a sacred way. As time went on, the interaction with the sacred became less frequent and sacred time only intersected with the temporal during certain ceremonies, events, and rites of passage (Grantham 2002, 63–65).

Franz Boas indicated that myths describe events that "happened at a time when the world had not yet assumed its present form." Yet mythical beings could play a role in the historically based folktale. Thus the mythological age had passed, but mythological figures, such as giants and animals who talked and acted like humans, could still be found somewhere in the world. According to Boas, the fact that a narrative contained mythological characters was not what determined whether it was a myth. The determining factor was the story's setting in time and space (Boas 1914, 378–379).

MYTHS AND HISTORICAL TIME

Mythic time describes that era when the world and its inhabitants were very different than they are now. However, myths, or what Boas called folktales, can also be set in *historical time,* when the earth—its landscape, its flora and fauna, and its people—was no different than it is today. Even though the mythical age is past, mythical beings and even mythical lands still exist somewhere in the present, and in these tales, mythical beings often interact with humans. Numerous myth stories tell of giant cannibals such as Dzonokwa who kidnapped children and carried them off into the woods. Other mythological figures include animals such as Blue Jay, Coyote, Mink, and Raccoon, who act like, or interact with, humans.

Tricksters also exhibit human characteristics and at times are seen as actual humans with supernatural abilities, especially when they are also Transformers who go about changing the land and the people living in it. One such individual is Manabozho of the Northeast Woodlands. A related figure also from the Northeast Woodlands is Glooskap, who is often seen as a culture hero.

He interacted with humans but also had a hand in transforming the land. His footprints can be seen yet today. Numerous islands and lakes dot the landscape in testimony of his adventures and journeys throughout the land.

Time has different meanings for different people. However, when considering the mythological literature of a culture, care must be taken to attempt to understand the appropriate cultural context. When studying the mythology of Native North American people, notions of linear time and its related limitations must be set aside. New concepts of time and space will challenge the reader to reflect on new meanings and possibilities.

3

DEITIES, THEMES, AND CONCEPTS

ADLIVUN
Central Inuit/Baffin Island, Arctic
The underworld realm of Sedna, the Sea Woman. A place where souls of the dead were taken.

After Sedna's dogs ate her father's hands and feet, he cursed them all. Suddenly the earth opened and they all fell down into the underworld region of Adlivun. There Sedna's large house was guarded by her dog, who moved only slightly to allow the dead souls to pass.

The Sea Woman became very angry when humans broke any of her taboos. She would then hide game animals from the hunters and the people began to starve. While in a ceremonial trance, the spirit of a shaman (*angakok*) traveled to Adlivun in order to appease her and win the release of the animals. But first he had to get past the guard dog and only the most powerful *angakok* could accomplish the task.

> *See also* Angakok; Sedna
> *References and further reading:*
> Boas, Franz. *The Central Eskimo.* Lincoln: University of Nebraska Press, 1964.
> Seidelman, Harold, and James Turner. *The Inuit Imagination: Arctic Myth and Sculpture.* Vancouver: Douglas and McIntyre; Seattle: University of Washington Press, 2001. First published 1994 by Thames and Hudson.

AFTERLIFE
A Menominee tale relates the story of a happily married couple. The husband often declared to his wife, "If you die first, I will go with you." His wife would say the same. Then one day the wife became ill and died. Her husband decided to be buried with her. His parents tried to dissuade him, but to no avail. And so it was that the husband was buried next to his dead wife.

The man could see the tracks his wife made as she traveled to the land of the dead and he followed her there to the west. When he arrived, he entered a large lodge and saw an old man. "Why did you come?" the old man asked.

The man explained that he loved his wife so much that he wanted to take her back home with him. The old man said it would be very difficult, but he would try to help. The old man arranged a dance and warned the husband to hide and not let his wife see him. The people filed into the lodge and began dancing. After a while the man peeked out and saw his wife dancing, but she did not go near the old man. Finally the old man used an object about the size of a flute to draw her toward him. When he had gotten her inside the object, he closed the ends. He gave it to the husband and warned him not to let her out, no matter what she said. As long as they could hear the old man's drum, he would not let her out. Finally, when he could no longer hear the drum, he released his wife, but held her firmly by the hand. They traveled back to where they were buried and leaped back into their bodies.

The man could hear his mother weeping, and called out to her. This frightened the old woman, who ran home to get her husband. The old man didn't believe her but finally went to the gravesite with his wife. There they uncovered the bodies and found that their son was indeed alive. The people quickly erected a ceremonial hut. The man and woman went into the hut while oil was poured over hot stones. The woman who had been dead cried out for a long time. Finally, she was no longer crying, and the people heard the man and his wife conversing. The man called for water to wash their faces and then the people opened the hut. The couple came out and the woman was alive.

Mechling included the Malecite narrative "The Man Who Followed His Wife into Spirit Land." Once there was a man who dearly loved his wife. When she became ill and showed no signs of improvement, the man made plans to follow her spirit. He cut a hole in their wigwam beside where she slept. Then he went outside and sat next to the hole watching for her spirit to leave. It wasn't long before he saw a wisp of what looked like smoke pass by him. He gathered his belongings for the journey and followed her spirit. He traveled all day, and at night he came to a camp where he asked an old woman if she had seen his wife pass by. "Yes, about noon," she said. The man asked if she thought he would be able to catch up. The old woman didn't know, but told him to continue his travels and he would come to the home of a much older woman who would probably know the answer.

So the man continued on his journey without stopping to rest. The next evening he came to another camp and found a woman who looked older than anyone he had ever seen previously. Again he asked if she had seen his wife. "Yes, last evening." He asked this old woman if she thought he could catch up. Again the reply was, "Continue on your journey and you will come to the house of a woman much older than I. Perhaps she will have the answer."

The man continued and arrived the next evening at the camp of an old woman who looked even older than the one before. He asked if she had seen his wife. "Yes, yesterday morning." When he asked if he thought he could catch up to his wife, the old woman told him that it would be difficult, but if he would do exactly as she said, it might be possible. She gave him a nut to take with him and instructed him to set out in a certain direction and to ignore all the noises he might hear, even if he heard his wife's voice. When he arrived at a certain wigwam, he was to sit in a corner. The spirits would dance around him, and when his wife danced near him, he was to open the nut. This would bring her back to life. When she passed by, he was to close the nut. Then he was to leave the wigwam and return in the direction he came.

On his way home, he stopped at the wigwam of the first old woman. She asked how he had fared. The man described what had happened, and the old woman asked to see the nut. She told him that it was full of oil, and when he returned home he was to dig up his wife's body and grease all of her joints with the oil. The old woman also gave him a comb to comb his wife's hair. The man thanked the old woman and in the morning proceeded on his way.

It took him a long time to reach his home, and when he did, he found that the people had all aged greatly in his absence. He made a shovel and dug up his wife's bones. He oiled her joints as he was instructed and when he was finished, his wife looked as she had before her illness. She asked for a drink of water. He then rushed to his mother-in-law's to get clothes for his wife. The old woman began to weep with joy that she would soon see her daughter again. The man returned to his wife, and when she had dressed they went to her parent's camp. The old people then became young again, looking as they did before the woman died.

A number of Native American myths about the afterlife are similar to the Greek "Orpheus" tale. In this tragic story, Orpheus's bride, Eurydice, died. Overcome with grief, Orpheus traveled to Hades and succeeded in persuading Pluto, the king of the dead, to let her return with him to the land of the living. There was a stipulation, however, and it required Orpheus to refrain from looking back at Eurydice while they traveled to the upper world. Unfortunately, Orpheus was unable to keep from looking at his wife, and she immediately was taken from him.

The following Comanche narrative was recorded by Ake Hultkrantz during an interview with Dr. Ralph Linton. Dr. Linton in turn heard it during his work with the Comanche in 1933.

There was a young man who loved his wife so much that when she died, he vowed to follow her. He made preparations and rode off to the west. He traveled so long that all of his provisions and everything he had with him gave out, including his horse. Finally, he arrived on foot to the region of the dead. He was greeted by children skipping around him. Then he found his father-in-law's home where his wife was staying. He asked his wife to return with him. She was unable to decide because although she loved her husband, she was happy where she was. Finally, her father settled the issue. He told his son-in-law, "You may take my daughter back to the land of the living. But as you travel east, you may not touch her until you get to the place where the buffalo are. Give her a buffalo kidney to eat and then she will become alive. You must never strike her, for if you do, she will return to us."

The young couple set off on their journey and eventually arrived on the plains. The husband killed a buffalo and gave a kidney to his wife to eat. She then became alive again and they happily returned to their village. Life went on well until autumn. One day as they lay together, the man wanted to pull the buffalo hide around himself and his wife. As he tugged on the robe, his hand slipped and struck his wife. "You hit me and now I have to return to the land of the dead!" she cried as her voice faded away.

See also Ghosts

References and further reading:

Bloomfield, Leonard. *Menomini Texts.* 1928. New York: AMS Press, 1974.

Hultkrantz, Åke. *The North American Indian Orpheus Tradition: A Contribution to Comparative Religion.* Monograph Series, Publication no. 2. Stockholm: Ethnographical Museum of Sweden, 1957.

Mechling, W. H. *Malecite Tales.* Memoir 49, Anthropological Series, no. 4. Ottawa: Government Printing Bureau, 1914.

ALARANA AND HER BROTHER

Inupiat (North Alaskan Eskimos), Arctic

A tale of a brother and sister who were eaten by wolves and then became caribou.

There was a famine at Point Barrow. Everyone died except for a girl named Alarana and her brother. The siblings set off to find other people, but on the way they were surrounded and eaten by a pack of hungry wolves (who were sometimes wolves and sometimes people). An old woman among them asked to have the children's bones. She spread caribou skins on the floor and then laid out the children's bones on top of the skins. Then she laid walrus guts over all the bones and sang a magic song. Soon the bones began to move and the children came back to life as humans wearing clothes made from caribou skins.

Eventually the brother and sister traveled inland. They came upon a herd of caribou and were surprised they could approach it without startling it. As the siblings walked among the caribou, they discovered that they had turned into caribou. During the following days, the brother and sister learned to live like caribou. They scraped snow from the ground to uncover moss. However, for Alarana and her brother, the moss seemed to taste like human food such as guts and whale skin. They also learned to graze while keeping watch for hunters and other enemies of the caribou.

When it came time for hunters to set traps for the caribou, Alarana and her brother were able to avoid being caught because they remembered how the traps worked. At night they would quietly approach the hunters' camp and hear them talking. Alarana missed humans so much that she and her brother finally removed their caribou coats and went into the camp. There they were welcomed and the hunters told about the poor results of their expedition.

Alarana held a séance and convinced the spirits to allow the animals to be caught. But she told the hunters that there was one condition. One special caribou was to be saved for her; no one else could have it. However, as it sometimes happens, there was a greedy hunter in the group who claimed the animal for himself. So Alarana and her brother donned their coats and returned to the forest as caribou. The hunters from that camp never again had good fortune when hunting caribou.

See also Transformation, Human-Animal

References and further reading:

Gill, Sam D., and Irene F. Sullivan. *Dictionary of Native American Mythology.* Santa Barbara, Calif.: ABC-CLIO, 1992.

Rasmussen, Knud. *The Alaskan Eskimos, as Described in the Posthumous Notes of Dr. Knud Rasmussen.* 1952. Report of the Fifth Thule Expedition, vol. 10, no. 3. New York: AMS Press, 1976.

ANGAKOK

Inuit, Yupik Eskimos (Alaskan Eskimos), Arctic

A shaman.

Angakoks (angakut) were most often men; however, a woman could also become an angakok.

How a person became an *angakok* depended on the situation. Sometimes a son would be trained to follow in his father's footsteps, or an established *angakok* might tutor a young person who exhibited a special gift or talent. Others were called through strange dreams or visions. During the training period, the novice learned not only the oral traditions and ceremonies that would need to be performed, but also the special language of the *angakoks.* This language was comprised of archaic words and expressions handed down over the ages by *angakoks* across the Arctic. Somewhere during the training period, the novice *angakok* would receive one or more familiar spirits (sometimes referred to as "helping spirits" and even "guardian spirits"). These spirits would be visible only to the *angakok.*

Angakoks lived as their neighbors did until intervention with the spiritual world was needed. Then they would be called upon to perform ceremonies to cure the sick or to discover the cause of misfortunes such as accidents, bad

Eskimo medicine man and sick boy. (Library of Congress)

weather, or unsuccessful hunting expeditions. Payment was expected for services rendered to an individual or a family, but ceremonies for the common good of the village or other group seem to have been performed without charge.

Often illnesses or difficulties resulted from a taboo being broken. The *angakok* would hold a ceremony in which his familiar spirits would assist him to travel outside of his body to far-off places where he would learn the cause of the problem and how to rectify the situation. Once he returned to his body, the *angakok* would question the individual or other persons in the household. The general belief was that the *angakok* knew who was at fault, so those he questioned were obliged to answer him truthfully. At times only a confession was needed, and then the *angakok* would announce that all would be well. At other times, however, he would declare that certain acts of penance must be performed, ranging from cleaning the urine pots before dawn to swapping wives.

One of the most widely reported rituals was the Central Eskimo's Sedna ceremony, which was performed each autumn to ensure that hunters would be successful. Sedna, the Sea Woman, became angry with humans when they broke her taboos. In order to pacify her, an *angakok's* spirit, while in a dream, had to travel down to Adlivun where Sedna and her father lived. Once inside her house, the *angakok* smoothed out Sedna's hair, which is difficult for her to do since she has no fingers. He also pleaded (some say fought) with Sedna to let the animals return to the hunters so the people would not starve. Sedna then informed him about the people's transgressions and her anger toward them. The *angakok* would assure Sedna that the people were sorry and would promise that from now on they would keep all of her taboos.

Once the *angakok*'s spirit returned to his body, there was a time for communal confessions, and then much rejoicing that Sedna had been tamed and the hunting parties would be successful.

See also Adlivun; Sedna; Shaman

References and further reading:

Boas, Franz. *The Central Eskimo.* Lincoln: University of Nebraska Press, 1964.

Rink, Hinrich. *Tales and Traditions of the Eskimo, with a Sketch of Their Habits, Religion, Language, and Other Peculiarities.* 1875. Reprint, New York: AMS Press, 1975.

Spencer, Robert F. *The North Alaskan Eskimo: A Study in Ecology and Society.* 1959. Bulletin, Smithsonian Institution, Bureau of American Ethnology 171. New York: Dover Publications, 1976.

Weyer, Edward Moffat. *The Eskimos: Their Environment and Folkways.* Hamden, Conn.: Archon Books, 1962. First published 1932 by Yale University Press.

ANI HYUNTIKWALASKI

Cherokee, Southeast

This story explains how man acquired fire through the actions of the Thunderers and the little Water Spider. The Thunderers, who inhabit the Darkening Land in the west, are the sons of the great spirits Kanati (The Lucky Hunter) and Selu (Corn). The spider is a culture hero that appears often in most Native American mythology but is otherwise absent from Southeastern stories.

Long ago, the world was without fire and was cold until the Thunderers set fire to a hollow sycamore tree with their lightning. The animals could see the smoke but could not reach the tree, because it grew on an island.

Various birds volunteered to fly to the tree and bring back the fire. The Raven went first, but while he was wondering what to do, his feathers were burned black, and he returned without fire. The little Screech Owl went next, but as he was looking down inside the tree, a blast of hot air nearly burned out his eyes. He managed to fly home, but it was some time before he recovered, and his eyes remain red to this day. The Hoot Owl and Horned Owl tried next, but the smoke from the now fiercely burning fire nearly blinded them, and ashes borne by the wind made white rings around their eyes that they could not rub away.

No other birds would venture to the island, so the Black Racer snake and the great Blacksnake both swam to the fire and were scorched black. At last the Water Spider volunteered to go and bring back the fire. She spun a small bowl, a *tusti* bowl, and fastened it to her back. The Water Spider crossed the water to the island, put one coal of fire into her bowl, and returned safely with it. Ever since, man has had fire.

See also Culture Hero(es); Kanati and Selu; Spider

References and further reading:

Hudson, Charles. *The Southeastern Indians.* Knoxville: University of Tennessee Press, 1992. First published 1976.

Mooney, James. *James Mooney's History, Myths, and Sacred Formulas of the Cherokees: Containing the Full Texts of "Myths of the Cherokee" (1900) and "The Sacred Formulas of the Cherokees" (1891) as published by the Bureau of American Ethnology; With a New Biographical Introduction, "James Mooney and the Eastern Cherokees."* Ashville, N.C.: Historical Images, 1992.

Ugvwiyuhi. *Journey to Sunrise: Myths and Legends of the Cherokee.* Claremore, Okla.: Egi Press, 1977.

AURORA BOREALIS

Algonquian tribes, Subarctic; Inuit, Inupiat (North Alaskan Eskimos), Arctic

For the people of the far northern regions, the aurora borealis is a spectacular phenomenon. Children were warned to hide when the aurora was active and adults thought it caused head and neck pain. Some groups believed that the lights were caused by spirits holding torches as they searched for the souls of those who recently died. These spirits also communicated with humans by making whistling sounds and the humans whispered back with messages for the dead.

One evening two brothers went outside to watch the *kiguruyat* ("spirits who gnaw with their teeth") play football. The older brother cautioned his younger brother not to talk loudly or to whistle; otherwise, the spirits might find them and carry them away. While hiding in some willows, the older boy told this story:

"Late one night there were two boys playing outdoors. Suddenly they heard hissing noises and saw colored lights flashing in the sky. It was the *kiguruyat* coming for them. The older brother told the younger one to cover his face and lie down in the snow. When the *kiguruyat* finally left, the boys crawled to a shelter under a willow. The lights of the *kiguruyat* were still flashing in the distance. The younger brother then asked, 'What is that ball that they are playing with?' His brother told him that it was the head of a disobedient child who had wandered off and was taken up to the sky by the *kiguruyat*. The team leader bit the child's head off with his sharp teeth."

When the older brother finished the story, the young boy asked, "Do you really think the *kiguruyat* are using a child's head for a football?"

"Yes," his older brother answered.

The younger brother was frightened and wanted to go home. So his brother waited until the flashing lights were far away and then said, "Run! Cover your mouth and breathe into your parka." Just as they neared their igloo the *kiguruyat* came swooping overhead. When they were safely inside, the younger brother said, "If you had not protected me, the *kiguruyat* would have carried me away." He then promised to keep watch over his little brother, too.

References and further reading:

Seidelman, Harold, and James Turner. *The Inuit Imagination: Arctic Myth and Sculpture.* Vancouver: Douglas and McIntyre; Seattle: University of Washington Press, 2001. First published 1994 by Thames and Hudson.

Spencer, Robert F. *The North Alaskan Eskimo: A Study in Ecology and Society.* 1959. Bulletin, Smithsonian Institution, Bureau of American Ethnology, 171. New York: Dover Publications, 1976.

Ticasuk. *Tales of Ticasuk: Eskimo Legends and Stories.* Fairbanks: University of Alaska Press, 1987.

BEAN WOMAN

Seneca, Northeast Woodlands

Beans, Corn, and Squash, pioneered by the Indians of central Mexico, were called "The Three Sisters" by many tribes in the Northeast. A narrative in the Curtin and Hewitt collection tells of Bean Woman.

Long, long ago there was a certain village located near a river. The people heard singing coming from downstream. It was Bean Woman who sang, "Who will marry me?" The first to answer her was Panther Man. Bean Woman asked, "If I marry you, what will you give me to eat?" Panther Man's reply was that he would keep her supplied with meat. But, Bean Woman said, "In that case, I cannot marry you as I cannot eat that kind of food."

So she again sang, "Who will marry me? Isn't there anyone who will marry me?" Soon Deer Man drew near and offered to marry her. "What will you give me to eat if I marry you?" she asked. Deer Man replied, "We will have buds and the bark from tender young saplings for our food." To that Bean Woman sighed, "That will not do. I have never had buds nor bark for food."

A third time Bean Woman sang out, "Is there anyone who is willing to marry me? Let him come and ask me." This time Bear Man came and said, "Yes, please marry me." Once again Bean Woman asked, "What sort of food will you provide for me?" Bear Man told her of all the many baskets of nuts that he had stored away. She could eat as many nuts as she wished. But, Bean Woman rejected his offer as well.

Again, Bean Woman began singing, "Is there anyone who will marry me?" The fourth suitor was Wolf Man, who said, "I am willing. Marry me." Bean Woman asked Wolf Man the same question that she had asked the others, "If I marry you, what will you bring me to eat?" Wolf Man said, "I will bring meat and venison for you to eat." But Bean Woman refused to eat that sort of food and sent him away.

Bean Woman sang again, "Is there anyone willing to marry me? Let him ask me." Corn Man approached and said, "I am willing, if you will accept me." Bean Woman asked him, "What sort of food would you provide for me, if I marry you?" Corn Man said, "You will have sweet corn to eat always." This was the answer Bean Woman had been longing for, and when she accepted his offer of marriage, Corn Man said, "Come to me." Bean Woman rushed to him and threw her arms around his neck. "This is what our Creator meant for us." Bean Woman and Corn Man continued to happily live together. This is why we find the bean vine embracing the corn stalk even to this day.

See also Corn

References and further reading:

Curtin, Jeremiah, and J. N. B. Hewitt. *Seneca Fiction, Legends, and Myths.* Thirty-Second Annual Report of the Bureau of American Ethnology to the Secretary of the Smithsonian Institution, 1910–1911. Washington, DC: Government Printing Office, 1918.

BEAR

Bear is one of the most common characters in Native American myths. In some stories, he is friendly and intelligent. He appears as a culture hero, friend, master of animals, and chief of the underworld. He has been known to give power and heal. Bear taught the Oneida gentleness and strength, but at times he was malicious and perverse. Ceremonies and rituals centering on the bear were practiced among a variety of cultures, particularly the Algonquians; the bear was revered in hunting practices, for example.

In the following story of the Cree, Bear is benevolent.

A bear found a boy in the woods and cared for him for several years as though they were father and son. During the summers, the bear would hunt, and together he and the boy would gather blueberries in the autumn. They would take their food to where they planned to spend the winter.

One fall, the child's father started to sing. His song was so powerful and strong, the bear was unable to oppose the father with his own song, because he forgot his own song and stopped singing.

During the following winter, the father sang again, and he defeated the bear's song once more. The next day, the bear told the child he sensed that the boy's father was preparing to come and find them.

The father started walking directly to where the bear and the child were staying. The bear tried to lead him off his path by throwing a porcupine out of his den, but the man kept walking straight. Next, the bear threw out a beaver. Then, he threw out a partridge, but the man still kept walking. The bear realized the man's power was stronger than his. The bear next tried to use his magic to defeat the man. He lay on his back with all four legs in the air, and an object came hurling out of the sky, causing a huge storm. But the father still kept coming toward the bear.

The bear knew that the boy's father was about to kill him, so he gave the boy one of his forelegs. He told the boy to keep it wrapped up and hanging in his tent, above where he always sat. He said that if the boy wanted to hunt bears, he should climb to get a good view of his surroundings and look for rising smoke. Only he would be able to see the smoke, and if he went to the place where the smoke was, he would always find a bear.

The child's father then broke the snow around the bear's den. The bear came outside and was killed. The man took his son home, and the boy watched over the bear's foreleg as he had been told.

Man dressed in a full-body bear costume, 1914. The bear had the duty of guarding the dance house. (Library of Congress)

The boy eventually got married and was an extremely successful bear hunter. His hunting group was able to live almost entirely on bear meat. Sometimes he told another hunter where to look for a bear, and he would always find and kill one.

This hunting group was visited by another. The women of this group were very jealous because the hero of the first group always found a bear and their husbands were never able to kill any. One day, while the hero was off hunting, one of the women of the second hunting group entered his tent in search of his source of power. There she found the package, and started to unwrap it. Immediately, the hero realized what was happening, and he returned to camp. He entered his tent and asked for the culprit. The woman confessed that it was her. He told her that she could find a bear the next day by going to a specific place he described.

The hero then removed his ammunition pouch and clothes and went to sit at his accustomed place. The leg instantly fell down, and both he and the leg disappeared underground without a trace. It was said that he had become a bear.

See also Girl Who Married a Bear; Great Bear Constellation; Qumu?uc

References and further reading:

Barnouw, Victor. *Wisconsin Chippewa Myths & Tales and Their Relation to Chippewa Life: Based on Folktales Collected by Victor Barnouw, Joseph B. Casagrande, Ernestine Friedl, and Robert E. Ritzenthaler.* Madison: University of Wisconsin Press, 1977.

Rockwell, David B. *Giving Voice to Bear: North American Indian Myths, Rituals, and Images of the Bear.* Rev. ed. Lanham, Md.: Roberts Rinehart, 2003. First published 1991.

Schaeffer, Claude E. *Bear Ceremonialism of the Kutenai Indians.* Studies in Plains Anthropology and History, no. 4. Washington, D.C.: U.S. Dept. of the Interior, Indian Arts and Crafts Board, Museum of the Plains Indian, 1966.

BLIND BOY

Inuit, Arctic

This tale about how the Narwhal got its tusk is known in many areas of the North American Arctic.

Once there was a blind boy whose mother was very cruel to him. Even though he helped kill a polar bear that wandered by, his mother would not let him have any of it to eat. He could smell meat cooking, but his mother denied it. The boy's sister, however, hid some of her supper and later gave it to him while their mother was out. The boy decided to find an opportunity to kill his cruel mother.

Sometime later, when the boy was outside, a large loon carried him off to its nest on the edge of a cliff. The loon then dove into the water with the boy. They did this several times until the boy's eyesight was restored. His vision was so good that he could see far in the distance to where his mother was. When he returned to his home, his mother realized that she must be careful and from then on she treated him more kindly.

One day the mother and son were hunting narwhal. The mother held the end of the harpoon rope by tying it around her waist, but she feared that a large narwhal would drag her into the sea. So she asked her son to aim for only the small ones. This he did, and they soon were feasting on the blubber. Another time they saw a large narwhal and a smaller one. The mother again asked her son to aim for the smaller narwhal, as she still feared being pulled into the sea. However, the boy aimed at the large narwhal and his spear struck deep. The narwhal struggled to get free and pulled away from shore. It was too strong and the mother was dragged into the water. She yelled for the boy to toss her a knife so she could free herself, but he refused, and the cruel woman was drowned.

Then the woman became a narwhal herself. Her hair, which was worn in a twisted knot on top of her head, became a tusk. From then on, narwhals have had twisted tusks.

See also Transformation, Human-Animal

References and further reading:

Kroeber, A. L. "Tales of the Smith Sound Eskimo." *Journal of American Folklore* 12, no. 44 (January-March 1899): 166–182.

Nungak, Zebedee, and Eugene Arima. *Inuit Stories: Povungnituk.* Hull, Quebec: Canadian Museum of Civilization, National Museums of Canada, 1988.

Seidelman, Harold, and James Turner. *The Inuit Imagination: Arctic Myth and Sculpture.* Vancouver: Douglas and McIntyre; Seattle: University of Washington Press, 2001. First published 1994 by Thames and Hudson.

BLOOD CLOT

Ute, Great Basin

In this tale of human creation, a baby boy born from a clot of buffalo blood derives power from this mighty animal. Another story in which a boy forms from the blood of a game animal is "Kanati and Selu," told by the Cherokee.

Long ago, an old man discovered some buffalo tracks and followed them until they stopped, where he came upon a large clot of blood. Since game was scarce and he and his wife were hungry, he wrapped it up and brought it home.

The old man's wife placed the clot in a kettle of water, but before the water came to a boil, they heard a voice cry out. The man reached into the kettle and pulled out a baby boy, who had somehow formed from the blood clot. The old couple named the boy Blood Clot and raised him as their son.

Eventually, Blood Clot learned to hunt game and birds. His father proudly noted his ability to track and kill a different kind of animal every time he went out: a cottontail, then a badger, a deer, an elk, a mountain goat, a mountain lion, an otter, a beaver. Now they had plenty of food.

One day, Blood Clot told the old man and his wife that he wanted to visit a village where many people lived. He promised to hunt for them one last time, day and night, before he left, so they would have plenty of food. Blood Clot instructed them to tie up their tent, put rocks on the edges to weigh them down, and fasten the door securely so the wind would not carry it away. He warned his mother and father that the wind would be strong, but they should not be afraid, and they should stay inside until he called them to come out.

Blood Clot hunted all night while they slept. When daylight arrived, he called his mother and father out of the tent. Upon opening the door, they saw dead buffalo lying all over on the ground. He instructed them to dry the meat and hides, and asked his mother to make him a lunch before he left. His parents cried and asked him to someday return.

After traveling a few days, Blood Clot reached the village, where he was invited to sit down with the chief and his daughter. The chief asked him where he came from and which tribe he belonged to. Blood Clot told him he did not know. The chief then stepped outside and invited his people to come and meet their visitor. The people asked Blood Clot if he belonged to various tribes—Deer, Elk, Otters, Beavers, and others—but he told them he thought not. Finally, one old man said that Blood Clot's power suggested he was one of the Buffalo. Blood Clot thought about this carefully and agreed.

Blood Clot was asked to stay in the village and marry the chief's daughter. On the eve of the wedding, Blood Clot asked his father-in-law to bring him an arrow, which he did. He told him to have all the tipis fastened securely and warn the people to stay indoors, because a great storm was coming. In the morning, Blood Clot called to the chief, who came outside to find dead buffalo lying before every lodge. The entire village was invited to partake of a great feast.

One day, a hunting party left the village to find buffalo. Long before, Blood Clot had warned his wife to never say the word "calf," as he was part of the Buffalo Calf and it was part of him. As the party was butchering its kill, another herd of buffalo thundered past. Blood Clot's wife pointed and cried out "Kill that calf!" Blood Clot instantly jumped on a horse and galloped away, changing into a buffalo as he did so. Forever after, he ran with the buffalo.

See also Kanati and Selu; Transformation, Human-Animal

References and further reading:

Erdoes, Richard, and Alfonso Ortiz, eds. *American Indian Myths and Legends.* New York: Pantheon Books, 1984.

Mooney, James. *James Mooney's History, Myths, and Sacred Formulas of the Cherokees: Containing the Full Texts of "Myths of the Cherokee" (1900) and "The Sacred Formulas of the Cherokees" (1891) as published by the Bureau of American Ethnology; With a New Biographical Introduction, "James Mooney and the Eastern Cherokees."* Ashville, N.C.: Historical Images, 1992.

BLUE JAY

Chinook, Northwest Coast

Blue Jay tales are found among many peoples of the Pacific Northwest region. Blue Jay is sometimes portrayed as a trickster character. What follows is part of a series of tales involving Blue Jay and his sister Ioi.

One night the ghosts decided to buy a wife and traveled to the village where Blue Jay and Ioi lived. They left a dowry of dentalia for her parents and then disappeared with her. After a year had passed, Blue Jay wished to see his sister again. So he said, "I'll go look for her." He wasn't sure which way to go, so he asked everyone he met, "Where do dead people live?" At last he was able to reach the Land of the Ghosts and was happily reunited with his sister. In that village he found that all the houses were full of bones. There was even a pile of bones near his sister that she introduced to him as his brother-in-law. "Ha, she's lying!" Blue Jay thought. "That pile of bones cannot be my brother-in-law!"

That night the houses were suddenly full of people. Blue Jay asked Ioi about the people, but she just laughed and said that they weren't people at all, but ghosts. Then she encouraged him to go along fishing with one of his brother-in-law's relatives, but warned him not to speak to the boy. However, when Blue Jay joined in the song the ghosts were singing, he found that the boy had become a pile of bones. A little while later, the boy was sitting in the back of the canoe again. Every once in awhile, Blue Jay would talk loudly, just to see the boy fall to a pile of bones again. He kept himself amused with this game until they came to the fishing spot. The boy told him to dip his net in, but when Blue Jay pulled his net out, it only contained twigs and leaves, so he threw them back into the water. A few leaves fell into the canoe, so the boy gathered them up. This happened several times until Blue Jay finally decided to keep some of the twigs and branches for sister's fire.

When they returned to Ioi's house, she told him that he should not have thrown the leaves and twigs back into the water because they were really fish. Blue Jay thought she was lying again. However, his sister went down to the beach and brought back two salmon she found in the bottom of the canoe. Blue Jay didn't know where she'd gotten them, but she told him they were ones that he had caught.

The next night, Blue Jay went fishing again with the boy, but this time, instead of throwing the leaves and branches back into the water, he piled them up in the canoe. On the way back home, Blue Jay delighted in shouting several times just to make the ghost people turn into piles of bones. His sister met them on the beach and helped carry the salmon back to her house.

On the following night, Blue Jay heard someone say that a whale had been found. His sister gave him a knife and urged him to hurry down to the beach. When he got there, all he saw was a big log. He yelled at the people, "Where is the whale?" But they all fell into piles of bones. In a while the people were back up and started peeling bark off the log. So Blue Jay did the same and hauled two large pieces of bark back to his sister's house. He threw them on the ground and then went inside to tell her that it was only a log on the beach. But his sister looked outside and exclaimed, "No, it is whale meat!" So Blue Jay went back to the beach. On his way he met someone carrying bark up the path. Blue Jay shouted at him and he fell into a pile of bones. Blue Jay picked up the bark and carried it home. He did this several times more and was able to get a lot of whale meat for his sister.

The next morning, Blue Jay decided to play tricks on the ghosts. He went into houses and changed the bones around. He put an old man's head on the bones of a child and the child's head on the old man. That night, the child could not sit up because his head was too heavy and the old man's head was too light. The next day, Blue Jay put the heads back with the right bones, but switched their legs around. The old man had the short legs and the child had the long legs.

Eventually, the ghost people complained about Blue Jay's tricks, and Ioi's husband told her to send him home. At first he didn't want to go, but he finally left. On his way, he came to a prairie that was ablaze, and Blue Jay burned to death. Then he went back to the land of the ghosts. His sister met him at the river and went over to him in her husband's canoe. Blue Jay thought the canoe was beautiful, but Ioi reminded him that he used to complain that it was full of holes and covered with moss. He thought she was lying to him. When they came to the village, the people were playing games and singing. Blue Jay shouted at them, trying to get them to fall into piles of bones, but the people just laughed at him. He kept pestering them to no avail until finally his sister told him that he was dead, too. And then he became quiet.

See also Ghosts; Trickster

References and further reading:

Erdoes, Richard, and Alfonso Ortiz, eds. *American Indian Myths and Legends.* New York: Pantheon Books, 1984.

Grinnell, George Bird. 1901. *The Punishment of the Stingy and Other Indian Stories.* Reprint, Lincoln: University of Nebraska Press, 1982.

Spence, Lewis. *The Myths of the North American Indians.* New York: Gramercy Books, 1994. First published 1914 by G.G. Harrap.

Thompson, Stith. *Tales of the North American Indians.* 1929. Reprint, Bloomington: Indiana University Press, 1971.

BUFFALO WIFE

Okanagon, Plateau

In the Buffalo Wife tale, Coyote is an anti-hero. His excesses and indiscretions are the reason the buffalo herds didn't venture very far west of the plains.

Coyote was traveling north when he saw an old buffalo skeleton and relieved himself on the skull. A short time later he heard a great noise, and when he looked back there was the old buffalo bull charging him. Coyote ran to a nearby boulder, but the buffalo chased him around and around. Finally, Coyote stopped and gasped, "Why are you chasing me?" The buffalo was angry because Coyote had urinated on his head.

To distract his attacker, Coyote asked, "What killed you?" The buffalo explained that he had been in a fight with a younger bull and lost because his old horns were dull. Then Coyote had an idea. He told the old buffalo that if he promised not to hurt him, Coyote would make his horns sharp again. So Coyote attached sharp roots to the buffalo's horns. Buffalo rammed a log with his horns and gave it a toss. The new horns worked so well that Buffalo declared to Coyote that they were now friends.

Buffalo asked Coyote to accompany him back to his herd. He would fight the young bull again to win his wives back. Buffalo even promised Coyote that he'd give one of the wives to him. They eventually found Buffalo's herd and the young bull with all of Buffalo's wives. Buffalo attacked the younger bull and killed him. Then Buffalo said to Coyote, "Chose whichever wife you want." Coyote picked a fat one, because she would be thin by the time they arrived back at Coyote's home. However, before Coyote and his new wife set out, Buffalo warned him, "Do not sleep with her for three nights. After that you may do what you want."

They started back to Coyote's home and on the second night, Coyote thought, "Buffalo's time is too long." So he grabbed his wife, but before he could begin what he intended, she vanished. Coyote assumed she had returned to her own people, so he went back. Buffalo was angry that Coyote did not obey him, but since they were friends, he let Coyote take his wife again.

This time Coyote decided to follow Buffalo's command. But before they arrived at his home, Coyote was getting hungry. He decided to kill his wife and eat her. Coyote told her to go one way up a ravine and he would go the other so he could hunt. However, he ran around the hill and was at the top before his wife climbed that far. Coyote shot and killed her. Then he cut her up and spread out her hide to dry.

Before he got around to enjoying any of the meat, he decided he had to defecate. But, he could not have a movement and was seized with pains and unable to get up. About that time, Magpie came and sat on the carcass, and then other birds and animals came as well. Coyote called them names but they kept on devouring the meat until the bones were clean. Finally, they all left. Then Coyote finally was able to defecate, but he was angry at his dung and beat it with a stick because it had caused him to lose all that meat.

He followed the animals' tracks and found a few bones and his wife's bladder. He roasted the bones and scraped the marrow into the bladder. Then he tied the bladder shut and put it aside to cool while he rested. He checked on it several times, but it was still hot. Coyote then decided to cool it off in a pool of water. But it still was taking a long time to cool off. He saw a muskrat swimming nearby and asked him to take the bladder and dive to the bottom of the pool so the marrow would cool and harden. The Coyote stomped his foot and scared Muskrat, who dove into the water. Coyote thought that was a lot of fun and decided to stomp his foot again when Muskrat returned. However, when he did it the second time, Muskrat jerked his head suddenly and the bladder tore. The contents of the bladder poured out onto the water.

Coyote jumped into the water to save the marrow, but all he got was hands full of water.

In the end Coyote had lost his wife and his food. If he had not been so foolish and had taken his wife home, there would have been buffalo all over the land. But now buffaloes do not venture any farther west than where Coyote killed his wife. And now some lakes have an oily surface because the marrow spilled on the water.

See also Coyote

References and further reading:

Bierhorst, John. *The Mythology of North America: With a New Afterword.* Oxford: Oxford University Press, 2002. First published 1985 by William Morrow.

Boas, Franz, ed. *Folk-Tales of Salishan and Sahaptin Tribes.* 1917. New York: Kraus Reprint, 1969.

BUTTERFLY

Butterflies are numerous in the mythology of Native Americans. The butterfly was an especially prominent figure in Hopi myth and ritual, occurring frequently on their prehistoric pottery in a ritual Butterfly Dance. There is a butterfly clan in one of the Hopi pueblos and a Hopi butterfly kachina.

The Navajo story cycle known as *Ajilee* tells of the origin of butterflies and features a hero that appears in a butterfly disguise. In a Jicarilla story of the emergence, beautiful butterflies lure girls from the underworld. A Zuni kachina, Paiyatemu, has a flute from which butterflies come forth as it is played.

The sheer beauty of many butterflies is explained in a legend of the Tohono O'Odham. According to this myth, the Creator, watching some children at play in a village, started to feel sorry for them when he realized that their destiny was to grow old and become wrinkled, fat, blind, weak, and gray-haired. The thought that the puppies he saw would age and grow mangy saddened him, as well as the knowledge that the flowers would fade and the leaves would fall with the coming winter. So, to gladden his heart, and give the children something to enjoy, he gathered beautiful colors from various sources such as the sunlight, leaves, flowers, and the sky. He put them into a magical bag, together with the songs of birds, and presented it to the children. When the children opened it, hundreds of colored butterflies flew out and thoroughly enchanted them, as they had never seen anything so lovely. These butterflies also sang, which further delighted the children. However, the songbirds became jealous and complained to the Creator because the butterflies were so beautiful *and* could sing. The Creator agreed that the songs belonged to the birds and took away the butterflies' ability to sing. This is why butterflies are so beautifully colored but now silent.

The origin of the first butterfly is told in the White Mountain Apache legend of the Flower Maiden, a story that emphasizes the importance of the role of obligation:

Long ago lived a young girl named Yu-Ti, which means "beautiful maiden." As the first-born child of the tribal medicine man and his wife, she was accorded special responsibilities. Because she was beautiful and possessed gifts and talents much sought after in a bride, she had many eager suitors among the braves of her camp. Few, however, compared with the tribe's two favorites.

The first was Ko-So-Wa, which means "hidden love." He was full of vigor, and excelled in running, climbing, and swimming. He was a powerful fighter with weapons and a skilled hunter and trapper. He had loved Yu-Ti since childhood.

The second was To-Mo-Ka, which means "iron courage." He, too, was a powerful hunter, warrior, and trapper, and, though not as handsome as Ko-So-Wa, he was still attractive. He had won the admiration and respect of the tribe during a confrontation with a wolf that had invaded the Ndee camp and almost killed a small child. Like Ko-So-Wa, he was considered a worthy candidate for Yu-Ti's hand.

Because Yu-Ti was the daughter of the medicine man, and his firstborn, she was not free to marry just anyone, because she was considered an extraordinary woman. According to custom, a special contest would be held to select a new chief, and her husband was to be chosen for her from among the champions. Yu-Ti was obliged to marry the winner, for his victory showed that he had special qualities that would mean a prosperous future for their people following their union.

An announcement was made that a husband would be sought for Yu-Ti during the celebration of the harvest, on the first day of the new moon. Each brave was eligible for the chance to win the hand of the most beautiful woman of the tribe and become the new chief. The young men, ready for the contest to begin, eagerly assembled in the center of the camp, dressed in their most impressive regalia.

The first trial was a running test, which required a brave to chase after a wild horse on foot and return it to camp. This could take several days and a great deal of endurance. Both Ko-So-Wa and To-Mo-Ka brought their horses back to camp after just two days.

The second trial required a brave to swim to the deepest part of a swiftly-flowing river and retrieve a specific colored stone from the bottom. The few who successfully met this difficult challenge included both Ko-So-Wa and To-Mo-Ka.

The third trial tested the braves' skill and cleverness. They were sent into the woods with only one arrow and their bows, and asked to return with a hunting trophy that would feed a family. Game was scarce and difficult to find, since this was the time when herds were moving. After a week, only Ko-So-Wa and To-Mo-Ka each returned with a large stag. Thus concluded the first trials, and it looked as though the winner would be selected from among the two of them.

The second phase of the trials began with a contest in which each of the braves was required to defend himself, unarmed, against several opponents at once, opponents who were armed with war clubs. Ko-So-Wa and To-Mo-Ka both disarmed their adversaries and were the ones left to face the final test.

At this time, Yu-Ti prepared her bridal dress and the people prepared for a celebration. Her heart belonged to Ko-So-Wa, and she hoped that he would win. However, she believed that To-Mo-Ka was a great warrior and she felt warmly toward him. Should he prevail when the contest was over, she was prepared to bury her feelings for Ko-So-Wa and marry To-Mo-Ka as required.

The final and most important trial was called the Gift of the Sky Father. Each brave who had come this far was obliged to go to the Spirit Mountain and bring back a spirit prize that would be presented to the medicine man in exchange for his daughter. In times past, such prizes included a herd of captured mountain sheep, an eagle, or the body of a great bear. Such prizes were rare and special, and it was thought they were awarded only by the Giver of Life himself.

Ko-So-Wa and To-Mo-Ka left for the mountain, while the tribe prayed that one would be blessed by the Great Spirit. A sad and troubled Yu-Ti waited for them to return. Finally, after many days and nights, Ko-So-Wa returned with a majestic, wondrous gift and presented it to the tribe: a white baby buffalo. The tribe cheered with joy, as here was a sacred animal they believed would protect them from all enemies.

To-Mo-Ka returned several days later, and the people eagerly gathered around him to see with what he had returned. He unveiled a colorfully painted drum, which many felt was a gift unworthy of Yu-Ti. Everyone, including the chief and the medicine man, felt that Ko-So-Wa was the clear winner.

As people started to walk away, To-Mo-Ka proclaimed that he had spoken with the Great Spirit. He declared that, from that day onward, there would be no more dry seasons, as the people would be blessed with plenty of rain. To dispel their doubts, he withdrew from a small pouch a brightly-painted drumstick, sat down, and began to beat the drum with a slow cadence. As soon as To-Mo-Ka began to chant, the rains started to fall. The people were astonished, then impressed and delighted at the thought of always having the rain they needed for the harvest. Truly, both of the warriors had been blessed, but who was the most worthy of Yu-Ti? Who would be chosen for her husband?

The decision was not to be made, as the contest was interrupted when the tribe was forced to go to war with savage invaders from the north. Yu-Ti and all the other women who expected to marry during the celebration had to wait.

After many months had passed, and many battles fought, the Ndee gained the final victory. However, it was not without the loss of many dead, including Ko-So-Wa and To-Mo-Ka. Yu-Ti was crushed, and her people shared her sorrow. Her tears were endless, and it was difficult for anyone to console her. Finally, she told her people she could not rest until their bodies were found and given a proper burial.

Yu-Ti left her village and searched the battle sites that had been revealed to her by the chief. Discouraged, she prayed to the Great Spirit for guidance, who told her that he had covered the bodies of those who had fallen with soil and grass to hide the terrible sight of their bloodstained bodies. Yu-Ti despaired of ever finding them, and the Great Spirit took pity on her. He decided to give her the chance to find her lost ones and told Yu-Ti that he hereby ordered the shield design and color of each warrior to display as flowers, so that she could recognize the resting place of her Ko-So-Wa and To-Mo-Ka. But the Great Spirit realized that Yu-Ti would never live long enough to complete her search of every battlefield. Thus, he transformed her into a lovely butterfly, so that her spirit could return to wander and search among the flowers for her beloved warriors, an event that occurs every spring.

References and further reading:

Cuevas, Lou. *Apache Legends: Songs of the Wind Dancer.* Happy Camp, Calif.: Naturegraph, 1991.

Erdoes, Richard, and Alfonso Ortiz, eds. *American Indian Myths and Legends.* New York: Pantheon Books, 1984.

Fewkes, J. Walter. "The Butterfly in Hopi Myth and Ritual." *American Anthropologist,* n.s., 12, no. 4 (October-December 1910): 576–594.

Haile, Berard, comp. *Love-Magic and Butterfly People: The Slim Curly Version of the Ajilee and Mothway Myths.* American Tribal Religions, vol. 2. Flagstaff: Museum of Northern Arizona Press, 1978.

CANNIBAL DWARFS

Arapaho, Plains

Cannibals were featured in the myths of a number of North American tribal groups, such as the Heiltsuk (Bella Bella), Eskimo, and the Nez Percé. Arapaho myths that focused on "Little People" often characterized them as being cannibalistic. The following tale relates how an ingenious man outsmarted one of them.

A man was hunting by himself along a river. Eventually he came to a place where he could see smoke back in the woods and decided to find out where it was coming from. When he got deeper into the woods, he saw a tipi. As he approached it, he heard a voice from inside saying, "Someone is coming. Someone is here. Someone wants to come in." So the man went inside. There he saw a small man—a dwarf—who was blind.

The dwarf was very pleased to have this visitor arrive and said, "You are a good person to bring yourself to me so I can eat you." The man replied yes, that indeed had been his intention. He also told his host that he was a very fat man, so the dwarf and all of his family would enjoy eating him. Then the man suggested that the dwarf get started right away with the meal preparations. But the dwarf wanted to wait for the rest of his family to come home first. So the man agreed to wait patiently.

In the meantime, however, the man went outside and found a stick that he sharpened on one end. When he returned to the tipi, the man asked the dwarf, "What are these things hanging around the walls of your tipi?" The dwarf explained that they were the hearts of all of his relatives. The man asked, "This first one, then, whose heart is it?" The blind dwarf answered that it belonged to his father. So the man pierced it with his stick. Now the dwarf's family was away on a hunt, and at the exact time when the man pierced the first heart, the dwarf's father dropped dead. Then the man inquired about the second heart and was told that it belonged to the dwarf's mother. Again, he pierced it with his sharpened stick and the woman dropped dead. One by one the man went around the tipi wall, inquiring about the owner of each heart. When the dwarf named the heart's owner, the man pierced it and the owner dropped dead while away on the hunting trip.

Finally there was only one heart left. The man asked to whom it belonged. The dwarf responded, "It is my own heart." So the man pierced it and the dwarf dropped dead on the spot. The man who killed the cannibal dwarfs was a great hero.

Other Arapaho tales describe instances when cannibal dwarfs kidnapped young women, or at least tried to, in order to take them as wives. One myth about cannibal dwarfs depicted them as being about three feet tall, with dark skin, large stomachs, and a powerful build. These dwarfs supposedly had homes hewn from rocks. They were fast runners and could easily catch an Arapaho trying to flee from them. One man, however, did manage to escape by jumping across a stream that was too wide for the dwarf chasing him to hurdle.

Eventually, the raids by the dwarfs were claiming too many lives, so the people decided to rid their land of them once and for all. The Indians surrounded the dwarfs, who were trapped in the bottom of a gorge, and set the brush on the canyon walls on fire. As the fire raced toward them, the dwarfs tried to figure out how best to save their wives and children. One dwarf suggested burying them in the sand; another suggested putting them in the stream that flowed through the gorge. Finally, they decided that the best place for them was high up in the trees. However, as the fire raced down through the gorge, it

A Dzoonokwa (or Tsunukwa) totem pole measuring over 20 feet tall, depicting a figure with hands outstretched to receive dowry from the wife's family, 1914. (Library of Congress)

jewelry. Dzonokwa told the princess to put them on and then she would become strong also. So the young woman put on the gifts and then said that they would have to go to her father's house so that the man who cut her eyebrows could do the same for Dzonokwa.

On the way Dzonokwa asked if the people of the girl's tribe would hurt her. The princess assured her that they would not. When they entered the chief's house, the princess told her father that the Dzonokwa had come and wanted her eyebrows cut so they would be beautiful also. She said to her father, "Please go out and bring back the man who cut my eyebrows, so he may come and cut hers."

The chief went out and called for his warrior to sharpen his stone chisel and to bring it and a stone hammer to the chief's house. The warrior was instructed to cut through the Dzonokwa's eyebrows and kill her. When he arrived, the princess said, "This is the man who made my eyebrows beautiful." The warrior spoke to the Cannibal Woman and asked her not to scream. She assured him that she wouldn't mind the pain. He then instructed her to lay back so he could cut her eyebrows quickly and get back to his work. "And shut your eyes," he said, "so you won't see the point of my eyebrow cutter."

When the Dzonokwa closed her eyes, the warrior quickly hammered his chisel into her forehead and killed her. They cut off her head and burned her body. Afterward, the chief asked his daughter if she had seen the Cannibal Woman's home. "Yes," she said, "and there are many things in the house." So they traveled to the Dzonokwa's home and saw many articles of clothing, tanned hides, blankets, and dried meat. In the bedroom the princess found a beautiful mask that had red cedar bark twisted around it and an eagle's nest on top. The Chief called it the Nightmare-Bringer-Nest-Mask.

burned the underbrush and everything in its path. When the fire reached the trees, it continued up the trunks and consumed the trees and all of the dwarfs in them. None of them escaped, and that is why there are no cannibal dwarfs around today.

See also Cannibalism

References and further reading:

Bierhorst, John, ed. *The Red Swan: Myths and Tales of the American Indians.* Albuquerque: University of New Mexico Press, 1992. First published 1976 by Farrar, Straus, and Giroux.

Clark, Ella E. *Indian Legends from the Northern Rockies.* The Civilization of the American Indian Series, vol. 82. Norman: University of Oklahoma Press, 1966.

Dorsey, George A., and Alfred L. Kroeber. *Traditions of the Arapaho.* 1903. Sources of American Indian Oral Literature. Lincoln: University of Nebraska Press, 1997.

CANNIBAL WOMAN

Alsea, Kwakiutl, Northwest Coast

The Dzonokwa was a hideous looking giantess who carried children away to her home deep in the forest. Kwakiutl parents warned their children what would happen to them if she caught them alone. Adults feared the Dzonokwa, too, and blamed their nightmares on her. The Alsea have a similar legend about A'sin, the Monster Girl of the Woods, who was feared by all. Anyone who disappeared was believed to have been carried off by her. Children were rarely left alone, since they were especially vulnerable.

Among the Kwakiutl tales about the Cannibal Woman is one that relates her demise.

The chief of a certain village had a daughter who had recently become a woman. The princess stayed in her small hut observing all of the necessary taboos for sixteen days and then returned to her father's house. There her eyebrows were plucked in the fashion of the women of her tribe.

One day the princess walked alone in the woods. Her father scolded her and reminded her that the Dzonokwa might catch her and carry her off. However, the young woman disobeyed her father and again went on a long walk near the river. There she saw a large woman who invited her to her house. But the princess declined, saying she feared that the Cannibal Woman would find her. Dzonokwa then spoke in a flattering tone, complimenting the princess about her beautiful eyebrows. The princess replied that her eyebrows had been cut. The Cannibal Woman asked her to bring the person who cut them to her so she could also have beautiful eyebrows.

The princess protested, saying that it would be very painful to have done. However, the giantess insisted and gave the princess gifts of clothing and burned the underbrush and everything in its path. When the fire reached the trees, it continued up the trunks and consumed the trees and all of the dwarfs in them. None of them escaped, and that is why there are no cannibal dwarfs around today.

See also Cannibalism

References and further reading:

Bierhorst, John, ed. *The Red Swan: Myths and Tales of the American Indians.* Albuquerque: University of New Mexico Press, 1992. First published 1976 by Farrar, Straus, and Giroux.

Clark, Ella E. *Indian Legends from the Northern Rockies.* The Civilization of the American Indian Series, vol. 82. Norman: University of Oklahoma Press, 1966.

Dorsey, George A., and Alfred L. Kroeber. *Traditions of the Arapaho.* 1903. Sources of American Indian Oral Literature. Lincoln: University of Nebraska Press, 1997.

CANNIBAL WOMAN

Alsea, Kwakiutl, Northwest Coast

The Dzonokwa was a hideous looking giantess who carried children away to her home deep in the forest. Kwakiutl parents warned their children what would happen to them if she caught them alone. Adults feared the Dzonokwa, too, and blamed their nightmares on her. The Alsea have a similar legend about A'sin, the Monster Girl of the Woods, who was feared by all. Anyone who disappeared was believed to have been carried off by her. Children were rarely left alone, since they were especially vulnerable.

Among the Kwakiutl tales about the Cannibal Woman is one that relates her demise.

The chief of a certain village had a daughter who had recently become a woman. The princess stayed in her small hut observing all of the necessary taboos for sixteen days and then returned to her father's house. There her eyebrows were plucked in the fashion of the women of her tribe.

One day the princess walked alone in the woods. Her father scolded her and reminded her that the Dzonokwa might catch her and carry her off. However, the young woman disobeyed her father and again went on a long walk near the river. There she saw a large woman who invited her to her house. But the princess declined, saying she feared that the Cannibal Woman would find her Dzonokwa then spoke in a flattering tone, complimenting the princess abou her beautiful eyebrows. The princess replied that her eyebrows had been cu The Cannibal Woman asked her to bring the person who cut them to her so s could also have beautiful eyebrows.

The princess protested, saying that it would be very painful to have do However, the giantess insisted and gave the princess gifts of clothing

When they returned to their village, the chief gave away the tanned hides that he had found in the house. He became known as Dzonokwa Chief because he had killed the Dzonokwa and claimed the Nightmare Bringer's mask and belongings for his people.

See also Cannibalism; Culture Hero(es)

References and further reading:

Boas, Franz, and George Hunt. *Kwakiutl Texts.* 1905. New York: AMS Press, 1975.

Frachtenberg, Leo. J. *Alsea Texts and Myths.* 1920. Temecula, Calif.: Reprint Services Corp., 1995.

Nagle, Geraldine. "The Nightmare's Mask." *Parabola* 23 (Fall 1998): 64–67.

CANNIBALISM

Mythological narratives may explain the origins of the earth as we know it or tell us about the stars, sun, and the moon. Others describe the relationship between humans and the natural world we live in. Still others instruct or warn about certain behaviors or characteristics to avoid, such as cannibalism—considered by many cultures as one of the most evil crimes that can be committed. Strictly speaking, cannibalism is eating the flesh of ones' own kind. Cannibalism is known to occur in the animal world, but it is especially disturbing when found to be practiced by humans.

Myths describing cannibalistic atrocities are found throughout the world, with the perpetrators appearing as humans, ghosts, giants, or other monsters. Several Native North American cannibal myths describe humans who became cannibals after tasting fresh blood, often their own, as in the following Nez Perce tale from the Coyote cycle.

There were five brothers, the eldest of whom was married. Every morning they would go out hunting together and, as was the custom among their people, they would share the meat they brought back from the hunt with their neighbors and relatives. One day when the brothers were out hunting, the eldest shot a deer. It didn't die right away, but ran down a hillside and into a canyon. The elder brother followed it until the deer collapsed. There he butchered the carcass. While doing this, he accidentally cut himself. Some of his blood got on the meat and when he ate it, something came over him. He wasn't interested in the deer any longer. He thought the new taste was delicious and wanted more. When he realized where the new blood was coming from, he cut off a piece of himself and ate it. This made him want even more, so he kept cutting away and eating his own flesh until finally he was just bones.

That evening when everyone had returned from hunting, the youngest brother said, "Our oldest brother has not returned." The word was sent through the village, "Our brother is missing. Tomorrow morning we will all go looking for him." Early the next day, the people set off to find the lost brother, including all four of his younger brothers. When they arrived at the place the brothers had been hunting the day before, they all split up and searched through the hills and the trees and called out for him. The second brother, who had been the last to see the oldest brother, called out, "Older Brother, Older Brother!" Suddenly, the second brother heard a voice calling him from down in the canyon, "Here I am, younger brother." So the second brother hurried down to see if his older brother was hurt. He was startled to see a skeleton with bloody bones coming to meet him, and he turned quickly to run away. But, he was not quick enough. With a rope made of intestines, the older brother caught him and tied him up. The elder brother killed and ate his younger brother, leaving only a pile of bones.

Later that evening, when everyone was returned from searching for the lost oldest brother, they realized that the second brother was missing. It was announced to the people that the second brother was now lost as well, and that the third brother would go search for him in the morning. The third brother set out early the next morning and again went to the place where the brothers had all been hunting several days before. "Older Brother, Older Brother!" called the third brother. Then he heard his brother call to him, "Here I am, come down this way." The third brother was happy to hear the sound of his oldest brother's voice and hurried down into the canyon. But when he saw the bloody skeleton, he turned to run away. The oldest brother caught him with the intestine rope and killed and ate him as before.

That evening when the third brother failed to return home, the people were all alarmed. "Something strange has happened." But they all thought perhaps the brothers had all been in an accident and were all taking care of each other. So they sent the fourth brother out the next morning by himself to find his lost brothers. As his other brothers had done, this brother went to the area where they had been hunting and called out, "Older Brother, Older Brother!"

"We're all down here. Come down to us," the Older Brother answered. So the fourth brother ran down the side of the canyon, eager to see how his brothers were doing. But when the fourth brother saw the bloody skeleton of his oldest brother, he turned to run. Just as with his older brothers, he was caught by the intestine rope, killed, and eaten. The oldest brother piled his bones along with the others.

When the fourth brother did not return that evening, the people wondered why all four brothers were missing. They agreed that the youngest brother would have to go by himself on the following morning to find his brothers. So, he set out very early in the morning and headed to the place where they had all been hunting. On his way, he captured a meadowlark and inquired, "Aunt

Meadowlark, can you tell me what has happened to my four brothers?"
Meadowlark explained about the oldest brother and that he had tasted his own
blood and it had made him crazy. She went on to tell that the oldest brother had
eaten himself down to the bones and that he had killed and eaten the other
brothers. Meadowlark then told the youngest brother how he could escape being captured. He was to go to a certain place where he would find many pieces
of sharp flint. He was to tie pieces of the flint all over his legs. This way when
his oldest brother tried to catch him, the flint would cut the rope that had made
from intestines.

The youngest brother did exactly as Meadowlark had instructed and then
proceeded cautiously toward the canyon. He called out, "Older Brothers, Older
Brothers!" Soon he heard the voice of his oldest brother calling to him, "We're
down here! Come down here with us." The youngest brother walked slowly
down the path. Suddenly he saw the oldest brother looking just as Meadowlark
had warned. The youngest brother turned and began running back up the
canyon but was caught by the intestine rope. He nearly fell over but urged his
legs to keep going. Finally the flint pieces on his legs cut through the intestine
rope and he broke free. When he arrived back at his village, the youngest
brother quickly told the people what had happened and warned that the cannibal brother would be coming for the rest of the people soon. "He will kill us all,
if we don't leave," the youngest brother warned.

Coyote announced that on the next morning they would all go east. So all
of the people packed up their belongings and prepared to leave. However, the
wife of the oldest brother refused to leave. She told them that she and their
small child would stay and wait for her husband to return. No amount of pleading would change her mind. So the people left the woman and her child behind
and fled to the east. One day, the woman heard her husband coming. He was
singing a strange song about killing and eating his brothers. When he arrived at
her tepee, he demanded the child, "Just one swallow, that's all it will take." The
woman quickly replied, "Let me take him down to the river to clean him up,
and then we will be back." On her way out the door she grabbed a wooden
spoon. When she got to the riverbank, she asked the willows to answer, "Ho!"
when her husband called after her. Then she ordered the spoon to turn into a canoe. When it did, she placed her child in it and then climbed in herself and hurried down stream to join their people.

Eventually, her husband wondered what was taking so long and called for
her to come back to the tepee. The willows replied, "Ho!" After several times,
the cannibal husband realized that it wasn't his wife's voice and went to the
river to see what taking so long. His wife and child were gone, but he vowed to
find them.

When the woman arrived at the new village, she quickly told the people what had happened and warned that her husband was now very vicious. A plan was made. Crane was buried in the dirt at the top of a cliff. When the oldest brother came along, Crane stuck his legs out and kicked the cannibal over the cliff and killed him. All of his bones tumbled down the cliff and ended up in a heap at the bottom. So Crane went back to the people and told them that the cannibal was dead.

    See also Cannibal Dwarfs; Cannibal Woman; Kivioq

    References and further reading:

    Gill, Sam D., and Irene F. Sullivan. *Dictionary of Native American Mythology.* Santa Barbara, Calif.: ABC-CLIO, 1992.

    Walker, Deward E. *Nez Perce Coyote Tales: the Myth Cycle.* Norman: University of Oklahoma Press, 1998. First published 1994 as *Blood of the Monster: The Nez Perce Coyote Cycle* (Worland, Wyo.: High Plains, 1994).

Chinook Wind

See Hot Wind and Cold Wind

CORN

Corn is featured in numerous myths across most of the Americas. Known in much of the world as maize, corn appears to have originated in Mexico or Central America and, over the past several thousand years, has evolved from a wild grass to the domesticated varieties grown around the world today. Whether the change was due to evolution, cultivation, or a combination of both is still being debated in scientific circles. But the significance of corn and other crops for the development of civilization in the Americas is undeniable.

Agriculture is more labor intensive than hunting and gathering. Fields must be guarded, watered, and weeded. Crops must be planted and harvested. Storage containers must be created. Both the work and workers must be organized and supervised.

As farming became more prevalent, small hunting and gathering bands evolved into villages and more people were available to help with chores, which resulted in the need for more crops to be raised.

The Origin of Corn

Several myths describe corn being created as the result of a woman's death. In one story from the Cherokee, two hungry young boys secretly watched their mother, Selu, harvest corn and beans for their meal by rubbing her stomach and armpits. The boys were appalled and thought she must be a witch. When they threatened to kill her, the woman instructed them, "When you have killed me, clear a large area near the house. Then drag my body around the circle seven times. Keep watch on the field overnight." The boys did as they were instructed and by morning corn stalks with mature ears had grown in that place.

A Malecite version with a similar ending was reported by Mechling.

In olden times, before the people had crops, an old chief had several beautiful daughters. One of the girls had golden hair. A stranger came to the village and in time fell in love with the golden haired girl. They married and lived together a long time. When she was old and about to die, she said to her husband, "If you want to have me with you always, just do as I tell you." The man didn't want to part from his wife, so he did exactly as she said. First he cut down the trees near their home and then he burned the timber. Next, his wife had instructed him to tie her hands with cedar bark and drag her around the clearing seven times, but he was

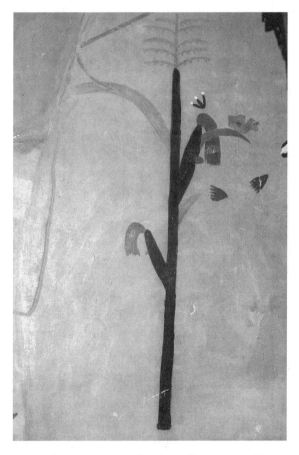

Native American fresco of a cornstalk on interior kiva wall, ca. 1500, Tiguex (Kuaua Pueblo) on the Rio Grande, New Mexico. (North Wind Picture Archives)

not to look back. When he finished doing this, the man looked back and saw just a skeleton remaining. The woman's flesh had been torn off by the tree stumps. The man was heartbroken and moved away immediately. But at the end of the summer, he wished to see the place again. To his amazement, the once charred field was now filled with corn the color of his wife's golden hair. Then he remembered that she had promised to be with him always.

Goodwin related a story about how the White Mountain Apache first received corn.

Long, long ago, when the animals all talked like people, Turkey overheard a boy and a girl talking about not having any food. So he shook himself, and all sorts of fruits and other food fell out of his feathers. The boy and girl ate all of it. Then Turkey shook himself again and four different kinds of corn fell out. The children ate some of it but saved the rest for seed. He showed them a place to plant the corn seed. The plants grew very quickly. The boy and girl also planted squash seeds. Then they asked Turkey for more corn to plant.

While they went to plant seeds in another field, Turkey stayed behind with their first crop. When they returned they heard Turkey hollering in the field and they saw that the plants had grown very tall. Turkey told them to keep back because snakes had come into the field for the corn tassel pollen. He said to wait four days and then the snakes would be gone. When they finally were able to get into their cornfield, the boy and girl found that all of the corn was ripe. Turkey explained that this was the only time that corn would ripen in just four days. Afterward it would take much longer. And so it has been ever since.

Marie McLaughlin related the Dakota (Sioux) tale "The Hermit, or the Gift of Corn."

A man lived alone, far from his people's village. He spent his time studying plants and roots to learn which could be used as food and which could be used as medicine. One night, just as he was dozing off, he realized a dark object was in his tent. It had something like a flint arrow in its hand and said, "I have come to invite you to my home." The hermit agreed to go, but when he got outside, he could not tell which way the mysterious object had gone. The next night the same thing happened. But the man decided to find out what this strange visitor wanted him to do.

On the following night, the hermit cut a hole in the side of his tent and stuck an arrow through it. He waited and soon the dark object came to the door and said, "I have come to. . . ." Before the sentence was complete, the hermit shot his arrow. It sounded as if the arrow had struck a bag full of pebbles. In the morning when it was light enough, the man saw a small pile of corn outside his door. There was a trail of corn leading away. The hermit followed the corn until he reached a spot where the grass had been scraped off leaving a circular area of bare ground. The trail of corn stopped at the edge of the circle.

The hermit realized it must be the home of the mysterious object that wanted him to follow. Using his bone ax and a knife, the man dug into the soil. He dug until he reached a sack of dried meat. Then he found a sack of turnips, one of cherries, and another with corn. Finally he found another sack. This one had only a small amount of corn in it along with the hermit's arrow. The hermit realized the meaning of the corn and the pit with the food. He taught the people how to keep their food safe while they were away traveling. He told them to dig a deep hole to bury their sacks and baskets of food. The people thanked him for instructing them how to preserve their food, and also for giving them corn.

The Three Sisters

Corn, beans, and squash are often planted together. Several kernels of corn are planted in "hills" where the soil has been mounded up. After the young corn stalks have been growing for several weeks, bean seeds are planted in each hill along with the corn. Squash seeds are also planted around the hills. Each of the three plants requires different nutrients from the soil. As the plants grow, the corn stalks become a trellis or stake for the bean vines and the large leaves of the squash cover the ground forming both a weed barrier and a moisture conserving shade for the soil.

Beauchamp reported in "Indian Corn Stories and Customs" that the Iroquois referred to corn, beans, and pumpkin (squash) as "Our Life, or Our Supporters." Beauchamp also described an Onondaga story told by Joseph Lyon.

A lonely young man lived alone on a hill. Each morning and evening he stood outside his house and sang, calling for someone to marry. Finally a lovely young woman came along and said she would marry him. But he refused, saying that she wandered too far from home and would not stay by his side. Finally, another young woman heard the man singing and approached his house. The slender young woman saw his fine looking robe and long plumes and said that she would marry him if he would love her in return. The man knew this young woman was the one he had waited for. They embraced, and since that time the corn stalk has supported the bean vine and the pumpkin roams all around them on the ground.

A narrative collected by Curtin and Hewitt, and titled "The Weeping of the Corn, and Bean, and Squash People," tells of an event from the "olden time."

An Iroquois village was situated in a fertile region. The people grew abundant crops of corn, beans, and squash. However, it came about that the crops began to fail and the game became scarce and the people became hungry. One day an old woman was walking near her fields, contemplating the dire situation, when she heard weeping coming from the field. She walked out among the shriveled corn, bean, and squash plants and, stopping next to a corn plant, asked, "Why are you weeping?" The corn explained that the people had not cared for the crops in the manner required. "The people do not cover us up well enough and do not make hills to give our roots a strong support. They do not give us enough water, and they allow our enemies to attack us and strangle us to death."

The old woman was distraught and returned home in tears. When the people of her village heard her weeping, they were moved to join in her grief. At last the chief of the people approached the old woman and asked what was causing her so much distress. After a time the old woman was able to explain. She told the chief and all of the people that she had heard weeping coming from the field. When she went to investigate, the corn plant told her that the people were not caring for the crops in the proper manner.

Then the chief met with the council and it was decided that from that time on, whoever planted corn or beans or squash was to cover the seeds with sufficient soil. The gardener must also dig around the hills in order for the water to nourish the roots. And lastly, the crops were to be guarded so that their enemies, the weeds, would not choke them out.

When planting time came in the spring, the people took great care to do just as instructed. The crops grew well, but as harvest approached, someone came to the fields and began stealing the corn and beans and squashes. The people were greatly distressed and wondered what they had done wrong. The next spring came and the crops were planted again. However, near harvest time thieves began to steal the corn from the fields again. One evening, the people then sent warriors to guard the fields. In the morning they saw certain strangers who were stripping ears off the cornstalks and gathering beans and squashes. The warriors captured the thieves. Every day these prisoners were brought out so the people could whip them. Eventually corn thieves led the people to their village far away. There the warriors killed many of the enemy but set the captives free. Then they were ordered to split the lips of the squash thieves so they could not eat squash again. The corn thieves who were released had stripes on their backs and rings around their eyes and tails from the beatings they received. They were the raccoons. The squash thieves who had their lips split were the rabbits.

A Selection of Other Stories Featuring Corn

A Tuscarora myth tells of a time long ago when the people were blessed with abundant harvests. They eventually began taking the situation for granted. They neglected the fields, wasted much of the food, and failed to store the corn carefully. They even forgot to thank their Creator for all he had provided for them. One man, however, did not forget how to carefully tend and harvest his crop, and he stored a portion of the kernels in well-constructed baskets. His name was Dayohagwenda. It caused him great pain to see how disrespectful the people had become. One day, while the man was walking in the woods and thinking about the way the people acted, he came to a trail that led to a lodge built on a hill. Weeds grew all around the lodge. Outside was an old man in ragged clothes who sat on the ground weeping. Dayohagwenda asked the old man, "Grandfather, why are you weeping?" The old man replied that he wept because the people had forgotten him. "Grandfather, why are your clothes torn?" The old man said, "Because the people had tossed him to the dogs." Dayohagwenda then asked, "Why are you so dirty?" The old man said,

Coyote petroglyph, near Galisteo, New Mexico. (North Wind Picture Archives)

create and transform, and often proves indestructible. Coyote stories were told to entertain young and old alike, to dramatize and convey the value of appropriate behavior, to instruct listeners in survival and getting along with each other, and to provide a sense of tribal identity.

Coyote occasionally assumes the role of beneficent culture hero, though sometimes the elements of life and culture he introduces have a negative aspect. The stories of several tribes reveal that Coyote brought the first fire, arranged the seasons, introduced salmon and taught how to catch and cook it, introduced work and suffering, played a role in the origin of Europeans, taught how to make bows and arrows, and introduced death to prevent overpopulation.

Many Coyote stories detail his erotic and incestuous adventures, complete with references to bodily functions and his insatiable sex drive. In a Navajo myth, Coyote tricks Younger Brother in order to sleep with his wife. Another Navajo story tells how Coyote is able to exchange skins with the unsuspecting hero and sleep with the man's wives, since the Coyote skin debilitates the man. In a Kawaiisu story, Coyote's lust is expressed through his attempts to have sex with three women by pretending he is a woman with a baby, though the "baby" is actually his penis. The Nez Percé tell of the widower Coyote's desire for his five daughters and how he tricks the eldest into marrying him. Coyote is credited with removing vaginal teeth in a number of stories, thereby explaining the origin of pleasure in sexual intercourse.

In other stories, nothing is beyond Coyote's powers, and he is credited with creating and transforming the West. He caused the Columbia River to form and gouged out Hell's Canyon along the Snake River. He changed animal beings into Beacon Rock, Rooster Rock, Latourell Falls, Mist Falls, and Horsetail Falls along the lower Columbia. Coyote created Mount Chopaka and two other peaks of the Okanogan Highlands from three young warriors. Coyote built waterfalls in several Washington rivers to keep salmon from reaching areas inhabited by people who refused his attentions toward their beautiful women. He changed the course of the Klamath River so that it runs only downstream instead of up-stream on one side and downstream on the other.

In the following story of the White Mountain Apache, "Turkey Makes the Corn and Coyote Plants It," Coyote as trickster is foolish, lazy, and mis-chievous—the ultimate example of what not to be.

A long time ago, when animals could talk like people do, Turkey overheard a boy begging his sister for food. Turkey asked the girl what her brother wanted, and she explained that he was hungry, but they had nothing to eat. When Turkey heard this, he shook himself all over. Various kinds of wild food and fruits dropped out of his feathers, and the brother and sister ate them up. Turkey shook himself yet again, and corn dropped out of his feathers. This corn was a variety that is very large. Turkey shook himself a third time, and yellow corn dropped out. When he shook himself a fourth time, white corn dropped out.

Bear saw what was happening, and came over. Turkey told him that he was helping to feed his sister and brother. Bear observed that it took Turkey four shakes to make food come out of him, but he had every kind of food on him, from his head to his feet. Bear then shook himself, and out of his fur dropped ju-niper berries. He shook himself again, and out dropped a type of cactus that is good to eat. He then shook out acorns, piñon nuts, a species of sumac, another kind of cactus, other acorns, more berries, then saguaro fruit.

Turkey told the boy and girl that he had four kinds of corn seeds for them and showed them a good place to plant them. The boy and girl made holes in the ground and planted all of their corn seeds in them. The next day, the corn had come up and was already about a foot and a half high. They still had some squash seeds, so they planted those too. The boy and girl asked Turkey for more corn seed. Turkey gave them the seed so they could make another farm and plant more corn. The boy and girl left him to look after their first farm while they started their second.

When they returned, they found Turkey hollering at the cornfield. Snakes had come to gather pollen from the tassels on the corn plants, so Turkey pretended to have a broken wing and dragged it along the ground as he made noise in an attempt to protect the boy and girl and lure the snakes away. Turkey warned them to stay away from the corn for four days, at which time the snakes would be finished. At the end of the four days, the corn had ripened. Turkey told them that this would be the only time when the corn would come up in four days, and that, in the future, it would take much longer.

By now the brother and sister had planted corn three times, and they gave seeds to others. Then Slim Coyote came and asked for some corn seeds so he could plant them for himself. He observed that the corn they planted was growing well and that the ears were coming out on it.

Coyote would need to do much work to raise corn, but that was not his desire. He decided he wanted to cook his corn first and then plant it, so he need not cook it after it ripened. Here is where Coyote made a huge mistake. He did indeed cook his corn first, ate some, and then planted a large patch of the rest. He felt very proud, and bragged how well he had done for himself, expecting to grow his already-cooked corn.

After planting his cooked corn, Coyote went off with the rest of the people to gather acorns. When they returned to their fields, Coyote's had nothing growing at all. He angrily accused the others of removing the hearts from the corn seeds they had given them. The people denied it and explained he was wrong to cook the heart out of the seeds before planting them. Coyote asked for more seeds and planted them the correct way. His corn grew, and the day after he planted it, it had grown about a foot and a half. He felt very satisfied.

The people who had planted their corn at the beginning were harvesting now and tying it up into bundles. Coyote saw these bundles and wanted some. People became angry with Coyote because he was always asking them for corn. He would always say he just wanted some green ears to feed his children and made promises to give the corn back when his own was ripe. The other people's squashes were still growing in the field. Coyote stole their squash, and the people came straight to his camp. They demanded to know if he was the one who stole the squash. Coyote pretended to be very angry and indignantly accused the others of always blaming him for stealing everything. He suggested people from other nearby camps could be the culprits. But the people were not fooled; they knew about Coyote's thieving ways and ordered him to move away to live some other place. Coyote declared that he no longer intended to repay the corn he was given because of the way he had been illtreated. So Coyote's family lived poorly, and they never bothered to cook any food before they ate it.

The Ponca story that follows, "Teeth in the Wrong Places," is an example of the many tales that tell of Coyote's sexual adventures:

Coyote was roaming around, looking for adventure and great deeds to perform, when he was told of an old woman, an evil sorceress who lived with her two wicked but beautiful daughters. Many young men went to visit them and sleep with the daughters, but they were never seen alive again. The one who told him of this place warned him to be careful to not sleep with these girls, or he would die. Coyote wondered how sleeping with two beautiful women would kill a man, and off he went to find them.

When Coyote arrived at her tipi, he found the old woman was very nice to him, and her daughters were as beautiful as he had heard. The mother invited him in. She complimented him on his appearance, and told him that he was just the kind of person she'd like to have for a son-in-law. Coyote entered the tipi, and the mother invited him to sit down so her daughters could serve him something good to eat. The girls brought Coyote much delicious food—buffalo hump, tongues, all kinds of meat. The eldest daughter told him how handsome he was. Coyote decided he did not believe what he had heard, that these were good people.

By nightfall, Coyote was full of food, and becoming drowsy. The mother suggested he was tired after his journey, that it was cold outside. She encouraged him to lie down to sleep between her two daughters, as they would keep him warm. Coyote snuggled between the two girls. He felt amorous, but he wondered about them. In the dark, the face of the younger girl brushed his; she whispered in his ear and warned him that her sister would soon ask him to sleep with her. She told him that he must not do it and explained that she was supposed to ask him to sleep with her as well. Coyote asked her why she was telling him this. The girl told Coyote that the old woman was a witch, that she was not really her mother. She explained she was the woman's prisoner, but the other girl was truly her daughter, and the witch had put teeth into both of their vaginas. Coyote heard that when a man came to visit, the witch would get him to copulate with the girls, that these teeth took hold of his penis and chewed it to bits, and the man would die. Afterwards, the woman would steal all of his things. Coyote did not believe her until he heard the grinding of the sharp teeth within their vaginas.

Coyote and the girl pretended to sleep. After a while the older girl, the old woman's daughter, tugged at his sleeve and invited him to enter her. Coyote could hear the teeth gnashing inside her vagina. He pretended that he desired her, took hold of a thick, long stick that was still warm from the fire, and inserted it into the girl's vagina. The teeth inside of her were chewing, and wood splinters were flying out of her all over Coyote. He quickly grabbed an arrow from his quiver and thrust it deep inside the girl before the teeth could snap shut. The teeth closed upon the shaft near the feathers, but the arrowhead had already reached the evil girl's heart, and she died.

Then Coyote killed the wicked old woman with his knife. He told the younger girl how grateful he was for saving his life, and invited her to marry him. She reminded him that she had teeth in the wrong place, but Coyote assured her he would take care of that. They set out for Coyote's house and walked an entire day. When evening fell, Coyote built a brush shelter for the two of them. He put sage into it for a bed. Coyote knocked out the teeth in the girl's vagina, leaving just one blunt tooth that was very thrilling when making love. Coyote and the girl were very happy together afterwards.

"Coyote and the Monster of the Columbia" is an example of how many of Coyote's exploits are associated with the Columbia River basin. In this Klikitat story, a monster that lived near Celilo Falls is rendered powerless, and Coyote assumes the role of a creator by naming all the animals and birds.

While traveling, Coyote learned that a monster was killing the animal people as they took their canoes up and down Big River. So many had been killed that some were afraid to go down to the water, even to catch salmon. Coyote promised to help stop the monster from killing the animal people. He had no idea what to do, however, so he asked his three sisters, who lived in his stomach in the form of huckleberries. They were very wise and knew everything.

At first, Coyote's sisters refused to tell him what to do, because he would claim it was his plan all along. Coyote threatened to send rain and hail down upon them if they did not tell him, which of course the berries did not like. However, the berries relented and told Coyote to take plenty of dry wood and plenty of pitch with him so he could make a fire. They also recommended he take five sharp knives. They explained that it was Nashlah at Wishram who was killing all the animal people, swallowing them as they passed in their canoes. The berries told Coyote that he must allow himself to be swallowed by Nashlah as well.

Coyote gathered together some dry wood and pitch, as his sisters advised, sharpened his knives, and went to the deep pool where Nashlah lived. Nashlah saw Coyote but did not swallow him, for he knew that Coyote was a great chief.

Coyote called Nashlah many mean names, because he knew he could make him very angry by teasing him. At last, the monster became so angry he took a big breath and sucked Coyote into his mouth. Coyote grabbed an armful of sagebrush just before entering and took it in.

Inside Nashlah, Coyote found many animal people, all of whom were cold and hungry. Some were almost dead from hunger, some from the cold. Coyote told the animal people he would build a fire and cook some food for them. Using the sagebrush and pitch, he built a fire under the heart of the monster. As they warmed themselves, Coyote declared that he would kill Nashlah. He assured the animal people he had come to help them and that they would soon join their friends.

Coyote cut pieces from Nashlah's heart and roasted them. While the people ate the heart, Coyote began to sever the cord that fastened the monster's heart to his body. He broke the first knife, but he kept cutting. He broke the second knife, but he kept cutting. He broke his third and fourth knives as well. He cut the last thread with his fifth knife, and Nashlah's heart fell into the fire. Just as the monster died, he gave one big cough and all of the animal people came out on to the land.

The grateful animal people gathered around Coyote on the shore of the river. He told them they would live a long time, and declared that he would give each of them names. Coyote named the best and bravest bird Eagle, the strongest animal Bear. The big medicine man with special powers became Owl. The largest fish in the rivers was named Sturgeon, the best of all fish for eating became Salmon. Coyote named Blue Jay, Beaver, Woodpecker, Deer, Cougar, and all the other animals and birds. Then he named himself Coyote, the wisest and smartest of all the animals.

Coyote then turned to Nashlah and laid down a new law. He sternly forbade him to kill people as he had been doing. He informed him that a new race of people was coming, that they would travel up and down the river. Coyote told Nashlah he could kill one now and then, that he could shake the canoes if they passed over him. Coyote explained that, for this reason, most of the canoes would go around Nashlah's pool and not pass over where he lived, so he would kill very few of the new people. Coyote told Nashlah that this was to be the law always, that he was no longer the powerful man he used to be.

The law Coyote made still stands, and the monster obeys it. He does not swallow people like he did before Coyote took away his power. Sometimes he draws a canoe under and swallows the people in it, but not often. The Indians usually remove their canoes from the water and carry them round the place where the monster lives, to avoid passing over his house. He still lives deep under the water, but he no longer possesses his great power.

See also Buffalo Wife; Culture Hero(es); Mountain Lion; Otters and Coyote; Seasons, Origin of; Skinkuts; Transformer; Trickster

References and further reading:

Angulo, Jaime de, and L. S. Freeland. "Miwok and Pomo Myths." *Journal of American Folklore* 41, no. 160 (April–June 1928): 232–252.

Blue Cloud, Peter. *Elderberry Flute Song: Contemporary Coyote Tales.* 4th ed. Buffalo, N.Y.: White Pine Press, 2002.

Clark, Ella E. *Indians Legends of the Pacific Northwest.* 50th anniversary ed. Berkeley; London: University of California Press, 2003. First published 1953.

———. "The Mythology of the Indians in the Pacific Northwest." *Oregon Historical Quarterly* 54, no. 3 (September 1953): 163–189.

Erdoes, Richard, and Alfonso Ortiz, eds. *American Indian Myths and Legends.* New York: Pantheon Books, 1984.

Linderman, Frank B. *Old Man Coyote (Crow).* Authorized ed. Lincoln: University of Nebraska Press, 1996. First published 1931 by John Day.

Lopez, Barry. *Giving Birth to Thunder, Sleeping With His Daughter: Coyote Builds North America.* New York: Avon Books, 1990. First published 1997 by Sheed Andrews and McMeel.

Lowie, Robert H. *Myths and Traditions of the Crow Indians.* Sources of American Indian Oral Literature. Lincoln: University of Nebraska Press, 1993. First published 1918 by American Museum of Natural History.

Mourning Dove. *Coyote Stories.* 1933. Lincoln: University of Nebraska Press, 1990.

Walker, Deward E. *Nez Perce Coyote Tales: the Myth Cycle.* Norman: University of Oklahoma Press, 1998. First published 1994 as *Blood of the Monster: The Nez Perce Coyote Cycle* (Worland, Wyo.: High Plains, 1994).

CULTURE HERO(ES)

A culture hero is responsible for providing or creating distinctive aspects or benefits of a culture and the natural world through discovery or invention. A Native American culture hero might be credited with the discovery of fire or agriculture. He or she may set the sun on its course, create humans, plants, and animals, or teach rituals and ceremonies. A culture hero may also be a deliverer who, for example, rids the world of the monsters that make it uninhabitable. The trickster character and the culture hero are sometimes combined in Native American mythology. The culture hero may give life to humans and bring them important features of their culture, but the cunning, thieving, or lustful urges he or she may possess give the culture hero a life of his or her own.

Culture heroes often appear in creation stories, though they usually belong to a world that already exists. Culture heroes may assume diverse forms; they may be human or animal, man or woman, young or old. They almost always have proper names and transformational abilities. A culture hero may have a non-human parent, and his or her birth may be surrounded by unusual circumstances. He or she often has a younger twin brother, and some have animal siblings, such as a moose or wolf.

Native American mythology features literally hundreds of culture heroes, a rich, diverse array that often reflects Native Americans's respect for and connection with nature. The Haida character Sin brings snow; the Milky Way and the pumpkin plant are the creation of a Seminole culture hero known as Hisagita misa, or Breath Maker.

In a story of the Montagnais, a wolverine causes the creation of rocks:

At one time, there were no rocks in the world, only one very large boulder. Wolverine approached it and boldly declared he could outrun it. The boulder agreed that was probably true and told Wolverine that he had been sitting in that one place for as long as he could remember. Wolverine seemed surprised. He told the boulder that even Lemming and Ant could run, and that he must be the lowest of the low if he really could not. Wolverine then gave the boulder a kick. The boulder did not like this, or Wolverine's insults, so it started rolling toward him. Wolverine continued to laugh at the boulder and started running away, down a hill, with the boulder rolling after him. Soon he complained and asked the boulder to slow down. Suddenly, Wolverine fell down, and the boulder rolled right on top of him. Wolverine yelled and screamed in panic, but the boulder just sat there, crushing his body. Wolverine called on his brothers Wolf and Fox to help him. They refused, however, and reminded Wolverine he had insulted the boulder, so it was only fair that it now lay on top of him. Frog tried to move it, but his hands were too slippery. Mouse declared that he was too small. Finally, Wolverine called on his brother Thunderstorm, who laughed when he saw him lying under the boulder. Wolverine admitted he was being silly again, and repeated his cry for help. Thunderstorm called on Lightning, who zigzagged down from the sky above and struck the boulder into many little pieces. That was how rocks were born. From then on, Wolverine spoke only kind words to those rocks.

Culture heroes can be credited with virtually every aspect of a culture, including how to fish or dig wells for water, the existence of light, games, and weaving, the origin of rituals and ceremonies, the location of genitalia, and the origin of marriage and funerary practices.

In a Shasta tale, the people are brought arrowheads:

A very long time ago, in the days of the first people, hunters used arrows that had pine-bark points. Ideally, they would have used obsidian, as obsidian made a sharp, strong, deadly point that always killed animals that were shot. But they did not know where to find it.

The only one who knew where Obsidian Old Man lived on Medicine Lake was Ground Squirrel. One day, he set out to steal some of his obsidian, so he took a basket filled with roots to Obsidian Old Man's house and offered him some. Obsidian Old Man ate the roots and enjoyed them so much, he sent Ground Squirrel to find more. As Ground Squirrel was digging for them, Grizzly Bear came along. Grizzly Bear sat in his lap and ordered Ground Squirrel to feed him the roots. As Ground Squirrel was very much afraid of Grizzly Bear, he obeyed. Grizzly Bear quickly gobbled up the roots and prepared to leave. He told Ground Squirrel, "Obsidian Old Man's mother cleaned roots for someone," and he walked away.

Ground Squirrel returned to Obsidian Old Man with only a few roots left to give him. Ground Squirrel told Obsidian Old Man that Grizzly Bear had eaten most of the roots he had gathered and what he had said. Obsidian Old Man was very angry at the insult to his dead mother and promised Ground Squirrel they would both go to find more roots the next day.

So, Ground Squirrel and Obsidian Old man went off together early the next morning. Ground Squirrel started digging, and Obsidian Old Man hid nearby. Ground Squirrel's basket was soon filled, and along came Grizzly Bear, who again ordered him to sit down and feed him the roots.

Ground Squirrel did as he was told, like before, and fed Grizzly Bear the roots by the handful as he sat in Ground Squirrel's lap. But then he saw Obsidian Old Man approach, and the bear rose to fight. The sharp obsidian cut into Grizzly Bear's flesh at each blow, but he kept fighting until he was cut to pieces, and fell dead. Ground Squirrel and Obsidian Old Man went home and ate the roots and were pleased. But Ground Squirrel awakened Obsidian Old Man early the next morning with his loud groans and complained that he was very sick and bruised because Grizzly Bear had sat on him. Obsidian Old Man felt sorry for Ground Squirrel, so he left to get wood, suspicious that Ground Squirrel might be trying to fool him. He crept back to peek at Ground Squirrel, but he was still lying down and groaning, so Obsidian Old Man decided he really was sick and went off in earnest. Clever Ground Squirrel, however, had been pretending the whole time. As soon as Obsidian Old Man was far away, he rose up, bundled up all the obsidian points, and ran off.

Upon his return, Obsidian Old Man noticed immediately that Ground Squirrel was missing. He dropped the wood he had gathered and took off in pursuit, almost catching Ground Squirrel before he ducked into a hole in the ground. He kicked dirt into the old man's eyes as he dug fast and tried to grab Ground Squirrel. Obsidian Old Man finally gave up and left, and Ground Squirrel ran out of the other end of the hole, crossed the lake, and returned home.

Ground Squirrel emptied his bundle of obsidian points on the ground and gave them to everyone. The people discarded the old bark points and tied the obsidian points onto their arrows. The new arrow points were used to hunt and kill a great many deer.

A story of the Lillooet tells of how the culture hero/trickster transforms himself into a dish in order to obtain some of the salmon it holds. He later assumes his true form and releases the salmon that have been withheld from mankind:

At the very head waters of the Upper Lillooet River lived two brothers who wished to become very great, so they spent most of their time training themselves in the mountains nearby. Suddenly, one became very ill and had to remain at home. After four years of this illness, he became very weak and thin. His brother grew anxious and ceased his training. He hunted regularly and brought his sick brother all kinds of meat. He also threw sticks into the water, where they turned to fish. He then caught them and also gave them to his brother to eat. But no food seemed to agree with him, and he continued to grow more and more weak and thin.

At that time, the invalid's brother decided to take him away to be cured. They embarked down the river in a canoe, naming all the places as they passed by. They arrived at a place they chose to call Ilamux, where a rock dammed the river. They made a hole in this rock so they could go on. Then they found themselves at a place they called Komelux, where two rushing creeks came together with very great force. The brothers made the water smooth enough for them to safely pass. They came to another place they called Kulexwin. Here, a steep, rocky mountain stood close to the river. The brothers threw their medicine mat at it, and the mountain became flat.

They continued to proceed down to Big and Little Lillooet Lakes and the Lower Lillooet River until they reached Harrison Lake. All along the way, they continued to name places, make the waters navigable, and change the features of the land. Finally, they reached Fraser River, traveled to its mouth, and went out to sea to the land of the salmon. When they arrived there, the well brother hid himself, and the sick brother transformed himself into a beautifully carved and painted wooden dish. In this form, he floated against the dam where the people kept salmon. A man found the dish and brought it to his admiring daughter, who used it to eat her meals. Whatever salmon she did not eat always disappeared overnight, but since salmon were very plentiful, she did not mind at all.

The sick brother in dish form was eating the salmon, and soon he became well again. His brother left his hiding place each night to visit his brother and eat salmon out of the basket into which were thrown the remnants. When his invalid brother had grown fat again, they departed one night and broke the dam that held the salmon. They set out in their canoe and led the salmon toward the mouth of the Fraser.

Because the salmon traveled very quickly, they reached the river by the next morning. As they proceeded, the brothers threw pieces of salmon into the various creeks and rivers, thus introducing salmon to the streams of the interior. They declared that the salmon would run every year at that time, and the people would discover and eat them. The two brothers returned to their home at the head of the Upper Lillooet, and made near their house the hot springs known as Tcîq, which they used to cook their food.

See also Ani Hyuntikwalaski; Cannibal Woman; Coyote; First Creator and Lone Man; Girl Who Married a Bear; Glooskap; Kanati and Selu; Kumokums; Mouse Woman; Old Man; Raven; Salt Woman; Trickster; Turtle; White Buffalo Woman; Wisaka

References and further reading:
Erdoes, Richard, and Alfonso Ortiz, eds. *American Indian Myths and Legends.* New York: Pantheon Books, 1984.

Jones, William. "Episodes in the Culture-Hero Myth of the Sauks and Foxes." *Journal of American Folklore* 14, no. 55 (October–December 1901): 225–239.

Swann, Brian, ed. *Coming to Light: Contemporary Translations of the Native Literatures of North America.* New York: Vintage Books, 1996. First published 1994 by Random House.

Thompson, Stith. *Tales of the North American Indians.* 1929. Bloomington: Indiana University Press, 1971.

DEER HUNTER AND WHITE CORN MAIDEN

Tewa, Southwest

Because their lives are so intertwined with nature, Native Americans are keen observers of the sky, stars, and planets, which figure prominently in their mythology. This story explains the origin of two stars.

Long ago, in an ancient village of the San Juan people, lived a special and most attractive young couple. The man was aptly named Deer Hunter because, even as a young boy, he was the only one who always returned home from the hunt with game. The girl was called White Corn Maiden, and she created the finest pottery and most beautifully embroidered clothing of any woman. Deer Hunter and White Corn Maiden thoroughly enjoyed each other's company and regularly sought each other out.

In time the couple married, as their parents and the other villagers expected. What they did not expect, however, was that the pair would spend so much time with each other. Both slighted their religious obligations. White Corn Maiden neglected her pottery making and embroidery, and Deer Hunter ceased hunting at a time his contribution was necessary to help spare many of the villagers from hunger. The people worried that the gods might become angry with the couple for not upholding tribal traditions and bring disaster upon them all. At their parents' request, the tribal elders called a council. But the pleas of the council to change their behavior merely drove Deer Hunter and White Corn Maiden even closer together.

Suddenly, following a very brief illness, White Corn Maiden died. Deer Hunter was consumed by grief. Refusing to eat or speak, he maintained a vigil by his wife's lifeless body until her burial the next day.

For four days, Deer Hunter wandered the village and its outer boundary, hoping to encounter his wife during the short period when her soul was expected to drift about the village in the form of a human shape, voice, wind, or dream. Meandering into the fields, Deer Hunter suddenly spotted a small fire at sundown on the fourth day after White Corn Maiden's death. At the same time, their relatives were gathering to perform a ceremony that would release her soul into the spirit world forever.

Deer Hunter approached the fire and encountered his wife, still beautiful and preparing herself for her last journey. Unable to accept his wife's death, he wept at her feet and begged her to return to the village before the releasing rite concluded. But White Corn Maiden implored her husband to let her go. Her return to the world of the living would anger the spirits, she warned, and soon she would lose her beauty.

Deer Hunter dismissed her pleas. Hearing him pledge his undying love and assurance they would always be together, White Corn Maiden eventually relented. The couple returned to the village to the horrifying stares of their relatives, who were just about to finalize the releasing ceremony. Both they and the village elders begged Deer Hunter to let her go, but he ignored their entreaties.

White Corn Maiden started to change profoundly following the couple's return to their home. She started to emit an unpleasant odor, her lovely face grew ashen, and her skin began to dry out. Deer Hunter started to shun her, as White Corn Maiden had predicted. Soon Deer Hunter could be sighted ducking among the houses and running through the fields, with White Corn Maiden chasing closely behind.

One morning a tall, imposing figure, sent from the spirit world, appeared in the small dance court in the village center. He commanded Deer Hunter and White Corn Maiden to come forward and appear before him. They meekly listened as he chastised them for their selfishness and violations of their tribal traditions. He commanded that they would be together for eternity in the sky, a visual reminder to their people how important it was to live and survive according to their traditions. Then he shot Deer Hunter into the sky on a huge arrow, placing him low in the west. White Corn Maiden followed on a second arrow, and was set right behind her husband, destined to chase him across the heavens forever.

See also Stars and Constellations

References and further reading:

Erdoes, Richard, and Alfonso Ortiz, eds. *American Indian Myths and Legends.* New York: Pantheon Books, 1984.

Fletcher, Alice C. "Pawnee Star Lore." *Journal of American Folklore* 16, no. 60 (January–March 1903): 10–15.

Miller, Dorcas S. *Stars of the First People: Native American Star Myths and Constellations.* Boulder, Colo.: Pruett, 1997.

DOG HUSBAND

Inuit, Arctic

There are several versions of this tale known across Greenland and the North American Arctic. In some areas it is part of the Sedna tradition, with the marriage to the dog occurring prior to the marriage to the bird. The tale explains the origin of the Indians and Whites.

There was a girl who refused to marry all suitors. None were good enough for her. Finally her father was so angry he said, "You should have a dog for a husband." Later that night, a dog in the form of a man came in and slept with the girl. When the girl became pregnant, her father rowed her out to a nearby island, but the dog swam after them and lived with the girl on the island. She gave birth to a litter of pups and human children.

Her dog husband would swim back to shore to get bags of meat that had been set out for them. One day, however, the girl's father placed stones in the bags and covered them with meat to conceal the stones. When the dog husband tried to swim back to the island he sank and drowned. Then the father began taking meat to the island for the girl and her children. But she was still angry at him for making her marry the dog in the first place. So she told her dog children to attack the old man the next time he came to the island. Her father was able to escape back to his village but was afraid to return to the island.

Soon the girl and her children were hungry and had no one to bring them any meat. So she cut off the soles of her boots and made boats out of them. She set the dog children in one boat and sent them off across the sea, telling them that they would be skillful with weapons. White men are descended from these dog children.

The girl then set her human children in the other boat and sent them across the water and ordered them to go inland. These became the ancestors of Indians who lived to the south of the Inuit. Then the girl returned home and lived with her parents again.

See also Sedna; Transformation, Human-Animal

References and further reading:

Boas, Franz. *The Central Eskimo*. Lincoln: University of Nebraska Press, 1964.

Fisher, John F. "An Analysis of the Central Eskimo Sedna Myth." *Temenos* 11 (1995): 27–42.

Millman, Lawrence. *A Kayak Full of Ghosts: Eskimo Folk Tales*. 1987. Northampton, Mass.: Interlink Press, 2004.

Rasmussen, Knud. *Iglulik and Caribou Eskimo Texts*. 1930. Report of the Fifth Thule Expedition, vol. 7, no. 3. New York: AMS Press, 1976.

EARTH DIVER

Crow, Plains; Seneca, Northeast Woodlands

Earth Diver myths relate the formation of the earth from a small bit of mud brought from the bottom of an ancient sea. Rooth compared nearly 300 creation myths from across North America and reported that versions of the Earth Diver myth were found in most all areas except portions of the southwest and Alaska. Rooth also described the elements of Earth Diver tales: first there is only water; some creature must retrieve mud or sand from deep below the surface of the water; the diver is away a long time; the mud or sand is used by a god (or animal) to form the earth; the earth must be stretched out or spread out; it increases in size over time and as humans or animals explore its circumference.

Leach retold a set of Crow tales collected by Robert H. Lowie.

Long ago Old Man and four ducks were the only creatures alive. There was only water at that time. Old Man was going along and saw the ducks. He asked them, "Is there any earth down there?" The ducks assured him that there was. Old Man spoke to a mallard, "Go down there and bring back some earth so we can make a world." The mallard dove down below the water and was gone a long time. When he finally returned, he did not have any earth in his beak. A second duck attempted to bring back a bit of earth and then a third duck did the same, but neither of them had any luck. Finally the helldiver (an aquatic bird) asked to be sent down. He, too, was gone under the water a long time, and Old Man and the other ducks were beginning to think he would not return. But when he did return, he brought back a little mud on the ends of his toes.

Old Man took the mud and began working it in his hands. He started spreading it out from the east to the west. He told the ducks that he would make streams and ponds for them to live in. Old Man also made mountains and hills and all sorts of trees and plants. Then he said he would make other creatures. But before he got started, a howling coyote came running from the west. Old Man declared that the coyote would be powerful because he had created himself. The Old Man then created the buffalo and all of the other animals. Finally Old Man made people and proceeded to teach them about making fire and arrows and how to set up their tepees.

In a Seneca tale, the earth had not yet been created when Iagen'tci began her fall from the heavens to the water below. Ducks were swimming on the surface and saw the young girl falling toward them. A council was quickly convened, and they decided on a course of action. Some of the ducks flew up to meet her, and with their wings outstretched, caught her and gently lowered her to the surface. Then the ducks took turns diving to the bottom of the water to bring back mud. This mud, when piled on the turtle's back, would form land where the woman could live. The ducks, however, died before returning to the surface. Several other animals were also unsuccessful. Finally Muskrat was able to retrieve a small amount of mud from the bottom. When he smeared the mud on turtle's back, it immediately grew, and the earth was formed.

As indicated by Fenton, a Wyandot (Huron) version of Woman Who Fell from the Sky was recorded by Sagard in 1623 and again by Jesuits ten years later. A very similar tale was told to Hewitt only a little over a hundred years ago by Iroquois informants. Fenton emphasizes the long oral tradition of this myth, which most likely is much older than we can guess.

See also Rabbit; Transformer; Woman Who Fell from the Sky

References and further reading:

Fenton, William N. "This Island, the World on Turtle's Back." *Journal of American Folklore* 75, no. 298 (October–December 1962): 283–300.

Leach, Maria. *The Beginning: Creation Myths Around the World.* New York: Funk & Wagnalls, 1956.

Parker, Arthur Caswell. *Seneca Myths and Folk Tales.* 1923. Lincoln: University of Nebraska Press, 1989.

Rooth, Anna Birgitta. "The Creation Myths of the North American Indians." *Anthropos* 52 (1957): 497–508.

EARTH MOTHER

Okanagon, Plateau

This tale of the earth's origins apparently has been influenced by Christian missionaries or by European contact.

Old One, the Creator, made the earth out of a woman. He rolled and stretched the earth and she became like a large ball. Old One shaped the animals from bits of mud from Earth Mother's skin. He made each kind of animal to have its own strengths and weaknesses. Some of the bits of mud he made into humans. These happened to be the most helpless creatures of all. Men were selfish and stirred up trouble. Then Old One sent his son Jesus to fix things. He told the people how to live right, but they didn't listen. Instead they killed him, so he went back to live in the sky.

Therefore Old One sent Coyote to set the world right. He taught humans how to hunt and fish, how to build shelters, and how to make clothes to wear. He taught them to talk and gave them names. He even put salmon in the rivers and showed the people the best way to catch them with spears and nets.

Coyote chased away the Ice People and killed them with heat. Only one remained—just to torment men for a time each year. Coyote did a lot of good things, but sometimes he did foolish things. One day he heard water making noise. He told it to stop, but it kept on dripping. So he became angry and kicked at the spot the water was dripping from. To his surprise, the drops turned into a gushing stream that swept him away and nearly killed him. Coyote's mistake became the mighty Columbia River.

Eventually, Old One returned to see what Coyote had done. He was pleased with Coyote's work and told him that it was time for him to rest. So Coyote left. Old One told the people that he, too, would be leaving, but he would send messengers to them at times. The people were to listen to them. He also told the people that when Earth Mother was very old, he would return again with the spirits of the dead and everyone would live together. The Okanagon say that the earth is very old now, so Old One will come back soon.

References and further reading:

Boas, Franz, ed. *Folk-Tales of Salishan and Sahaptin Tribes.* 1917. New York: Kraus Reprint, 1969.

Leach, Maria. *The Beginning: Creation Myths Around the World.* New York: Funk & Wagnalls, 1956.

Sproul, Barbara C. *Primal Myths: Creating the World.* 1st Harper Collins ed. San Francisco: HarperCollins, 1991. First published 1979 by Harper & Row.

EMERGENCE

Southwest

Well-known and respected, the emergence creation stories explain the existence of various populations in the current world and often account for their diversity in culture and language. Especially prevalent among Native Americans of the Southwest, emergence stories are by no means exclusive to this region. However, the ties to complex ritual and ceremony among the people of the Southwest, such as the initiation of boys and curing ceremonies, is what makes their emergence stories distinct from those of other cultures.

Typically, the emergence describes how humans, plants, and animals were conceived and gradually matured in one or more underworlds. The underworld is sometimes populated by people, and sometimes by animals. They are usually taught by a representative of a supreme being, and the existence of their food, work, and customs is explained. They come forth from the underworld(s) and migrate to their present location.

A Hopi story explains the emergence as initiated by two goddesses.

Long ago, the earth contained only water. In the east, a goddess of rock, minerals, and other hard substances lived in the ocean. She was Huruing Wuhti. A ladder led into her house, or kiva, to which two fox skins, one yellow, one gray, were usually tied. Another Huruing Wuhti lived in the west, in a similar kiva. A turtle-shell rattle was attached to her ladder.

The sun rose and set on this watery world. It would leave the Huruting Wuhti's kiva in the east and don the skins of the foxes as it moved across the sky—first the gray skin, creating the white dawn of the Hopi, then the yellow skin to create the bright yellow dawn. When it arrived at the Huruting Wuhti's kiva in the west, the sun announced its arrival by fastening the rattle to the top of the ladder. It would then continue under the water, back to the east.

One day, the two goddesses caused the waters to part and recede, causing some dry land to appear. The one from the east traveled to see the one in the west, over a rainbow, to discuss putting living creatures on the earth. They decided to create a little bird, so the Huruting Wuhti of the east fashioned a wren of clay and covered it with a cloth. Both goddesses sang a little song, and a live bird came forth. It was sent to fly over the earth. When it returned, it reported that it saw no living being anywhere. This was actually not true, as the bird failed to notice Kohkang Wuhti, or Spider Woman, who lived in her kiva in the southwest. The Huruting Wuhti of the west created more birds of many different kinds, and together the two goddesses made them real in the same manner as before. They taught the birds to sing and allowed them to scatter in all directions.

Next, the Huruting Wuhti of the west made various animals and taught them to make certain sounds before sending them into the world. The goddesses decided to make humans after that. So, the Huruting Wuhti from the east made a white man and woman from clay and brought them to life. The goddesses taught them their language, and then they selected a place to live.

Spider Woman heard about what the others were doing, and she, too, created a man and woman of clay. However, she taught them Spanish and made two burros for them, and they decided to live near her.

She continued to create other people, giving a different language to each pair. But she once forgot to make a woman for a particular man, and this explains why some single men exist. She also forgot to create a man for a certain woman, so she told the woman to go find one of the single men and see if he would accept her. The two finally met, and decided to stay together. He built a house for them, but it wasn't long before they began to quarrel. The woman decided she wanted to live alone, since she knew how to cook, but the man suggested they remain a couple. After all, he knew how to gather wood and work the fields. They made up, but it didn't last. They soon quarreled and separated, reunited, and separated again. Other couples learned to quarrel like them, which is why husbands and wives have so many arguments. This was the type of rough-mannered people the Spider Woman created.

The Huruting Wuhti of the west heard about the people the Spider Woman was creating. She told the goddess from the east that she did not want to live alone but around good people. So, she created more pairs, who ran into trouble whenever they encountered the people Spider Woman had created.

Eventually, the goddess from the west told the people that she was going to live in the middle of the ocean to the west. She instructed them to pray for her if they wanted anything. Her people were sorry to see her go. The Huruting Wuhti from the east did the same thing. Whenever the Hopi want something, they deposit their prayer offerings in their village, thinking of the two goddesses who still remember them.

Another emergence story, from the Northern California coast, tells of the earth's formation by a dragon and a god. Like so many stories from this area, it was recorded as a fragment because of the negative impact of early contact with Europeans.

Before the present world was formed, there existed another with a sky of old sandstone rock. Two gods, Thunder and Nagaicho, noticed that the sky was being shaken by thunder. They decided to fix the rock by stretching it above and far to the east.

They walked onto the sky to do so, and under each of its four corners, they set a great rock to hold it up. Then they added various things to make the world pleasant and attractive to people. Flowers were put in the south, and clouds in the east. To form these clouds a fire was built, and a large hole opened in the sky so that they could float through. In the west, another opening was made so the fog could drift in from the ocean.

Next, the gods created people. They formed a man from earth and made a stomach for him of grass. They used grass for his heart, too, round bits of clay for the liver and kidneys, and a reed for a windpipe. To create his blood, they mixed pulverized red stone with water. The gods put the man's parts together and then took one of his legs, split it, and turned it into a woman. They also fashioned a sun to travel during the day, and a moon at night.

It rained every night and day, however, and so the gods' creations did not last. Land and animals disappeared because of the water, and all the people slept. The oceans flowed together and joined, and there were no more mountains, fields, or rocks. All living things washed away, and there was no wind, snow, frost, rain, or sun. It was just very dark.

The earth dragon then walked down from the north, traveling underground with the god Nagaicho riding on its head. As the dragon walked along beneath the ocean, its glances and movements caused a coastal ridge, an island, and a great mountain range to form in various places. When it reached the south the dragon lay down. Nagaicho spread gray clay between its eyes and on each horn. He covered the clay with reeds, and then applied another layer of clay. On this clay he put some small stones and then set blue grass, brush, and trees in it. He declared there should be mountain peaks on the earth's head, against which the waves of the sea would break. So the mountains appeared, and brush sprang up on them. The stones he had placed on the head became large, and it could no longer be seen.

Next, people appeared, people with animal names such as Seal, Sea Lion, Whale, and Grizzly Bear. When Indians came to live on earth later, these "first people" were changed into their animal namesakes.

Nagaicho created various kinds of sea foods that grew in the water for the people to eat, such as seaweed, abalones, and mussels. He created salt from ocean foam, and arranged for the ocean to move in waves. Next, he traveled all over the earth to make it a pleasant place to live. He made redwoods and other trees grow on the dragon's tail, which lay to the north. He created oak trees to supply acorns to eat. He formed creeks with fresh water for drinking by dragging his foot around.

When Nagaicho had finished, he walked all around the new land with his dog to see how everything looked. Being satisfied, and finding himself close to his original home, he decided to stay in the north.

References and further reading:

Bierhorst, John. *The Mythology of North America: With a New Afterword.* New York: Oxford University Press, 2002. First published 1985 by William Morrow.

Erdoes, Richard, and Alfonso Ortiz, eds. *American Indian Myths and Legends.* New York: Pantheon Books, 1984.

Leeming, David, and Jake Page. *The Mythology of Native North America.* Norman: University of Oklahoma Press, 1998.

Newcomb, Franc J. *Navaho Folk Tales.* 2nd ed. Albuquerque: University of New Mexico Press, 2000.

FIRST CREATOR AND LONE MAN

Mandan, Plains

Myths regarding First Creator and Lone Man tell of the creation of the earth, its people, and its animals. The version retold here appears to have been influenced by contact with early European missionaries.

Before there was an earth as we now know it, water covered everything. First Creator and Lone Man were walking along on top of the water when they saw something in the distance. They soon discovered that it was Duck. As they watched her, she dove under the water and came back up with a bit of mud. First Creator and Lone Man asked Duck to bring up some mud for them also. They thought it would be a good substance from which to form the earth and its creatures.

They decided to divide up the responsibilities. Lone Man went to the north and First Creator went to the south. They left some water in between them and this is now the Missouri River. First Creator made hills, mountain streams, valleys, buffalo, elk, and antelope. While he was doing this, Lone Man created a level country with lakes and small streams scattered across the region. He made animals that lived in water part of the time, such as the beaver, otter, and muskrat. He also created cattle and moose. After First Creator and Lone Man had each completed their tasks, they inspected each other's work. First Creator thought his land and animals were superior. But, Lone Man replied that he created what he thought would be useful to mankind.

After a while, First Creator and Lone Man went separate ways. Lone Man walked among humans, but they didn't see him. So he devised a way in which to be born as a human and chose a young virgin to become his mother. He changed himself into corn and was eaten by the girl. Later, she was found to be with child even though she was still a virgin. Eventually the baby boy was born and grew as any normal boy, although he hated evil and never married. He promoted peace and harmony and settled disputes with calming words. He caused buffalo herds to come near the people so they had plenty to eat. He also directed rain to fall on the corn fields when there was drought everywhere else.

Lone Man joined a group of twelve men who were setting out to sail to an island where the inhabitants were known for their fabulous feasts. During the journey, evil spirits rose up out of the water, but Lone Man rebuked them and commanded them never to return. While they were still on the river, willows along the banks turned into evil spirits and challenged Lone Man to fight. He went on shore and killed all who attempted to wrestle with him. The remaining evil spirits fled. Then Lone Man reprimanded the willows. He reminded them that he was their creator and ordered them never to turn into evil spirits again.

Once on the sea, a whirlpool threatened to consume the boat. The other men on the boat were terrified and thought that they would perish, but Lone Man finally rebuked the waves and told them to "Be still!" From then on, their journey was peaceful. When they arrived at the island, Lone Man discerned that the chief of the island was plotting to kill him and his companions by making them overeat at the feast. So Lone Man told the other men to only eat as much as they felt comfortable eating. Lone Man, however, found a hollow bulrush and inserted it into his mouth and down through his whole digestive system until it penetrated far down into the earth. When the bowls of food were passed to him, Lone Man appeared to eat vast quantities. But in reality the food passed through the bulrush and down into the earth. The chief and his people were amazed that the strangers did not die from overeating.

The chief attempted to kill them in several other ways, but Lone Man always knew ahead of time what was planned. The chief became suspicious and eventually said, "You must be Lone Man!" But Lone Man denied it. When they all returned to their own homes, Lone Man taught them how to perform ceremonies in remembrance of him. As part of the preparation, the people were to find a cedar tree and set the trunk in the middle of the village. They were to paint it red and then burn incense and offer sacrifices nearby. Lone Man told the people that he would be going away, but that he was leaving his body (the cedar) behind.

The four day Mandan Okipa (O-kee-pa) Ceremony was conducted not only to provide the necessities of daily life, but also to underline the bond between the people and the supernatural forces around them. The sacred cedar pole representing Lone Man was a focal point for prayers and many of the ceremonial activities of the Okipa. In the winter of 1832, Prince Maximilian recorded what elders of the tribe described to him of the ceremony, and during the summer of that year, the artist George Caitlin and fur trader James Kipp actually witnessed it. Several titles listed below have summarized both Maximilian's and Catlin's reports.

See also Culture Hero(es); Tansformer

References and further reading:

Beckwith, Martha Warren. "Myths and Hunting Stories of the Mandan and Hidatsa Sioux." *Publications of the Folk-lore Foundation* 10 (1930): 1–116.

Bowers, Alfred W. *Mandan Social and Ceremonial Organization.* 1950. Reprint, Moscow: University of Idaho Press, 1991.

Peters, Virginia Bergman. *Women of the Earth Lodges: Tribal Life on the Plains.* Norman: University of Oklahoma Press, 2000. First published 1995 by Archon Books.

Taylor, Colin F. *Caitlin's O-kee-pa: Mandan Culture and Ceremonial, The George Caitlin O-kee-pa Manuscript in the British Museum.* Wyk auf Foehr, Germany: Verlag für Amerikanistik, 1996.

FLOOD(S)

Mythological narratives regarding a great deluge abound worldwide. In North America, flood stories are found not only where people lived near large bodies of water, but also in the drier interior of the continent.

An Inuit version of the great flood states that one spring a tremendous storm blew across the earth, destroying the homes of people living on the Arctic coast. The people hurried to their skin boats and, as a safety measure, lashed them together. The sea began to rise and soon covered everything as far as the eye could see. Terrified, the people drifted in their boats, unable to save themselves. At night many people died from the bitter cold, and their bodies fell into the sea. But by morning the wind and sea had calmed and the sun beat down on the people in the boats and the waters began to steam. The sun was so intense that some people died. Finally a sorcerer struck the water with his bow and yelled, "Enough! Enough! We've had enough!" Then the man tossed his earrings into the sea and again cried out, "Enough!" Soon the water began receding and eventually formed the rivers and streams. The sea retreated to the place it is today.

Teit described a Lillooet flood story.

A great rain fell on the area where the Lillooet once lived. It rained heavily and continued raining until the lakes and rivers overflowed. The people were afraid. A man named Ntci'nemkim put his family in a large canoe. The other people began climbing up a large mountain. When they saw the family in the canoe, they begged Ntci'nemkim to let their children in the canoe. However, the man said the canoe was too small to hold all of the children. So he took one child from each family—a boy from one family and a girl from the next. The rain continued falling and soon all of the land, except for Split Mountain, was covered with water. The people drifted in the canoe until the water receded. When the land was finally dry, the man and his family built their home near where the canoe came to rest. They made the other children marry each other and sent the young couples off in different directions to make homes where the game was abundant.

Another myth tale from the Pacific Northwest explains cause of the flood. According to the Haida tale included in the Erdoes and Ortiz anthology, *American Indian Myths and Legends,* there was a village near Frederick Island with many people residing in it. A group of boys and girls were playing on the beach. They noticed a strange looking woman wearing an unusual fur cape. A curious little boy walked up to her to find out more about her and other children followed him. One boy pulled up the back of her garment and they were surprised to see what looked like a plant that grows near the shore sticking out of her back. The children all laughed and made fun of her. But the elders of the village warned the children not to make fun of the woman.

The woman sat down at the water's edge. Since it was low tide, the sea was a long way from the village. However, as the tide began to rise, the woman got up and moved a little closer to the village. Each time the water touched her feet, she moved back towards the village. Finally she was sitting at the edge of the village. The people were amazed and terrified. They didn't have any canoes, so they tied logs together to form rafts. Then they placed their children and baskets of food and water on the rafts. The woman continued to back up each time the water touched her feet and she moved higher and higher up the mountainside. Eventually the entire island was covered by the water and the people floated around on the rafts. Finally they saw a few mountain peaks protruding from the water. One of the rafts came to rest on one peak while the other rafts landed on others, and this is how the people spread across the earth.

According to a tale from the Skidi Pawnee, the flood was caused by arrogant people who offended the sun. The god Tirawa destroyed them and monsters in a great flood and then created new people for the earth.

Long ago, Tirawa had created everything, including men, animals, and monsters. The people were giants and could do marvelous things. They thought they were as good as any of the gods in heaven. These giants became so proud they began behaving disrespectfully to Sun. When it rose in the morning they would call it rude names. They even went so far as to turn their backs and expel flatus at it.

This displeased Tirawa greatly and he asked the minor gods for their advice, "What shall I do with them?" But they replied, "It is not up to us. You made them; they are yours." So Tirawa decided to destroy them. He ordered Paruxti to send a cloud from the west to pour heavy rain on these evil people. But the people did not care. So Tirawa ordered a second cloud sent. This one also poured heavy rain down on the evil giants. But they were not concerned. So Tirawa ordered Paruxti to send a third cloud, and this time it was to rain until everything on earth was drowned. When the cloud burst, the water that had been in the ground also rose. The people realized that the situation was serious and ran to higher ground. But the water continued to rise until it covered everything, even the highest hills. All the people were killed by the flood and so were all of the monsters.

Tirawa then sent a little bird to see if the ground was dry. Then he sent another bird, a crow, and told him that he would find streams and people and animals, but he was not supposed to touch them while he was down there. The crow, however, when he saw the dead people, ate from them. Tirawa was displeased by this and refused to let him back into the heavens. "You shall remain on earth and live off of carcasses."

The other bird that had been sent to earth was told by Tirawa that he would become the chief of the birds because he had obeyed. Tirawa also said that the new people who were to be created would honor this bird and include him in sacred pipe bundles.

Then Tirawa, knowing that the streams and lakes had been restored, instructed Lightning to collect the people in a sack and rid the land of their carcasses. When Lightning returned to Tirawa, the other gods were commanded to create mankind. Paruxti, the Evening Star, created the first men, and then the other gods followed, and this way the earth was replenished with humans.

See also Tirawa

References and further reading:

Bruchac, Joseph, and Diana Landau, eds. *Singing of Earth: A Native American Anthology.* Florence, KY: The Nature Company, 1993.

Dorsey, George A. *Traditions of the Skidi Pawnee.* 1904. Reprint, Kraus Reprint Co., 1969.

Erdoes, Richard, and Alfonso Ortiz, eds. *American Indian Myths and Legends.* New York: Pantheon Books, 1984.

Teit, James. "Traditions of the Lillooet Indians of British Columbia." *Journal of American Folklore* 25, no. 98 (October–December 1912): 342.

FOX

The beautiful but clever and cunning Fox is another animal character commonly found in Native American myths and stories. He is one of Coyote's most common companions, but Fox often proves to be a deceitful friend and steals Coyote's food. In an Achomawi story, the two are co-creators who disappear from the world just before humans arrive. The Yurok tell the story of how the Foxes, angry with the Sun, caught him and tied him to a hill, causing him to burn a great hole in the ground. An Inuit tale features Fox as a beautiful woman who marries a hunter, but resumes her skin and leaves him when he offends her.

Fox proves to be an untrustworthy friend to Wolf in a story of the Menominee.

Fox and Wolf were living together and making maple sugar. They made one *mokok* ("bark box"), of sugar, and then they buried it. They agreed to let their cache remain hidden until they were very hungry.

Fox was a good hunter. He never failed to return home with chickens or small game every time he went out. But the greedy Wolf never killed anything or brought anything home, so Fox decided to play a trick on his chum for being so lazy. Fox suggested that Wolf visit a nearby house and see if the people living there would give him something to eat. He told Wolf that he had been given a chicken when he went there.

Wolf did as he was told. But when he arrived at the house, Wolf did not hide himself. The owner of the house saw the Wolf approach, so he set his dogs on him to drive him away. The man decided it was Wolf who had been stealing their chickens. Wolf escaped only by running into the river. When Wolf arrived at his home, he told Fox of his narrow escape. Fox explained that the man did not recognize him, but Wolf did not reply. One day Fox lied to Wolf and told him he had to leave the house, as he wanted to give a name to a child. But Fox went instead to their cache of maple-sugar and ate some of it. When he returned, he told Wolf in response to his question that he named the baby Mokimon. This word means to "reveal" or "dig out" something one has hidden.

Another time, while he and Wolf were sitting together, Fox pulled the same trick. This time, Fox told Wolf he had named the baby Wapiton, which means "to commence to eat." The next time, he told Wolf he had given the baby the name Hapata kiton, or, "half eaten." Finally, Fox claimed he had named a baby Noskwaton, which means "all licked up."

At that point, Wolf finally caught on and angrily guessed that Fox had been eating their stored maple sugar. But Fox just laughed at him. Then Wolf went to look at their cache. Sure enough, all he found was the empty box, with its former contents missing.

In the meantime, Fox went and hid in the branches of a large tree by a stream. Wolf returned home to find Fox gone and tracked him to the tree. He climbed part way, but fell into the water in surprise and fury when Fox startled him. He tried four times to jump out of the water to catch the laughing Fox but soon grew tired and gave up. Wolf finally suggested they make up and go home, knowing that Fox was feeding him regularly anyway.

Winter returned, and Fox frequently left their home to catch many fish. Wolf asked him how he caught so many, and Fox explained to him how he used his tail for a line. He suggested Wolf try this technique himself.

Fox was hoping he could get Wolf to freeze to death in the ice, so he would no longer have to feed him. So, he took him out and cut five holes in the ice—one for each paw, and one for Wolf's tail—explaining that he could catch more fish that way. Wolf remained there to fish all night. As his limbs and tail became heavy, he thought he was catching a tremendous load of fish, so he remained on the ice longer, unknowingly freezing fast. When he finally realized what was happening, he struggled to free himself, wearing out his tail and pulling the claws and bottoms of his feet off. He believed Fox's story that this was caused by all the fish he had caught.

Since this trick proved unsuccessful in killing Wolf, Fox persuaded him to climb a tree and take honey from a wasp's nest. Wolf was nearly stung to death. Fox ran away, over a wagon road to conceal his tracks, where he met a man hauling a load of bread. Fox lay down on the side of the road and pretended he was dead. The man stopped and put him in his wagon behind his load. Fox came to and, as they rode along, threw a loaf of bread to the ground every so often. Finally, he jumped off the wagon and took the loaves he had stolen to a secret place, where he built a shelter in which to live.

Wolf eventually stumbled along, half-starved and injured from his experience with the fishing and the wasp's nest. Fox fed him upon his arrival and suggested he steal some bread the same way he did.

The next morning, Wolf watched the same road, and the man approached with his load of bread. Wolf played dead on the ground, but the man was determined to not be fooled again after losing some of his bread to what he had thought was a dead fox the previous day. He stopped his team and knocked Wolf over the head with a big stick and killed him. Ever since then, Fox has eaten alone.

References and further reading:

Curtin, Jeremiah. "Achomawi Myths." *Journal of American Folklore* 22, no. 85 (July-September 1909): 283–287.

Russell, Frank. "Myths of the Jicarilla Apaches." *Journal of American Folklore* 11, no. 43 (October–December 1898): 253–271.

Skinner, Alanson. "European Folk-Tales Collected Among the Menominee Indians." *Journal of American Folklore* 26, no. 99 (January–March, 1913): 64–80.

GAMBLERS AND GAMBLING

Contrary to what many assume, the gambling that has arisen on Indian land across the United States during the past decade is not a ruinous element of capitalism newly adopted by Native Americans. Gambling was actually deeply rooted in the culture, myth, and religion of nearly all of the indigenous peoples of North America long before contact with Europeans. Historically, gambling was part of sacred tribal rituals, ceremonies, and celebrations, and was an informal mechanism for redistributing wealth within a given community. Today, many Indians view gaming as a viable source of employment and revenues, an integral part of tribal economies, and a previously unparalleled opportunity to gain self-sufficiency.

Native Americans were enthusiastic recreational gamblers and participants in a variety of games that stressed chance, skill, strength, and endurance. A favorite among Dakota (Sioux) women was played with dice made from beaver's teeth, bones, or other materials. Turtles, spiders, or lizards were painted and carved on the dice, which were kept in a round basket. A woman tossed the dice into the air and caught them in the basket. Designs were assigned different values, so points were scored depending on which designs faced upwards. Hair strings and beaded chokers were wagered on the luck of the throw. Especially popular among the Mohave was a hoop-and-pole game during which the participants themselves wagered heavily on the outcome. To play, a hoop was rolled and a player slid a pole along the ground, hoping that the hoop would fall on top of it when it stopped rolling. A favorite for betting among men of other California tribes was a guessing game that used objects hidden in the hands, a contest of wits that could go on for days while fortunes in shells, bows, skins, and baskets were wagered. One player held a marked and an unmarked bone and rapidly switched them from fist to fist. He then challenged his opponents to guess which hand held the marked bone.

Gamblers and games of chance appear frequently in Native American stories. In a Yana myth, Gopher tells Rabbit they will always gamble when they meet. A series of games results in Gopher losing everything, even his body, to Rabbit. A Kawaiisu story features Inipi, a spirit of the dead and keeper of doves who gambles with Coyote. Coyote wins the doves, and they are released for the Kawaiisu people. During seasons when no doves are seen, Coyote is believed to be losing the gambling match. In a story of the Alabama, about a moccasin game called *thlakalunka*, a man of considerable means wagers first his family fortune, then his clothes, then all of the world's water, and loses. People begin to die of thirst because the rivers, streams, and ponds have all dried up. Woodpecker discovers a canoe as large as a tree and pecks a hole in it, causing all the water to gush back into place. The story of the divine gambler Noqoìlpi tells of how a great pueblo, Kintyèli, frequently found in Navajo legends, came to be built.

In a Chilcotin story, two men played the game lehal, and one lost everything he owned. He finally bet his wife, lost her too, and was very unhappy. He

Group of Indians from the Sinkiuse-Columbia tribe, Colville Reservation, Washington state, playing a game of chance, 1911. (Library of Congress)

went away and lay down beneath an overhanging rock. As he lay there thinking about ways he might recover his wife and property, he heard some ducks flying over. Looking up, he was surprised to find that he was able to see the ducks right through the rock. He then laid his lehal bones on top of the rock and found that they, too, were visible through it, and he could see which one was black and which one was white. Joyful at his discovery, he returned home. He spent that summer alone in the mountains, hunting groundhogs, the skins of which he made into many blankets.

When the salmon were running, he went to fish, and encountered the man who had won his wife. Since he had blankets to wager, he suggested they play lehal again. The game began, and the man found that this time he could see the lehal bones right through the other's hands. He allowed the other man to win a few times to make him overconfident and careless. Soon, he started to win and gradually won back all his possessions, until his rival had nothing left. He then suggested they play for his wife again. But the other man said he preferred to keep his wife, and was willing to bet his own wife instead, as he didn't care for her. So, they played on, and he soon won the man's wife. Then they played for his own wife, and when he had won back half of her, the other man suggested they stop the game so he could stay with her for one more night. However, the man refused, as they had not made this kind of arrangement when they had played previously. The man finally won both women, and his revenge was complete.

See also Otters and Coyote

References and further reading:

Culin, Stewart. *Games of the North American Indians.* 2 vols. 1907. Lincoln: University of Nebraska Press, 1992.

Farrand, Livingston. *Traditions of the Chilcotin Indians.* 1900. Memoirs of the American Museum of Natural History, vol. 4, Anthropology, vol. 3, pt. 1. Publications of the Jesup North Pacific Expedition, vol. 2, pt. 1. New York: AMS Press, 1975.

Gabriel, Kathryn. *Gambler Way: Indian Gaming in Mythology, History, and Archaeology in North America.* Boulder, Colo.: Johnson Books, 1996.

Matthews, Washington. "Naqoìlpi, the Gambler: a Navajo Myth." *Journal of American Folklore* 2, no. 5 (April–June 1889): 89–94.

Pasquaretta, Paul. "Contesting the Evil Gambler: Gambling, Choice, and Survival in American Indian Texts." In *Indian Gaming: Who Wins?*, edited by Angela Mullis and David Kamper, 131–151. Contemporary American Indian Issues Series, no. 9. Los Angeles: UCLA American Indian Studies Center, 2000.

GHOSTS

Most Native North Americans viewed death not as the end of life, but as the beginning of the next life. Although traditions and beliefs surrounding death varied across the continent, there appears to have been general agreement that the spirit of the deceased often remained nearby for a time. Ceremonial mourning periods also varied and may have coincided with the length of time a spirit was considered to be present. Numerous mythological stories include or focus on ghosts. In some stories ghosts have dangerous power and elicit fear, while in others they come as messengers to warn the living of peril.

Some myths tell of mourning spouses who went to the land of the dead to bring their loved ones back. Often in these myths the deceased spouse was able to come back (or be brought back) home and the living spouse was admonished to follow certain directives. Failure to do so would result in the loved one becoming a ghost again and returning to the land of the dead. Several of these myths have been included here in the entry entitled *Afterlife.*

J. Owen Dorsey and George Bushotter recorded several ghost myths from the Teton Dakota. In one of these a young man wished to marry a certain girl. One day when he returned from gathering wild horses to give to her father, he found the village deserted except for one lodge. In it he found a burial scaffold, and looking down from it was the girl. He stayed there with her until one day

Hand-colored woodcut of a Dakota family offering gifts to the dead in an elevated grave, Montana. (North Wind Picture Archives)

he was very hungry and thought to himself that he must leave the lodge to hunt for food. The ghost said to him, "You said you were hungry. Go ride to the bluffs and there you will find a herd of buffalo. Shoot the fattest one and then bring me some of the roasted meat before you eat your meal." When the young man brought the food into the lodge, the girl climbed down from the scaffolding. This startled him, but she knew what he was thinking and reassured him saying, "Don't be afraid."

Eventually, the couple decided to leave that place, traveling by night and resting by day. As they went along the young woman kept her head covered and walked silently through the grass. Whenever her husband was thinking about something, the young wife knew exactly what it was, even if he did not speak a word. That is because a ghost knows everything, even when the wind will blow or the rains will fall from the clouds. The young man and his wife continued to travel around, but they were never seen by people. Eventually the man became a ghost, too.

According to Dorsey's translations of over 200 myths and other texts recorded by Bushotter in his native language, ghosts were not always visible to the living, but sometimes they could be heard. Occasionally, ghosts would become visible and live as humans, eating, drinking, and marrying. When someone was sick, the ghost of dead relatives would come to coax the person away. To keep the ghosts away, cedar logs were laid around the home to protect it. At other times cedar wood was burned to make smoke.

In order to make travel to the ghost world easier, Dorsey and Bushotter reported that Teton people received a tattoo on their foreheads or on their wrists. An old woman sat along the road to the ghost world and examined each ghost that tried to pass. If she did not find the appropriate tattoo, she pushed them over a cliff and they fell back to earth. That is why some ghosts are forever wandering around here on earth.

An Ojibwa myth relates the story of a man and his wife who were longsuffering in their hospitality to two strangers.

The husband was out hunting, and as the time grew late, the wife worried about him. When she heard footsteps outside, she thought it was her husband. Instead there were two strange women. The wife invited them into her home. The strangers sat in a far corner, kept their heads covered, and didn't speak. Much to the wife's relief, her husband finally arrived home. He brought in with him a carcass of a large, fat deer. The two strangers jumped up and tore off large pieces of fat from the deer and ate eagerly. The man and his wife were very surprised by their behavior but didn't say anything out of respect for the strangers.

The two women continued to stay with the man and his wife throughout the remainder of the winter, and except for this one thing that they did each time the man returned with meat, their behavior was above reproach. They were quiet, kept to themselves, and were no trouble at all. Hunting had been good since the women arrived, so the couple thought the two women had brought good luck. One day, however, when the man returned very late, the two strangers immediately tore into the carcass he brought back. The wife became angry at their behavior, but didn't say a word. Still, her husband knew that she was upset by the incident. Later that night, there was weeping coming from the corner where the strangers stayed. The man asked the two women why they were crying and said, "Have we been inhospitable to you?"

The women replied that they had been treated with kindness. They told the man that they had been sent on a mission from the land of the dead. The Master of Life had heard the cries of people who lost loved ones and wished to have another chance to make them happy. The test he devised was to see if humans were really sincere. The two women gave the couple advice and instructions about the future, promised the hunter great success, and then they departed into the night.

See also Afterlife; Bluejay; Ghosts

References and further reading:

Bierhorst, John, ed. *The Red Swan: Myths and Tales of the American Indians.* Albuquerque: University of New Mexico Press, 1992. First published 1976 by Farrar, Straus, and Giroux.

Bushotter, George, and J. Owen Dorsey. "A Teton Dakota Ghost Story." *Journal of American Folklore* 1, no. 1 (April-June 1888): 68–72.

Dorsey, J. Owen. "Teton Folk-Lore." *American Anthropologist* 2, no. 2 (April 1889): 143–158.

Weltfish, Gene. *Caddoan Texts: Pawnee, South Band Dialect.* New York: AMS Press, 1974. First published 1937 by G.E. Stechert.

THE GIRL WHO MARRIED A BEAR

Haida, Tlingit, Tsimshian, Northwest Coast

This story recounts how the people were taught to respect bears and to perform the proper ceremonies to appease the spirits of the bears they had hunted and killed.

The chief of a village had four sons who were excellent hunters and fishermen. His daughter gathered berries with the other girls from the village. One day, when the girl and her companions were some distance from the village, her basket line broke and all of the berries tumbled out. The other girls told her to just leave them on the ground and return to the village as it was getting dark. However, the girl insisted on picking up all the scattered berries and stayed behind.

Soon two young men came along and offered to help carry her basket. They led her to a village that she had never seen before. She was ushered into the house of the chief of that village. Mouse Woman came to her side and advised what food to eat and what food to decline. Mouse Woman also explained that she was now in the village of the Black Bears and that the people she saw were not really people at all, but bears.

The girl married a son of the Black Bear chief and lived with them through the summer. When the fall came, the bears prepared to go to their winter homes. The Bear chief called everyone together and asked which dens they wanted to live in. The other families chose their dens and then the chief asked his son and daughter-in-law which one they wanted. The girl's husband named a nearby place, but she said, "No, it is near where my brothers and their dogs hunt." So the husband named other dens, but each time the girl refused to go there. Finally the chief asked where she wanted to spend the winter and she replied, "Somewhere far away that would be difficult for my brothers' dogs to find." So the chief gave them a den on the far side of the mountain.

That winter the girl's brothers went hunting. The older ones were very successful and brought home many bear hides and much meat. But, the youngest one did not have any luck, so he kept searching farther into the mountains. One day his dogs picked up the scent of bear and ran up a snowy mountainside. The brother had a difficult time following but finally made it to the opening of a den. When he peeked inside he saw his sister and her husband. His sister asked him to wait while she gave birth. After a while, she gave him her two babies and he tucked them inside his clothing. Then the girl asked her brother not to kill her husband with a spear, but to build a fire at the mouth of the den. At first the brother said that he would spare her husband, but the girl said, "No. Kill him, or he will kill you."

So her brother built a fire at the mouth of the bear's den and after a while they could no longer hear the bear's moans and they knew he was dead. The hunter pulled the bear outside and while he butchered it, the girl sang the songs her Bear-husband had taught her. They prepared the bear's head, heart, tail, and hide as she had been instructed and she sang a song for each part of the ceremony.

Then the girl, her children, and her brother returned to her father's village. All of the people were glad to see her again, and her father gave a feast for his grandchildren. The children grew and played rough-and-tumble inside and out. One day, as they were wrestling inside the house, they knocked their grandmother over. The old woman complained angrily, and the children were so ashamed that they asked to return to their father's people. So their mother sent them off with a sorrowful heart. She asked them to bring food at times and to let their younger uncle have successful hunting trips.

See also Bear; Culture Hero(es); Mouse Woman

References and further reading:

Reid, Bill. *The Raven Steals the Light: Native American Tales.* Boston: Shambhala, 1996. First published 1984 by University of Washington Press.

Swann, Brian, ed. *Coming to Light: Contemporary Translations of the Native Literatures of North America.* New York: Vintage Books, 1996. First published 1994 by Random House.

Tate, Henry W. *The Porcupine Hunter and Other Stories: The Original Tsimshian Texts of Henry W. Tate.* Vancouver: Talonbooks, 1993.

GLOOSKAP

Northeast Woodlands

Across the northeastern region, variations in the spelling of this culture hero's name include Gluskap, Gluskabe, Glukoba, and Kuloskap. Although he was not the creator, Glooskap worked to set the world right. He also instructed both people and animals in the way they should live. In many areas of the Northeast, evidence of Glooskap's handiwork can be found in the lakes, hills, and islands he formed. Eventually his tasks were finished, and he left for the west.

Glooskap's birth is reminiscent of the birth of the twins in the myth "Woman Who Fell from the Sky."

Glooskap and his twin brother Malsum (called "Wolf") discussed how they would be born. Glooskap wanted to be born the usual way, but his brother came out through their mother's armpit, causing her death. The boys raised themselves and eventually grew to be very powerful. Glooskap then went around doing good, while Malsum was bent on making trouble for man and beast.

Malsum became envious of his brother, Glooskap, and one day asked him, "How would a person be able to kill you?" Glooskap suspected trouble, so he lied and said, "If someone would strike me on the head with a tail feather from an owl, I'd never know what hit me." Later, the brothers were on a hunting trip. While Glooskap was sleeping, Malsum found an owl and plucked out one of its tail feathers. He quietly crept up to Glooskap and struck him on the head with the feather. Glooskap woke up and was so angry he killed his brother, but later revived him in the form of a wolf (though some say he was turned into a mountain on the Gaspe Peninsula).

In a Passamaquoddy tale Glooskap (Kuloskap) defeated a family of cannibalistic Ice-Giants. The family had been friends of Glooskap when he was young, but later on he heard about their grisly ways. He decided to see for himself, and if it was true, he would destroy them. So he disguised himself to look like one of their kind and set off on his journey. When he arrived at the old man's wigwam, he went in and sat down. The old man's sons looked in but could not tell Glooskap and their father apart.

They devised a series of tests. First, the old man's daughter brought in food and placed it in front of Glooskap. However, before he could start eating, one of her brothers picked up the platter and took it outside. Glooskap was hungry so he merely willed the platter to return, and it did. Next they gave the old man a whale's jaw, but he could not bend it. Glooskap, however, snapped the huge bone as if it were only a pipe stem. The old man's sons marveled, but they tested him again. This time they brought strong tobacco that only a great wizard could smoke. But Glooskap burned the whole pipe full in just one puff.

Then the Ice-Giants said, "Let's have a game." They all went outdoors and started kicking a ball around. It wasn't just any ball, but a live human head that tried to bite off their feet when they kicked it. Glooskap took a branch from a tree and turned it into an even more gruesome ball. The others all ran away in terror. Then Glooskap caused a great flood of water to rush down the mountain, and he turned the Ice-Giants into fish. The fish were swept out to sea with the rushing water.

One myth retells the events from the time when Glooskap saved a village from a water monster.

The only source of water for a certain village had dried up. A man went to find out why. He walked to the source of the spring and learned that a huge monster had dammed up the water. The man pleaded with the monster to release the water for the thirsty people down stream. But, the monster just threatened to kill him. The man ran back to his village to report that the situation was hopeless. Glooskap, however, knew of their problem and decided to intervene. As he prepared for battle, Glooskap formed a flint knife from a nearby mountain. Then he went to the place where the water monster lived. When Glooskap demanded the release of the water, the monster just laughed and said that he would swallow Glooskap. The earth shook with Glooskap's rage. He made himself taller than the tree tops, and the monster was not able to swallow him. Glooskap pulled out his flint knife and split the monster's belly open. Suddenly, the water gushed out and ran down the hill and toward the sea.

Eventually, Glooskap had defeated all of the monsters. The land had been transformed to its present shape, and all living creatures had been instructed in how to live in peace and harmony. But the people were a rebellious lot and Glooskap became weary of living among them. So he made a great feast for them and then said his goodbyes and left for the west. It is said that the horned owls and the loons call out for him to return even today.

See also Culture Hero(es); Transformer
References and further reading:
Erdoes, Richard, and Alfonso Ortiz, eds. *American Indian Myths and Legends.* New York: Pantheon Books, 1984.

Hemmeon, Ethel. "Glooscap: A Synopsis of His Life; The Marked Stones He Left." *Canadian Forum* 12 (1932): 180–181.

Ives, Edward D. "Malecite and Passamaquoddy Tales." *Northeast Folklore* 6 (1964): 1–81.

Prince, John Dyneley. "Passamaquoddy Texts." *Publications of the American Ethnological Society* 10 (1921): 1–55.

GREAT BEAR CONSTELLATION

Northeast Woodlands, Plateau, Subarctic

The constellation Ursa Major is commonly called the Big Dipper in modern North America; to the ancients around the world, it was known as the Bear.

In the mythology of the Carrier Indians, a young man was away on a hunting expedition. He woke up and looked up at the Great Bear to check the time. Then he went back to sleep. Some time later, he looked at the Great Bear again, but it had hardly moved. The young man was angry at the Great Bear, since he was anxious for morning to come. So he yelled up at the stars, complaining that the Great Bear must be lame.

In the morning, the hunter's dog caught the scent of a bear near the camp and set off after it. The young man ran after them but had a difficult time keeping up. Finally, in the evening, the dog stopped, and instead of a bear an old man was sitting on a log. The old man asked the hunter if he'd been running all day. "Yes," he replied, "that's why I'm so exhausted." At that the old man reminded the youth what he'd said the night before. "In the sky I travel a great distance, but it appears that I travel slowly. Today I walked slowly, but you couldn't catch up to me." Then the young man was embarrassed at his harsh words, and the Great Bear returned to the sky.

The Skitswish (Coeur d'Alene) have several myths about the stars. One relates the story of three brothers who had a grizzly bear brother-in-law. Two of the brothers did not like the bear and plotted to kill it. The younger brother tried to warn his brother-in-law, but his brothers had followed him. As the young man called out to the bear, the other two shot and killed it. They were all suddenly transformed into the four main stars of the Great Bear Constellation.

Among the Algonquian-speaking people of the Northeastern Woodlands, there were a number of myth stories similar to the following from the Fox (Meskwaki) people.

Early one winter morning, three hunters set out along with their dog. They followed the river into the woods. After a while they found a trail that led to a bear's den. The oldest hunter crawled into the cave and poked the bear with his bow. The startled bear ran out of the den and the hunters and their dog gave chase.

At first the bear headed toward the frigid north. The youngest hunter ran quickly to turn him away from there. Then the bear ran to the east where the sun rises in the sky. The middle hunter ran in that direction to turn the bear back toward the others. Next the bear ran to the west where the sun sets. The oldest hunter and his dog ran after the bear. He called to the other hunters, "Hurry!" And then he looked down and saw Grandmother Earth far below. "Let's go back," he said, "before it's too late." But the bear had led them high into the sky, and they couldn't return.

The hunters finally caught the bear and killed it. They gathered branches from maple trees and sumac and butchered the bear on them. The blood of the bear is what causes those leaves to turn red in the autumn.

The four bright stars in the shape of a square are the bear. The three bright stars and one faint star are the hunters and their dog chasing after the bear. All year round they chase the bear around the sky.

See also Bear; Stars and Constellations

References and further reading:
Clark, Ella E. *Indian Legends from the Northern Rockies.* The Civilization of the American Indian Series, vol. 82. Norman: University of Oklahoma Press, 1966.
Jenness, Diamond. "Myths of the Carrier Indians of British Columbia." *Journal of American Folklore* 47, no. 184/185 (April–September 1934): 248–249.
Marriot, Alice, and Carol K. Rachlin. *American Indian Mythology.* New York: New American Library, 1986. First published 1968 by Crowell.

HOT WIND AND COLD WIND

Wasco, Plateau

Stories about the forces of nature abound in Native American mythology. Some explain their origins while others describe how things were different back in the distant, mythological time.

The Cold Wind brothers and their little sister made a sport of challenging anyone who came near to a wrestling match. While the brothers were wrestling, their sister would throw a bucket of icy water on their opponents, which caused great distress for the opponents and resulted in the Cold Wind brothers winning every time. Coyote thought he was actually the winner in these events, since he was able to cut off the heads of every unsuccessful challenger.

Not far away lived Eagle, his wife, and his son and daughter-in-law. With them also lived the five Chinook Wind brothers. Eagle's son heard the taunting of the Cold Wind brothers but was never tempted to wrestle them. But one day he finally gave in. The Cold Wind sister poured icy water over him, and he fell. Coyote was there to immediately cut off his head. So the Cold Wind brothers bragged loudly about their prowess.

Then the Chinook Wind brothers decided to avenge the death of their friend. One by one they wrestled with the Cold Wind brothers. But each time, the sister was there to pour icy water over them. Each of them fell, and Coyote cut off their heads. There was no one who could defeat the Cold Wind brothers.

Eagle's daughter-in-law was expecting a child, so she went back to her parents' home. Before she left, she left a sign for her in-laws: if a red feather fell from the top of her bed, they would know that the child was a girl. But if a white feather fell, it was a boy, and he would come back and avenge his father's death.

At last, the white feather fell and her in-laws knew they had a grandson. They were happy to know that he would come soon to fight the Cold Wind. While they waited for that day, the Cold Wind sister began tormenting them by coming to their house every day and pouring cold water on them.

Eagle's daughter-in-law instructed her son well. She told him about the Cold Wind brothers and how he must prepare himself to defeat them. When he arrived at his grandparents', he had a large salmon with him. He asked his grandmother to roast it over the fire and carefully save all of the fat that dripped out. He put the fat into five baskets. The young man and his grandparents hid the baskets with the fat, and then they traveled by canoe to where the Cold Wind brothers were waiting to wrestle.

The young man instructed his grandmother to let the Cold Wind sister pour out her water first, and then the grandmother was to pour the oil over top. The young man began wrestling with the first Cold Wind brother. The sister then poured her bucket of water on him. He called for his grandmother to quickly pour the oil on them. When she did, the Cold Wind brother fell and Coyote pounced on him and cut off his head.

And so, the young man wrestled the second brother. Again the Cold Wind sister poured her bucket of icy water on him and then the grandmother threw the second container of oil. The second Cold Wind brother fell and Coyote cut off his head. This happened with the third and fourth Cold Wind brother. When the fifth brother fell, he pleaded for his life, but the young man answered that the Cold Wind brothers had not shown mercy, so he would not receive any.

The Cold Wind sister ran away. But she knew she would not get far because the Chinook Wind avenger would come for her, too.

References and further reading:

Boas, Franz, ed. *Folk-Tales of Salishan and Sahaptin Tribes.* 1917. New York: Kraus Reprint, 1969.

Trafzer, Clifford E., ed. *Grandmother, Grandfather, and Old Wolf: Tamánwit Ku Súkat and Traditional Native American Narratives from the Columbian Plateau.* East Lansing: Michigan State University Press, 1998.

HOW BLUEBIRD GOT ITS COLOR

Pima, Southwest

This story explains why Bluebird and Coyote possess their characteristic colors. They appear together in other stories from the Southwest as well, in which Bluebird loans feathers to Coyote so he can fly.

A long time ago, the beautiful Bluebird was once a very dull and ugly color. Every morning for four mornings, he bathed four times in a lake that no river flowed in or out. Each morning he sang this magic song:

> *"There's blue water. It lies there.*
> *I went in. I am all blue."*

On the fourth morning, Bluebird shed his feathers and came out of the lake dressed only in his skin. The next morning, when he came out of the lake, he was covered with rich blue feathers.

Coyote had been watching Bluebird bathe all this time. He wanted to eat him, but he was afraid to jump into the water. On that last morning, when Coyote saw that Bluebird had acquired his lovely new feathers, he asked him how he lost his ugly color. "You are more beautiful than anything that flies in the air," Coyote said. "I want to be blue, too." At that time, Coyote was bright green.

Bluebird told Coyote that he had gone into the water four times on four mornings. He taught Coyote the magic song. Coyote went into the water four times, and the fifth time he came out as blue as the little bird.

Coyote became extremely vain because of his new color. He was so vain that as he strolled around he looked from side-to-side, attempting to see if anyone was noticing just how fine was his shade of blue. He looked to see if his shadow was blue as well. Coyote was so busy looking to see if anyone was paying him attention that he neglected to keep an eye on the trail. Suddenly he ran into a large stump and fell into the dirt. Coyote was covered with dust.

This is why Coyote is no longer blue and is the color of dust today.

See also Coyote

References and further reading:

Judson, Katharine Berry. *Myths and Legends of California and the Old Southwest.* Lincoln: University of Nebraska Press, 1994. First published 1912 by A. C. McClurg.

Parsons, Elsie Clews. "Pueblo-Indian Folk-Tales, Probably of Spanish Provenience." *Journal of American Folklore* 31, no. 120 (April–June 1918): 216–255.

KANATI AND SELU

Cherokee, Southeast

This story of The Lucky Hunter and his wife, Corn, two great spirits of the Upper World, tells of the origin of game and corn. Once held very sacred by the Cherokee, it is one of the best-known of their myths and one of the most famous of the Southeastern narratives. It contains incidents that have numerous parallels in Native American myths of various culture areas. Reflected in the text is the belief of the Indians of the Southeast that hunting was a man's occupation and agriculture the woman's domain. The frequent recurrence of the number seven is an indication of its importance in Cherokee ritual.

Kanati and Selu lived together with their only child, a son. One day, when playing by the riverbank, the boy found a wild boy who claimed he was his elder brother and told him his mother had been cruel to him and threw him into the river. Kanati and Selu then realized the wild boy had sprung from the blood of game Kanati had killed and Selu had cleaned at the river's edge. Eventually, Kanati and Selu brought the boy home and tamed him, though his disposition continued to be wild and cunning. His parents soon discovered he had magical powers, and they named him Inage-utasunhi, "He-Who-Grew-Up-Wild."

Inage-utasunhi led his brother into every mischief. One day they followed their father and discovered that he knew of a hole where deer are shut up under a rock, and that he let them out and shot them with his arrows whenever he needed meat. The boys returned later, raised the rock, and unintentionally let out all the deer, then raccoons, rabbits, all the other four-footed animals, turkeys, and other game birds. An angry Kanati discovered their deed and reminded them they now must hunt all over the woods for deer and may not find one. Then he sent them home to their mother while he stayed behind to attempt to find something to eat.

The boys returned home and their mother offered to feed them. Peeking between the logs of their storehouse, they saw Selu lean over a basket, rub her stomach, and make corn appear in half of it. Then she rubbed her armpits and the basket filled to the top with beans. The boys decided their mother was a witch, the food would poison them, and they must kill her.

When they re-entered the house, the boys admitted their intentions, but Selu knew the boys' thoughts before they spoke. She told them that after she was dead, they should clear a large piece of ground in front of the house and drag her body seven times around the circle, then drag her seven times over the ground inside the circle. When they were finished, they should stay up all night and watch, and in the morning there would be plenty of corn. After they killed her, the boys only cleared seven small spots, instead of a full area, which is why corn grows in only a few places and not everywhere in the world. They dragged Selu's body around the circle, and corn sprang up wherever her blood fell on the ground. But instead of dragging her body across the ground seven times, they only dragged it twice, which explains why Indians raise just two crops in one season. The boys stayed up all night to watch their corn grow, and in the morning it was mature and ripe.

When Kanati returned home, and did not find Selu, he asked the brothers where their mother had gone. "We killed her because she was a witch," they said, "and there is her head on top of the roof of the house." Kanati became very angry, and said, "I will not stay with you any longer; I am going to the Wolf people." Not long after he left, Inage-utasunhi changed himself into a tuft of down and landed on Kanati's shoulder. When he came upon the Wolf people's settlement, they were holding a council in the townhouse. When the Wolf chief asked him to present his business, Kanati said, "I have two bad boys at home, and I want you to go in seven days from now and play ball against them." The Wolves knew the true meaning behind his words, that he wanted them to kill the boys, and they promised to do so. The bird's down, which he never noticed, blew off Kanati's shoulder and was carried through a hole in the roof of the townhouse. When it landed on the ground outside, Inage-utasunhi assumed his true form and went home to tell his brother all he had heard. Kanati left the Wolf people, but did not return home.

The boys prepared for the arrival of the Wolves. They ran a wide circle around the house until a trail was made, except on the side from which the Wolves would come. Here a small open space was left. The brothers made four large bundles of arrows and placed them each at different points on the outside of the circle, after which they hid in the woods and waited. After a day or two, a party of Wolves arrived and surrounded the house. They did not see the trail, as they came in through the opening, but the moment they entered the circle, the trail changed to a high brush fence and shut them in. The boys began shooting them down with their arrows. As the Wolves were trapped by the fence and could not jump over it, they were all killed, except for a few that escaped through the opening to a nearby swamp. The boys ran around the swamp, and a circle of fire broke out in their tracks, setting fire to the grass and bushes and burning up nearly all the other Wolves. Only two or three escaped, and from these have sprung all the other wolves that exist in the world.

Not long afterward, some strangers came to visit who had heard that the brothers had a wonderful grain from which they made bread. Only Selu and her family were already familiar with corn. The boys gave them seven grains of corn and told them to plant them the next evening on their way home. They were to sit up all night to watch the corn, which would have seven ripe ears by morning. These they were instructed to plant the next evening and watch in the same way, and so on every night until they reached home, a journey of seven days. By that time, they would have enough corn for all their people. The people did as they were told the first night, and the second, but the way home was long, the sun was hot, and they grew tired. On the last night before reaching their destination they fell asleep and did not watch the corn as before, so by morning they found what they had planted had not even sprouted. They brought home what they had and planted it, and were able to raise a crop. Even since, however, corn must be watched and carefully tended for half a year, when previously it would grow and ripen in just a night.

Kanati had still not returned, so the brothers decided to leave home to go find him. Inage-utasunhi rolled a gaming wheel in various directions, including toward the Sunland, from which it did not return. So, they went toward the east and finally came upon Kanati walking along with a little dog by his side. They knew the dog was the wheel they had sent to find him. "You bad boys," said their father. "Have you come here? Well, as you have found me, we may as well travel together."

They soon approached a swamp. Kanati warned the boys to keep away from it, as there was something dangerous there. He went on ahead, but as soon as he was out of sight, Inage-utasunhi said to his brother, "Come and let us see what is in the swamp." They went in together, where they found a large, sleeping panther. The boys shot the panther several times with arrows, but it merely looked at them. It was not hurt and paid no more attention to them. The boys left the swamp and soon found Kanati, who was waiting for them. Kanati was surprised when they told him the panther did not hurt them, but he said nothing.

After walking farther, Kanati warned the boys of their approach to a tribe known as the Anadaduntaski (Roasters, or cannibals). Then he went on ahead. The boys approached a tree that had been struck by lightning, and Inage-utasunhi told his brother to gather some of the splinters. As they came to the settlement, the cannibals came running out, crying, "Good, here are two nice fat strangers. Now we'll have a grand feast!" They caught the brothers and brought them inside their townhouse, where they made up a great fire, brought water to boil in a large pot, and put Inage-utasunhi down into it. His brother, who was not frightened and made no attempt to escape, simply knelt down and put the splinters into the fire, as if to make it burn faster and stronger. When the cannibals thought their meat was ready, they took the pot from the fire. At that instant, a blinding light filled the building, and lightning began to dart from one side to the other, striking the cannibals until not one was left alive. The lightning then traveled up through the smoke hole, and suddenly the boys found themselves standing outside as though nothing had happened. They went on again and soon overtook Kanati, who appeared much surprised to see them. "What did the cannibals do to you?" Kanati asked.

"We met them and they brought us to their townhouse, but they never hurt us." the boys answered. Kanati said no more, and they traveled on.

The brothers soon lost sight of Kanati, but they kept on until they came to the end of the world, where the sun comes out. The sky was just coming down as they arrived, so they waited until it went up again and then went through, climbing to the other side. There they found Kanati and Selu sitting together. They received the boys kindly and told them they might stay there for a while, but they must then go live in the Darkening Land, where the sun goes down. After staying with their parents for seven days, the brothers left for the west, where they still live.

The adventures of the sons of Kanati and Selu are found in various Cherokee stories. Known as Anisgaya Tsunsdi (Little Men) or Thunder Boys, it is believed that low, rolling thunder is heard in the west whenever they speak to each other. A sequel tells of how the boys are summoned by the nearly starving people to teach them songs and ceremonies with which to call the deer so they can be hunted.

See also Ani Hyuntikwalaski; Blood Clot; Corn; Culture Hero(es)

References and further reading:

Hudson, Charles. *The Southeastern Indians*. Knoxville: University of Tennessee Press, 1992. First published 1976.

Lankford, George E. *Native American Legends: Southeastern Legends: Tales from the Natchez, Caddo, Biloxi, Chickasaw, and Other Nations*. Little Rock: August House, 1987.

Mooney, James. *James Mooney's History, Myths, and Sacred Formulas of the Cherokees: Containing the Full Texts of "Myths of the Cherokee" (1900) and "The Sacred Formulas of the Cherokees" (1891) as published by the Bureau of American Ethnology; With a New Biographical Introduction, "James Mooney and the Eastern Cherokees."* Asheville, N.C.: Historical Images, 1992.

Ugvwiyuhi. *Journey to Sunrise: Myths and Legends of the Cherokee*. Claremore, Okla.: Egi Press, 1977.

KIVIOQ

Inuit, Arctic

Those in Greenland as well as the Central Eskimo of Canada know numerous tales of the hero Kivioq. Details within the tales vary from place to place but often involve an unfaithful wife, an abandoned son, and many harrowing adventures.

Kivioq mourned for his dead wife and decided to travel to a distant place, leaving his son behind. But one day the boy ran into the house and said that his mother was outside with another man. Kivioq did not believe the son at first but finally went to see for himself. Sure enough, there was his wife embracing another man. Kivioq was furious. He killed them both and buried them together in another grave.

That night when the boy was asleep, Kivioq left in his kayak. As he was hurrying away, he thought he heard his son calling for him, but he kept paddling and narrowly escaped being sucked into a whirlpool. Then his kayak was attacked by sea-lice. Only by covering his paddles with a pair of gloves was Kivioq able to get away. He soon came upon two huge icebergs with a narrow passage between them. As the icebergs moved in the water, the passage opened and closed. Kivioq paddled quickly and just as he got through the·passage it closed again.

Kivioq was relieved to reach the shore, but his troubles were just beginning. He met two women and was invited into their house. The old woman offered him some berries mixed with fat. When Kivioq commented that the dish was very tasty, the old woman replied that "the fat is from a very young fellow." Then Kivioq noticed the row of human heads lined up under the sleeping ledge. Later, Kivioq pretended to be asleep and heard the two women plotting to kill him. The old woman wanted his head, but the younger woman wanted his genitals. At this Kivioq jumped up, ran out the door, and jumped into his kayak.

After some time Kivioq came to another house. A baby with a huge, bloated stomach was the only person in it. When the baby saw Kivioq, he exclaimed, "Grandmother has sent more food!" Immediately, Kivioq ran back to his kayak thinking that the sea was less dangerous than the land.

He paddled on and in time the ghosts of people who had drowned climbed onto his kayak in the hopes of drowning him, too. However, Kivioq kept paddling. Eventually, the ghosts of his wife and her lover attempted to climb onto the kayak, but the other ghosts told them that there wasn't enough room. The wife and her lover managed to get onboard anyway. Kivioq continued paddling and over the years traveled all along the coast and back. His kayak kept getting heavier as more ghosts piled on, and yet he kept going.

Finally, he came upon some other kayaks that were pulling a large whale. Standing on top of the whale was a young man. When Kivioq got close enough, he could see that it was his now grown son. He called out, "My son, I'm your father!" But the young man did not believe him and replied, "That could not be. My father died a long time ago when he was pulled down into a whirlpool. You're only an old man with a kayak full of ghosts."

At that, Kivioq's heart sank, and he wept.

See also Cannibalism; Ghosts

References and further reading:

Millman, Lawrence. *A Kayak Full of Ghosts: Eskimo Folk Tales.* 1987. Northampton, Mass.: Interlink Press, 2004.

Norman, Howard, ed. *Northern Tales: Stories from the Native Peoples of the Arctic and Subarctic Regions.* Selected, edited, and retold by Howard Norman. Pantheon Fairy Tale & Folklore Library. New York: Pantheon Books, 1998. Originally published as *Northern Tales: Traditional Stories of Eskimo and Indian Peoples* (1990).

Rasmussen, Knud. *Observations on the Intellectual Culture of the Caribou Eskimos.* 1930. Report of the Fifth Thule Expedition, vol. 7, no. 3. New York: AMS Press, 1976.

Rink, Hinrich. *Tales and Traditions of the Eskimo, with a Sketch of Their Habits, Religion, Language, and Other Peculiarities.* 1875. New York: AMS Press, 1975.

KOKOPELLI

Southwest

Images of the mythic Kokopelli, the mysterious, humpbacked, priapic flute player, are found widely in rock art within a large geographic region of the Four Corners states (Utah, Colorado, Arizona, and New Mexico). Sacred to Native Americans of

Dish decorated with Kokopelli. (Werner Forman/Art Resource, NY)

the Southwest since prehistoric times, his image was also a design element on ancient pottery. He is ever-present in contemporary Native American arts and crafts, including jewelry, ceramics, sculpture, textiles, and paintings. Kokopelli has generated widespread fascination and popular appeal, as demonstrated by his appearance in mainstream American culture. Kokopelli-inspired institutions of all kinds exist, including hotels, restaurants, stores, and galleries, to name but a few examples. Kokopelli appears as a decoration on a variety of contemporary items such as knick-knacks, souvenirs, business cards, and T-shirts, and he has been showcased in popular mainstream literature.

The origin, significance, and meaning of Kokopelli remain a mystery. He is a variable and inconsistent character, and has been interpreted as a rain priest, fertility symbol, deity, roving minstrel or trader, shaman or medicine man, hunter, warrior, magician—and even as an insect. He is not universally regarded as a trickster, though he does share traits with many trickster characters of other Native American cultures.

Kokopelli is a figure in Hopi stories as well as rituals and ceremonies of the Pueblo, Hopis, and Zunis. As a Hopi kachina, he is known as a bearer of gifts and babies, a seducer of maidens, and a tutelary of hunting. Kokopell' Mana is Kokopelli's female counterpart, portrayed by a man, as all kachinas are. Passionate toward men, "she" beckons to them in a sexual manner and entices them to race with her. If she catches one, she flings him to the ground and imitates copulation, much to the delight of onlookers.

The following myth explains the nature of the Kokopelli kachina:

When the village of Oraibi was first inhabited, the kachina Kokopelli was living nearby with his grandmother. Within Oraibi there lived a beautiful girl who was so vain she rejected the advances of all the young men. Kokopelli informed his grandmother that he had his own intentions for this girl. His grandmother laughed at him because he was humpbacked and far less handsome than many of the Oraibi boys, but Kokopelli insisted he would try his luck.

Kokopelli noticed that every noon, following lunch, the girl would regularly go to a particular spot at the edge of the mesa to perform her natural functions. He intended to take advantage of her habit in order to win her over. He dug a trench leading from his house to the spot where the girl was accustomed to visit. Then he cut and hollowed out a number of reeds, from which he created a continuous pipe, and laid it in the ditch. Having done this, Kokopelli filled in the trench and smoothed it over so the girl would find nothing disturbed.

The next day the girl came to her spot as usual and bent down to relieve herself. After she finished, she felt something stirring beneath her, and, enjoying the sensation, made no attempt to investigate. It was Kokopelli's penis that she felt, for he had so cleverly arranged his hollow reed that on inserting his organ into it he was enabled, thanks to its unusual length, to direct it into the girl's vagina. From then on, Kokopelli never failed to take advantage of his device; nor did the girl cease her regular visits to this spot. Finally, she found herself pregnant, but neither she nor any of the village people had the slightest idea of her lover's identity. No one in the village ever succeeded in identifying the girl's sweetheart, and when she gave birth to a baby boy his paternity remained a great mystery.

That spring, one of the men in the village announced a special foot race intended to reveal the father of the girl's baby. He made a speech to the young men and boys, inviting them to gather a bouquet of pretty flowers. The race would take place in front of the girl as she nursed her son. Each man would extend his bouquet upon finishing the race, and the baby would grab the one held by his father.

Many of the young men still desired the girl very much, so each was eager to win the race and be the first to offer his flowers in the hope that the baby would grasp them. When Kokopelli heard of the race, he very much feared the loss of his mistress. He informed his grandmother that he would compete with the others. Again she discouraged him and expressed her fear that he would be unlucky because the baby would not like a man as unattractive as he. Kokopelli was persistent in his quest, however, and went out with the others to pick a bouquet the day before the race. Kokopelli was no match for the other runners, and finished far behind them. But none of the other racers, including the winner, made an impression on the baby. No sooner had the winded Kokopelli offered his bouquet than his son grasped it eagerly, and everyone was duly astonished. The sponsor of the race told the girl to take Kokopelli as her husband.

The girl lived happily with Kokopelli, who was a good provider and brought lots of rain to the village in his role as kachina. The Kwitavi group did not appreciate his kindness, however, because they were jealous of Kokopelli's pretty wife. Eventually, news of their plot to kill him and take her away reached him. They planned to invite him to their kiva to spin yarn, where they would beat Kokopelli to death with hidden weapons. He consulted his grandmother, who advised him to seek help from the Spider Woman.

Spider Woman promised to aid Kokopelli by giving him good medicine. She warned him that the Kwitavi would kill him when the time arrived to rest and eat, upon extinguishing the fire. Kokopelli was told to chew up the medicine and spurt it everywhere as soon as it became dark. The men would then all become humpbacked just like himself, and be fooled into beating each other as they tried to find him by his hump. Spider Woman told Kokopelli to jump up and hang on to the rafters so he would be safe.

The next day, the troubling events unfolded just as the Spider Woman predicted. Yarn was spun from dark until midnight and then the men gathered for a feast. They had hardly begun their meal when the kiva chief extinguished the fire and plunged the kiva into total darkness. Kokopelli immediately chewed and spurted his medicine and made his way safely to the rafters while the evil Kwitavi men, fooled by each other's humps, began to attack each other. Finally, they called for light, realizing there seemed to be many humpbacks present and not just one. They discovered some of their own men of the kiva had been killed or injured, but that Kokopelli was unharmed.

The men from Kwitavi were witches and "two-hearted," so they soon lost their humpbacks and were healed of their wounds or restored to life. However, they did not escape their just punishment, for within a few days they all died.

Alarmed by his narrow escape from death, Kokopelli moved his family to his grandmother's home just outside Oraibi. Here he lived peacefully and prospered. After a few years he had more children, enough for him to stage a dance for his former neighbors.

References and further reading:

Hill, Stephen W. *Kokopelli Ceremonies*. Santa Fe: Kiva, 1995.

Malotki, Ekkehart. *Kokopelli: The Making of an Icon*. Lincoln: University of Nebraska Press, 2000.

Slifer, Dennis, and James Duffield. *Kokopelli: Fluteplayer Images in Rock Art*. Santa Fe, N. Mex.: Ancient City Press, 1994.

Titiev, Mischa. "The Story of Kokopelli." *American Anthropologist*, n.s., 41, no. 1 (January–March 1939): 91–98.

Wright, Barton. *Kachinas: A Hopi Artist's Documentary*. Revised ed. Flagstaff, Ariz.: Northland Publishing with the Heard Museum, [1998?]. First published 1973 by Northland Press.

KUMOKUMS
Modoc, Plateau

Kumokums (alternately spelled Kumukumts or Gmukamps) was a trickster-transformer who used mud from the bottom of Tule Lake to create the surrounding land. With his fingernails, he scratched grooves in the mountains so the water could flow to the lakes. Then he went about putting people on the earth and setting it all in order. The following Modoc tale relates the story of Kumokums and his daughter.

At that time all was well in the world and there was plenty of food for everyone in summer and in winter. Many babies were being born and every place was getting crowded. So Porcupine discussed the problem with Kumokums. He suggested that when old people died they should no longer stay around the village but should travel to a new home in the Land of the Dead. Kumokums considered this plan and decided it was a good one. So he proclaimed that once people died, they should go to the Land of the Dead.

Five days later, when Kumokums returned from fishing, he heard a dreadful wailing sound coming from his house. He ran there and asked his wives what had happened. They told him that his daughter, whom he loved dearly, had died. Kumokums was overcome with grief and quickly sent for the medicine man. But even though the medicine man performed all of his ceremonies, the daughter did not return to life.

At last Porcupine went up to Kumokums and reminded him that once a person died, they must travel to the Land of the Dead and not return. The new way applied to everyone, even Kumokums's beloved daughter. But Kumokums decided to visit the chief of the Land of the Dead to try to persuade him to let his daughter return to the living. To do that Kumokums had to send his spirit over to the Land of the Dead.

The chief of that land asked why he was there. So Kumokums explained that he wished to take his daughter back home with him. The chief told him that she was his daughter now dead and called her out of the house. Then out walked a thin skeleton. The chief said to Kumokums, "Surely you don't want to take her back home now that she looks like this." But, Kumokums said, "Yes." He wanted his daughter back home.

So the chief of the Land of the Dead let her return, but he gave strict instructions to Kumokums: "On your way there, press her hand four times. That way she will once again be alive by the time you reach your own home." He also gave a warning, "Do not look back to the Land of the Dead no matter what."

Kumokums and his daughter started off. As he pressed on her bony hand, he could feel the flesh returning. When they reached the borders of the land of the living, he was overjoyed and turned to look at his daughter. But she was just a pile of bones. When Kumokums opened his eyes, he was once again in his own house.

From then on there has always been death in the world.

See also Culture Hero(es); Transformer; Trickster

References and further reading:

Leeming, David, and Jake Page. *The Mythology of Native North America.* Norman: University of Oklahoma Press, 1998.

Marriot, Alice, and Carol K. Rachlin. *American Indian Mythology.* New York: New American Library, 1986. First published 1968 by Crowell.

Sturtevant, William, ed. *Handbook of North American Indians.* Vol. 12, *Plateau.* Washington, DC: Smithsonian Institution, 1998.

LAND OTTERS

Haida, Heiltsuk (Bella Bella), Tlingit, Tsimshian, Northwest Coast

Land Otters were greatly feared by many people in the areas along and near the Pacific Northwest Coast. They were known for their cunning and treachery. Land Otter People were believed to cause canoes and small boats to capsize. They would then seize the souls of people who drowned and gradually turn them into Land Otters like themselves. Shamans were called upon to intervene and free the drowned spirits from the Land Otters' control.

There are several myths about humans who were captured by Land Otters after their canoes capsized and became like them. The following tale, however, relates the story of a man who refused to yield to the Land Otters.

A certain man declared that even if he capsized he would never be captured by the Land Otter People. But one day when he was in his canoe with his sister, the canoe tipped over and they were thrown into the water. The man swam to shore and soon had built a fire to dry and warm himself. It wasn't long before he heard a canoe pull up on the beach. He quickly looked away, since he did not intend to be tricked if the people in the canoe were really Land Otters. When they approached his campfire, the man jumped up and ran down to the canoe. He grabbed the paddles and then threw them into his fire. Suddenly the canoe and its crew were revealed to be just an old driftwood log and several minks.

On another occasion, when he was nearly asleep, he heard a woman's voice calling to him. She brought him food and urged him not to be afraid. But the man had heard about the deceitful tricks Land Otters use to lure their victims away. The woman continued to attempt to get him to eat from the bowls of food she brought, but he just yelled at her and accused her of being a Land Otter.

This went on for several days. The woman would bring food, but the man would refuse to have anything to do with her or her gifts. Finally, one night it seemed as if the woman's voice sounded like that of his drowned sister. She admitted to him that she was indeed the spirit of his sister. So the man thought, "I should not fear my sister." At that, he ate some of her food and regained his strength. But the man was still careful and watched for other Land Otters. Any time a canoe came to where he camped, he would burn the paddles as before. That way he exposed the Land Otters for what they were. After he had been stranded there one month, a canoe with real humans came and the man was rescued at last.

See also Tcaawunkl; Transformation; Human-Animal; Shaman

References and further reading:

Barbeau, Marius, and William Beynon, collectors. *Tsimshian Narratives*. Vol. 1, *Tricksters, Shamans, and Heroes*. Mercury series. Ottawa: Directorate, Canadian Museum of Civilization, 1987.

Beck, Mary Giraudo. *Shamans and Kushtakas: North Coast Tales of the Supernatural.* Anchorage: Alaska Northwest Books, 1991.

Boas, Franz. *Indian Myths & Legends from the North Pacific Coast of America: A Translation of Franz Boas' 1895 Edition of "Indianische Sagen von der Nord-Pacifischen Küste Amerikas."* Vancouver: Talonbooks, 2002.

LOON WOMAN

Modoc, Shasta, Wintu, California

The loon is a popular character in Native American mythology due to its unforgettable cry and distinctive appearance. The Loon Woman is the most widely known of the loon stories and explains how this rare water bird acquired its characteristic neck markings. It is also a story of incest between siblings, a theme commonly found in Native American myths.

There was once a couple who had many children, nine boys and one girl. As their first child was a handsome boy, named Talimleluheres, they hid him away from the attention of females.

The girl grew into a woman. One morning she went to a stream, where she found a long hair. She wondered whose it was. She decided to go west and wished to take along a guide. Her mother offered each of her brothers, but the woman rejected them one by one, noting the hair she found did not match that of any of them. Finally, her mother offered Talimleluheres as a guide, and the woman was happy, as she could see his hair matched the one she had found.

After making preparations, the woman and Talimleluheres left on their journey. When evening fell, she started a fire, made supper, and prepared a bed. The woman wanted to have intercourse with her brother, who fled back to their family.

When Talimleluheres reached their home, he urged their mother and father to go quickly. They set their earth lodge on fire, and the entire family went whirling upwards toward the sky in the smoke.

The woman sleeping in the west woke up. When she saw that Talimleluheres had gone, she became very angry. She came toward the east, to the burning earth lodge, where she saw no one. She chanced to look up and saw her family going up. "I want to go, my mother, my father, I want to go," she cried.

When they had almost reached the sky, one child looked down, and the entire family plunged down into the fire and burned up. As they burned, their hearts burst from their bodies. After the fire had gone out, the woman found and gathered up the hearts, strung them on a cord, and hung them around her neck. She did not find Talimleluheres's heart, which had exploded and gone to another place, where it fell down.

Far away lived two sisters. Every afternoon they gathered wood. One day, the older one heard singing and listened before they returned home. The next afternoon, the singing had grown louder. The older woman went nearer and nearer until she was upon the sound and saw damp ground. She saw something black on the ground, which said, "Woman, come. Don't be afraid." The woman thought to herself, "This must be the person who was lost long ago. It must be Talimleluheres." The one on the ground said, "Woman, don't be afraid of me. Come!" And the woman said, "Yes." Then she looked at the one on the ground. It was dusty, and many deer had been there. To the east, and to the west, were many deer tracks. The woman carried wood back to where her younger sister was standing. The girl said, "Where did you go? You were gone long." They brought the wood home. In the evening they slept, and the woman still said nothing. The next morning they arose, and when they were ready to go after wood, she put a little soup into a basket cup and carried it hidden under her clothes. As her younger sister gathered wood, the woman took the soup and fed it to the one who lay on the ground. He seemed a little better after he ate the soup. After she fed him, the woman gathered wood and brought it back to the house.

The next morning, the two women got up and ate. The older one left, carrying the soup. The younger girl thought, "What is the matter?" She followed her elder sister, wanting to see, and she saw. Her sister was sitting and feeding someone soup. The younger girl went to her sister and said, "Have you discovered this one?"

"Yes. The one who went away long ago, the person who was lost, the person not found, this is the one," she told her younger sister. They went home, ate, and went to bed.

In the middle of the night the two women woke up and saw that a man lay between them, a beautiful man. He who had been found by the two women had come back to life and come to the house. He stayed there a while, and the two women bore children, two boys. They grew and played and played, shooting at birds. They once saw a bird and shot at it with an untipped arrow and hit it on the lower leg. The bird shrieked, "Tuwetetek, tuwetetek, why did you shoot me, cousins?"

They went and came to the woman. They sat down and she talked to them. "Let me tell you something," she said. "You are getting older. Over there is a pool, there is a raft on the pool. Don't shoot with these. Prepare good untipped arrows of pitch wood. There, to the pool, comes every evening she who made us kinless. She'll come from the east around the hill. And after she comes out, this is what she does. She stands flapping her wings. Watch carefully and shoot well, look well and shoot, don't miss her."

When she had finished talking, the boys returned to their home, playing, not saying anything. They stayed home the next day. The day after they got up, ate, and played. They went to the pool. The sun set and it grew dark. The boys got on the raft and rowed about, shooting at the ducks that were on the pool. Suddenly, they heard her coming with roaring wings. She alighted on the pool "Wuuuuk," she said. Then she dived. She came close to the raft and got out beside it, flapping her wings. The boys kept her in their sight the whole time, and shot and hit her exactly at the hollow of her underarm with the untipped arrows of pitch wood. Then she dived into the pool and suddenly rose to the surface, dead. The boys dragged her to the edge of the raft and threw her on top. Then they left and returned to the house, where they told their father they had killed the Wukwuk.

The next morning, the boys led their father to show him the one they had killed. "Yes," he said, "this is she who made us kinless." He took hold of her and saw that she was wearing a necklace of human hearts. The man untied his father's heart, his mother's heart, and the hearts of his younger brothers. Then he cut her flesh into strips and left it. He returned to the house, bringing the hearts of his family with him. He put them in water, with stones over them, and went to bed in the evening. At dawn the next day, his mother, father, and younger brothers came back to life.

References and further reading:

Angulo, Jaime de. *Coyote Man & Old Doctor Loon.* San Francisco: Turtle Island Foundation, 1973.

Demetracopoulou, D. "The Loon Woman Myth." *Journal of American Folklore* 46, no. 180 (April–June 1933): 101–128.

MANABOZHO

Northeast Woodlands

Also known as Nenabush, Nanabozho, Wenebojo, Manabush, Manapus, and other variations among the people of the north central Woodlands region, the meaning of the name is frequently given as "Great (or Giant) Rabbit."

Manabozho tales are numerous and depict him as a sly trickster, a foolish buffoon, or a culture-hero. According to Helbig and Radin, Manabozho myths developed over time, with the earliest being predominately of the trickster-buffoon genre while the culture-hero aspect was a more recent (although still ancient) addition.

One tale in which Manabozho exhibits Trickster characteristics also explains why the buzzard's head lacks feathers.

Buzzard saw Manabozho walking along below him. He swooped lower and heard Manabozho ask for a ride on his back. Buzzard consented and landed nearby. Manabozho saw that Buzzard's back looked slippery, so he said, "You'll need to be careful, or I might fall off while you are flying." Buzzard appeared to agree, but he was really thinking up a trick to play on him.

Manabozho climbed on Buzzard's back and soon they were flying high over the trees. Manabozho was frightened but held on tightly as Buzzard dipped and circled in the sky. Eventually, Manabozho managed to look down at the ground, but just as he did, Buzzard swerved sharply and Manabozho lost his grip. He plummeted to the ground, landed in a crumpled heap, and hit his head so hard he was knocked unconscious. Buzzard continued circling overhead to keep an eye on Manabozho.

When Manabozho woke up he saw someone staring at him. He reached out, but since he was still bleary-eyed from his ordeal, didn't realize it was his own buttocks until he grabbed them. Buzzard laughed heartily, but Manabozho jumped up and threatened to get even. "I've got more power than you!"

Buzzard disagreed. "You can't fool me. I can watch everything you do."

So Manabozho walked away. When Buzzard flew off, Manabozho went to a clearing that was visible from all directions. He knew that Buzzard only ate dead fish and animals, so he changed himself into a dead deer. It wasn't long before bugs and worms and all sorts of creatures that live off of carcasses were drawn to him. Buzzard saw what was going on and decided to take a look. He was leery at first, thinking it was one of Manabozho's tricks. But he was finally convinced that it really was a dead deer lying there. Buzzard landed next to the carcass and began pecking at its thigh. He dug deep into the flesh until his head and neck were buried in it.

Manabozho suddenly squeezed his flesh around Buzzard's head and jumped up. "Ha! See if you can get out of this one!" he yelled. Buzzard pulled and pulled and after some time was able to free his head. But in doing so, all of the feathers were stripped off of his head and neck. Manabozho declared, "From now on you'll go around with a bare head and you'll stink from the food you eat."

Radin and Reagan collected a large number of myths that they called "The Manabozho Cycle." Among these tales is one in which Manabozho plays a trick on his neighbor but is the one who suffers in the end. Manabozho and his neighbor entered into a partnership. They would fish and dry their catch together and then share it equally. It was a very productive business, and all of the members of both families worked very hard. When the fishing season was over and everyone was preparing for the long winter, Manabozho convinced his neighbor that they should all eat his neighbor's share of the fish first. The unsuspecting neighbor agreed. By mid-winter the neighbor's supply of fish was gone, but Manabozho's was still untouched. This would not have been a problem if Manabozho had shared his fish just as his neighbor had done. But the crafty Manabozho refused to give any fish to his neighbor.

In order to keep his family from starving, the neighbor went into the woods each day to hunt what he could. But it was not enough to keep them from being hungry, and before winter was over their situation was getting desperate. One day the neighbor was in the woods and heard someone talking to him. When he turned around there was a man who instructed him to go out onto the lake, chip a hole in the ice, and fill up his sack with the ice chips. Then he was supposed to go straight home. "You'll hear voices calling your name. Do not say a word or turn around. When you get to the cup-shaped depression near your home, toss the sack of ice into it and go on home."

Manabozho's neighbor did exactly as he was told. When he heard the voices calling after him, he just kept going. He returned home empty handed, and this did not set well with his family. They made him leave early in the morning to go hunt for their breakfast. When he walked by the spot where he had tossed the sack, he was amazed to see a pool of water full of fish. He took some home to cook and everyone ate their fill of fish. Then the family brought the remaining fish home to dry.

One day Manabozho walked by and saw smoke coming from the home. He had expected them all to be dead by then. Eventually his curiosity got the best of him. Manabozho peeked in and saw fish roasting on the fire. "Where did you get that fish?" he asked his neighbor. "Down at the lake," was the reply.

Eventually Manabozho's supply of fish ran out, but spring had not yet arrived. So Manabozho had to resort to hunting in the woods and gathering thorn apples. One day he heard someone behind him call his name. The man said, "You are hungry. Go to the lake and chip a hole in it. Gather the chips in your bag and then go home immediately. You will hear voices calling to you, but do not speak to them, and do not turn around."

He decided to do as instructed. However, when the voices started calling after him, Manabozho forgot to do as he was told. Instead, he grabbed his axe and spun around to face the enemy. But, no one was on the path, so Manabozho started out for home again. Soon, however, the voices started yelling at him.

Manabozho again drew his axe and faced his attackers. But as before, there was no one behind him. He continued without any further problems and tossed his bag into the dry pool near his home. Before he reached the door, he turned around and saw the pool was full of fish. That night his family went to sleep happily dreaming of the feast they would have in the morning. However, when Manabozho returned to the pool, he found only his ice filled sack because he had not obeyed the instructions.

Before long Manabozho returned to his neighbor and asked, "How do you get all of that fish?" So the neighbor shared what he claimed was his secret: "I have a fishing hole on the lake. Early each morning I go out there and dive in with my spear. I can catch more fish than we need in just a short time." Manabozho thought that sounded easy. So he went to the lake, cut a hole in the ice, and then went home to wait until morning. His neighbor was secretly watching and later that night took a scrawny sturgeon from his pool and pushed it down into Manabozho's fishing hole. In the morning, Manabozho returned to the lake. He stripped off his clothes and dove into the hole with his spear. Soon he saw the sturgeon that had been placed there. After spearing the fish and tossing it onto the ice, Manabozho dove back in. He searched in vain for more fish. The water was near freezing, so he had to climb out onto the ice, but time and again, he dove back into the water searching for more fish.

At last Manabozho gave up and climbed out of the fishing hole empty-handed. His neighbor was waiting for him, and said snidely, "Don't you want to find more fish?"

Bloomfield recorded several Eastern Ojibwa tales about Nenabush (known by other tribes as Manabozho or other variations). Nenabush was hungry so he took some rope and went down to the river. There he saw a large number of ducks floating near the river bank. Quietly Nenabush slipped into the water and dove underneath them. When he had tied their legs together, he surfaced right in the middle of them. The startled ducks flew into the air, dragging Nenabush, who was still hanging onto the rope, behind them. Eventually the rope broke. Nenabush fell to the ground and landed in a hollow tree.

He was stuck and pondered how he could get free. Finally he heard some women talking as they walked along the path. When he could tell that they were nearby, Nenabush called out, "White porcupi-i-ine! White porcupi-i-ine!" The women decided to catch the animal and began chopping the tree with an axe. However, they were afraid the porcupine might get away, so one of the women took off her skirt to throw over him if he should try to escape. As they continued to chop and the hole became larger, the other women took their skirts off, too. Then suddenly, Nenabush darted out through the hole and ran off with all of the women's skirts.

Barnouw also collected a series of myths from the Wisconsin Ojibwa. In these the Manabozho figure is called Wenebojo. These tales tell of the origin of Wenebojo. Long ago there was an old woman and her daughter living alone. The daughter would go out berry picking by herself. One day a strong gust of wind came and blew her dress up. After awhile the wind subsided and the girl continued to pick berries. Later the old woman grew suspicious about her daughter and asked her if she ever saw anyone when she was out in the woods. But the daughter denied ever seeing anyone. In time the daughter realized that something was wrong and asked her mother about it. Again the old woman questioned the girl whether or not she had ever seen anyone in the woods. Finally the girl remembered the incident with the wind. And then her mother knew that Sun had impregnated the girl.

The girl eventually gave birth to triplets. The first was like a normal baby boy. She held him in her arms and then heard a voice tell her to put him on the ground. The young mother didn't do it. Finally the voice scolded her and said, "If you had put the baby on the ground he would have walked right away like baby animals do, but now human babies won't walk for a year."

The second baby was born, but it didn't exactly look like a human child. Finally the third baby was born, but it was a stone. The boys, who were spirits, grew up quickly. Wenebojo, the oldest, went around killing all the little animals he could find. His mother told him not to, but he didn't listen to her.

The stone boy stayed at camp, but Wenebojo and the second boy went traveling around the country. One day on their way back to camp, Wenebojo suggested that the two of them would be able to leave and explore more of the world if they killed their stone brother. The second brother didn't say a word. Wenebojo kept asking him, but his brother replied, "You're the one thinking about it."

Wenebojo didn't realize it, but the youngest brother knew what he had been talking about doing. So when the two brothers returned to camp, the youngest brother said, "Go ahead and do what you intend to do." So Wenebojo took a long handled axe and struck the stone brother. The axe didn't have any effect. So the brother said, "You won't succeed unless I tell you what to do."

Wenebojo then said, "Well, what do I need to do?" He was then instructed to build a fire and put the stone brother into it. The brother kept telling Wenebojo to add more wood to the fire. Then finally he said, "It is time now." So Wenebojo poured water over his brother and the stone cracked into pieces. That was the first time anyone had died on earth and there were only the two brothers left.

Then Wenebojo and his remaining brother started traveling all over the earth, but eventually his brother became tired and unable to keep up. So Wenebojo made a hole in the ground and put his brother in it. He covered him up and set a stone over the top so he could find him again. He promised his brother that he would be back in four days. But Wenebojo had such a good time traveling around that he forgot about his brother. When he finally remembered and went back, his brother was gone.

Wenebojo cried and cried. Finally his brother heard him and spoke to him, telling Wenebojo not to cry. Wenebojo replied, "Why did you come back? Just go back to where you were."

His brother said, "Now you will make it difficult for people. I will make a road for people to travel on when they die."

Among the Menominee there is a tale that explains why we have to work so hard to make maple sugar. Nokomis said to her grandson, Manabush, "Go fetch some birch bark for me. I'm going to make maple sugar." This was new to him, but Manabush went to the woods and stripped off some birch bark. His grandmother made cups from the bark and then at each maple tree she cut a hole into the bark and inserted a stick into each hole. Then she attached the cups below the sticks. In this way, the sap ran into the cups.

Manabush went to check this out and saw the cups were full of thick maple syrup. He stuck a finger into the syrup and then tasted it. The syrup was wonderfully sweet. However, he returned to his grandmother and told her that even though the syrup was the best thing he had ever tasted, it was too easy to make. He was sure that the people would become too lazy and would only want to sit next to the maple trees and eat maple syrup all day long.

So Manabush climbed up a maple tree and sprinkled water over top of it. This caused the syrup to run thin. From then on people had to work hard to collect and boil down the syrup to make it just right.

See also Culture Hero(es); Rabbit; Trickster

References and further reading:

Barnouw, Victor. *Wisconsin Chippewa Myths & Tales and Their Relation to Chippewa Life: Based on Folktales Collected by Victor Barnouw, Joseph B. Casagrande, Ernestine Friedl, and Robert E. Ritzenthaler.* Madison: University of Wisconsin Press, 1977.

Erdoes, Richard, and Alfonso Ortiz, eds. *American Indian Trickster Tales.* New York: Viking, 1998.

Helbig, Aletha. "Manabozho: Trickster, Guide, Alter Ego." *Michigan Academician* 7 (1975): 357–371.

Leeming, David, and Jake Page. *The Mythology of Native North America.* Norman: University of Oklahoma Press, 1998.

Makarius, Laura. "The Crime of Manabozho." *American Anthropologist,* n.s., 79, no. 2 (June 1973): 663–675.

Radin, Paul. *The Trickster: A Study in American Indian Mythology.* London: Routledge and Kegan Paul, 1956.

Radin, Paul, and A. B. Reagan. "Ojibwa Myths and Tales: the Manabozho Cycle." *Journal of American Folklore* 41, no. 159 (January–March 1928): 61–146.

THE MICE'S SUN DANCE
Arapaho, Plains

The following tale concerns one of the many adventures of Nihansan.

Nihansan was traveling across the prairie. He stopped when he heard drumming and shouting. It sounded like a Sun Dance. He looked around and finally realized that the noise was coming from inside an elk skull. He peeked in through one of the holes and saw a mouse tribe's Sun Dance going on. Nihansan was a very curious sort and wanted to see more, so he shoved his head in farther and farther. The frightened mice scattered out through other openings.

Then Nihansan realized that his head was stuck inside the elk skull. He wandered around bumping into all sorts of trees. Each time he encountered a tree, he asked what kind it was. They replied, "dogwood," "bow wood," "Pawnee wood," "praying bush," "cottonwood," "willow." With each reply, he knew he was getting closer to the river. Eventually Nihansan came to the riverbank and fell into the water.

He floated downstream for a while until he came to a place where the women were bathing. When he drew near, he pleaded with them to hit him hard across the middle of the skull. So they did. The skull cracked open, and the broken pieces became the scrapers the women use when working with hides.

In a similar story, the trickster Veeho came upon mice holding a powwow in an elk skull. He watched the intriguing ceremonies and dances until he could no longer stand it. He, too, pushed his head into the skull as the mice fled. Veeho, however, found his way home to his wife. He asked for her help, and she willingly obliged by whacking him over the head with a large stick. Of course, many of her blows missed the mark and landed on his back and shoulders instead. She complained that he was not standing still, but finally she cracked the skull open with a hefty wallop from the stick.

See also Nihansan

References and further reading:

Bierhorst, John, ed. *The Red Swan: Myths and Tales of the American Indians.* Albuquerque: University of New Mexico Press, 1992. First published 1976 by Farrar, Straus, and Giroux.

Erdoes, Richard, ed. *The Sound of Flutes and Other Indian Legends.* Transcribed and edited by Richard Erdoes. New York: Pantheon Books, 1976.

MOUNTAIN LION
Kawaiisu, Great Basin

Both Mountain Lion and Coyote figure prominently in Kawaiisu mythology. As with many Native American myths, this one incorporates explanations for the peculiarities of a particular species.

One day, while the twin sons of Mountain Lion and his wife, Jackrabbit, were being cared for by their grandmother, Coyote kidnapped them and hid them in a canyon. When Jackrabbit returned home to find her sons missing, she cried, putting fire and ashes on her head as she did so. The brown spot found on the back of cottontails' heads is from the ashes. She searched for Coyote and the children but found no trace of them.

When Mountain Lion returned home and found his sons gone, he cried all night. He left his home to search for them and roamed all over the mountains and the plain for years, but found no trace of them. His tears of sadness caused streaks on his face that are visible on mountain lions' faces to this day. In the meantime, both his wife and the grandmother died, and Coyote raised Mountain Lion's sons with his own children.

Finally, Mountain Lion discovered his sons when they were out hunting deer. He approached them and explained that Coyote was not their father, which they suspected because they looked different from his other children. Mountain Lion told them how Coyote had stolen them from their grandmother, and how he had been searching for them for many years.

Mountain Lion and his sons tricked Coyote by luring him to a deer carcass lying under an oak tree, where Mountain Lion took his revenge by killing him. He then went to Coyote's house and killed his wife and children. Mountain Lion and his sons went to live in the mountains. Ever since that day, mountain lions have had no homes and wander about.

See also Coyote

References and further reading:

Kroeber, A. L. "Indian Myths of South Central California." *University of California Publications in American Archaeology and Ethnology* 4, no. 4 (1906–1907): 167–250.

Zigmond, Maurice L. *Kawaiisu Mythology: An Oral Tradition of South-Central California.* Socorro, N. Mex.: Ballena Press, 1980.

MOUSE WOMAN

Haida, Tlingit, Tsimshian, Northwest Coast

Mouse Woman appears in a variety of myths. A secondary but nonetheless important character, she exhibits great wisdom and offers sound advice to humans and other animal-persons.

In the Tsimshian tale "The Prince who was taken away by the Spring Salmon," the young son of a chief had an encounter with Mouse Woman.

The boy was scolded severely by his mother for stealing a piece of dried salmon that she'd been saving in a box for two years. So that night the boy ran away and hid in a place downstream. Later a canoe pulled up, and the men in the canoe told him to get in so they could take him to his father. Instead, they took him to another village, where he was escorted into the great chief's house.

When he sat down, Mouse Woman came up next to him and asked the boy if he knew why he was there. "No," the boy replied. Then Mouse Woman told him that he was in the house of the great Spring Salmon chief. The chief had been very ill for two years, but when the boy took him out of the box, he began to feel better.

Mouse Woman asked him for his woolen ear ornaments. After they had been toasted in the fire, she ate them. Then she told the boy, "When you get hungry, go out and club one of the children who are playing on the hill behind the village. Then roast and eat him. Be sure to gather all of the bones and burn them in the fire."

The next day when the prince was hungry, he did just what Mouse Woman had told him to and immediately the child turned into a Spring Salmon. Mouse Woman also advised the boy that right after eating salmon, he should drink fresh water. That way the salmon would have water and would be renewed again.

The boy had more adventures in the land of the Spring Salmon, but finally headed home. When he arrived, he told his father and the rest of the people what he had learned from Mouse Woman: don't keep dried salmon in a box; if fresh salmon is cooked, all of the bones should be burned; and drink fresh water after eating a meal of salmon. By observing these things, the people would always have a good supply of salmon.

See also Culture Hero(es); The Girl Who Married a Bear

References and further reading:

Boas, Franz. *Indian Myths & Legends from the North Pacific Coast of America: A Translation of Franz Boas' 1895 Edition of "Indianische Sagen von der Nord-Pacifischen Küste Amerikas."* Vancouver: Talonbooks, 2002.

———. *Tsimshian Mythology.* 1916. Landmarks in Anthropology. New York: Johnson Reprint Corp., 1970.

Bringhurst, Robert. *The Black Canoe: Bill Reid and the Spirit of Haida Gwaii.* Vancouver, B.C.: Douglas & McIntyre, 1995. First published 1991 by University of Washington Press.

Shearar, Cheryl. *Understanding Northwest Coast Art: A Guide to Crests, Beings, and Symbols.* Vancouver, B.C.: Douglas and McIntyre; Seattle: University of Washington Press, 2000.

NALUSA FALAYA AND KASHEHOTAPOLO

Choctaw, Southeast

The Nalusa Falaya are anthropomorphic beings about the size of a man, with shriveled faces, very small eyes, long noses, and long, pointed ears. They walk upright and speak with voices that sound human. They live in dense woods near swamps and resemble Kashehotapolo.

A Nalusa Falaya will appear at dusk and call to hunters, who become so affected they fall to the ground and sometimes even lose consciousness. It will then bewitch the hunter by inserting a small thorn into his hand or foot, giving him the power to do evil to others. However, the hunter remains unaware of this power until it is evidenced by his malevolent actions. Young Nalusa Falaya children possess the ability to remove their internal organs at night, causing them to appear as small, luminous bodies that may be seen along the edges of marshes.

Kashehotapolo is part man, part beast. His head is small, and his face is shriveled. His body is that of a man, but his legs and feet are those of a deer. He utters a sound that resembles a woman's cry; hence his name (*kasheho,* "woman," and *tapalo,* "call"). He lives in low-lying, swampy areas and delights in slipping up behind hunters who venture near his home and frightening them before running swiftly away.

> **References and further reading:**
> Hudson, Charles. *The Southeastern Indians.* Knoxville: University of Tennessee Press, 1992. First published 1976.
> Lankford, George E. *Native American Legends: Southeastern Legends: Tales from the Natchez, Caddo, Biloxi, Chickasaw, and Other Nations.* Little Rock: August House, 1987.

NAUGHTY GRANDCHILDREN
Pima, Southwest
The following story explains why the saguaro cactus and palo verde grow in the Southwest.

There was once an old woman who had two mischievous and disobedient grandchildren. Although she tried hard to please them and teach them manners, she was unsuccessful. Every morning she ground maize to make them porridge, but the children would always run round around the fire and kick over the olla water, so more would have to be brought from the spring.

The grandmother finally told them she was tired of their bad behavior. If they wanted to eat, she told them, they would have to go get more water themselves. So, the grandchildren went to the spring and brought more water. But again they ran around the fire, knocking the olla over. They went to get more water, and ran around the fire again after their return, spilling the water. This occurred over and over.

Finally, one of the grandchildren, tired of fetching water, decided to turn himself into a saguaro, so he could store water inside himself all the time. The other grandchild decided to turn himself into a palo verde, so he could store water inside himself, too, and so the mountains would be green.

Soon afterwards, the grandmother started searching for her grandsons, but the thorns of the saguaro and the palo verde kept her away. And so these plants grow everywhere in that place, the children of those mischievous children.

References and further reading:

McNamee, Gregory, ed. *The Bearskin Quiver: A Collection of Southwestern American Indian Folktales.* Einsiedeln, Switzerland: Daimon Verlag, 2002.

NIHANSAN

Arapaho, Plains

Nihansan (also spelled Nihanca or Nihancan) is depicted in some myths as the one who commanded Duck to bring up mud from below the water. From this mud, Nihansan formed the earth and created people. Other stories, such as the following, show him to be a selfish buffoon, with many trickster-like qualities. Frequently, these stories relate how his impulsiveness and voracious sexual appetite got him in trouble.

Nihansan was traveling along when he came upon a man who was tossing his eyes up into the top of a tree. Nihansan was very curious and watched from a distance. The man tossed his eyes up and then shortly afterward commanded them to return to him. Finally, Nihansan approached the man and asked to be taught how to do this trick. At first the man hesitated and told Nihansan that he was surely smart enough to figure it out himself. But Nihansan kept asking. Finally the man relented and explained how to do it. However, he warned that the trick should not be done too often and only when necessary.

Then they parted, each going off in a different direction. Nihansan came to some trees and decided to try out his new skill. He tossed his eyes up into the top of one of the trees and then commanded them to return back to their sockets. This went flawlessly. Nihansan continued walking until he came to another grove of trees and then a third. Each time he tossed his eyes up into the trees and they returned when he commanded them.

Later on he was stalking something through tall grass. When he came to some trees, he decided to get a better view of his prey by tossing his eyes into the trees. However, this time when he commanded them to return, they did not. He gave the command again and again, but without success. Blindly, he felt his way down to the riverbank. He could hear small animals scamper by him. He asked a mouse if he could borrow his eyes. The mouse complied, but they were too small and fell out of Nihansan's eye sockets. He gave them back and then went on asking other animals he met for the use of their eyes. None of them worked for him. Finally an owl gave Nihansan his eyes. That is why his eyes are now yellow. (Another version of this myth ends with Nihansan receiving eyes from a mole—and that is why moles are blind to this day.)

Nihansan took advantage of women in many of his exploits, but in the case of Whirlwind-Woman, he was rebuffed and overpowered.

Nihansan was traveling along and met Whirlwind-Woman. "Get out of my way!" he growled at her. So she spun away leaving a trail of dust behind her. Later he met her along the road and said, "Go away!" At this she quickly moved on. Still later, their paths crossed again. This time Nihansan was very emphatic and told Whirlwind-Woman that he did not want her around and that he really didn't like her at all. She whirled away as before, but not long afterward came to the spot where Nihansan was walking along the river.

Nihansan began to have second thoughts about Whirlwind-Woman. He approached her and said he thought they should be sweethearts. Whirlwind-Woman said that would not be possible, as she was forever traveling around. Nihansan said, "Me, too. I'm always traveling." And then to prove that they would be compatible, he started spinning around and around and stirred up a lot of dust. She wasn't impressed, so he spun faster and faster and threw dust higher in the air. She still refused his offer. When he brought up the subject again, she lost patience with him and with a great whirl she spun all around him. The powerful wind picked him up and threw him down head first. By the time Nihansan had collected his wits about him, Whirlwind-Woman was already far away.

> See also Earth Diver; The Mice's Sun Dance; Trickster; Whirlwind Woman
> References and further reading:
> Carroll, Michael P. "The Trickster as Selfish-Buffoon and Culture Hero." Ethos 12, no. 2 (Summer 1984): 105–131.
> Dorsey, George A., and Alfred L. Kroeber. Traditions of the Arapaho. 1903. Sources of American Indian Oral Literature. Lincoln: University of Nebraska Press, 1997.

OLD MAN
Siksika (Blackfeet), Plains

Old Man shaped the mountains, hills, streams, and prairies. Then he created vegetation, people, and animals. Old Man also, at times, exhibited trickster-like qualities.

Old Man was traveling around. As he traveled he formed the earth's features and then created the grasses, shrubs, and trees to cover them. He made the animals and placed them where they would be best suited. Then he decided to make a woman and a child. He formed them out of clay and four days later they came alive. He told them that his name was Napi (Old Man.) Later the woman asked Old Man what would become of them. Would they live forever, or would they die? Old Man decided on a test. He told the woman that he would toss a buffalo chip into the river. If it floated, then people would live, but if it sank, then they would die. He tossed the dried buffalo chip into the river and it floated. However, the woman picked up a stone and said, "If it floats we will live forever, but if it sinks, there will be death." So the woman tossed the stone into the river and it sank. Therefore all people must die. Sometime later, the woman's child died. She regretted the law about death and asked Old Man if they could change it. "No," he said, "What has been made law is unchangeable. People will die and not live forever."

At first the people did not know how to hunt. Instead, the buffalo had weapons and would capture and eat humans. But, Old Man decided that would not do at all. So he taught the people how to hunt animals, and how to gather plants, nuts, and fruit for their food. He also taught them about the power of medicinal herbs. Old Man taught them how to make fire so they could cook their food and keep warm.

There are numerous stories about Old Man and his "trickster" adventures. A few of them are related here:

Old Man was traveling around with Coyote when they passed a large rock. Old Man was tired of carrying his heavy buffalo hide blanket. So he left it on top of the rock and they continued on their journey. A little later the sky looked as if it would rain, so Old Man sent Coyote back for the blanket. However, the rock refused to let him have it, saying, "Once you give a gift to a rock, you can never take it back." Several times Old Man sent Coyote back, but the rock would not let go of the blanket. Finally, Old Man went himself. He grabbed the blanket off the rock and then started back on his travels with Coyote. Suddenly they heard an ominous rumble behind them. When they looked back there was the rock quickly rolling in their direction. They both ran up a hill, but the rock could not follow them. That is why rocks cannot roll up hill today.

Old Man and Fox were out hunting but had not been successful. One day they spotted four buffalo bulls lying at the bottom of a hill, but Old Man could not see a way for them to sneak up on the buffalo. Finally, he had a plan. It was the only way he could think of to get close enough to the buffalo. The plan called for Old Man to pluck out all of Fox's hair, except for at the very end of his tail. Then Fox would walk down to the buffalo and prance around them. The theory was that the buffalo would find the sight of a bare naked Fox hilarious. They would laugh so hard that Old Man would be able to sneak right up to them and kill them. Fox could not think of a better idea, so he finally agreed. The plan worked exactly as Old Man had predicted.

While Old Man was butchering the buffalo, the weather turned colder and the wind picked up. He kept talking to Fox as he worked, "Little brother, you were wonderful. The bulls laughed so hard, and I nearly died laughing myself. What a funny sight!" Fox didn't answer because he was shivering so hard that his teeth were chattering. The wind became colder and snow started falling. Old Man just kept on working and kept on talking about the comical performance Fox had given.

Finally all of the buffalo were skinned and butchered. Old Man got up and said, "It's getting cold. But we won't mind. We have enough meat to last all winter." But Fox did not answer. Old Man was irritated and said, "What's the matter with you? Didn't you hear me?" Still there was no response from Fox. So Old Man walked over and gave Fox a shove, but Fox fell over. He had frozen to death in the cold.

Old Man was traveling. One day he came to where the Sun lived and was invited to stay a while. Sometime later, all of the meat was gone, so Sun suggested that they go hunting for some deer. Then Sun retrieved a pair of beautiful leggings he had stored in a bag. He explained that the leggings had great medicine. When he was hunting, he would walk through the brush and the leggings would set it on fire, thus driving the deer out of hiding.

So they went hunting, and just as Sun had said, the leggings started the brush on fire. Old Man and Sun were each able to kill a deer when they ran out of the brush. That night, Sun removed his leggings, and Old Man watched where he stored them. While everyone else was sleeping, Old Man stole the leggings and hurried off. He traveled a long way and finally was too tired to go any farther. He made a pillow out of the leggings and then went to sleep. In the morning, he was awakened by Sun asking him, "Why do you have my leggings?" When Old Man opened his eyes, he was back in Sun's lodge. Old Man thought he must have gotten lost and accidentally ended up back there. That night, after everyone was asleep, Old Man again stole the leggings and fled. This time he kept running until it was almost morning. Finally he was too tired to go any farther. But when he awoke, he was back in Sun's lodge. He didn't realize that the entire world belonged to the Sun and he could never run away from him. But Sun decided to let Old Man have his leggings since he liked them so much.

Later on, when Old Man's food was nearly gone, he decided to put on the leggings and set fire to some brush. However, as he was taking aim at some deer, he realized that the fire was burning toward him. He tried to run away, but the flames caught up with him and set the leggings on fire. Just then he came to a river and jumped in. But it was not in time to save the leggings.

Old Man had been traveling around for a long time. He decided that it was time to settle down and get a wife. Wherever he went he asked the people if there were any single women around who wanted to get married. Finally, he learned about a woman whose husband had died and left her with two daughters who were nearly grown. Old Man went to visit the woman and asked her to marry him right then. Much to his surprise, she said, "Yes." So they began living together that day. Life went on smoothly until one day when Old Man had a close look at his stepdaughters. He began thinking that they would soon have young men courting them. Suddenly he felt jealous and decided that he wanted the girls for himself.

About that time someone in the village died and was buried under a pile of stones on a hilltop. That gave Old Man an idea. He began to act sick and became worse as the days went by. Finally, he told his wife and stepdaughters that a spirit had visited him and told him that he would soon die. The spirit also said that a stranger would come to their tipi four days after he died. The stepdaughters were to marry this stranger. Old Man also told them that the spirit gave instructions about how he should be buried. They were not to cover his body with stones, but with only a few thick robes.

And so it was that Old Man breathed his last breath. His lifeless body was carried to the hilltop and buried as they had been instructed. Old Man, of course, was not really dead. He waited several days under the robes, and when no one was around, he sneaked away from the grave site. Meanwhile, his wife and stepdaughters waited in their tipi for the stranger to arrive. Four days later a man who was painted with yellow earth came to the tipi and took the girls for his wives. Eventually, one of the girls noticed a long scar on the man's right leg. She reported this to her mother and sister. "It looks exactly like the scar our stepfather had on his leg." Over the next few days, the mother and daughters tried to get a look at the man's scar. Finally, they were convinced that it was Old Man. One day the three women waited inside the tipi with clubs in their hands. When Old Man came in, they all started beating him, but he ran out and kept on running because he realized that the women had figured out what he had done.

See also Culture Hero(es); Skinkuts; Transformer; Trickster; Why Stories

References and further reading:

Bullchild, Percy. *The Sun Came Down*. San Francisco: Harper & Row, 1990.

Grinnell, George Bird. *Blackfoot Lodge Tales: The Story of a Prairie People*. Lincoln: University of Nebraska Press, 2003. First published 1892 by Scribner.

———. *Pawnee, Blackfoot and Cheyenne: History and Folklore of the Plains*. New York: Charles Scribner's Sons, 1961.

Linderman, Frank B. *Indian Why Stories: Sparks from War Eagle's Lodge-Fire*. 1915. New authorized ed. Lincoln: University of Nebraska Press, 2001.

Rides At The Door, Darnell Davis. *Napi Stories*. Browning, Mont.: Blackfeet Heritage Program, 1979.

Wissler, Clark, and D. C. Duvall. *Mythology of the Blackfoot Indians.* Sources of American Indian Oral Literature. Lincoln: University of Nebraska Press, 1995. First published 1908 by American Museum of Natural History.

OTTERS AND COYOTE

Navajo, Southwest

A story about gambling that incorporates explanations for the characteristics of different species of animals.

One day some Otters were entertaining themselves by gambling. Coyote approached them and asked if he could take part in the game. Having heard what a rascal Coyote was, the Otters refused and told him to go away. Coyote stayed and pleaded with them, and eventually the Otters invited him to join them.

Coyote foolishly bet his skin and lost. The Otters rushed him and tore the hide off his back, beginning at the root of his tail and pulling forward, despite his piteous cries of pain. He wailed terribly when they reached the end of his nose, which was most sensitive. When they were finished, Coyote jumped into the water, as he had seen the Otters do, and hoped his skin would come back. He jumped into the water again and again, but he always came out as bare as before. Coyote had had a glossy, beautiful pelt like the Otters, but now it was gone.

Finally, Coyote grew exhausted and lay down in the water. Taking pity on him, the Otters pulled him out and threw him into a badger hole, and covered him with dirt.

When Coyote had dug his way out of the badger hole, his fur had reappeared, but it was not like the fur he had once had. Now, it was coarse and rough and dull, and Coyotes have worn such fur ever since.

Coyote did not learn any kind of lesson from this experience, however. He challenged the Otters to further play and bet his new skin. The Otters just scoffed at him and told him to go away, as no one would play for his skin now. This angered Coyote, who retired to a safe distance and began to taunt and deride the Otters.

"You are nothing but braggarts," he cried. "You pretend to be brave, but you are cowards. Your wives are ugly, just like you." After a while, he retreated to a cliff and continued his taunts and insults from there.

The Otters decided they would suffer his abuse no longer, so they sent word to the chiefs of the Spiders and asked for their help. The Spiders crept up the cliff behind Coyote and wove strong webs in the trees and bushes. When they had finished, they told the Otters what they had done. The Otters went up the cliff to attack Coyote, who pretended to be unconcerned and allowed them to come very close. He turned to run but was soon caught in the webs.

The Otters seized Coyote and dragged him down to the foot of the hill. The Cliff Swallows flew down from the canyon walls and tore Coyote to pieces, carrying off fragments to their nests. They tore his skin into strips and made them into bands that they put around their heads. This is why these birds have bands on their heads today. Eventually, Coyote came back to life, but he resented how badly the Otters and Spiders and Cliff Swallows had treated him, and so he plotted his revenge.

See also Coyote; Gamblers and Gambling

References and further reading:

McNamee, Gregory, ed. *The Bearskin Quiver: A Collection of Southwestern American Indian Folktales.* Einsiedeln, Switzerland : Daimon Verlag, 2002.

OWL

The nocturnal owl, viewed with mystery and awe, is a prominent figure among Native Americans north of Mexico. To some tribes, he is a wise and friendly advisor. To others, he is a protector that warns against danger or an approaching enemy, or a prophet that foretells the weather, impending death, or the coming of good news. He is also a benefactor or source of power; sometimes, he is a destructive and malevolent figure who can cause death or disease. Some tribes honor and respect the owl, believing it to be a sacred creature. The owl is often found on Indian pottery, stoneware, and basketry.

In the following Pawnee story, a poor boy is pitied by owls, who give him nocturnal vision:

Long ago, the people moved south to a forested area and made their village. Here, they found much game, which kept them well fed, and a peaceful life, as enemies appeared to be far away and there were no wars.

Living among these people was a poor orphan boy with no relatives. He made his home with an old woman who lived in a grass lodge. He would sit outside and watch the men carrying home deer and other game. The boy decided to leave his people and the village, as he thought it would be better if he died.

He made his way through the timbered land for many days, expecting to be killed by wild animals. Finally, he stopped and cried. His strength had given out, as he had not eaten since he left his village. He stayed in this place for several days.

One night, as the boy stood in despair and was about to kill himself, a voice from the tops of the trees spoke to him and said, "My son, leave this place; go back toward your home, and you will come to a lone, dry oak tree, standing in the open. Inside this tree is our home. Stop there and we will speak to you, and then you shall see us. So the boy went back toward his village, and by daylight had found the tree. Here he stopped, and he cried all day.

Owl totem pole. (SEF/Art Resource, NY)

During the night, another voice spoke to him. He looked up at the tree and saw two owls sitting on a limb. One was white, the other red. The white owl said "We know you are poor; we know you want to kill yourself, so we brought you here. You can see us plainly, even though it is dark. We are the leaders of all the other owls who live in this forest. We go out in the night and kill all kinds of birds to eat. We will each give you one feather and ask you to start for home at once. Put them in your scalp-lock, then leave the lodge, close your eyes, and you will see as you do in the daytime; you will see raccoons, otter, and deer, but to them, you will be invisible."

The owl then told the boy to make a bow and some arrows, and to put the two feathers in his hair. The owl instructed him to kill first a raccoon, then a turkey, an eagle, and several deer. After he had killed the deer, the boy was to come back to talk to the owls again. He obeyed them and went home.

The old woman was very happy to see the boy. She took care of him and fed him, and he became strong again. He did as the owls told him and made a bow and arrows. He put the two owl feathers in his hair and left the lodge. He closed his eyes, and as he walked along he opened them, and could see a raccoon beside a creek. He shot at it and killed it. The proud boy took it home—and killed several rabbits along the way. The woman was very thankful, because before she had been obliged to beg for meat.

The next night, the boy killed several turkeys and put some of their feathers on his arrows. The night after that, he killed an otter along the bank of the stream. The woman took the hide to a medicine man and exchanged it for flints, which the boy put on the ends of a new set of arrows he made.

The boy went out with his flint-tipped arrows and killed several deer. He continued to go out and bring in game, and he and the old woman now had a lot of meat and many types of buckskin, which the woman had tanned.

White traders arrived at this time, and the boy sold them his furs and buckskins. Some he traded for knives and steel to make arrow points. He went out to hunt more often during the night and was able to acquire enough skins to trade for a rifle. He got many more hides and furs, and traded them to another Indian for a pony. He traded more game to hunters for buffalo hides, so the woman was able to have a buffalo-hide tipi.

One night, the boy went back to the owls and stayed until one spoke to him. It told him they were glad he was having success, and to get many ponies, and keep them, for he would soon leave and go north.

So the boy went home again and traded more furs and hides for several ponies. He continued to kill more game and traded it for more ponies and clothing and blankets.

Again he went to the tree to see the owls. One told him they were glad he was now so well off, that he should now find a woman, and then return to them. The boy returned home and the old woman found a girl who consented to marry him.

The boy returned to the owls again. One of them said, "The power that we gave you to see while hunting is gone, but we give you the feathers so that you can wear them. When you try to take ponies from your enemies, you can see clearly. Now, the only time we give you power to see will be in February, when all animals are abroad at night seeking their mates. Return home and we will come to you in your dreams, so that you will learn to be a medicine man."

The boy went home and stayed in the village for a while. He joined a party that went north. He became a great warrior and, in time, a great medicine man. His power to see in the dark eventually left him, but he became a power among his people.

An Iroquois story explains why the owl has such big eyes.

The Everything-Maker, called Raweno, was working to create various animals. He was busy with Rabbit, who told him he wished to have long legs and ears like a deer, and the sharp claws and fangs of a panther. Roweno liked to give the animals exactly the characteristics they asked for.

Owl was sitting nearby in a tree, awaiting his turn and watching. He told Raweno that he wanted to be turned into the fastest, most beautiful and most wonderful of all the birds. He asked for Swan's long neck, Egret's long beak, Cardinal's vibrant red feathers, and Heron's crown of plumes.

Raweno was displeased. He ordered Owl to be silent and turn away or close his eyes, because no one was allowed to watch him do his work. At that moment, he was making Rabbit the long ears for which he had asked.

Owl refused to do as Raweno commanded. "Whoo, whoo," he replied. "I can watch if I want to. No one can forbid me to do so or order me to close my eyes. I enjoy watching you, and watch I will!"

This made Raweno angry. He grabbed Owl and pulled him down from his branch, stuffing his head deep into his body, shaking him until his eyes grew large with fright, and pulling at his ears until they were sticking up on both sides of his head.

"There! That will teach you," said Raweno. "Now you cannot crane your neck and watch things you should not watch. Your eyes are large but not so large that you can watch me, as you will be awake only after dark, and I work during the day. Your ears are now large, so you can listen when someone tells you not to do something. And as punishment for your disobedience, your feathers will be gray, not red like Cardinal's"—and with that remark, Raweno rubbed Owl with mud. Owl flew off, pouting "Whoo, whoo, whoo."

Raweno turned his attention back to Rabbit, who was quivering with fright, even though Raweno's anger was directed at Owl. Rabbit ran off only half completed. As a result, only Rabbit's hind legs are long, and he can only hop about instead of walk or run. Because he took such fright at that moment, Rabbit has remained afraid of almost everything, and he was never given the claws and fangs he wanted in order to defend himself. Rabbit would have become quite a different animal if he had allowed Raweno to finish his work.

As for Owl, he remained as he was formed by Raweno in anger, with large eyes, a short neck, and ears that stick up prominently on each side of his head. In addition, he now sleeps during the day and comes out only after dark.

References and further reading:

Dorsey, George A. *Traditions of the Skidi Pawnee*. 1904. New York: Kraus Reprint Co., 1969.

Erdoes, Richard, and Alfonso Ortiz, eds. *American Indian Myths and Legends*. New York: Pantheon Books, 1984.

Wilson, Eddie W. "The Owl and the American Indian." *Journal of American Folklore* 63, no. 249 (July–September 1950): 336–344.

PEOPLE BROUGHT IN A BASKET

Modoc, Plateau

A Modoc explanation of how people came to be in this world.

Old Man (Kumush) traveled to the land of the underworld spirits. He followed a long, steep road and came to a place where a vast number of spirits lived. At night the spirits danced and sang, but in the morning they went back to their houses and were dry bones. After spending several days there, Kumush missed the sun and decided to return home with some of the spirits' bones. He wanted to use the bones to make people for the earth.

He selected various bones to be used for the different tribes, thinking some would be good for one tribe and other bones better for other tribes. When the basket was full, Kumush started up the steep road. But near the top he tripped and the basket fell off his back. The bones turned into spirits that sang as they hurried back to their homes in the spirit world.

Kumush filled his basket a second time and started to climb up the trail. But once again he stumbled and the spirits escaped. Then he went back and filled his basket again. This time he scolded the bones and told them that once they saw his world and the sunshine, they would be happy to stay with him. So up the steep trail he went and when he neared the edge, he tossed the basket up onto the ground.

Then he set about the task of putting the bones in various places and giving the people names. He tossed some to the west and declared that they would be the Shastas and would be brave warriors. He told other people, the Pit River Indians and Warm Springs Indians, that they would be brave warriors also. Then just to the north he tossed the bones that would become the Klamath, saying that they would be easily frightened and would not make good warriors.

Finally he chose the bones that would become the Modoc Indians. He spoke to them, saying, "You will be the bravest." He told them that they would be his chosen people and would be able to fight off all who came against them. He also instructed all the people that certain ones would need to go to the mountains if they sought wisdom or special powers.

Kumush also created the fish and animals and the plants and berries for the people to eat. He also made the laws about how people would work. Men, he said, would be the warriors, hunters, and fishermen. Women would stay near their homes to gather wood and water as well as the berries and roots to cook for their families.

After Kumush had created his world, he traveled with his daughter to near where the sun rises in the east. From there they traveled along the sun's path until they reached the middle of the sky. That's where they still live today.

References and further reading:
Clark, Ella E. *Indians Legends of the Pacific Northwest.* 50th anniversary ed. Berkeley; London: University of California Press, 2003. First published 1953.
Erdoes, Richard, and Alfonso Ortiz, eds. *American Indian Myths and Legends.* New York: Pantheon Books, 1984.

Indian dancers at Potlatch, Chilkat, Alaska, 1895. (Library of Congress)

POTLATCH, ORIGIN OF

Various, Northwest Coast

Potlatches are formal ceremonies that combine feasting, dancing, athletic competitions, storytelling, and the distribution of gifts to audience members. Often they were held in conjunction with other events such as naming ceremonies, puberty rites, marriages, funerals, totem pole raising, or house building. The prestige of the host was at stake, for the more generous he was, the more he was respected. But elaborate potlatches did not necessarily impoverish the host, because as others held their own ceremonies, gifts would be given in return. Because Europeans did not understand the socioeconomic function of the potlatch and related ceremonies, potlatches were banned in Canada from 1884 until 1951.

In times past, a potlatch, which had religious as well as economic significance, could last for several days. Today, potlatches often are concluded in one day. Although the potlatch was widespread across the Northwest Coast culture area, it varied in form and scale among the tribes. Here is a Quileute version of how the potlatch originated.

Once, an unusual-looking bird appeared near the village. All the young hunters went out to kill it, but none were successful. Every day they went out, but no one could kill the bird. Then Golden Eagle said to Blue Jay, his slave, "My daughters could get that bird." Blue Jay was surprised at what Golden

Eagle said, because girls did not hunt. But Golden Eagle's daughters overheard what was said. The next day they went to the woods and stayed all day. For several days they went back, but did not tell anyone where they were going or what they were doing.

Then one day, after the hunters had gone out in their canoes to hunt the strange bird, the girls ran to the woods to get the bow and arrows they had made. They disguised themselves and paddled out until they were near the bird. The older sister shot her arrows and one killed the bird. Later that night, they told their father what they had done. "We've hidden the bird in the woods and want to give the beautiful feathers away as gifts," she said.

So Blue Jay went around inviting people to ceremony. When everyone was gathered in the house, the girls gave the colorful feathers away. Yellow and brown feathers were given to Meadowlark, red and brown ones to Robin, yellow and black to Finch, and so on until they had given away all of the feathers.

Since that time, birds have feathers of those colors. And that was the first potlatch where people gave gifts to the people who were invited.

References and further reading:
Clark, Ella E. *Indians Legends of the Pacific Northwest.* 50th anniversary ed. Berkeley; London: University of California Press, 2003. First published 1953.

Hirshfelder, Arlene, and Paulette Molin. *Encyclopedia of Native American Religions: An Introduction.* Updated ed. New York: Facts on File, 2000.

Vancouver Art Gallery. *People of the Potlatch: Native Arts and Culture of the Pacific Northwest Coast.* Vancouver: Vancouver Art Gallery, 1956.

PRAIRIE DOG
Jicarilla, Southwest

The Jicarilla told two stories that reflected their belief that the prairie dog had powers associated with water. In the first story, a warrior dying of thirst is saved when a prairie dog takes pity on him, leads him into his home, and gives him a vessel of water. Although it is but a small amount, the water saves him from death and lasts for four days, enough for him to return home to his people.

In the second story, a man is very thirsty but does not know where to find water—so thirsty that he has done everything he can to lighten his load, including throwing away his arrows, quiver, and everything heavy. He lies down to beg for water at a prairie dog's hole. Eventually, the prairie dog brings out a very small cup of water and gives it to him. The man doubts that it would be enough to quench his thirst, but he takes the cup and drinks and from it. He finds that he cannot not finish it. His mind begins to clear, and he soon feels much better.

Prairie Dog tells the man to pick up his bow and arrows and his blanket and start walking, and he would find more water. The man does as Prairie Dog says, and he soon arrives at a place where there has been much rain, and he knows that Prairie Dog sent it.

References and further reading:

Opler, Morris Edward. *Myths and Tales of the Jicarilla Apache Indians.* Sources of American Indian Oral Literature. Lincoln: University of Nebraska Press, 1994. First published 1938 by American Folklore Society.

QUMU?UC

Ute, Great Basin

Qumuʔuc is the hot-rock medicine that Bear hides in the hollow of a tree and from which he gains his strength as he dances and sings.

In one story, the chief Sunawavi (Wolf) heard that Bear was approaching his village. Bear had been murdering people, so Sunawavi told the men to watch for him. He instructed them, "Track him backwards, because we have heard that he always puts his medicine near a village. Take plenty of water jugs and put out the fire of the rock. Take many boys with you."

They searched and found the red-hot rock hidden in the trees and poured water on it, which turned it black. The villagers rushed home to report their success to Sunawavi. Bear was then invited to a dance in the village and told to sing a song. He sang "My hot rock, I am here, help me." The rock would then usually come to kill people, but this time it did not. He repeated the song, but nothing came, because the *qumuʔuc* had been extinguished. Then all hit Bear over the head and disabled him.

See also Bear

References and further reading:

Lowie, Robert H. "Shoshonean Tales." *Journal of American Folkore* 37, no. 143–144 (January–June 1924): 1–242.

RABBIT

Ottawa, Northeast Woodlands; Natchez, Southeast; Ute, Great Basin

In the myths from the Northeast Woodlands related by Brinton, this figure is called Michabo, Giant Rabbit, the greatest of all animals. Rabbit instructed mankind how to hunt and fish and how to perform religious ceremonies. He was also instrumental in the creation of the world as we know it. The following is an Earth Diver myth, this time with Rabbit as the creator of the earth.

In the beginning water covered the earth. A raft floated on the water, and on the raft was Rabbit and several other animals. They all wished for land to live on, so Rabbit ordered beaver to dive to the bottom of the water to bring up some mud. Beaver willingly obeyed but returned after a long time without having reached the bottom. Next Rabbit ordered the otter to try. He, too, returned

Western cottontail rabbit near the Rio Grande, Bosque del Apache National Wildlife Refuge, New Mexico. (North Wind Picture Archives)

after a long absence, but without having succeeded. Finally Muskrat volunteered to dive to the bottom, and Rabbit consented. She was gone so long that the others on the raft gave up on ever seeing her alive again. At last, Muskrat floated to the surface of the water and was pulled, unconscious, onto the raft. In one of her paws was a tiny bit of mud. She had succeeded on her mission! The other animals were soon able to revive her.

Rabbit took the tiny bit of mud and formed an island and then a mountain. As the earth grew and grew, Rabbit walked around its edges to see what it was like and how big it was. Rabbit then created trees by shooting his arrows into the ground.

One version of the story explains that Rabbit and Muskrat married and humans are their offspring. Rabbit cared for his children and taught them many things that they would need to live on their own.

In the Southeast, there were numerous tales about Rabbit and his adventures. The following tale, related by Swanton, is from the Natchez.

The chief of all the animals let them each chose the kind of food they wished to eat. Squirrel chose acorns; Opossum, Raccoon, and Fox chose persimmons; the birds selected grapes; and so on. Rabbit decided he wanted the balls that hang from the sycamore tree. He sat under a tree and waited for a ball to drop. But when it did, it just scattered everywhere. Finally he got hungry and went to the chief to ask for something else. The chief said, "If you get me something I want to eat, I'll fix it so you can have something you want."

So Rabbit took off and soon arrived at the place where Alligator lived. He called for Alligator to come out. "Why should I?" he asked.

"Well, the chief wants you to hew a post for him," Rabbit replied.

"Well, then I'll come with you," Alligator said. However, as they were going along, Rabbit grabbed a club and hit Alligator over the head, but didn't kill him. Alligator ran back home.

Rabbit returned to the chief and said that he had not had any luck. The chief told Rabbit that if he didn't eat, then neither would Rabbit. So Rabbit headed back toward Alligator's home. On the way, he killed a fawn, skinned it and covered himself in the fawn's hide. Again he told Alligator that the chief had summoned him, but this time Alligator was wary. "I don't want to go," Alligator said. "They'll hit me on the head again."

"Who did that?" Rabbit asked.

"It was Rabbit," said Alligator, thinking he was talking to Fawn.

"Well, I won't do that. You can trust me," Rabbit told him.

So Alligator agreed to go along. On the way, Rabbit asked Alligator. "So where is the spot that if someone were to hit it you would die?" Alligator explained about the tender place on his back. It wasn't long before Rabbit found a club and hit Alligator on the back and killed him. Then he took off the fawn hide and carried the alligator to the chief.

To his surprise, the chief was not happy. "Those things aren't fit to eat!" he said. Then the chief ordered Rabbit to find his food in old women's gardens where he'd have to watch out for their dogs. Since that time rabbits have been fond of garden vegetables, and dogs are forever chasing them.

The Ute tale "Little Rabbit Fights the Sun" begins when Ta-vwots, Little Rabbit, was sleeping with his back to the sun and got burned. His children woke him up. "Father, your back is covered with holes!" they told him. Little Rabbit knew that Sun had burned him and decided to go out and fight him.

While traveling, Little Rabbit came to a wonderful valley with a cornfield. The corn was ripe and ready to roast. But Little Rabbit had never seen corn before, so he examined it closely. Then he realized it was corn and set about roasting some ears. After he had his fill of roasted corn, Little Rabbit wondered if the field belonged to anyone, so he decided to hide. When the owner came, he realized right away who the culprit was and declared to his warriors that he wanted the thief dead.

They searched all over for Little Rabbit and finally found the hole he was hiding in. They shot arrows into the hole, but Little Rabbit just blew them back out. Then they started digging near the hole, but while they were occupied doing that, Little Rabbit escaped out a different hole. The warriors had dug a deep hole and Little Rabbit tossed a magic ball onto the rim of earth above them. It caused the ground to collapse and buried them all.

Little Rabbit traveled on and came to a place where two men were shaping arrowheads out of hot stones. He watched them from behind a tree for a while before he made his presence known. "Let me help you," he said. "These stones will not harm me."

The men thought he was crazy and asked him, "Are you a ghost?"

"No, I'm not a ghost," Little Rabbit replied, "but I am powerful enough not to be harmed by the hot stones." The men thought he would surely be burned, but Little Rabbit just blew on the stones and cooled them with his magic breath. Then he said, "All right, now it is your turn." He made the men lie down on the hot stones, and they were immediately destroyed. Little Rabbit thought this was great practice for fighting with Sun.

The next day Little Rabbit saw some women picking berries. He instructed them to blow the berry bush thorns into his eyes. The women did as they were told and Little Rabbit just blew the thorns away. "Are you a ghost?" they cried.

"No, I'm not a ghost," said Little Rabbit. "I'm just a regular person like you. Let me blow the thorns into your eyes. They won't hurt you." So, the women agreed, but unlike Little Rabbit, they were blinded by the thorns. He thought this was also good practice for fighting with Sun.

Later on he saw some other women standing on a cliff. They recognized him and decided to kill him by throwing rocks off the cliff as he passed by. But Little Rabbit realized what they were up to and stopped while still out of range. He cooked a mixture of dried meat and chokecherries and began eating. The women asked, "What are you eating?"

Little Rabbit told them and said he'd share it with them. "Just come to the edge of the cliff and I'll toss some up to you," he said. The women moved to the edge, but Little Rabbit tossed the food just short of where they were. He did this several times, and finally the women leaned far over the cliff to try to reach the food he was tossing to them. They leaned so far that they fell to their deaths. Little Rabbit then continued on his way.

Later he happened upon another group of women weaving baskets. They saw him coming and decided to kill him. But Little Rabbit knew what they had planned. He suggested that they weave a closed basket with him in it. The women thought this would fit into their plan. However, Little Rabbit broke free of the basket. "You must be a ghost!" they exclaimed.

"No, I'm not a ghost," Little Rabbit said, then asked the women, "Why don't you try getting into the baskets?" The women did just that, but they got stuck in the pitch they had used to make the baskets waterproof. Little Rabbit kicked the baskets around and then finally threw his magic ball at them and killed them all. "I'm getting good at this!" he declared.

Next Little Rabbit met Great Bear, who told him that he was going to hide from Little Rabbit, since he was going around killing everyone. Little Rabbit said, "Me, too. Let's hide together." So they dug a huge hole and hid inside. But Little Rabbit escaped out a small hole in the back. When Great Bear discovered this, he tried to go out the same exit but got stuck. Little Rabbit tossed his magic ball at him and killed him on the spot. "Now I am ready to fight Sun," said Little Rabbit as he went on his way.

Then he met Tarantula, who had already heard about Little Rabbit's exploits. Tarantula had a magic stick that would kill other people, but not himself. He said to Little Rabbit, "Here, beat me with this stick." But Little Rabbit knew what he was up to and quickly exchanged Tarantula's stick for his magic ball and killed Tarantula.

Little Rabbit finally arrived at the eastern edge of the world. He was careful not to step over the edge while he waited for Sun to make his appearance. When Sun began to rise, Little Rabbit hit him in the face and it shattered into tiny flames all over the world. The flames burned all of Little Rabbit except for his head, which rolled around in the fire. The heat of the flames caused his eyes to explode, and this caused a flood of tears that covered the earth and extinguished the flames. Eventually Sun and Little Rabbit recreated themselves, and Little Rabbit learned that killing is not the answer.

See also Earth Diver; Manabozho

References and further reading:

Brinton, Daniel G. *American Hero-Myths: a Study in the Native Religions of the Western Continent.* 1882. Series in American Studies. New York: Johnson Reprint Corp., 1970.

Erdoes, Richard, and Alfonso Ortiz, eds. *American Indian Trickster Tales.* New York: Viking, 1998.

Swanton, John R. "Animal Stories from the Indians of the Muskhogean Stock." *Journal of American Folklore* 26, no. 101 (July–September 1913): 193–218.

RACCOON

The wily raccoon appears often in Native American myths and displays many characteristics of a trickster. In a Missisauga tale, Raccoon is very fond of crawfish. He lies on a lakeshore and lets his tail and hindquarters into the water and pretends to be dead. Gradually many crawfish gather around him, pinching him. He suddenly jumps up and catches them, and has a great feast. In a story of the Abenaki, Raccoon is a deceitful prankster who employs his cunning to obtain food from other beings. In a Kathlamet story, Raccoon's grandmother hits him in the face with a fire poker after she discovers he has eaten all of her stored acorns, thus explaining the origin of the markings on his masked face. In stories of the Iroquois, Raccoon often outwits other animals. Some stories of the Achomawi tell of lightning taking the form of a raccoon.

Raccoon and fellow trickster Coyote appear together in a story of the Shasta.

After going to a dance, Raccoon and Coyote were returning to their homes. On the way, a squirrel ran across the road and into a hole. Coyote told Raccoon to scare him out the other side. Raccoon did so by putting his hand into the other opening of the hole. Coyote put his hand in at the other opening, seized Raccoon's arm, and pulled. Thinking it was the squirrel, Coyote ignored Raccoon's protests. He eventually pulled off Raccoon's arm, and he died.

Coyote brought Raccoon's body home and distributed the meat among his children. The youngest boy, angry because he was not given an equal share, went to Raccoon's five children and told them Coyote had killed their father. The next day, while Coyote was gone, Raccoon's children killed the other children of Coyote. Then they returned to their own house, prepared themselves, and ran away with Coyote's remaining child into the sky.

Coyote returned home to find his children dead. He ran to Raccoon's house but found no one. He hunted Raccoon everywhere, asking questions. The dust began to rise in eddies, and looking up, he saw the children of Raccoon and his own son rising. He ran after them, calling and weeping, but they would not listen, and he could not catch them.

Raccoon's children remained in the sky as stars. They are the Pleiades. Coyote's surviving child is the smallest, the red star. The Pleiades are their most brilliant and continually visible in the winter, when raccoons are less active and spend much time in their holes. During the summer, when the raccoons are out and about, the Pleiades are not seen.

See also Coyote; Stars and Constellations

References and further reading:

Chamberlain, A. F. "Tales of the Mississaguas I." *Journal of American Folklore* 2, no. 5 (April–June 1889): 141–147.

Farrand, Livingston, and Leo J. Frachtenburg. "Shasta and Athapascan Myths from Oregon." *Journal of American Folklore* 28, no. 109 (July–September 1915): 207–242.

RAINBOW(S)

Rainbows appear widely in Native American stories and prophecies. The Cherokee believe a rainbow forms the hem of the Sun's coat. In a story of the

Yana, Rainbow's son overcomes Moon in a pole-bending contest and hurls him to the sky. Kiaklo, a Zuni kachina and the keeper of Zuni history, bears the imprint of a rainbow on his cheek. A rainbow is a toy or charm used by the Creator to stop a rainstorm, according to the Mohave of Arizona. Children of northern California tribes are warned that their fingers will become crooked and fall off if they count a rainbow's colors. These tribes also believe great healing powers are bestowed upon a medicine person who walks through a rainbow. Rainbows may carry dreams across vast canyons and are sometimes made from the souls of wildflowers.

Rainbows are occasionally portents of evil, or an evil force. They can prevent rain from falling, either by stretching across the sky and catching it, or by exuding a stench that causes the clouds to retreat.

More often, rainbows are regarded as bridges or ladders from one world to another, from this world to the next. In the mythology of the Navajo ritual healing process known as Waterway, the character Sunlight Boy journeys to the sky on crossed rainbows. In the mythology associated with the Navajo Nightway ceremony, the hero is transported back to his home on a rainbow. Among the Keresan, a rainbow forms the gateway through which people entered Shipap, the home of the dead and the supernatural.

Navajo sandpaintings, which have been used in religious rituals for centuries, often feature rainbows. They frequently function as protectors against evil influences by encircling the painting, with an opening on the east side, where two guardian figures are often found, such as Sun and Moon. Sometimes rainbows represent the Rainbow God, with the body circling northeast to a head and feet at the southeast. Rainbows that appear in the shape of short, straight rectangles represent symbols of protection in these pictures.

References and further reading:

Gill, Sam D., and Irene F. Sullivan. *Dictionary of Native American Mythology.* Santa Barbara: ABC-CLIO, 1992.

Malotki, Ekkehart, ed. *Hopi Tales of Destruction.* Collected, translated, and edited by Ekkehart Malotki. Lincoln: University of Nebraska Press, 2002.

Matthews, Washington. *The Mountain Chant: a Navajo Ceremony.* Salt Lake City: University of Utah Press, 1997. First published 1887 by Bureau of American Ethnology.

Newcomb, Franc J., and Gladys A. Reichard. *Sandpaintings of the Navajo Shooting Chant.* 1937. New York: Dover Publications, 1975.

RAVEN

Arctic, Northwest Coast, Subarctic

Among the tribes of the Northwest Coast, many mythological stories were told only at certain times and by certain people. Some myths were historical and

Shaman's rattles. (Library of Congress)

could only be related or performed by the people who owned them. These individuals belonged to the clans that descended from a character in the story. Other tales were accessible to all. Many of the myths of the Raven cycle were of the second type. These were most numerous in the northern part of the region among the Haida, Tlingit, and Tsimshian groups and in the western Subarctic. They were less prominent to the south and east. Raven myths were also widespread on the other side of the Pacific Ocean among the people living in the far northeastern corner of Asia, such as the Koriak and the Chuckchi.

Raven was central to the mythology of the Northwest Coast, where he was depicted as a significant force in shaping the world as we know it. He was more of a changer than an original creator, and this was best seen in the way he reconstructed the earth and populated it after a great deluge. One myth tells that when all the people had been destroyed, Raven created new ones from leaves. This explains why people die, especially in autumn when the leaves fall off the trees. A different tale relates that Raven was walking on the beach when he heard high-pitched noises coming from a shell. He opened the shell and freed the people. A variation of this tale states that Raven found a shell on the beach and, being a lusty fellow, had relations with it. Nine months later when he walked back that way, he heard little voices coming from inside the shell. When he opened it, he found that he had fathered the first people.

In the tale often entitled "Raven Steals the Light," Raven's greed for light ended up being a benefit to all.

Long ago, while everything was still dark, there was a great chief who kept light hidden away in three boxes. Raven, who had been busy forming the land and seas, decided that he needed light to proceed with his work. So Raven set off on his quest to steal the light, but he could not figure out how to get inside the chief's house undetected.

One day when the chief's daughter left the house to fetch water, Raven devised a plan. He changed himself into a small leaf and floated into the girl's drinking water. The girl was very thirsty. She drank the water quickly but didn't realize she had swallowed the leaf. Inside her body Raven transformed himself once more and caused her to become pregnant. Raven grew as all babies do and eventually the girl gave birth to a son. No one suspected that this was not an ordinary little boy.

The grandfather was delighted with his new grandson and began to spoil him from the very first day. As the baby grew he became more and more demanding. His mother and grandfather tried to keep him entertained and happy by giving him anything he wanted. One day Raven, disguised as the baby, put his arms out as if trying to reach the boxes that stored the light. The adults tried to distract him by giving him other toys to play with, but Raven just threw those things across the room.

Raven cried and cried until his grandfather finally took down the first box. The old chief told the little boy that he could play with the box, but he was not allowed to open it. Raven took the box and played quietly. When no one was looking, he opened the lid and out flew the stars. They ascended high in the sky and are there to this day. The old man scolded his grandson for disobeying, but later when Raven demanded the second box, he took the box down and gave it to the boy.

Again, Raven played quietly with the second box and waited for the right opportunity. When it came, he opened the lid and out flew the moon. Now the grandfather was more than a bit upset. But sometime later, when Raven began crying and demanding to be allowed to play with the third box, his grandfather eventually relented and handed the box to the little boy on the condition that he would never open it.

Raven quickly changed back to his raven form, and with the box in his beak, flew out the smoke hole and into the starlit sky. When he was far away from the chief's house, he opened the lid of the third box and immediately a blazing ball of light appeared in the once dark sky. The light was much too bright for many of the people. They ran away, some to live in the forests on the mountainsides, some to live in caves, and some to live under the water. That is how the different animals came to be.

At times Raven was a transformer who could change himself or others into a variety of animate beings or inanimate objects. Once Raven came to a raspberry bush. When he shook the bush, it turned into a man who became his slave. The man traveled with Raven and was supposed to be his spokesperson when they encountered other people. However, the man didn't always relay Raven's messages correctly and Raven would end up being the one who was tricked. On another occasion, Raven held a great feast and invited all of the animals. While they were dining on fish, Raven let out a shout and all of his guests were changed into stones.

Raven was wily, deceitful, lusty, impulsive, curious, mischievous—an all-around complex individual. It was these "human" attributes that endeared him to the audiences who listened to his exploits.

A story from the Arctic region illustrates Raven's impatient nature.

In the beginning, Loon and Raven were both completely white. One day they decided to tattoo each other. First Raven worked on Loon. When he finished, the colors and designs on Loon looked very attractive. Then it was Loon's turn to tattoo Raven. However, Raven would not sit still. He kept complaining that the procedure hurt, and he would jump and pull away. Loon scolded him and told him to calm down and sit quietly. But Raven continued to squirm. Finally, Loon threatened, "If you don't sit still so I can finish, I'm going to explode." It wasn't long before Raven started fidgeting again and Loon grabbed the oil lamp and hurled the contents at him. As Loon was fleeing the house, Raven picked up the oil lamp and threw it at Loon striking him in the legs. That is why loons have great difficulty walking on land and why ravens are all black.

The trickster dimension of Raven's personality can be compared to tricksters found in other parts of the world. Coyote was an important trickster character in the mythologies of western North America. Other tricksters included Spider, or Iktomi, on the Plains, Hare (also known as Manabozho, Glooskap, and other names) in the Northeast region of America, and Anansi in Africa.

Sometimes Raven's tricks backfired, as in this tale from the Tlingit:

Raven was traveling and happened on a village where the fishermen were catching a lot of halibut. The people invited Raven to stay with them and proved to be very hospitable and generous hosts. It wasn't long, however, until Raven thought up some mischief to do. When the fishermen went out the next day, Raven dove in and swam underwater to where the fishing lines were dangling. At first he just nibbled on the bait, but his greediness got the best of him and he took a big bite. When the fisherman felt the tug on the line, he started hauling in his catch. Raven fought against the line and finally grabbed on to the bottom of the boat. The other fishermen also pulled on the line and at last Raven's nose broke off.

Then Raven swam to shore and transformed himself into an old man. He glued a piece of bark on his face in place of a nose and walked back to the village. The people at the first house invited him in and fed him well. During dinner, the man of the house told how they had caught a nose that day. Raven asked what had become of the nose. So the man told him it was at the chief's house. When Raven arrived there, the chief served him a big meal and shared the story of how the fishermen had caught a nose. Raven asked to see it and then, after examining it closely, declared that it was a bad sign. "If you keep this nose, many people will come to fight you." That frightened the people so much that they pleaded with Raven to take the nose away with him. Thus Raven's beak was restored.

See also Culture Hero(es); Transformation, Human-Animal; Transformer; Trickster

References and further reading:

Boas, Franz. *Indian Myths & Legends from the North Pacific Coast of America: A Translation of Franz Boas' 1895 Edition of "Indianische Sagen von der Nord-Pacifischen Küste Amerikas."* Vancouver: Talonbooks, 2002.

Borgoras, Waldemar. "The Folklore of Northeast Asia, as Compared with That of Northwestern America." *American Anthropologist*, n.s., 4, no. 4 (October–December 1902): 577–683.

Deans, James. "The Raven in the Mythology of Northwest America." *American Antiquarian and Oriental Journal* 10 (1888): 109–114.

Norman, Howard, ed. *Northern Tales: Stories from the Native Peoples of the Arctic and Subarctic Regions.* Selected, edited, and retold by Howard Norman. Pantheon Fairy Tale & Folklore Library. New York: Pantheon Books, 1998. Originally published as *Northern Tales: Traditional Stories of Eskimo and Indian Peoples* (1990).

Reid, Bill. *The Raven Steals the Light: Native American Tales.* Boston: Shambhala, 1996. First published 1984 by University of Washington Press.

Swanton, John R. *Tlingit Myths and Texts.* 1909. Reprint, Brighton, Mich.: Native American Book Publishers, 1990.

ROADRUNNER

Tohono O'Odham, Southwest

According to Cuevas, the Apache today tell a story of the swift roadrunner that teaches a lesson: if one seeks greatness in size, then greatness tends to go unnoticed. The following story of the Tohono O'Odham teaches that same lesson.

One day when the world was new, the people returned from the hunt to find that their fire had died down into gray ashes. They asked Roadrunner to go quickly to the Lightning God, keeper of the fire, and ask him for one of his fire sticks. Roadrunner agreed, and with his strong legs, ran up the mountain to his destination.

The Lightning God asked him what brought him there, and Roadrunner told him. But the Lightning God angrily refused to give Roadrunner a fire stick.

Realizing it was useless to ask a second time, Roadrunner grabbed a stick from the blazing fire, placed it across his back, curled his tail feathers over it, and scurried away. Lightning God started shooting at Roadrunner with flaming arrows. Roadrunner saw an arroyo and scampered into it to escape them. But the beautiful feathers on his head were burnt off, leaving him with just a small of tuft. His eyes were red from the smoke, and his back was singed a brownish color.

But Roadrunner brought the fire stick back to the Indians. When the women saw what was left of his beautiful, long plumage and noted his tired, red eyes, they cried, "Shoik, shoik, shoik." Roadrunner wailed, "Poi, poi, poi."

Roadrunner has lived in the desert ever since. When he finds a fat lizard to eat, he gaily chants "Thra, Thra, Thra!" The people remember what he did for them and are grateful whenever they hear this melodic sound.

References and further reading:

Cuevas, Lou. *Apache Legends: Songs of the Wind Dancer.* Happy Camp, Calif.: Naturegraph, 1991.

McNamee, Gregory, ed. *The Bearskin Quiver: A Collection of Southwestern American Indian Folktales.* Einsiedeln, Switzerland: Daimon Verlag, 2002.

SALMON

Chinook, Heiltsuk (Bella Bella), Pacific Northwest Coast; Skitswish (Coeur d'Alene), Plateau

Salmon was, and is, an important part of the culture and economy in the coastal and plateau regions of the Northwest. Various groups throughout the area, and especially those living near the great rivers, have mythological tales relating to the origin of salmon as well as tales that reflect the people's beliefs and taboos regarding salmon.

A Heiltsuk (Bella Bella) myth story tells about a chief's son who was out shooting with his bow and arrows. Three of his arrows struck a salmon bone lying on the beach. As he gathered up his arrows, he sighed to the bones, "If only you were a real salmon, you could guide me to the Salmon chief's home." Suddenly a bone spoke and told the young man to toss all of the bones into the sea. When he obeyed, the bones became a live salmon. The salmon instructed the young man to climb on his back, and swam away.

The two eventually reached the entrance to the Salmon chief's country, but the hole was guarded by an eagle that would not allow them through. The salmon made several passes trying to get through the hole until finally, the eagle was distracted, and the salmon with the young man on his back was able to get through. Once in that country, the boy was able to see what the Salmon People and their villages were like.

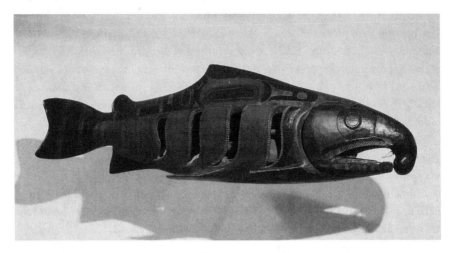

Tlingit salmon rattle. (Werner Forman/Art Resource, NY)

When they approached the village of the Salmon chief, the guide told the young man to hide near where Salmon chief's daughters were bathing. Later the boy grabbed one of the girls and carried her off. He told her that he wanted to marry her, and in time the girl delivered twins. Her father, the chief, was angry and tried to find out who had fathered the babies. At first, Wren spoke up, but the girl denied it was him. Then Thrush claimed to be the father, but again the girl denied it. Finally the young man came in, the chief asked him if he was the father, and he said yes. The girl confirmed his statement, and her father eventually allowed the young people to marry.

After a number of years, the young man was very hungry for salmon. The chief noticed that something was wrong and asked his daughter. "My husband wants to eat salmon," she replied. So the chief instructed the young man to take one of the children who were playing near the river and toss him into the water. When the young man did this, the child turned into a salmon that he took home and cooked for his meal. The young man and his wife were very careful to catch all of the bones and eyes on a mat and then they threw the remains of the salmon back into the water. The bones and eyes immediately turned back into the boy who had been tossed into the river.

Sometime later the young man was very homesick, so the Salmon chief promised to send him home in four days. During that time four large boxes were prepared and the chief sent the young man, his wife, and their children back to his family. When he arrived at his father's village, it seemed to the young man as if he had been away only four days, but actually he had been away four years. They were met on the path by his younger brother, who ran to the village to tell the news of the lost brother's return. The father had thought his older son was dead. So when the younger boy told him about seeing his brother, the father did not believe it. Finally the old chief was persuaded to see for himself.

The people of the village rejoiced to see the young man again and held a dance in his honor. He sent people to the canoe to bring the boxes sent by the Salmon chief, but the boxes were too heavy. Finally the salmon wife carried them to the village and told her father-in-law to have a large house built and to have the people gather. When the boxes were opened they were found to contain never-ending supplies of salmon, berries, meat, and tallow.

Farther to the east, James A. Teit recorded a Skitswish (Coeur d'Alene) tale relating how Coyote brought the salmon.

Coyote heard about four women living on the Columbia River who ate anyone who ventured into their land. A dam near their house prevented salmon from ascending any farther upstream. So Coyote decided to travel there and destroy their dam.

Coyote floated downstream disguised as a board. When he neared the dam, he made himself look like a baby. The four women were fishing near their dam when they saw the baby in the water. Since they didn't have any children or any husbands, the women decided to raise the baby as their own. Coyote lived with them for a time and grew quickly. One day he asked to go to the river to get a drink. While he was there, he began pulling out a small part of the dam.

Each day when he went to the river to drink, he would remove another piece of the dam. On the fourth day, the women became suspicious when Coyote was away longer than usual. When they went down to the river to see what had become of him, Coyote was just pulling down the last of the dam. They tried to attack him, but Coyote jumped onto the far bank as the river rushed through the opening.

Coyote led many salmon past the broken dam and upstream to areas where the people had never seen salmon before.

See also Coyote

References and further reading:

Boas, Franz. *Bella Bella Tales*. 1932. Memoirs of the American Folklore Society, vol. 25. Millwood, N.Y.: Kraus Reprint Co., 1973.

———. *Chinook Texts*. 1894. Temecula, Calif.: Services Corp., 1995.

———. *Folk-Tales of Salishan and Sahaptin Tribes*. 1917. New York: Kraus Reprint, 1969.

Gunther, Erna. "An Analysis of the First Salmon Ceremony." *American Anthropologist*, n.s., 28, no. 4 (October–December 1926): 605–617.

SALT WOMAN

Zuni, Southwest

The Salt Woman or Salt Mother is a very important Zuni deity who lives at the sacred Zuni Salt Lake, located in present-day New Mexico. Since time immemorial, the Zuni, Acoma, Laguna, Hopi, Navajo, Apache, and other Southwestern tribes have followed pilgrimage trails to the lake to collect salt for ceremonial and domestic purposes. This story recounts how the ancestors of the Zuni people took this natural resource for granted and nearly lost an important part of their culture. It also establishes the manner in which the Zuni conduct the pilgrimage and gather the salt.

The priest at Itiwana proclaimed that all the people should go to nearby Black Rock Lake, where the Salt Woman lives, for salt. They liked to go, for they always had a good time. The men took fawn-skin bags to fill with the salt, and the girls dressed up in their finery and brought the food. The girls went two-by-two, as did the boys. Everyone looked for their sweethearts; two boys would invite two girls to eat with them, and the girls would spread out the food.

Salt Woman was waiting for them. She sat and watched them, since this was the first time the boys and girls had come. All were careful and behaved well. At last they started home, the men carrying the fawn-skin bags filled with salt.

They used the salt freely, since it was easy to get it nearby. When the people's supply was gone, the priest made another proclamation, and another trip was made to the salt lake. Later, a third proclamation was made. But this time the people were careless and ill-behaved, and they left the Salt Woman no offerings. When they brought the salt home they wasted it, so they could make another trip soon and enjoy themselves again. The Salt Woman was sad and offended that they wasted her flesh.

Turquoise Man lived near the salt lake. The priest proclaimed that the men should go there to gather turquoise. They found much pretty turquoise and wasted it, treating it as if it were a common thing. Turquoise Man noticed the waste, just as Salt Woman did. Salt Woman and Turquoise Man decided to leave and go far away, so that the people would find it harder to get their flesh and value them more.

That same day at Itiwana, yet another proclamation was made to go and get salt. The people went to the salt lake, but saw very little salt. Salt Woman did not sit and watch them as she had before, but stayed inside her house. The people worked hard to get a few handfuls of salt and got sores on their hands from digging. They said, "We shall come again. There will be more next time." They returned home with their bags only half filled.

Salt Woman and Turquoise man departed as planned, and eventually came to the home of the Tenatsali Youths. They went in and were asked, "What have you come to ask of us?"

"We were living at Black Rock and the people did not value our flesh. We are going farther away, then the people will have a hard time to get us," said Salt Woman and Turquoise Man. The Tenatsali said, "What do you want before you go?"

"Will you give me some meal and some tenatsali sticks? I will take it where I am going and leave it there," said Salt Woman. So they went into the other room and brought out a bunch of tenatsali. Salt Mother said, "I shall take this to my house, and it will be valuable. She thanked them and left.

Salt Woman and Turquoise man traveled until they came to Salt Lake. There Salt Woman turned to Turquoise Man and said, "This is where I wanted to be. I shall stop here. Go to the east and make your home there." So Turquoise Man went east and eventually settled in the white man's country, and that is why they had better turquoise than the Indians could get.

After a few days, the people of Itiwana had no salt. Again the priest made a proclamation for them to get salt. When they came in sight of where the lake had been, they found it had disappeared and only a damp place remained. They were sad and did not have a good time. They were worried about how they would obtain more salt. They went home to their village empty-handed. The priests of the council and the village priest met to talk. "Why did Salt Woman do this?" they asked themselves.

"We were careless with her flesh," they lamented. "The people played nearby when they went after it, and we wasted it as if it were common. She did not like this and has gone away." They chose their best runners to go look for her, and decided that two of the priests should also go to carry a bundle of prayer sticks.

So they made feathers and prayer sticks. The runners carried the food, and the priests carried the prayer sticks, and they journeyed to the east to Black Rock Lake. There they followed Salt Woman's tracks, all the way to Tenatsali Place. Her trail was barren and salty, and she had created landmarks on her journey to show which way she was going, for even though she was angry for being disrespected, she also felt sorry for the people. Here the priests and runners came to the home of the Tenatsali Youths, who instructed the priests in the uses of tenatsali in divining.

The priests and runners went on toward Salt Lake, south and then east. Finally, they saw a great lake before them but were afraid to approach because they had been unkind to Salt Woman. When they got close, the priests went first and the runners hung back. The priests took off their moccasins and waded into the lake. As punishment for the misuse of salt, the salt in the lake cut their feet. They were close to Salt Woman's house, but they could not bear the pain. They ran out of the lake and sat down where they had started. Again they waded into the lake, and again the salt cut their feet. They had almost reached her house, but they ran back because the pain was too much. They came just to the door. Their feet were bleeding. The priests waded into the lake a third time, but the salt cut them so badly they had to run back. So they rubbed their feet with clay. They waded out the fourth time and went into her house. She was glad to see them and asked, "What is it that you have come to ask? Why have you come this long way?"

"My dear daughter, we are looking for you," said the priests. "We have had a hard time finding you."

"Yes," she said, "it was too easy for you to get my flesh. You were careless and spat and eased yourself on me. I do not want these boys and girls to play and step on me. You know better. Did you think young people knew better than you? After this I want the older people to come for my flesh. I want the men to come for my flesh and bring prayer sticks." She instructed the priests to make prayer sticks with duck feathers to show the maker had been initiated into the kachina society.

Then she told them, "You shall take a little salt with you. When you near Zuni, call out for your fathers' sisters to come wash your bodies. They shall give you a present, and you shall give them a little salt in return. If other men wish to come, they may come also for my flesh. Their fathers' sisters shall wash them the first time, but when they come a second time, their aunts shall not wash them. I shall be valuable now that I am far away."

"All right," the priests replied. "We shall do as you say."

They came out with their fawnskin bags full of salt. Just before they left, Salt Woman said, "Do not go around by the way you came. You can go straight to Zuni. There is a road there."

They set out, but they could not find the road. Like the cutting of their feet with the salt, this was punishment for the people's carelessness at Black Rock Salt Lake. It took them four days to make their journey. They ran out of food and killed butterflies to eat. On the fourth day they climbed a mountain and saw Itiwana. To signal their impending arrival, they burned a pile of wood, but it frightened the people. They feared the Navajo were coming.

About noon the priests and runners came in past Sand Hill and called, "We are coming in. When we arrive home our fathers' sisters shall come to wash our bodies before we have anything to eat. They shall bring us a present."

The aunts ran to their nephews' houses to be ready. The men came in, and everyone was watching. Their moccasins were worn out and their hands and faces were covered with clay from Salt Lake. They entered their houses, spread the buckskins, and poured out the salt. They put a perfect ear of corn with it, covered it with a blanket, put beads with it, and scattered prayer meal. They prayed, "Salt Mother, we are glad that you have come to this house, we are glad of your flesh. Increase and come many times again."

Their fathers' sisters broke up soap-weed root and made suds to wash the men's hair. They brought in bowls of grain to give to their nephews and they washed their entire bodies. The head aunts filled up the bowls with salt and all of the fathers' sisters took them home. That is why the salt is still brought in in this fashion.

See also Culture Hero(es)

References and further reading:

Benedict, Ruth. *Zuni Mythology.* 1935. 2 vols. Columbia University Contributions to Anthropology, vol. 21. New York: AMS Press, 1969.

Bunzel, Ruth Leah. *Zuni Ceremonialism.* Albuquerque: University of New Mexico Press, 1992.

Stevenson, Matilda Coxe. *The Zuni Indians: Their Mythology, Esoteric Fraternities, and Ceremonies.* 1905. Landmarks in Anthropology. New York: Johnson Reprint Corp., 1970.

Tedlock, Dennis. "Zuni Religion and World View." In *Handbook of North American Indians.* Vol. 9, *Southwest,* Alfonso Ortiz, ed., 499–508. Washington: Smithsonian Institution Press, 1979.

SAPIYA

Creek, Southeast; Seminole, Oklahoma and Southeast

Magic stones of red, blue, or yellow that are greatly respected and believed to bring their owners great power in matters related to love, war, and the hunt. This might include success in pursuit of a love interest or game, protection from enemies, or strength in battle. According to the lore, *sapiya* are capable of breeding and moving around, at times hopping like fleas. They are controlled with special procedures and songs, and must be attended carefully. If not fed with squirrel blood and given dew to drink, the *sapiya* will give their owner sores. Some choose not to keep any *sapiya* because of their potential to turn on their owners. It is said that *sapiya* sing during the Soup Dance, or Horned Owl Dance, the final event of the Seminole's ceremonial year.

The *sapiya* are kept in a special container with vermilion paint. When the owner is ready to use them, he or she goes into the woods alone, away from others, and builds a small earthen mound. The container is placed intact on top of this mound, and the owner sings the proper songs. Then some of the paint is applied to the outer corner of each eye using a grass stem, and the owner immediately sparkles, causing others to want to be with him or her.

References and further reading:

Howard, James H., in collaboration with Willie Lena. *Oklahoma Seminoles: Medicines, Magic, and Religion.* The Civilization of the American Indian

Series, vol. 166. London; Norman: University of Oklahoma Press, 1990. First
published 1984.

Sturtevant, William C., ed. *Seminole Source Book*. New York: Garland, 1987.

SEASONS, ORIGIN OF

Many Native American cultures have stories that explain the origin of the seasons. In the Tsimshian story of the Four Great Winds, various conflicts and alliances between the North, South, East, and West Winds and their children eventually result in the four of them agreeing that each would have the earth for three months. In a Seneca story, a hunter challenges Hotho, or Winter, to a contest with a claim that Hotho cannot make him freeze no matter how hard he tries. The outcome is that the hunter is successful, and it begins to grow warm and thaw, demonstrating that Winter can be conquered.

The following is a Northern Paiute tale:

Coyote summoned a large crowd to decide how many months there should be in each season. He proposed there be ten spring months, ten summer months, ten autumn months, and ten winter months. He said, "I am strong. I shall be able to get along in the winter." The others present did not say anything in reply, since they did not like Coyote's speech or his plan. Hearing no protests, Coyote decided they should smoke to bind what he thought was an agreement. His pipe and tobacco were at his home, so he left to get them.

As soon as we had gone outside, the others said, "Let us hurry and decide about the moons before he returns."

One bird that lived on the mountains rose and said, "There shall be three spring months, three summer months, three autumn months, and three winter months." The bird and the others felt that Coyote wanted the seasons to be too long.

When Coyote returned, no one was there. He called out, "Where is everybody? Come, we'll speak about it."

In response, he heard, "We have talked about it already and we are all through." Coyote stood for a moment in surprise, and finally went back home in defeat.

In a Zuni story, *Coyote Steals the Sun and Moon*, the origin of winter is explained:

Coyote was a bad hunter who never managed to catch anything. After watching Eagle catch rabbit after rabbit, he suggested they hunt together. "Two can catch more than one," he told Eagle. Eagle accepted Coyote's suggestion without reservation. But Eagle continued to catch many rabbits, and Coyote only caught some bugs.

The world was still dark at this time, because the sun and moon had not yet been placed in the sky. Coyote lamented that the lack of light was the reason he could catch nothing. He asked Eagle if he knew where they could find some light so he could see well. Eagle agreed there should be some light. He suggested they go west, since he thought there might be some there.

After traveling for a while, they came upon a pueblo where kachinas happened to be dancing. They invited Eagle and Coyote to sit and eat while they watched the sacred dances. Eagle told Coyote he thought the powerful Kachinas had light. Coyote noticed two boxes, one large, one small, and pointed them out. The people opened them whenever they wanted light. The larger box, which gave off more light, held the sun. The smaller box, which gave off less light, held the moon. Coyote nudged Eagle and urged him to steal the big box. Eagle suggested they borrow it, but Coyote told him the people would never loan it to them. Eagle agreed and indicated that he was willing to steal the box.

Finally the Kachinas went home to sleep, and Eagle flew off with the large box. Coyote ran along, panting and trying to keep up. He yelled up to Eagle and begged him to let him carry the box a little way. Eagle refused, telling Coyote that he never did anything right. But Coyote ran along and kept trying to convince Eagle to let him carry the box. Eagle continued to refuse. Finally Eagle could stand no more pestering and told Coyote that he could carry the box, but he had to promise not to open it.

"Oh, yes, I promise!" said Coyote. They continued as before, with Eagle flying and Coyote running. Soon Eagle was far ahead, and Coyote was hidden behind a hill where Eagle could not see him. He decided to peek in the box, thinking that there must be something extra that Eagle wanted to keep for himself. Coyote opened the lid and found that Eagle had put the moon in the large box with the sun. The moon escaped and flew high into the sky. Instantly, the plants shriveled and turned brown, and the leaves fell off the trees. It was now winter. Coyote ran after the moon and tried to put it back in the box as it bounced away. Meanwhile, the sun flew out of the box and rose into the sky. It gradually floated far away, causing the peaches, squashes, and melons to shrivel in the cold.

Eagle turned back to see why Coyote lagged behind. "You fool," said Eagle. "Look what you've done!" It began to snow, and Coyote shivered. "It's your fault the cold has come into the world," said Eagle.

Indeed, if it weren't for Coyote's curiosity and mischief-making, winter would not exist, and it would be summer all the time.

See also Coyote

References and further reading:
Barbeau, Marius and William Beynon, collectors. *Tsimshian Narratives.* Vol. 1, *Tricksters, Shamans, and Heroes.* Mercury Series. Ottawa: Directorate, Canadian Museum of Civilization, 1987.

Erdoes, Richard, and Alfonso Ortiz, eds. *American Indian Myths and Legends.* New York: Pantheon Books, 1984.

Lowie, Robert H. "Shoshonean Tales." *Journal of American Folklore* 37, no. 143–144 (January-June 1924): 1–242.

SEDNA

Central Inuit/Baffin Island, Arctic

Also called Sea Woman and Nerrivik, Arnarkusuagsak (or Arnakuagsak), Nuliajoq, or Kannakapfaluk and other names by various Inuit groups. Versions of the following tale differ in details but tend to have similar beginnings and outcomes.

Sedna was a beautiful girl who spurned all of the young men who sought her as their wife. Finally one spring, Sedna was swayed by the songs a handsome young stranger sang about his beautiful home and his friends who would provide all she wanted or needed. She agreed to marry the young man and to go with him to his home far across the sea. However, when they reached his home, she discovered that she had been deceived. Her husband was not a handsome young man after all, but a fulmar (a sea bird) in disguise. His home was not beautiful as he had described, but a drafty tent made of fish skins. Her bed was made of hard walrus hide instead of the soft bearskins he had promised, and his friends, the birds, brought her nothing but fish to eat.

Sedna realized her mistake and sang to her father, Anguta, pleading for him to rescue her. A year later when the sea ice had melted again, the father arrived for a visit. When Sedna told him about her dreadful life with her bird-husband, her father became so angry he killed the fulmar. They quickly left in the father's kayak and paddled toward home. However, when the other fulmars returned and found the body of their friend, they flew over the sea searching for the murderer.

The pursuing birds caused a huge storm to rise, and the boat was in danger of sinking. Fearing for his life, Anguta threw his daughter over the side, but she grabbed onto the edge of the boat. Desperate to save himself, her father chopped off her fingers at the first joints. These fell into the sea and became the whales. Sedna still clung to the boat. So her father cut off her fingers at the second joints and these became the seals. The fulmars saw this and thought Sedna would drown, so they flew away and the storm subsided. Anguta then let Sedna back in the boat, but she deeply hated her father for what he had done. Later, when they had arrived on the shore and her father had gone to sleep, Sedna ordered her dogs to gnaw off Anguta's hands and feet. He awoke and cursed his daughter and her dogs. Suddenly, the earth opened up and Sedna, her father, and the dogs fell down into Adlivun, the realm beneath the earth and sea.

Because the sea mammals came from Sedna's fingers, she controlled them. Sedna allowed them to be hunted or hid them from humans, whom she hated because of her father's cruelty. She demanded respect and the observance of certain cleanliness rituals and of taboos regarding hunting and the treatment of animals. Offenses by humans enraged her, and it was then that she kept the animals from being found by hunters or created storms to hamper hunting parties' success.

In order to pacify Sedna's rages, a shaman's spirit would travel to the underwater realm of Adlivun. The journey itself was a dangerous one requiring the spirit of the shaman to travel to the depths of the sea, get past Sedna's guard dog, and then appease her by smoothing out her tangled hair. He also promised that the people were repentant of their erroneous ways and were committed to obeying her rules for conducting their lives.

A Sedna Ceremony was held each autumn on Baffin Island. During this time, an *angakok* (shaman) entered into a dream-trance during which his spirit would travel to Sedna to ask her to send the animals and good weather for the hunters. Some accounts say that the shaman battled with Sedna in order to win seals for the hunt. There were also ceremonial confessions of wrongs committed against the taboos Sedna enforces and a tug of war between teams comprised of people who were born during the summer and during the winter. This competition determined how much food would be available for the people.

See also Adlivun; Angakok; Dog Husband; Shaman

References and further reading:

Bierhorst, John. *The Mythology of North America: With a New Afterword.* New York: Oxford University Press, 2002. First published 1985 by William Morrow.

Boas, Franz. "The Eskimo of Baffin Land and Hudson Bay, from Notes Collected by Captain George Comer, Captain James S. Mutch, and Rev. E. J. Peck." *Bulletin of the American Museum of Natural History* 15 (1907): 4–570.

Carmody, Denise Lardner, and John Tully Carmody. *Native American Religions: an Introduction.* New York: Paulist Press, 1993.

Hirshfelder, Arlene, and Paulette Molin. *Encyclopedia of Native American Religions: An Introduction.* Updated ed. New York: Facts on File, 2000.

Thompson, Stith. *Tales of the North American Indians.* 1929. Bloomington: Indiana University Press, 1971.

SHAMAN

A shaman is a person who receives—or finds within himself—a supernatural power. The term is not derived from any Native American language but has found its way into the English from either a Sanskrit term for an ascetic or from a Manchu term with a meaning similar to its current anthropological use. A shaman can be either male or, less frequently, female. The scope of a particular shaman's status within his tribe or village is dependent upon the type of supernatural power the shaman possesses and the extent that he, or she, uses that power. Among some groups, a shaman was known to receive a helping spirit who would

A Wintun Native American shaman wearing a kilt, shirt, feather headdress, and collar and holding a split rattle stick. (Denver Public Library, Western History Collection, X31198)

guide the shaman's thoughts, words, and actions for a specific purpose, such as finding a cure for a disease or locating game animals for the hunters.

When an Eskimo shaman received a helping spirit, he would often make an amulet or a mask to represent the spirit. He might also give amulets to patients to aid in their cure, or he might make one for someone who has asked for a blessing or good luck in hunting or in another endeavor. Novices trained for a period of time and learned the shamans' secret language, various songs, techniques such as séances, and about the special relationship between himself and his helping spirit. Séances were held to help determine why the weather was bad, why there was illness, or why the hunting was poor. Shamans were responsible for the good of the community. As part of their duties, they were charged with finding out who had broken a taboo (often thought to be the cause of some illness or misfortune such as an accident or scarce game) and to elicit a confession from the guilty party. Shamans also were the intermediaries between the deities or spirits and the people. In the Sedna ceremony, a Shaman (or his helping spirit) traveled to Sedna's undersea realm and convinced her to release the game so the people would not go hungry. Among the people of the Arctic, shamans were both held in high regard for their help in difficult times and feared because of their connection with the spirit world.

Among the Ojibwa and related groups of the upper Great Lakes region, shamans handed down celestial legends to their apprentices. With this knowledge the shamans were able to predict seasonal changes and regulate various rituals and rites. Thor Conway's essay in *Earth & Sky: Visions of the Cosmos in Native American Folklore* describes the custom of familial transmission of shamanistic knowledge. Ritual items, personal spirit helpers, and the like could be passed on from father to son or from grandfather to grandson. Like the people farther north, the people of the Great Lakes region regarded shamans with both awe and distrust, because shamans were capable of misusing their powers to the detriment of an individual or society as a whole.

In the Pacific Northwest, shamans were also feared because of the supernatural power they possessed but were regarded as a necessary part of society because of their ability to mediate between mankind and the spirit world. Shamans were also able to do battle with the *kushtakas* (Land Otters) to reclaim the spirit of someone in danger of drowning.

Shamans have also been called medicine men (or women), herbalists, and doctors. Their diagnosing and healing powers were frequently sought.

See also Angakok; Land Otters; Sedna; Tcaawunkl

References and further reading:

Beck, Mary G. *Shamans and Kushtakas: North Coast Tales of the Supernatural.* Anchorage: Alaska Northwest Books, 1991.

Lyon, William S. *Encyclopedia of Native American Shamanism: Sacred Ceremonies of North America.* Santa Barbara, Calif: ABC-CLIO, 1998.

Sturtevant, William, gen. ed. *Handbook of North American Indians.* Vol. 5, Arctic. 1984. Washington, DC: Smithsonian Institution.

Williamson, Ray A., and Claire R. Farrer, eds. *Earth & Sky: Visions of the Cosmos in Native American Folklore.* Albuquerque: University of New Mexico Press, 1994. First published 1992.

SKELETON HOUSE

Hopi, Southwest

Many Native American stories refer to death, the dead, and the place where the dead live, such as this one:

In Shongopavi, long ago, a very curious young man would often sit at the edge of the village and stare at the graveyards, wondering what happened to the dead. He was interested in knowing if they really were not dead, if they perhaps continued to live in another place. He asked his father, the village chief, but his father could tell him very little.

The chief asked the other chiefs and his assistants and the village criers if they knew anything that would help his son. The criers told him that Badger Old Man possessed the medicine that would answer his son's questions. They summoned Badger Old Man and told him about the young man. Badger Old Man consented to use his medicine to show him about the dead.

Badger Old Man selected the appropriate medicine and took it to the village chief. He instructed him to put a white kilt on his son and blacken his chin with black shale. He told him to also tie a small eagle feather to his forehead, since these were the very preparations used for the dead.

The next morning, they dressed the chief's son this very way, and Badger Old Man told him to lie down on a white robe he had spread on the floor. He gave the young man some medicine to eat, and also placed it in his ears and on his heart. He then wrapped him in a robe, and the young man appeared to die, but he only fell asleep. This was the medicine that would help the man find out what he wanted to know.

As he slept, the young man saw a path leading westward, which was the road to the skeleton house. He followed it and came upon a woman sitting by the roadside. She asked him what he had come for, and he told her he wished to find out about her life in that place. The woman explained that she was forced to wait there, because she had not listened and followed the straight road. After a certain number of days had passed, she could proceed a little, and then go on, but it would be a long time before she reached the skeleton house.

The young man continued to follow the path westward and finally arrived at the rim of a steep bluff, where a buffalo chief was sitting. He asked the young man why he had come, and the young man told him. The buffalo chief pointed him in the direction of the house, but a great deal of smoke hid it from the young man's view. Then, the buffalo chief spread the young man's kilt on the ground, placed him on it, and lifted it up. He held it over the edge of the cliff, and the young man was carried down slowly like a giant bird.

Upon arriving on the ground, he put on his kilt again and proceeded. He came upon Skeleton Woman and asked what the column of smoke was that he saw rising in the distance. Skeleton Woman explained that some people who were wicked while they lived had been thrown there. She told him the bad chiefs send people down the road, and then they are destroyed. She warned him not to go there, to keep on the road and go straight toward the Skeleton House.

At last, he arrived at the Skeleton House, where he saw only a few children playing. By the time he had gone into the village, all the skeletons living there had heard about him, and gathered to stare. The young man explained that he came from Shongopavi, and that he was the chief's son. The skeletons pointed toward the Bear clan and told him that they were the people he should see, because they were his ancestors.

A skeleton took him to the house where his clan lived and showed him a ladder that led up to the house. It was made of sunflower stems, which broke when he stepped on the first rung. So, the skeletons brought some food to him. The skeletons laughed at the man when he ate. They were lighter than air because they never eat the food, only its odor. That is the reason why clouds into which the dead are transformed are not heavy and can float in the air. The food itself the skeletons threw out behind the house, and this is where they had found his meal.

The young man explained to the skeletons why he had come, and that Badger Old Man had given him the medicine that took him there. The skeletons told the young man all about where they lived, how it lacked light, and how they lived poorly. They told him to work for them after his return home, to make ritual food and scarves they could tie around their heads to represent dropping rain. In return, they promised to send rain and crops.

As he looked around, the young man noticed some of the skeletons walking around with huge burdens of millstones and bundles of cactus on their backs. He was told that some of them had to submit to such punishments for a time before they could go live with the others. At another place in the Skeleton House, he saw the chiefs who had been good when they lived, and they had built a good road for others. They had set up their protective medicine bundles there, and when people in the villages conduct their ceremonies, and smoke, the smoke makes its way down to this world to the bundles or to the mothers, and rises up from there in the form of clouds.

After the young man had seen everything, he started home for his village. When he had just about arrived, his body, which was still lying where he had fallen asleep, began to stir, and he awoke. He was uncovered and washed, and the feather charm removed from him. He was given food, and he recounted his experiences in detail to his mother and father and Badger Old Man. Then he told them about the prayer offerings he was asked to make and explained what the skeletons would do in return. They agreed it would be good to do as he had been asked.

From that time on, the living and the dead worked to benefit each other.

References and further reading:

McNamee, Gregory, ed. *The Bearskin Quiver: A Collection of Southwestern American Indian Folktales.* Einsiedeln, Switzerland: Daimon Verlag, 2002.

SKINKUTS

Kootenai, Plateau

This tale explains why coyotes have long, thin legs.

Long ago Old-Man had only animal persons as companions. One day he was walking and felt lonely. He wished he had some Person to talk with. Then he saw Skinkuts, the Coyote, walking up the path and asked him to join in on his travels. Skinkuts asked, "Where are you going?" to which Old-Man replied, "Everywhere!"

So Skinkuts agreed. He didn't mind traveling with his companion, but the Old-Man talked on and on. Skinkuts listened, but after a while wasn't paying much attention to what Old-Man was saying. They walked a long time and were deep in the forest when Old-Man cautioned the coyote about a nearby danger. "When you hear crying up ahead coming from behind a pine tree, don't pay any attention," Old-Man said, "just keep on walking. It is Bad-Person just trying to cause trouble."

Now Skinkuts couldn't help but listen for the sound that he was supposed to ignore. They climbed higher up the mountain side, and Old-Man just kept on talking and talking. He was talking about the pine trees and that made Skinkuts think of the crying he had been warned about. Soon Old-Man sat down for a rest. Skinkuts thought he heard a crying noise coming from the trees, but Old-Man did not appear to have heard anything.

It sounded like a baby, but Skinkuts could not tell what sort of baby Person it was. Old-Man got up and continued walking up the trail. Skinkuts could not believe that Old-Man had not heard the cries. "He must be hard-hearted," thought Skinkuts. The crying continued until finally, the coyote could no longer stand it. "I'm not afraid of babies!" he assured himself.

When Skinkuts looked behind the tree, there wasn't any Person there. He walked around the tree, but didn't see anyone. Just when he was ready give up and follow Old-Man, he saw a Baby tied up in the tree. Coyote tried to calm the Baby as he took it down. The Baby, however, kept on crying. Finally, the coyote stuck his fingers into the Baby's mouth to quiet it. The Baby quit crying and started sucking on Skinkuts's fingers. It sucked until Skinkuts's hand, and then his whole arm up to the shoulder, disappeared.

When Skinkuts remembered Old-Man's warning, it was too late. Old-Man had ignored the crying and kept walking. By now he was too far up the trail to help. So Skinkuts gave a shout to the Echo-Person and eventually Old-Man heard his call. Old-Man wasn't happy about having to turn back, and it was nighttime by the time he reached the place where Skinkuts and the Baby were. He scolded Skinkuts for not heeding his warning and then clubbed the Bad-person to death.

It took a long time, but Old-Man was finally able to pull Skinkuts's arm out of the Bad-person's mouth. It came out all long and skinny. Old-Man thought it served Coyote right for not listening to him and said that from then on Coyote and all of his children would have long, skinny arms and legs.

See also Coyote; Old Man; Why Stories
References and further reading:
Gill, Sam D., and Irene F. Sullivan. *Dictionary of Native American Mythology.* Santa Barbara, Calif.: ABC-CLIO, 1992.

Linderman, Frank B. *Kootenai Why Stories.* Authorized ed. Lincoln: University of Nebraska Press, 1997. First published 1926 by Scribner's.

SPIDER
Teton (Lakota), Dakota (Sioux), Plains

Numerous myths have been recorded about Iktomi, an ancient trickster who is also called "Spider." As with other tricksters, Iktomi (also known as Iktome, Unktomi, or Ictinicke) was bent on deceiving others for his own gain but often was the one who suffered the consequences of his schemes. Tales about Iktomi frequently begin with introductions similar to Coyote stories: "He was traveling."

Iktomi's scalp was itching because he had lice. Then he saw two girls tanning a hide. So he went over and lay down next to where they were sitting. With his head in one girl's lap, he asked them to pick out the lice. As they combed his long hair, Iktomi fell asleep. The girls stopped what they were doing and filled his hair with burrs. When Iktomi awoke the girls were gone. When he sat up his hair pulled away from his face from the weight of the burrs. He tried in vain to remove the burrs and in the end had to cut off all of his hair. What a funny sight he was and the whole village laughed at him.

Iktomi went on and soon came to a burial ground. "Oh, this dead person smells very bad!" Iktomi exclaimed. The dead man's ghost heard Iktomi's complaint and grabbed him, demanding to know what he had just said. "I said, 'It smells wonderful here, like wildflowers and grass,'" Iktomi replied. That seemed to appease the ghost and he released Iktomi. But Iktomi had had quite a fright and quickly ran away.

Soon Iktomi saw an old man. He was a medicine man and he began to sing. When he had finished singing four songs, a buffalo rolled off the cliff above and fell dead at his feet. The old medicine man explained that his buffalo song was very powerful and kept him well fed. Iktomi pleaded with the old man to teach him the buffalo songs. At first the old man refused, because Iktomi appeared to be a foolish fellow and didn't merit such a wonderful song. But, Iktomi pleaded with the old man, saying that he only needed the song to help out the hungry people in his village. So, the old man taught him the song. Later, when he had traveled far enough away from the old man, Iktomi decided to give the song a try. It worked! A buffalo rolled down a cliff and fell dead at his feet. But Iktomi wasn't hungry; he had just wanted to see if the song worked for him, too. So, he left the dead buffalo there and traveled on. Iktomi sang the powerful song two more times. The result was just as it had been the first time. But when he sang it a fourth time, he was nearly crushed to death when the buffalo landed on top

Spider Rock in Canyon de Chelly, Arizona, home of the Navajo deity Na'ashje'ii Asdzau (Spider Woman). (North Wind Picture Archives)

of him! If it weren't for the coyotes that came to eat the buffalo, that would have been the end of Iktomi.

Another time Iktomi was traveling north. After a few days he became very hungry. Soon he found a stream with numerous ducks floating in it. He devised a plan that would get him the most ducks with the least amount of effort. First he packed his bag full of grass, and then walked along the edge of the stream. The curious little ducks asked what was in his bag. "Oh, it's full of songs I'm taking to a big dance. I'm the featured singer, so I must be on my way," Iktomi said. The ducks begged him to stay and let them hear some of the songs. Appearing very annoyed, Iktomi finally relented. He told the ducks that the songs were very special and they had to do exactly what the songs told them to do. The first song, he said, was the "shut-eye" song. Everyone who heard it was required to close their eyes tightly as they danced in the grass. The ducks obeyed and danced around with their eyes shut. As Iktomi sang the "shut-eye" song, he struck each duck as it came near him. However, one duck was a bit suspicious and opened his eyes. He let out a loud quack and warned the others what that trickster Iktomi was doing. The ones who survived quickly flew away.

Iktomi found a spot to cook the ducks near a grove of trees. When there was a thick bed of coals, he covered the ducks with them and prepared to take a nap while they roasted. However, about the time he was drifting off to sleep, branches from two trees began beating against each other in the wind. Finally, Iktomi could not take it any longer and climbed up one of the trees so he could separate the clashing branches. Just as he was doing that, the wind subsided and the branches came to rest with Iktomi's arm stuck in between them. He struggled in vain to get free. It wasn't long before he could smell the wonderful aroma of his roasting ducks.

As Iktomi gazed around from up in the tree, he saw a hungry-looking fox wandering near the edge of the woods. The fox seemed to have picked up the scent of Iktomi's ducks but then lost it and began moving farther away. Iktomi couldn't help himself and yelled at the fox, "You get away from here! I'm cooking my ducks in the embers and I'm not going to share any with you!" At that the fox turned around and headed straight to the fire pit. When the ashes cooled off, the fox dug out one of the ducks and began eating. Iktomi screamed at the fox to go away, but the fox continued his meal. The fox invited Iktomi to stop hanging out in the tree and join him on the ground. When he was finished eating the first duck, the fox started on another, and then another. Finally he decided he'd better leave just a few ducks for Iktomi since he had been so generous to share his meal. The fox thought about it for a while, but then remembering just how tasty the ducks were, decided to have just one more. However, when he reached into the ashes, he found that the ducks were all gone.

The fox was tired so he stretched out near the cooking pit and took a nap. Before continuing on his way, the fox thanked Iktomi for being so gracious and asked that he be invited the next time Iktomi decided to cook more ducks. After the fox departed, a gust of wind came up and separated the branches that had held Iktomi captive. Back on the ground, Iktomi stormed around his campsite. He was furious because all that was left of his supper were cold ashes and a big pile of duck bones.

Another day Iktomi was hungry and went looking for food. He came to a river, but it was too deep for him to cross. So he began to cry. Sometime later a bull buffalo came along and asked Iktomi why he was crying. Iktomi explained that he wanted to cross the river but couldn't. The bull was going across anyway, so he offered to let Iktomi ride on his back. "Your back is much too broad for me to hold on to," Iktomi exclaimed, "I'd surely slip off." So the bull then offered to let Iktomi hold onto his tail as they crossed. But, this time Iktomi declined by saying, "If you'd flick your tail, I'd go flying into the water." Next the bull offered to let Iktomi ride on top of his head and hang onto his horns. Iktomi said that would not work either. "If you bent your head down to get a drink, I'd fall into the river." The buffalo was out of ideas and asked Iktomi if he had any. Iktomi then explained what he thought would work best. "You could swallow me and then I'd be able to cross safely. When you get to the other bank, just cough me up." That sounded reasonable to the buffalo. But when he got on the other side, he forgot about Iktomi and found a nice place under a tree to take a nap. Iktomi tried to get the bull's attention, but he was sound asleep.

Finally in desperation, Iktomi took his knife and cut his way out through the bull's side. Iktomi left the dead buffalo there and again went on his way.

Sometime later he saw some mice playing an interesting game. They were tossing their eyes into the air. The one who could toss theirs the highest would win. Iktomi asked to join them. When he tossed his eyes up, they landed high in a tree. The mice ran away, fearing Iktomi would blame them for being blind. Now Iktomi had to feel his way around. He could no longer cry, so he just made pathetic moaning sounds.

One day someone nearby said to him, "Why are you crying like that?" Iktomi explained about losing his eyes. He didn't know he was talking with the Spirit-Chief, but when the person told him to take his walking stick and make a circle on the ground, Iktomi obeyed.

"Now," the Spirit-Chief said, "we will stay inside the ring, and you will try to catch me. If you do, your eyes will be returned to you." So Iktomi tried to catch the Spirit-Chief, but he couldn't. For three days they ran around inside the ring. Finally on the fourth day, Iktomi grabbed hold of the Spirit-Chief and his eyes were restored immediately. Iktomi was grateful to have his eyes back.

Again Iktomi was traveling and came to a river he couldn't cross. He saw a large buzzard circling overhead and asked the bird to help him get to the other side. The buzzard obliged. At first Iktomi was afraid of the heights, but soon he began to enjoy soaring above the trees. He noticed a village nearby and asked the buzzard to fly over the people. When the people on the ground saw Iktomi flying overhead on the back of the buzzard, they were amazed. Iktomi was feeling a bit too sure of himself and made a fist at the buzzard's head. However, the buzzard saw the shadow of Iktomi's fist and quickly deposited him in the top of a hollow tree trunk. Iktomi was stuck in there and could only cry. Finally, he heard some women walking nearby. He began singing out, "I'm a fat raccoon. Whoever finds me will have plenty of grease." So the women began chopping down the tree. When it toppled over, Iktomi crawled out. He thanked them and went on his way once again.

See also Ani Hyuntikwalaski; Trickster; Wind

References and further reading:

Beckwith, Martha Warren. "Mythology of the Oglala Dakota." *Journal of American Folklore* 43, no. 170 (October–December 1930): 339–442.

Deloria, Ella C., comp. *Dakota Texts.* 1932. Reprint, Freeman: University of South Dakota Press, 1992.

Erdoes, Richard, ed. *The Sound of Flutes and Other Indian Legends.* Transcribed and edited by Richard Erdoes. New York: Pantheon Books, 1976.

LaPointe, James. *Legends of the Lakota.* San Francisco: Indian Historian Press, 1976.

Melody, Michael Edward. "Maka's Story: a Study of a Lakota Cosmogony." *Journal of American Folklore* 90, no. 356 (April–June 1977): 149–167.

Wallis, Wilson D. "Beliefs and Tales of the Canadian Dakota." *Journal of American Folklore* 36, no. 139 (January–March 1923): 36–101.

SPIDER WOMAN

Pawnee, Plains

In various tales from around North America, Spider Woman was frequently seen as a kindly being who helped or gave advice to people in need. However, in the following story from the Pawnee, she was a cannibal who met her end by the quick wits of two young boys.

Long ago Spider Woman and her daughters lived off by themselves and tended a garden. People would travel there to get corn, bean, and squash seeds from the woman, but she would tell them that first they had to play a dice game with her. In this game the people would jump up and down just as dice do when tossed in a basket. While the people were jumping up, Spider Woman would send storms and the people would freeze to death. Then she hung the skulls of her victims from the walls of her lodge.

Finally the people decided that something had to be done about the Spider Woman. There were two young boys in their village who seemed to possess great powers. The people asked these boys to visit Spider Woman. The boys traveled several days until they came to a cornfield with a grass lodge nearby. Skulls were hanging from the walls of the lodge. They spoke with a girl outside the lodge who warned them to go away quickly. If her mother saw them, she would make them eat poisoned human flesh. The boys told her that they would leave for a short time and then return.

When they were on the far side of the cornfield, the boys ate a piece of root from their medicine bag and then returned to Spider Woman's lodge. This time she saw them draw near and called to them to come into her lodge. She suspected that they had come for her daughters and decided to kill them like all the others who had approached her lodge. "You must be hungry," she said to them. The boys replied that they were, indeed, very hungry from their long journey.

Spider Woman set bowls of food in front of them containing human brains cooked into a mush. Behind her they could see the daughter shake her head, warning them not to eat, but they did anyway. When they were finished the boys excused themselves to go outdoors for awhile. Spider Woman feared they would go away, but the boys promised her they would be right back. When they had walked far enough away and were out of sight from the lodge, the boys vomited the poisoned brains and then returned to the lodge. Spider Woman thought it was strange that they appeared normal, so she gave them bowls of what appeared to be black corn, but were really human eyes. Before they began eating what she had prepared, they each took a bit of the medicine root from their bag. Again, when they had emptied the bowls, they went outside and vomited all they had eaten.

Spider Woman decided that she couldn't kill them with poison, so she asked them to stay until the next morning and play a dice game with her. In the morning she gave them what looked like squash but was actually human ears. The boys used their medicine again, and when they came back to the lodge, Spider Woman told them that it was time to play the dice game. The boys once again walked out of sight of the lodge, but when they came back they were covered with white clay and had black streaks painted below their eyes. They sat down and Spider Woman began to sing and call for a windstorm to come. That didn't kill the boys, so she sang for a snowstorm to come. But, the boys turned into snowbirds, and when the sun returned, they turned into larks.

Finally the woman decided she could not harm the boys so she told them to go back to her lodge with her and they could have her daughters. But the oldest boy said, "No, let me sing and you can dance." First he called the blizzard, but Spider Woman had power over snowstorms, so it didn't harm her. Then he called for boiling heat. She begged for him to stop, but he kept singing. Then she felt herself being raised off the ground as the boy sang for a swarm of grasshoppers to come. The grasshoppers flew all around her and lifted her up into the sky. The boy kept singing the grasshopper song as the woman was taken up to the moon where the grasshoppers left her. Then the grasshoppers flew on to the sun, and that is why on hot summer days we see grasshoppers swarming around in the sky. Today we can still see something on the moon. It is Spider Woman's dress.

References and further reading:

Dorsey, George A. *The Pawnee Mythology.* 1906. Sources of American Indian Oral Literature. Lincoln: University of Nebraska Press, 1997.

———. "Wichita Tales I, Origin." *Journal of American Folklore* 15, no. 59 (October-December 1902): 215–239.

Erdoes, Richard, and Alfonso Ortiz, eds. *American Indian Myths and Legends.* New York: Pantheon Books, 1984.

Hazen-Hammond, Susan. *Spider Woman's Web: Traditional Native American Tales about Women's Power.* New York: Berkley, 1999.

STARS AND CONSTELLATIONS

Keenly aware of the sky above them, Native American storytellers wove many tales about the origin of stars and constellations. Coyote is sometimes credited with creating constellations, as are the Navajo Black God and the culture hero Glooskap. Sometimes a culture hero becomes a star. The Juaneño people of

California believed the deceased turned into stars. Stars played, and continue to play, important roles in ritual as well as mythology, particularly among the Pawnee. Among the Navajo, a trained practitioner employs the skill of star gazing to diagnose an illness that cannot be determined by visible symptoms, and prescribes ceremonial treatment to cure the patient.

Native American storytellers often wondered why a star appeared to be missing from an incomplete circle in the sky called the Northern Crown. An explanation is offered by many versions of a favorite tale; the following was told by the Ojibwas:

Long ago, a young hunter was returning to his village. He paused in a clearing when he came upon a strange, circular path. He could find no path leading to the circle or away from it. He crouched down in the shadows of a birch grove to wait and watch and see what might have made this circle. After night had fallen, the hunter heard music and noticed a cluster of stars in the sky, traveling toward him. He caught his breath as the cluster alighted in the clearing.

The hunter saw twelve beautiful maidens climb out of a basket and begin to dance around the circle. He decided they must come there often, as they seemed to be very familiar and comfortable with their surroundings. The hunter stepped out of the shadows and approached the maidens. At once, the music and dancing stopped, and they flew to their basket. It rose into the night and went back from where it came.

The hunter returned to the clearing the following evening, determined to discover whom or what he had seen. Events unfolded as they had before, though this time he did not allow himself to be seen so soon. Again, the maidens ran to their basket and disappeared. The hunter noticed that one of the maidens was more beautiful and graceful than the others. He decided he wanted to know her, so he decided to come to the circle again.

On the third night, the hunter changed himself into a mouse and hid in the grass. As he watched quietly, the basket came down from the sky as before. Each dance the maidens performed flowed into the other, and they remained in the clearing until the stars had traveled from one horizon to the other.

The hunter inched his way forward as he watched the maidens. His heart pounded for the one maiden, who was the youngest, as he crept toward her feet. Again, the music suddenly ended, and the maidens ran to their basket. As he sprang forward, the hunter became himself again and grasped the maid. The others cried out for their youngest sister, but she was held fast by the hunter's arms, and the basket vanished back into the sky.

In time, the hunter won the star maiden's heart, and they became husband and wife. Eventually they had a son, and the star woman was happy.

The star maiden came from the land of the star people, however, and she could not live on earth forever. One night, while her husband and son slept, her eleven sisters came down in their basket again and brought her back to the sky. The star people were glad their dancing circle of sisters was complete again, but they noticed the younger sister never smiled anymore, and she wept for the family she had left behind.

The star people finally took pity on the youngest star sister. One night, they brought the hunter and their son to the sky for a visit, but only for that night. The father of the star people warned that they were earth people who must return to their home or they would die. So the hunter and his wife and child made the most of their brief time together.

The star people were moved as they watched the family. Because they wished to help them, the father of the star people changed all three into white falcons. Now they are neither earth people nor sky people and are free to visit both whenever they desire. The remaining star maiden sisters of the Northern Crown still dance together, but it is said that they will never leave the sky again.

The Milky Way, the broad band of billions of stars that arches across the night sky, is featured in many Native American stories. Some tribes believed that it was the path of migrating birds; some believed it was the road taken by the dead. Others thought it was formed when Coyote sprayed stars across the sky. In a story of the Snohomish, whalers and fishermen of the Northwest Coast, the Milky Way is a river, the site of a conflict between earth and sky people.

There was once a time when the entire world was dark and cold, and a man lived who made the strongest and tightest of canoes. He enjoyed making them so much, he would start his work every day at dawn, while the stars could still be seen in the sky, and he would continue late into the night, hammering, pounding, rubbing, and scraping to make the finest and most seaworthy of vessels.

The great chief of the sky was enraged by the endless noise he made, and sent four of his men to capture Canoemaker and restore silence.

When Canoemaker's people discovered he was missing, they searched everywhere for him, as he was the only one across the land who made canoes of such quality. They finally found an old man at the far end of the village who spent much of his waking hours watching the world outside of his window. It was he who told them of Canoemaker's capture, and the villagers were very upset by this news. While they wailed and complained and cried, the old man told them that when he was a child, he used to hear storytellers say that the sky could be reached by making a chain of arrows.

The desperate and unhappy villages raised their bows and shot arrows into the air, but not one rose high enough to stay there. Robin came forward to help them. He took one arrow and flew it high up into the sky, and Canoemaker's people were able to add theirs until an entire chain of them hung down into the village. The villagers quietly climbed into the heavens, so the great sky chief would not hear them.

When the last of the villagers had reached the sky, Robin decided to snoop around. He discovered the village of the sky people along the Great White River. He then discovered the Canoemaker tied to the roof of a house. He assured him that help was on its way and quickly left to alert his people.

By this time, Robin was growing cold, but he wanted to continue snooping. As he went about, he began to feel something warm and decided to investigate. Along the Great White River, he encountered a group of the sky people huddled around a fire. As the lower world still had no fire, Robin did not know what this strange glowing thing was. But he enjoyed the warmth and decided the village should have some of it. Robin tried to ease his way toward the fire, so he could take some back to earth. But each time he drew near, the sky people pushed him back, which made Robin angry. He found Beaver and they conceived a plan.

Beaver floated down the river to where the sky people were gathered around the fire. Some of the children saw him and began to tease and chase him. Beaver played along with their game, all the while inching closer to the fire. Just as Beaver drew right up to the fire, the people of Canoemaker's village arrived to rescue their friend. The angry sky people charged after them. In the confusion, Beaver saw his chance and approached the fire, snatched a flaming stick, and fled to a hole in the sky. In the meantime, Robin led Canoemaker's people to the rooftop where he was captive and untied him. All ran along the shore of the Great White River to a hole in the sky. The chief of the sky people followed, but all escaped safely down the chain of arrows.

Afterward, as the village people enjoyed the warmth of Beaver's fire, Canoemaker thanked them for his rescue. He gave them his solemn promise that he would never anger the great chief of the sky people again. This is why Canoemaker and his people no longer build their canoes early in the morning or late at night.

See also Deer Hunter and White Corn Maiden; Great Bear Constellation; Raccoon; Tirawa

References and further reading:

Clifton, James. *Star Woman and Other Shawnee Tales*. Lanham, Md.: University Press of America, 1984.

Grinnell, George Bird. "A Pawnee Star Myth." *Journal of American Folklore* 7, no. 26 (July–September 1894): 197–200.

Hagar, Stansbury. "The Celestial Bear." *Journal of American Folklore* 13, no. 49 (April–June 1900): 92–103.

Haile, Berard. *Starlore Among the Navaho*. 1947. Santa Fe, N. Mex.: William Gannon, 1977.

Mayo, Gretchen Will. *Star Tales: North American Indian Stories about the Stars.* New York: Walker, 1987.

Miller, Dorcas S. *Stars of the First People: Native American Star Myths and Constellations.* Boulder, Colo.: Pruett, 1997.

Thompson, Stith. *Tales of the North American Indians.* 1929. Bloomington: Indiana University Press, 1971.

STRONG MAN WHO HOLDS UP THE EARTH

Tsimshian, Northwest Coast

This myth relates the story of the man who supports the earth and causes earthquakes. In some versions of this tale, he was called Am'ala, meaning "smoke hole," or Dirty.

At one time there was a chief who had four nephews. The oldest three worked hard for their uncle, but the youngest nephew slept all day and didn't do any work. His brothers ridiculed the boy because he was lazy and slept in the ashes near the fire. He didn't go to the beach to bathe in the morning as they did, nor did the brothers ever see him leave the house to relieve himself. They called him Dirty.

The chief's three older nephews prepared themselves for the upcoming sea lion hunt. Because it was a dangerous undertaking, only the strongest men were allowed on the hunt. So the three brothers bathed every morning in the cold sea water. Then the chief whipped them with branches, rubbed their muscles with a concoction of boiled roots, and gave them cups full of devil's-club tea to drink. The chief had his nephews train to improve their strength by pulling branches off of trees. The brothers also continued to deride the youngest one because he was so dirty and lazy.

However, the lazy brother would go out at night to bathe in the sea and to follow the training regime that his brothers did during the day. He would return to his bed in the ashes before anyone else in the house was awake. That way he kept his increasing strength a secret. The rest of his household were ashamed of him and mocked him continuously, except for a younger uncle and his wife. They felt pity for him and would give him food when no one else was around, but they did not know about his nightly baths and training.

One night when Dirty was at the beach, a loon swam near and spoke to him. The loon told him to grab his feet so they could dive under the water to a cavern where there was a special spring. The young man was instructed to bathe in the spring water in order to receive great strength. After he bathed, Dirty returned to his sleeping space in the house. As his nightly training continued, the loon said to the young man, "Go to a large spruce tree and after you tear its branches off, you must bend the tree until its top reaches the ground." The young man did as instructed and then went back to the ashes to rest.

When it came time for the sea lion hunt, the three older brothers jeered at Dirty and called him names. Then they told him that he should at least help the slaves carry the sea lion meat from the canoes to the house when they returned. The brothers set off for the hunt, each in the canoe of one of their uncles. But the youngest uncle did not have anyone to go with him. Then Dirty announced that he would go along on the hunt. The men all laughed and accused him of being lazy and said that he would only be a hindrance to them. However, his youngest uncle said, "Come with me. You can at least just sit in the canoe."

So the four canoes set out on the hunt and headed to the island of the sea lions. It was always stormy there with huge waves crashing on the rocky shore. There was a danger that if a man missed the jump from the canoe to the rocks, he would drown in the sea. If he did make it to shore, he might be attacked by the sea lions. And so it happened that the first two uncles and everyone in their canoes perished while trying to land on the island. Then Dirty said he would jump onto the rocks. The men in the other canoe, however, wanted to turn back home since the expedition was a failure. But Dirty, the youngest nephew, was insistent. His uncle paddled the canoe to near the rocks and at the crest of the next wave, the young man jumped to the rocks. A great sea lion charged him, but Dirty grabbed the sea lion and broke its back. He killed more sea lions until the others fled into the sea.

Each time the canoe rose on the crest of a wave, the young man stood on the rock and placed one of the dead sea lions in it until the canoe was full. Then they returned to the village and the other hunters who had ridiculed him and returned with empty canoes were ashamed. The next day, he said to his younger uncle, "Let's go back for more sea lion meat." They continued to do this every day until the uncle's house was full of meat. The uncle became a very wealthy man because everyone had to come to him for their food.

Then the neighboring tribes gathered for strong-man competitions. Many of the men had been in training for a long time. But Dirty didn't participate in their training. He continued to sleep in the ashes but secretly went out at night to bathe and train. By now he was no longer just bending trees over but was pulling whole trees out of the ground and carrying them to the beach, where he threw them into the water.

The first competition was stone throwing. Each man took turns throwing a large rock as far as he could. A giant of a man from another tribe threw the rock the farthest. He called for the champions of the other tribes to try to do better than his throw, but no one could. Then Dirty went down to the contest field. His fellow villagers called to him to go back and not embarrass them any more, but he didn't pay any attention to them. When he saw the rock that the contestants were throwing, he asked why they were using such a small stone. He found a much larger boulder and effortlessly tossed it farther than the distance anyone else had reached. The people were all amazed, but the young man went back to his uncle's house and sat in the ashes.

Then the wrestling competitions started. A huge man from another tribe was winning every match. No one could defeat him. Finally he challenged the people to send their strongest man out to meet him. No one dared to try. Then the young man whom everyone called Dirty went to the beach to wrestle this giant. The people from his village cried out, "No, don't let him! He'll be an embarrassment to us." When the wrestling began, the young man grabbed the giant and threw him high in the air. When he fell back to the ground his bones were all broken. No other wrestlers came forward to challenge him, so Dirty went back home.

The last contest was for overall strength. The winner would be the one who could uproot the largest tree and toss it onto the beach. Several men attempted to do this, but all failed. Finally a man from one of the other tribes was successful, and no one else could match what he had done. Then that man and people from his tribe called out for Dirty to try to do better, since he had won the first two contests. When Dirty arrived at that place, he asked why they had used such a small sapling. He then proceeded to shake a large tree. He pulled out the branches and then lifted the tree and its roots completely out of the ground. Then he carried it down to the beach.

Everyone was amazed and word about him spread far and wide. Finally the animals, the mountain lion, the grizzly bear, and the wolf, came to challenge him. But the young man was able to conquer them all. Then the forests and finally the mountains themselves pushed down against the village, but the young man drove them back.

Life for the young man and his people went back to normal. But one night a canoe pulled up to the beach near his house and a stranger went in and woke him. The stranger told the young man that his grandfather had sent for him and he must go back with them. Quietly the young man left the house and went with the stranger. The others in the canoe eventually removed their human appearances and took the form of loons. Only his guide kept his human form. When they reached an island, the guide told the young man that his grandfather was very old and weak and needed him to replace him. So they followed a path through the island. They came to a place where the stranger pulled back a covering over a hole in the ground. The young man was led down a long ladder until they arrived at a platform. There sat a very old man who was holding a huge pole. The old man had been holding up the earth since it was formed and was now ready to rest. "That's why you were trained to become so strong. I needed you to be able to take over my job." He continued instructing the young man, telling him that the loons would be his messengers and would constantly oil his joints so he would not become stiff. He also warned the young man to keep very still, because each time he shifted position he would cause earthquakes, and if he would happen to collapse, the world would come to an end. And so the young man took his place as the one who held up the earth.

When the people in his house woke up and found him missing, they thought he had been kidnapped. But the younger uncle said, "No, he is super-natural. Nothing can harm him. He must be away doing something good." The people looked for him, but never found where he had gone.

References and further reading:

Barbeau, Marius and William Beynon, collectors. *Tsimshian Narratives.* Vol. 1, *Tricksters, Shamans, and Heroes.* Mercury Series. Ottawa: Directorate, Canadian Museum of Civilization, 1987.

Boas, Franz. *Tsimshian Mythology.* 1916. Landmarks in Anthropology. Reprint, New York: Johnson Reprint Corp., 1970.

Feldmann, Susan, ed. *The Storytelling Stone: Traditional Native American Myths and Tales.* New York: Laurel, 1991. First published 1965 by Dell.

SWEET MEDICINE
Cheyenne, Plains

Details of Sweet Medicine's birth and parentage vary somewhat in versions of this myth. In one he was an orphan who was being raised by an old woman. Another version tells that he was born to a virgin girl who left him near a stream, hoping someone would find and care for him. Here, too, he was raised by an old woman whom he called Grandmother.

Sweet Medicine grew quickly and while still a boy performed his first mira-cle. The people's food supplies were running very low, and the hunters could not find any game. One day Sweet Medicine asked his grandmother to find an old buffalo hide, soak it in the stream, and scrape it clean. While the hide was soaking, he proceeded to cut four pointed sticks out of cherry wood. He also formed a hoop from a willow branch. When the hide was clean and dried, Sweet Medicine cut it into one long, thin strip. With this he wove a net across the hoop, but left the center of the hoop open.

The next morning Sweet Medicine and his grandmother went to the middle of the village and began playing a game. The old woman would roll the hoop to-ward Sweet Medicine and he would try to throw a stick through the center open-ing. People of the village came out to watch. On his first try, Sweet Medicine only managed to knock the hoop over. He laid the first stick aside and sent the hoop back to the old woman. Twice more she rolled the hoop toward him, but he could not send the sticks through the opening. However, on the fourth try the stick hit the center of the hoop and as it did, the hoop changed into a buffalo calf. The calf, with the arrow in its side, took a few steps and then collapsed dead on the ground. Sweet Medicine called for the people to get meat for themselves and their families. The meat did not run out and the people had plenty to eat.

Sometime later, Sweet Medicine was old enough to go on his first buffalo hunt. While the other men and boys were aiming at the main herd, he found a small group of buffalo off to the side and was able to kill one of them. When he was nearly finished cutting meat off the carcass and piling it on the hide, an old man came up and said he wanted the hide for himself. During the ensuing argument about who would get possession of the hide, Sweet Medicine picked up one of the buffalo's leg bones and hit the old man on the head.

Then Sweet Medicine rolled up the hide with the meat inside and took it back home to his grandmother. When the other hunters returned to the village, they were angry about what had happened to the old man. The men came to the tipi, but Sweet Medicine had already left. The next morning someone saw him standing on the hill behind the village. Some of the people ran up the hill to get him. But when they got to the top, he was already on the next hill. He motioned for them to come after him, but they could not catch up with him. The first time they saw him, he was dressed like a Fox Society warrior. The second time they saw him, he had the weapons of an Elk warrior. When they saw him a third time, he was wearing feathers and red paint like a Red Shield warrior. The fourth time he looked like a Dog Society warrior. And the fifth time they saw him, he was dressed like a Cheyenne chief. After that they did not see him again.

Sweet Medicine traveled across the prairie feeling that he was being drawn to a sacred mountain. When he arrived there he found a large tipi filled with many old people, both men and women. However, they weren't people at all, but spirits or gods who taught him many new things to take back to the Cheyenne. They taught him about the Four Sacred Arrows. Two of the arrows were for hunting and two for war. The arrows had great powers, and there were many ceremonies and rules connected with them. The Old Ones taught him new laws for governing the people and about the council of forty-four chiefs that were to lead them. They also taught him how to set up the warrior societies, how to honor women, and many more things that would benefit the people. The teaching went on for four years. Finally it was time for Sweet Medicine to return home and teach the people what he had learned. As he prepared to leave, one of the Old Ones burned sweet grass to purify him and the sacred arrow bundle he carried.

As he neared his village, some children who were hunting for mushrooms were the first to see him. He learned from them that food was scarce again, so he turned their mushrooms into buffalo fat and the children ate until they were full. Sweet Medicine instructed them to take what was left to the village and to tell the people that he had returned. Two young men went out to find him, but all they saw was an eagle fly up to the sky. The next morning they set out and again saw the eagle spread its wings and take flight. The same thing happened on the third day. But on the following morning they found Sweet Medicine standing on a hill with the arrow bundle in his arms.

Sweet Medicine ordered them to tell the people that he was coming with a powerful gift and that they should set up a large tipi in the center of the village. The people were to spread sage on its floor and burn sweet smelling grass. Then all of them were to wait inside for him to come.

When the preparations were complete, Sweet Medicine began to walk slowly to the village center. As he did, he called out four times, announcing to the people that he was bringing them the sacred and powerful arrows that would help them learn the right way to live. That night and for many nights to follow, Sweet Medicine taught them what he had heard from the spirits about the sacred arrows, the new laws, and new governing council.

The spirits had given Sweet Medicine the blessing of a long life, and he outlived several generations. But finally, when his end was near, he instructed the people to carry him to a place near the sacred mountain. There they built a shelter and laid him in it. He ordered them to camp several miles away. But before their last parting, he reminded the people what he had taught them and cautioned them to remain faithful to his teachings. He also warned them of things that would transpire in the future—the coming of horses and of white men, the end of the buffalo, and many other strange things that would change the way the people lived.

References and further reading:

Coffin, Tristam P., ed. *Indian Tales of North America: An Anthology for the Adult Reader.* Publications of the American Folklore Society, Bibliographical and Special Series, vol. 13. Philadelphia: The Society, 1961.

Dorsey, George A. *The Cheyenne.* 1905. Fieldiana, Anthropology, vol. 9, no. 1–2. Glorieta, N. Mex.: Rio Grande Press, 1971.

Erdoes, Richard, and Alfonso Ortiz, eds. *American Indian Myths and Legends.* New York: Pantheon Books, 1984.

Stands In Timber, John, and Margot Liberty. *Cheyenne Memories.* 2nd ed. New Haven, Conn.: Yale University Press, 1998.

TCAAWUNKL

Haida, Tlingit, Northwest Coast

This tale is named for the main character, who becomes a shaman, and for the spirit who speaks through him.

One day a baby's parents set him down in his cradle and wandered along the shore to hunt for mussels. Then they remembered their baby and returned for him. The parents saw a flock of crows sitting above him and heard what sounded like singing. When they looked at their baby, he was acting like a shaman. The parents picked him up and returned home, but they soon forgot about the incident.

A few years later, people began to die because of him, and before long nearly everyone in the village shunned him. Only his youngest uncle's wife took pity and brought him food. Eventually the boy went to live with his grandmother, away from the village. The old woman eventually learned that the boy had been given supernatural powers and helped him with the ceremonies of a shaman. He learned how to build deadfalls and was very successful at killing bear. Soon the boy and his grandmother had to build a larger house to hold all of the meat, fat, and furs.

At night, some people from the village secretly came out to watch him perform his ceremonies. About that time food in the village began to run out, so the boy shared food with his youngest uncle's wife, because she had been kind to him. Then the chief's son became sick. Shamans were called in from around the land, but none of them could cure the boy. Tcaawunkl heard the drums and went to the door of the house. Because of his supernatural powers, he could tell that the chief's son could be healed. So one day he sent word with his grandmother offering to heal the boy. At first people laughed, but those who had sneaked out to his house at night knew that he acted like a shaman. They encouraged the chief to invite him to try. Tcaawunkl was successful and the boy was cured. From then on he was welcome in the village again. He brought meat to sell to the people and continued to work as their shaman.

Eventually his fame spread across the land. Then the son of the Chief of the Land Otter people became ill. None of the Land Otter shamans could cure him. So the chief sent Land Otters to bring Tcaawunkl to their land. The unsuccessful shamans were jealous and taunted him. But Tcaawunkl eventually prevailed, after throwing rotten urine on the other shamans, and saved the chief's son. The chief sent him back home with a canoe full of hides, boxes of grease, and halibut hooks. They arrived at night and the Land Otters set the boxes and hides on the beach and departed. In the morning when he went back to the beach, there were only piles of seaweed and logs where the hides and boxes of grease had been stashed. The halibut hooks had disappeared as well.

See also Land Otters; Shaman

References and further reading:

Gill, Sam D., and Irene F. Sullivan. *Dictionary of Native American Mythology.* Santa Barbara: ABC-CLIO, 1992.

Swanton, John R. *Haida Texts and Myths: Skidegate Dialect.* 1905. Bulletin, Smithsonian Institution, Bureau of American Ethnology 29. Brighton, Mich.: Native American Book Publishers, 1991.

THUNDERBIRDS

Thunderbird myths were found in nearly all regions of North America.

According to a Teton (Lakota) myth, Inyan, who created Maka (the Earth), also created the Wakinyan (at times called the Winged-One, Thunderbird, or Thunderstorm) to be his messenger. The Wakinyan had mighty wings, a huge beak, sharp teeth and claws, and lightning flashed from his eye. The sound of his voice was the booming thunder. The little wakinyan echo after the great thunder is heard. It was Wakinyan who oversaw the growth of living things, controlled the clouds and weather, and destroyed those bent on evil. This purpose was given to Tate, the Wind, as well. One of the great enemies of the Wakinyan was the water monster. The Wakinyan lived on a high mountain in the west, near the west wind.

Beckwith related an Oglala myth that includes thunderbirds. A young man named Plenty Horses was an only son and helped raise his father's large herd of horses. All of the new colts that were born one spring were strong and healthy except for one that was sickly and pathetic looking. The young man found a good mare to care for this colt, but the colt did not improve. Finally the young man decided to kill the other colts, so he could spend all of his time and energy caring for the sickly one. Still, the colt did not improve. This exasperated the young man, and he decided to punish the colt by riding him into the west as fast as he could go. When Plenty Horses decided to stop to rest, the colt kept on galloping toward the west. The young man began to cry, but the colt said to him, "Don't cry. I'm taking you to a wondrous place."

Eventually, they arrived at a camp where a contest was under way to see who would marry a beautiful young woman. A bone ring was suspended from a wooden scaffold. The young men would ride their horses past the ring and try to throw a dart through it. One by one the others tried and failed. But when Plenty Horses took his turn, his dart sailed through the ring. That night the young woman disappeared. Plenty Horses found a trail heading east, so he rode off in that direction until he came to a great lake. He didn't know what to do, so he sat on the back of his horse and cried.

The horse told Plenty Horses not to cry, but to shut his eyes tight. When he finally opened his eyes, he was on an island. He found an old woman in a tipi and told her that he was searching for the young woman he was supposed to marry. The old woman told him to wait. "Your uncles, the four winds, will be back soon," she said, "and perhaps they can tell you where your bride was

Thunderbird with lightning and rain, fresco on interior kiva wall, ca. 1500, Tiguex (Kuaua Pueblo) on the Rio Grande, New Mexico. (North Wind Picture Archives)

taken." The first to arrive came in a black cloud with thunder and lightning. His name was Owner-of-the-Water. But he had been too busy watering the land in the west to see the young woman. Next to arrive was Owner-of-the-Hail, who came out of the north. He, too, had been busy taking care of his territory in the north and did not know anything about Plenty Horses' bride. The third to arrive had also been too busy to see where the girl had gone. But when Owner-of-the-Wind arrived amid a storm from the east, he told Plenty Horses that the young woman was to be married the next day in the country of the Thunderbirds.

The old woman opened up a large rawhide blanket and told Plenty Horses to sit in the middle. The four winds carried him away. Sometime later, Plenty Horses found himself in the midst of another large gathering. The young woman was about to be married. When she saw him approach, she ran to him and they disappeared.

Now when someone goes far away to marry, he says, "I'm going to be Thunderbird's son-in-law."

In the following Skidi Pawnee myth, two boys saved a nest of young thunderbirds from a water monster.

Two boys went hunting and stayed near a lake for quite some time. There they lived on small game and fruit that grew in the area. One night they heard strange noises coming from the lake. The boys stayed awake for a long time, wondering what caused the commotion. They finally fell asleep, and when they awoke they were in the lodge of some animals. The boys learned that they had been brought there because of a monster in the lake that the animals wanted killed. The water monster was destroying all of the young animals, and while the older animals had tried to kill the water monster, they could not.

The animals gave the boys some blunt-ended arrows and instructed them to use only these special arrows to shoot the monster. They also instructed the boys that if the monster came near them, they were to shoot it in the mouth. The boys took the arrows, and suddenly they were back at their campsite. They stayed in that place for some time, expecting that the water monster would appear any minute, but they did not see or hear it again. Eventually they decided to climb a nearby hill and found it had a flat top and steep banks on three sides. On one edge of the hill top was a large rock with a nest on it. The boys looked in and found two small thunderbirds.

They decided to stay with the little birds and help care for them by bringing them worms and insects. Occasionally, the mother thunderbird would come with food and didn't seem to mind that the boys were there. One day a cloud approached and the boys thought they would get drenched, but they felt only a few drops. The cloud moved on and hovered over the lake. The boys saw two thunderbirds flying above the clouds. When the huge birds opened their mouths, thunder rang out and lightning flashed. After a while the cloud returned to the hilltop. The boys looked down the hill and could see the monster coming up from the lake. Lightning struck it, but the monster wasn't affected. It then began climbing up the hill. The mother thunderbird called to the boys, "Help me save my children! I'll give you the power of thunder and lightning if you help me."

The boys rushed to the edge of the hilltop and pulled out their arrows. They shot at the monster, but the arrows just bounced off. Then the thunderbird called out, "Use the blunt arrows!" Just then the monster opened its mouth wide to swallow the little birds. The boys grabbed the blunt arrows and shot straight into its mouth. The force of the arrows flung the monster on its back. The arrows grew into large trees with deep roots so the monster could not move, and it soon died.

The little thunderbirds were saved and the mother kept her promise. The boys received the power of the thunder and lightning. However, they didn't tell anyone about it until one year when the land was parched. They prayed for rain and the rain came. Then they shared the story of the thunderbirds and the water monster.

In some myths from the Pacific Northwest the Thunderbird was able to change into human form, as in the following brief story.

Two brothers went to the woods for several months. During their stay, they purified themselves by washing in a lake and rubbing their skin with evergreen branches until they no longer had the scent of humans on them. Then the young men climbed a nearby mountain to the home of the Thunderbirds. When they entered the house, a woman welcomed them in and told them that her husband and his brother were away but would return soon. She hid the men in a corner, and soon the Thunderbirds returned with the sound of a great wind. The Thunderbirds were not fooled by the men. They told the woman that they could smell men in their house. So the woman had the young men come out of hiding. The Thunderbirds removed their belts and feather garments and then took the appearance of men.

Many of the people in the Northeast Woodlands also told of great Thunderbirds. A Passamaquoddy myth tells of two men who wanted to locate the source of thunder. They began walking north until they came to a certain mountain. The mountains in this area did strange things, including moving together and then parting again. The men's path went through these mountains, so one of the men said, "I'll go first. If I get caught between the mountains, then you go on alone to find the thunder." The first man went through the pass before it closed, but the second one was smashed between the mountains.

The first man went on by himself and soon found a village where some people were playing ball. After some time, one of the players said to the others, "It's time to go now." They all went into their wigwams, put on their wings, and gathered outside with their bows and arrows. Then they flew off over the mountains. This is how the man found where the thunderbirds lived. The old men of that village who stayed behind asked the man, "What are you doing here? Who are you?" So he told them about his quest and about his friend who died trying to get through the mountains. The old men thought about what to do. Finally they put the man in a mortar, ground him up, and then formed him into a new shape with wings like a thunderbird. Then they gave him a bow and arrows and sent him on his way back home. But, they warned him not to fly too close to the tree tops or he'd get stuck in them.

At first the thunderbird-man was unable to reach his home because a great enemy bird stirred up a strong wind that blew him off course. Over time, though, this new thunderbird became very powerful and kept guard over the Passamaquoddy people.

See also Thunderers; Wind

References and further reading:

Beckwith, Martha Warren. "Mythology of the Oglala Dakota." *Journal of American Folklore* 43, no. 170 (October–December 1930): 339–442.

Dorsey, George A. *Traditions of the Skidi Pawnee.* 1904. New York: Kraus Reprint Co., 1969.

Fewkes, J. Walter. "A Contribution to Passamaquoddy Folk-Lore." *Journal of American Folklore* 3, no. 11 (October–December 1890): 257–280.

Melody, Michael Edward. "Maka's Story: A Study of a Lakota Cosmogony." *Journal of American Folklore* 90, no. 356 (April–June 1977): 149–167.

THUNDERERS
Northeast Woodlands

Natural phenomena such as thunder and lightning have been a cause of awe and fear across the ages. Some myth stories ascribe the booming sound and flashing light to great thunderbirds, while others tell of great, human-like gods who are known as Thunder or the Thunderers.

The god of thunder and/or rain was often thought beneficent. One myth reported by Barbeau tells of seven brothers who lived in the heavens. Henon (also spelled Hinon or Hinun) was good natured but more energetic and boisterous than his brothers, who worried about him because of his strength. They feared that someday Henon might become angry and destroy them all. So the six brothers debated about what could be done. Finally, they decided on a plan. They invited Henon on a hunting trip to a distant island. There the brothers said they would each go off in a different direction to chase the deer towards Henon. However, instead of doing that, the brothers headed back to their canoes and quickly set off for home. Before they were out of sight, Henon sensed that something wasn't right. He ran down to the shore and called out to his brothers to come back for him.

The brothers yelled back, "It's safer for everyone if you stay on the island." Henon thought about it, then good-naturedly agreed. He remained on the island by himself, but occasionally his voice would be heard booming out across the water. If thunder was heard during the winter, people would smile and say, "Oh, something must have awakened Henon from his nap."

In a Haudenosaunee (Iroquois) myth retold by Beauchamp, three men were returning from a raid on a distant land. One of the men broke his leg. His friends carried him for many days but eventually tired of their burden. There was a crevice nearby and the men tossed the injured fellow into it. Then they quickly returned home and reported that the third man had been mortally wounded by the enemy and died as they tried to bring him home. His mother grieved for many days for her only son.

However, the injured man was not the only one at the bottom of the crevice. An old man who was crouching in the corner asked him, "What did your friends do to you?" The injured man replied that he'd been tossed in there to die. But the old man said, "You will not die if you promise to do what I say." When the injured man inquired what that would be, the old man said that all he needed to do was to hunt for him.

So, the injured man agreed and the old man then proceeded to treat the broken leg with herbs and cared for him as he recovered. By winter the young man was able to go out hunting. The old man offered to help carry bundles of meat if there was ever more game killed than the injured man could carry. As the winter progressed, the man had to search for game farther and farther away from the crevice. One day he saw three men approaching who appeared to be dressed in clouds. They told him that old man who also lived in the crevice was not what he appeared to be. They were Thunderers and had been sent on a mission to find and destroy serpents and all who devastated crops. When there was a drought they were to bring beneficial rain. They promised if the young man would help them, he would be returned home so he could care for his mother.

The young man agreed. He went back to the crevice and told the old man that he had killed a bear and needed help carrying all of the meat back to their shelter. The old man was wary and asked if there were any clouds in the sky. "No, the sky is clear." So the old man went along, urging that they hurry about their task. While they were packing up the meat they had cut up, a cloud quickly arose. When the old man saw it, he dropped his pack and ran back toward the crevice. As he ran, he became a huge porcupine. The Thunderers hurled bolts of lightning down and killed the animal just as it got to its den. Then, as promised, they returned the young man to his village. His mother was overjoyed to see him safe and sound. It wasn't until the next spring when the Thunderers returned that the young man told the people of his adventures with them. He explained the good works they did for the people.

A Seneca myth tells of a young boy who was out hunting. As he was walking through the woods he noticed a brightly colored worm on a branch of a nearby tree. He watched it for quite some time and then went home. The next day, on his way home, he walked past the same tree. The colorful worm was still there, so the boy tore off a piece of one of the birds he had killed and fed it to the worm. This became a routine with the boy feeding the worm each day on his way back home. However, the worm began to grow quickly and needed more and more food. Soon he was feeding the worm a whole bird, and then two birds. Finally the worm became so heavy that the branch could no longer hold it and it fell to the ground.

One day some of the boy's friends were with him and saw the worm. They had great fun feeding the worm the game they had caught. By now the worm was eating rabbits and growing larger every day. Then one day, the boys were jostling each other to see who would get to feed the worm next when one small boy was knocked on the ground. The worm immediately swallowed the boy. The others ran home, but didn't tell what had happened. The parents of the missing boy questioned them, but all they said was that they'd seen him earlier in the day. The great worm held the boys in its spell and caused them to push others of their group close to the worm so they were eaten, too. One day the remaining boys came to where the worm was and realized it had killed a deer. They were so frightened they ran back to the village without feeding it as usual.

The next morning the village, which was situated on the top of a hill, was surrounded by the monstrous worm. Some people tried to escape, but were swallowed by the worm. Finally, the boys confessed and told the whole story. The people who remained discussed their plight. In the end they decided to plead for their lives to Henon, the Thunderer. They burned sweet-smelling tobacco and offered prayers. Soon they saw a dark cloud approaching and heard the peals of thunder. Lightning struck the huge worm and severed it into pieces. These pieces rolled down into the valley and were turned into a lake.

See also Thunderbirds

References and further reading:

Barbeau, Marius. *Huron and Wyandot Mythology, with an Appendix Containing Earlier Published Records.* Memoir 80, Anthropological Series, no. 11. Ottawa: Government Printing Bureau, 1915.

Beauchamp, William M. *Iroquois Folk Lore Gathered from the Six Nations of New York.* 1922. Empire State Historical Publication 31. Port Washington, N.Y.: Kennikat Press, [1978?].

Curtin, Jeremiah, and J. N. B. Hewitt. *Seneca Fiction, Legends, and Myths.* Thirty-Second Annual Report of the Bureau of American Ethnology to the Secretary of the Smithsonian Institution, 1910–1911. Washington, DC: Government Printing Office, 1918.

Hale, Horatio. "Huron Folk-Lore. III, The Legend of the Thunderers." *Journal of American Folklore* 4, no. 15 (October–December 1891): 289–294.

TIRAWA

Pawnee, Plains

The Pawnee's supreme deity was known as Tirawa. Sometimes this god was also referred to as Tirawahat or Tirawahut, although this term may also mean the abode of the gods.

Tirawa created the sun, moon, and stars, set them in the heavens, and assigned their individual roles and powers. He then set about creating the earth and living creatures. Animals were given knowledge and power and functioned as messengers from Tirawa to men.

The humans of today were not the first people Tirawa created. Long ago there were giants on the earth. These giants did not respect Tirawa, their creator, and were very wicked and rebellious. Tirawa decided to destroy them with lightning. But since the giants were very large and powerful, the lightning had no effect on them. So Tirawa sent a heavy rain. Much of the land was covered with water and the giants fled to high ground. But the rain continued and the ground became soft. The giants sank in the mud and were buried. Their bones can be found today in many places, especially where rivers have eroded away the banks.

Tirawa instructed the gods of the Winds, Clouds, Lightnings, and Thunders to create the things that humans would need—the trees and plants, streams and lakes. The son of the Moon and Sun and the daughter of Bright-Star and Great-Star became the first humans on earth. At Tirawa's command, the gods taught the people how to hunt and plant, and how to make weapons, fire, shelters, and clothing. They also instructed the people about ceremonies they were to perform and gave them the sacred bundles.

Far from being distant and disinterested, Tirawa (also called A-ti'-us, meaning "father") was described in several myths as feeling compassion for his creation. One of the tales relates the story of a poor, orphaned boy who was raised by a widow who had two children of her own. There was a famine and the people traveled south hoping to find buffalo or other game. Finally, the orphan was so weak he could go no farther. When the people moved on, he stayed behind and gathered sticks to make a fire. After a while he fell asleep, and when he awoke, he saw two dark spots in the sky. He kept watching them as they drew closer and they appeared to be swans. But he grew tired and soon was asleep again. The next time the orphan awoke he found himself in front of a very large lodge with paintings of animals on the walls. The orphan boy pulled himself up and walked to the door of the lodge. There across from the door sat A-ti'-us. He was large and handsome and dressed in beautifully embroidered clothes and a white buffalo robe. There were many other chiefs sitting on the sides of the lodge. They were also dressed in wonderful clothes.

The boy entered the lodge. A-ti'-us welcomed him and instructed one of the chiefs to give him something to eat. The chief cut off a small piece of meat. The boy was starving and thought that the piece of meat was much too small, but he started eating anyway. No matter how many slices the boy cut off, the piece of meat remained the same size. He soon had eaten his fill and there was still meat left over. When the boy was finished eating, A-ti'-us told him that he had seen the suffering of the people and explained what the boy should do. Eventually the boy was sent back with new clothes and weapons. When he was led out to the swans, a deep sleep came over him, and the next thing he knew he was waking up next to his fire.

He stood up and felt strong again. He started to run and by evening caught up with his people. When he reached the woman's lodge, she was cutting up the last of a buffalo robe to cook for their meal. The boy went back outside and the woman heard what sounded like a buffalo snorting and then the sound of something heavy collapsing in the snow. The boy came back in and told the woman to go outside and bring in some meat. The woman was amazed, but did what he said and outside she found a buffalo cow. After skinning it she cooked some of the meat. When her children and the boy had eaten, she sent for her relatives and friends to come and share in the feast. When they had all eaten, they prayed to the Father, thanking him for giving them food.

Then the orphan told the woman's son to run to the top of a nearby hill and report what he saw. He returned, saying that there was nothing but snow as far as he could see. The orphan told him to go back and look again. He returned with the same report. So the orphan went there himself. When he looked out over the valley he could see that it was full of buffalo. He signaled for the people to follow him. The buffalo could not get away from the hunters because they were stuck in the deep snow. In time the orphan boy became very wealthy and a great man among the people.

See also Flood(s); Stars and Constellations

References and further reading:

Dorsey, George A. *The Pawnee Mythology*. 1906. Sources of American Indian Oral Literature. Lincoln: University of Nebraska Press, 1997.

———. *Traditions of the Skidi Pawnee*. 1904. New York: Kraus Reprint Co., 1969.

Grinnell, George Bird. *Pawnee Hero Stories and Folktales: With Notes on the Origin, Customs and Character of the Pawnee People*. 1889. Lincoln: University of Nebraska Press, 1990.

Williamson, Ray A., and Claire R. Farrer, eds. *Earth & Sky: Visions of the Cosmos in Native American Folklore*. Albuquerque: University of New Mexico Press, 1994. First published 1992.

TOBACCO

Native to the Americas, tobacco has been cultivated and used by tribal groups of the North American continent since before the arrival of Europeans. Research has led to the conclusion that precontact tobacco use originated with the Native peoples of South America and spread gradually north. Prior to European contact, the most common species of tobacco used was *Nicotiana rustica*, not the *Nicotiana tabacum* that is smoked today. It was used primarily by Native Americans of the eastern United States and the Great Plains.

Tobacco was used for a variety of ceremonial and religious purposes. Supplies were small, and it was considered sacred. Tobacco smoke represented contact between this world and that of the supernatural. Tobacco was also smoked as a medicine in curing and healing, to suppress hunger, and in agricultural rites. Tobacco societies existed among tribes of the Plains, and certain duties were required of initiates. These included the selection of medicine, sweat lodge rituals, and the planting of sacred tobacco. Frequently, tobacco was used to cement agreements between tribes, as offerings, to show respect, or as payment.

Piegan man holding a medicine pipe, 1910. (Library of Congress)

Because of its long-standing importance and widespread use, it is not surprising that tobacco is featured in many Native American myths and stories, many of which tell of its origin.

In a Siksika (Blackfeet) story, four medicine men kept the sacred tobacco for themselves, instead of sharing it with others and teaching them how to use it. But a young man and his wife, determined to bring tobacco to the tribes, were given the seed and taught the songs, prayers, dances, and ceremonies that go with it by four man-beavers.

Another Siksika story tells how a poor young man, Apikunni, was publicly humiliated when his love for the youngest wife of the old chief was discovered. He wandered away from his village and spent the winter living with an old beaver, who told him how to defeat his enemy and instructed him on how to use certain medicines, including tobacco seed. Apikunni pierces his foe—the first man ever killed in war—with an aspen stick given to him by the beaver. He subsequently returns to his village with great honors. The old chief retires and makes Apikunni the new chief. He then marries the youngest of the former chief's wives and acquires the other two wives as servants. At a village council, he shares the information the beaver gave him and teaches the people how to use the Beaver Medicine (tobacco) in their ceremonies.

Several Cherokee stories tell of the origin of tobacco.

There was a time when tobacco, with which they had been made acquainted by a wandering stranger, was not readily available to the Cherokee. Having smoked it in their large stone pipes, the Cherokee were anxious to obtain abundant supplies. They determined that the area where it grew in the greatest quantities was situated on the big waters, and that the mighty mountain gorge that led to it was guarded by little people or spirits.

A council of brave men of the nation was called to discuss bringing back some tobacco from the dangerous and unknown country. A bold young warrior stepped forward and volunteered to undertake the task. He departed but never returned, and the Cherokee Nation was now in great tribulation. Another council was held to consider and decide upon another strategy. A celebrated magician stepped forward and volunteered to visit the tobacco country and see what he could do. He changed himself into a mole and made his way east of the mountains; however, he was pursued by the guardian spirits and was forced to return home empty-handed. Next, he turned himself into a hummingbird, and succeeded, to a very limited extent, in obtaining some of the precious tobacco. Upon his return, he found several friends at the point of death because of their intense desire for it. He placed some of the fragrant weed in a pipe and blew the smoke into the nostrils of those who were ill and happily revived them.

The magician became the sole possessor of all the tobacco in the unknown land and decided to avenge the young warrior's death. He turned himself into a whirlwind, and, passing through a mountain gorge on his way, stripped the mountains of their vegetation and scattered large rocks in the valley, frightening away the little people and guardian spirits. He found the bones of the young warrior in a stream bed and brought him back to life as a man. They returned to their home country laden with tobacco, and ever since then it has been plentiful throughout the entire land.

References and further reading:
Grinnell, George Bird. *Blackfoot Lodge Tales: The Story of a Prairie People.* Lincoln: University of Nebraska Press, 2003. First published 1982 by Scribner.
Hirschfelder, Arlene, and Paulette Molin. *Encyclopedia of Native American Religions.* Updated ed. New York: Facts on File, 2000.
Ugvwiyuhi. *Journey to Sunrise: Myths and Legends of the Cherokee.* Claremore, Okla.: Egi Press, 1977.

TRANSFORMATION, HUMAN-ANIMAL

Human-animal and animal-human transformation, sometimes referred to as shape-shifting, is a common theme in mythological narratives across the length and breadth of North America. Occasionally, evildoers transform themselves into benign creatures in order to facilitate their wicked ways. In other tales, the transformation occurs as the outcome of an event or series of events in which the individual finds himself or herself.

Parker noted the Seneca belief that "any being possessing orenda may transform himself into any form, animate or inanimate." This *orenda* was described as a magical power or a type of supernatural power that would give its possessor the ability to overcome the laws of nature. Humans could transform themselves into whatever form they wished and then transform back again, if they so chose. Animals possessing *orenda* could transform themselves into humans and live as one of them.

Often times, a Trickster, such as Raven or Coyote, transformed himself in order to manipulate a situation. Raven wished to obtain light, so he traveled to where the chief who kept the light lived. Raven devised a plan and turned himself into a small leaf that fell into a drinking cup. After being swallowed by the chief's daughter, Raven became a baby inside of her, and eventually he was born as the chief's grandson. The chief naturally doted on the baby and spoiled him terribly. The baby soon demanded to be allowed to play with a special box that the grandfather kept high on a shelf. In time the grandfather gave the little boy the box—with the stipulation that he must never open it. Raven promised the grandfather that he'd keep the lid on tightly, but of course, as soon as he was left alone, Raven opened the box. Out flew the stars, moon, and the sun.

Some transformations occur in order that lovers may live together happily ever after. The Shawnee told of a young hunter named Waupee who roamed far from home one day and approached a clearing in the forest. As he entered the open space, he saw a circular path worn in the grass, but without any path leading to it from the forest. Curious to find out who or what had made the circle, Waupee hid himself at the edge of the clearing. Soon he heard a faint sound of music coming from the sky. When he looked up, he saw something coming down toward the clearing. The small spot in the sky quickly grew larger until Waupee saw it was a large basket containing twelve beautiful sisters, daughters of a star.

He continued to watch as the sisters jumped out of the basket and sang and danced around the clearing. Although the sisters were all beautiful to behold, Waupee was smitten with the youngest. Finally he rushed out from his hiding spot and attempted to capture her. But the sisters all rushed back to the basket and returned into the sky.

Waupee returned home but could only think about the lovely young girl he had seen. So on the following day, he decided to go back to the ring where the sisters had danced. This time he changed himself into an opossum and hid at the edge of the forest clearing. Again the basket came down from the sky and the sisters danced around the ring. Waupee, in the form of an opossum, slowly moved toward the ring. But the creature frightened the sisters and they ran back to the basket and returned to the sky. Waupee, changing back to his original form, sadly walked home.

The next day Waupee returned to the clearing. He spotted mice running in and out of an old stump. Waupee thought, "Perhaps the young women will not be afraid of a little mouse." So he moved the old stump close to their dancing ring and changed himself into one of the mice. Soon the basket with the sisters returned. They began to dance as before, but one of them noticed the stump and said, "That has not been here before!" The youngest sister became frightened and started to run back to the basket, but the others laughed and gathered around the stump. With sticks, they began hitting the stump, and soon mice were running out. The sisters killed all of the mice with their sticks, except for one. That one was caught by the youngest sister. As soon as she grabbed the small mouse, Waupee changed into his normal form and held on tightly to the young girl. The other sisters were able to escape back to the sky in their basket.

Kwakiutl man, wearing a mask depicting a loon to facilitate the loon's changing into the form of a man, 1914. (Library of Congress)

Waupee gently wooed the young girl. He told her about his skill as a hunter, and about the wonderful earth she now lived in. By the time they reached his home, Waupee was the happiest of all men.

Time passed, and a son was born to them. But Waupee's wife had not forgotten her home among the stars and longed to return. On days when her husband was out hunting, the young woman would work on constructing a wicker basket and collecting many delicacies from the surrounding region. When everything was prepared, the young woman took the basket and supplies to the clearing, and along with her son, climbed into the basket. As she began to sing, the basket rose into the sky. Waupee recognized the song and ran to the clearing. But he was too late; they had risen far up into the sky.

Waupee was heartbroken at the loss of his wife and especially his son. Meanwhile, his wife and son arrived at her former home. She would have forgotten all about her husband and life on earth, if it had not been for her son. Each time she saw him, she was reminded of his father. As the child grew, he became more and more anxious to learn more about his father and wanted to visit the place where he was born.

Finally the young woman's father gave his blessing for them to return to earth. "Take your son to his father, but ask the man if he would return back here with you. Ask him also to bring along one of each kind of bird and of each animal he kills. So, the young woman took the child and returned in the basket to where her husband lived. Waupee heard the singing as the basket descended and ran to the clearing. He was overjoyed to hold his wife and son in his arms again.

The young woman told him about her star-father's request. Waupee set out immediately to find the objects his father-in-law asked for. When everything was ready, he joined his wife and son in the basket and soon they were ascending into the heavens. The star chief called a feast and everyone was invited to choose a gift from what Waupee had brought along. Those who chose tails or claws suddenly became animals and ran off. Others became birds and flew away. Waupee chose a white hawk's feather for himself, his wife, and their son. Soon they spread their wings and flew with the other birds down to the earth and their kind are still found on earth today.

Sometimes the change takes place in a person's spirit long before it is made evident by a physical transformation.

Once, long ago, a young Zuni woman was captured by a Navajo raiding party. She was tied to the back of a horse and the group galloped back to the Navajo village. The young woman was taken to the home of a Navajo man to become his younger wife. However, by the second night, she chose to sleep alone outside. Very early the next morning, when the young woman awoke, she found the older wife standing beside her. The Navajo woman offered the Zuni girl a blanket, food, and container of water, and then pointed to the east where the sky was just beginning to turn light. The Zuni girl gratefully took the items and ran from the Navajo village toward the rising sun.

She ran quickly through the underbrush and covered her tracks when she walked on sandy riverbanks. Finally she reached the top of a high mesa and looked back in the direction she had traveled. No one was following her, so she unwrapped the package of food and ate it all and drank most of the water. After the refreshing meal and rest, the Zuni girl began to run again until evening. She dug into the ground under a large tree and slept in the depression. Later, when she awoke, she was hungry again, but found that she'd consumed all of her food on the mesa. Then she tried the water container, but it, too, was empty. The girl was frightened, cold, and tired, but she got up and began running toward home again.

Another night came and she fell asleep huddled under the Navajo blanket. Snow fell and covered the ground. When she awoke, the girl pushed the cold, wet blanket away and started running again. However, exhaustion soon caught up with her and she collapsed on the snowy ground. A large, white, furry animal came to examine her nearly lifeless body. The animal looked toward the heavens and let out a spine-tingling howl and trotted off. The girl tried to sit up, but collapsed again. The white wolf returned quickly, pulling a freshly killed animal. He pulled it up over the girl to give her warmth. Then the wolf tore off a piece of the prey's flesh and pushed it into the girl's mouth. She ate the raw meat and was grateful for the warmth of the dead animal covering her.

When she had recovered the young girl began running toward home once more. She ran all day and again collapsed in the snow when her strength was gone. Soon the white wolf found her and lay in the snow beside her to keep her warm. For four more days the two traveled together toward the east. On the morning of the fifth day, the girl could see her village and ran down the slope toward it with the white wolf running beside her. The girl called out to the people who only stared at the strange sight. She told them her name and how happy she was to have returned home. Some men grabbed their bows and arrows and pointed them toward her and the wolf. The girl stopped suddenly, confused by what she saw. The men ordered her to move away from the wolf so they could kill it. Just then the girl realized that the men thought the wolf was chasing her. "No! Stop! This wolf saved me and brought me home."

The men lowered their bows. As they approached her, the wolf disappeared and the girl sank to the ground. She was carried to her father's home. When the girl awoke she was lying on the floor next to her father's corpse. As she looked around, she realized the house had been stripped bare. Her father had died while she was gone and no one was there to prepare his body for burial. Tenderly she washed her father's hair, dressed him, and covered him with a blanket. No one spoke to her as she made her preparations, nor while she pulled his body to the Cliff of Death. The young girl continued to live in her house alone. Occasionally food was left at her door overnight, but no one dared speak to her.

Over time the young girl became an old woman. She knew there would be no one to take her to the Cliff of Death when the time came, so she decided to prepare her body and dress in her burial clothes. Unable to stand any longer, the woman dragged herself through the village—the village that had been her home. The people watched as she made her way up the hill. They saw her turn to look back at the village and suddenly a chilling howl pierced the air. The howl came from the old woman as her body changed into a white wolf. The White Wolf Woman howled again and then with strong legs loped away over the hills. She still roams the area today and White Wolf Woman Canyon is named for her. People tell of being lost in that canyon, but White Wolf Woman shows them the way home.

See also Alarana and Her Brother; Blind Boy; Blood Clot; Dog Husband; Land Otters; Raven

References and further reading:

Bierhorst, John, ed. *The Red Swan: Myths and Tales of the American Indians.* Albuquerque: University of New Mexico Press, 1992. First published 1976 by Farrar, Straus, and Giroux.

Pijoan, Teresa. *White Wolf Woman: Native American Transformation Myths.* Collected and retold by Teresa Pijoan. Little Rock, Ark. August House Publishers, 1992.

TRANSFORMER

The word *transform* means to alter, change, and modify. Many of the transformers in Native American mythology were individuals who were active in changing or reforming the earth and getting it ready for the coming of animals and humans. Often the transformer changed the shape of the land, set the mountains and lakes in their places, and taught humans and animals how they should live. Coyote, Glooskap, Manabozho, Old Man, and Raven were all transformers as well as culture heroes or tricksters. Ives stated that Kluskap (Glooskap) is "the Wabanaki culture hero. He is not a god; that is, he is neither a judge of man nor a creator. He is a transformer. The world was here when he arrived, and all he did was to fix it up a little."

Franz Boas, in discussing origin myths, indicated that the concept of the creation of the world and everything on it from nothingness or from the imagination of a Creator was generally unknown to most Native American groups. Instead it was widely believed that the earth had some sort of form previously and that *a creator*, but not necessarily *the Creator*, molded, rebuilt, or rearranged the existing substance and "created" a new earth. Humans, animals, and vegetation were also frequently transformed from a past state into the way they are now.

The Earth Diver myths are an example of a transformer's work in changing the shape of the world and making it ready for mankind. Radin and Reagan related that Manabozho was floating on a raft after a flood covered the whole world. He had forgotten to take some soil along with him, so he chose four divers from among the animals that were swimming along beside the raft. After several unsuccessful tries, Muskrat was able to bring up mud and some seeds from the bottom of the sea. Manabozho dried the lump of mud and seeds and then began to blow on them. An island formed around the raft. After a time, Manabozho sent a raven out to see how large the land had become, and the raven returned in two days. Manabozho decided that it was not big enough, so he continued to blow on the dirt until the land extended farther than anyone could see. This time when he sent the raven out, it did not return. So

Manabozho knew the land was big enough. Then he set about establishing the plants and the forests. When he was finished, Manabozho returned home.

Among the people who lived along or near the southern portion of the Pacific Northwest coast, a number of transformer myths are known. The Kwakiutl knew the transformer as Kánekelak. Their father, Heron, made Kánekelak and his younger brother go hungry. One day Heron and the boys' red-headed stepmother went to the river and found a salmon in the trap. Heron asked his wife, "How can we keep this salmon away from the boys?" The step-mother said, "Scare them." So the father called to the boys, "Hurry! Run! A ghost is coming!" When the boys ran off to hide, the parents roasted their catch and ate it all before the boys returned home.

The next day the parents found two salmon in the trap, and again they told the boys to run away and hide. On the following two days the same thing hap-pened, except that on each day subsequent there was more salmon in the trap. But, the greedy parents would not share their roasted salmon with the boys. However, on the fourth day, Kánekelak peeked through a hole in the side of the house and saw his parents eating the roasted salmon. Then he heard Heron say, "Hurry, let's eat all of the salmon and hide the bones, so the boys won't find them." At that Kánekelak ran inside and threw his father in the air. "Now," he said, "you will become the heron." Then he turned to his stepmother and threw her into the air. "And you will be the redheaded woodpecker."

Kánekelak now named his brother Only One and built a huge house for him to live in. Then he killed four whales so Only One would have plenty of food to eat. Kánekelak then began traveling around and having many adven-tures. Once he came upon a man by the name of Deer. This man was sharpen-ing mussel shells. When Kánekelak asked what he was doing, the man replied, "Don't you know? Kánekelak is coming and I need to be ready to defend my-self." Kánekelak had a better idea. He attached a mussel shell to the man's ears and said, "You will now become the deer." At that Deer jumped and ran off into the woods. Kánekelak continued his travels and met many people whom he recreated as the animals we know today.

See also Coyote; Earth Diver; First Creator and Lone Man; Glooskap; Kumokums; Old Man; Raven; Wisaka

References and further reading:
Bierhorst, John. *The Mythology of North America: With a New Afterword.* Oxford: Oxford University Press, 2002. First published 1985 by William Morrow.

Boas, Franz. "Mythology and Folk-Tales of the North American Indians." *Journal of American Folklore* 27, no. 106 (October–December 1914): 374–410.

Ives, Edward D. "Malecite and Passamaquoddy Tales." *Northeast Folklore* 6 (1964): 1–81.

Radin, Paul, and A. B. Reagan. "Ojibwa Myths and Tales: The Manabozho Cycle." *Journal of American Folklore* 41, no. 159 (January–March 1928): 61–146.

TRICKSTER

The trickster is featured in myths and legends in many parts of the world, and numerous scholars have attempted to analyze the trickster's meaning in social, psychological, and religious contexts. The character is a complex blend of personalities. Although most often portrayed as male, the trickster is occasionally depicted as female. The North American trickster is frequently seen as a creator or re-creator of the world. He is the one who taught mankind and the animals how to live and gave them the necessities of life: daylight, fire, and water. He is what Ricketts called a "'trickster-transformer-culture hero' (or 'trickster-fixer' for short.)"

On the other hand, the trickster can be a self-centered prankster who is forever on the lookout for his next scam, meal, or sexual encounter. Often his schemes are foiled when humans or animals see through his devious and lecherous ways; at other times, they backfire on him. Carroll suggested that the term *trickster* has been used too broadly and argues against classifying a "clever hero" such as Robin Hood, or even Brer Rabbit, as a trickster. The North American trickster, he argues, is undoubtedly a "culture hero" and at times a "buffoon."

Carroll also noted that scholars have grouped North American trickster tales into seven broad categories: Coyote is found most often west of the Mississippi River; Nanabush (and variant names such as Manabozho and Winabojo) in the Northeast; Raven in the Northwest; Rabbit in the Southeast; Hare and Iktomi, the Spider, among the Siouan people; and Napi in the Plateau and northern Rockies. Each of these tricksters exhibits human characteristics while often, but not always, being associated with particular animals such as the coyote, raven, hare (rabbit), and spider.

Erdoes and Ortiz compared Coyote to some of the gods from Greek and Roman mythology who used an assortment of tricks and disguises, including transforming themselves into animals, to seduce young women. Like the North American tricksters, the gods of classical mythology were at times creators, benefactors, and meddlers in the lives of humans. For more discussion on this topic, see Radin's *The Trickster: A Study in American Indian Mythology.*

Nanabush, according to Ridie Wilson Ghezzi, was a culture hero who transformed the world after a great flood, interceded between the gods (or spirits) and mankind, and taught important life skills to the people. As a trickster, however, Nanabush exemplified the type of actions and attitudes to avoid. Thus the nar-

Coyote chasing Rabbit. 1941 painting by Quincy Tahoma. (Manuscript Acee Blue Eagle Papers: Paintings and Prints by Indian Artists: Tahoma, Quincy, Smithsonian Institution National Anthropological Archives/NAA INV 08806500)

ratives of the Nanabush cycle were meant to educate the entire society by illustrating what was moral and what was considered immoral behavior.

Spider (called Iktomi by the Teton [Lakota] and Dakota [Sioux]) was originally named Ksa, the god of wisdom. As Ksa, he created time, named the animals, and gave men their languages. But after disgracing a goddess, Ksa was banished from the feasts of the gods and became Iktomi, the Spider. He used both his wisdom and his trickster traits to plot deceptions against men and animals. Iktomi was famous for his sexual appetite and abilities, and even broke a nearly universal taboo when he made love to his daughters. This often despised and mischievous creature is nevertheless considered *wakan* (sacred).

In the Pacific Northwest, Raven was the one who reformed the land after a great deluge and brought the people salmon. But in other tales, Raven is greedy and lacks foresight. Although Hays referred to Raven as a trickster, he noted that "he also shades into culture hero and magician—with episodes in which he is pure schlemiel."

Rabbit was seen as a culture hero in some trickster tales found in the Southeast. However, the Creek told of a deceitful, conniving Rabbit who tried the people's patience far too long. A trial was held and Rabbit was found guilty and condemned to death by drowning. True to his nature, Rabbit found a way to foil the plan and escaped with his life. He later returned to the people and deceived them yet again.

Napi, the Old Man of the Siksika and related tribes, ordered mud to be brought to the surface from the bottom of a lake and thus formed the earth. He was the creator of man and animals, and taught them how to hunt, marry, and procreate. In other tales, however, Old Man exhibits various trickster qualities and often gets himself or someone else in trouble.

In trickster tales we see the good, the bad, and the ugliness of humanity. We can relate to a culture hero–trickster who can do so much good; at the same time, we know what it's like to be selfish and a buffoon. Trickster tales are entertaining as well as enlightening and instructive. From Trickster we can learn a lot about life and how to live it well.

See also Blue Jay; Coyote; Culture Hero(es); Kumokums; Manabozho; Nihansan; Old Man; Raven; Spider

References and further reading:

Carroll, Michael P. "The Trickster as Selfish-Buffoon and Culture Hero." *Ethos* 12, no. 2 (Summer 1984): 105–131.

Erdoes, Richard, and Alfonso Ortiz, eds. *American Indian Trickster Tales.* New York: Viking, 1998.

Ghezzi, Ridie Wilson. "Nanabush Stories from the Ojibwe." In *Coming to Light: Contemporary Translations of the Native Literatures of North America,* edited by Brian Swann, 443–463. New York: Vintage Books, 1996.

Hays, H. R. *Children of the Raven: The Seven Indian Nations of the Northwest Coast.* New York: McGraw-Hill, 1975.

Radin, Paul. *The Trickster: A Study in American Indian Mythology.* New York: Schocken Books, 1976. First published 1955 by Routledge and Paul.

Ricketts, MacLinscott. "The North American Indian Trickster." *History of Religions* 5 (1966): 327–350.

Wissler, Clark, and D. C. Duvall. *Mythology of the Blackfoot Indians.* Sources of American Indian Oral Literature. Lincoln: University of Nebraska Press, 1995. First published 1908 by American Museum of Natural History.

TURTLE

The slow and plodding Turtle appears often in Native American stories, many of which have been shaped by his ability to dig with his claws, retract into his hard shell, and live both on land and in water. Because he is clumsy and at times clownish, he is often ridiculed by others. In some cultures, however,

Turtle is respected as a powerful shaman, guardian of spirit health, or destroyer of monsters.

The following Seneca story illustrates their belief that Turtle is a warrior:

There was once a turtle that lived near a river. One day, feeling lonesome, he decided to go on the warpath. He got into a canoe and started paddling up the river, singing as he traveled along, "I am on the warpath! I am on the warpath!"

After going a short distance, Deer came to the riverbank. Calling out to Turtle, he asked him to stop and told him that he wanted to go with him. Turtle told Deer that first he wanted to see him run to the mountain and back. He explained that they might be defeated and need to run for their lives to avoid being scalped and killed. Deer ran to the mountain and back in no time, but Turtle was unwilling to take him because he did not run fast enough.

Turtle set out again in his canoe, singing "I am on the warpath! I am on the warpath!"

A Native American ritual shield. It is made of yellow ochre rawhide and buckskin and has red strouding, eagle feathers, and a wire handle. Images of a turtle, butterflies, lizard, and a bird are painted in green, black, red and yellow on the front face of the shield. It was possibly used in Sun Dance rituals. (Department of Material Culture, Colorado Historical Society, CHS X20010)

Soon Skunk came to the river and called out to Turtle. He wanted to go on the warpath, too. Turtle paddled ashore and told Skunk he must see him run, and that he could not take him along unless Skunk could run very fast. Turtle told skunk to run to the second mountain. Skunk showed his strength as he started out, so Turtle called him back and told him he could come along. The two got into the canoe and set out, with Turtle singing, "I am on the warpath! I am on the warpath!" Turtle commented on Skunk's odor.

Soon Bear called to them and asked them to stop. He, too, wanted to go along. Turtle landed and told him to run to the mountain. Bear started off and soon returned. However, Turtle told him he was not fast enough and refused to take him.

As they paddled along in their canoe, Hedgehog called to Turtle and Skunk. He wanted to go on the warpath, too. Turtle told Hedgehog he could come along if he was a good runner. He asked Hedgehog to run to the mountain. Hedgehog turned and started to run, but his feet crossed and he stumbled, nearly rolling over. He took only a few steps before Turtle said, "Stop! You'll do. Come and get into the canoe."

The three set off, with Turtle singing, "We are on the warpath! We are on the warpath!" Again, he commented on Skunk's odor. Referring to Hedgehog's quills, he told him that he had many arrows.

Now it was Elk that called from the bank and asked to go on the warpath with them. Turtle paddled ashore and told Elk to run to the second mountain and back as quickly as he could. Elk set out and returned in a very short time, smashing and breaking limbs, boughs, and bushes as he came. Turtle told Elk he could not go and started off, singing as before.

Soon, Rattlesnake appeared on the bank, and called out to them, asking to go along. Turtle told Rattlesnake he would only take along fast runners, explaining that they may have to run for their lives. He told him to run to the second mountain. Rattlesnake rose up to go, and Turtle suddenly told him he was welcome to come along.

So, the four started out, Turtle, Skunk, Hedgehog, and Rattlesnake, with Turtle singing as before. Again, he made comments about Skunk's odor and Hedgehog's arrows. He told Rattlesnake he had a black face.

The band of warriors decided to make war on the Seven Sisters, whose home was not far away. When they reached their destination and pulled the canoe out of the water, Turtle told them to each choose the place best suited to his fighting technique. Skunk chose the fireplace and said he would attack the first person he saw. Hedgehog chose to hide near the house in a pile of wood, and said he would attack the first person who came for it. Rattlesnake said he would get into the skin bucket in which there was dried corn. Turtle chose to station himself by the spring.

Early in the morning, the mother of the Seven Sisters went to build a fire. Skunk attacked her and she fell back, unable to open her eyes. The Seven Sisters heard their mother scream and ran to her. They began to fight with Skunk. Eventually, they pounded Skunk with clubs and killed him. They threw him outdoors and made a fire. One of the sisters went to the woodpile. Feeling a blow on her arm, she saw that it was full of hedgehog quills. The girl started screaming and fighting with Hedgehog, and her sisters came to her rescue. Seeing

Hedgehog, they struck him on the head and back with pieces of wood until they killed him.

One of the sisters then went to the skin bucket for dried corn for breakfast. When she put her hand in, she felt a sharp blow. Seeing Rattlesnake, she called to her sisters, who armed themselves with sticks and beat Rattlesnake until he was dead. But the sister he had bitten was dead as well.

After some time passed, the mother of the girls sent one of her daughters to the spring to get water. As she bent over to dip up the water, Turtle bit down on her big toe and wouldn't let go. She tried and tried to get him off but was unsuccessful, so she walked back to the house, dragging him along. When her mother saw her daughter with Turtle attached to her toe, she became very angry, so angry she suggested that Turtle be thrown on the fire and burnt up. But Turtle laughed and told the old woman that he could not be destroyed by fire, since he came from fire and liked to be in it more than anywhere else. So she changed her mind and decided to take him to the river to drown him. Turtle begged her not to do it, and told her he would die. He begged hard, but it was no use. He was taken to the river and thrown in. He sank to the bottom but soon rose to the top in the middle of the stream. He held out his claws as if showing scalps and laughed. He declared himself to be a brave warrior and told her that the river was where he lived. Then he sank out of sight.

See also Culture Hero(es)

References and further reading:

Curtin, Jeremiah. *Seneca Indian Myths.* Mineola, N.Y.: Dover, 2001. First published 1922 by E. P. Dutton.

Hertzberg, Hazel W. "The World on the Turtle's Back: An Iroquois Creation Myth." In *The Indian Peoples of Eastern America: A Documentary History of the Sexes,* J. Axtell, ed., 173–179. New York: Oxford University Press, 1981.

Tall Bull, Henry. The *Turtle Went to War: Northern Cheyenne Folk Tales.* Indian Culture Series, Stories of the Northern Cheyenne, BB-12. Billings, Mont.: Montana Reading Publications, 1971.

TUTOKANULA, LEGEND OF

Yosemite Valley, California

Two little boys who once lived in the valley went for a swim in the river. After splashing and frolicking in the water, they went ashore and climbed on top of a huge boulder that stood by the bank. Tired from playing for so long, they fell asleep. They slept so soundly that they did not realize the boulder grew and rose by day and by night, until they were lifted up and out of sight of their people, who searched for them everywhere. The rock continued to grow so high the boys were lifted far up above the sky, until their faces scraped against the moon. The boys continued to sleep among the clouds, year after year.

Then the animals held a great council to see who could bring the boys down from the top of the rock. Every animal attempted to leap as high as it could to no avail. Mouse could only jump as high as one's hand, and Rat twice that. Raccoon could make it only a little further. Grizzly Bear leaped quite high, but fell back. Lion made an attempt, and he managed to jump higher than anyone else, but he also fell.

Then it was tiny Measuring Worm's turn. He gradually began to creep up the face of the rock, inch by inch. Eventually, he reached as high as all the other animals had jumped and kept going. For one entire snow, Measuring Worm climbed, until at last he reached the top. He awakened the boys and brought them down to the ground safely. Thereafter, the rock was called Tutokanula, the measuring worm. To the white man, it is known as El Capitan.

References and further reading:

Judson, Katharine Berry. *Myths and Legends of California and the Old Southwest.* Lincoln: University of Nebraska Press, 1994. First published 1912 by A. C. McClurg.

WHIRLWIND WOMAN

Arapaho, Arikara, Plains

There are myths among the people of the Northeast Woodlands that depict the Whirlwind as a masculine figure, but stories about a female, Whirlwind Woman, were told on the upper Plains. Whirlwinds were sometimes thought to be ghosts.

All the people from a certain village were traveling west to hunt for buffalo. At the back of the group was a woman with two small children, a girl and her younger brother. As they crossed a stream, the children fell off the horse, but their mother didn't realize it until the people stopped to make camp. Some men went back but could not find the children because the youngsters had walked off in a different direction.

Eventually the children found a cave and the girl left her brother there while she looked for food. But while she was gone a Whirlwind grabbed her and took her away. She returned soon afterward, but from that day on the girl would leave and be gone for days at a time. Upon her return, the girl was always very happy.

The boy soon was big enough to hunt for rabbits, and his sister brought him a bow and some arrows. And then she left again. Sometime later, he told her that he needed a bigger bow and more arrows, since he was becoming a good hunter. The next time the sister returned, she brought just what he had asked for. This pleased the boy very much. Each time before the girl returned, her brother would hear the sound of an approaching storm and then suddenly she would come into view.

One day while the boy was hunting, an owl spoke to him. The owl told him that the animals had taken pity on him because his sister had become a whirlwind and was going around killing people. The owl told him that the whirlwind would eventually try to kill him, too. It wasn't long before the sister returned. She threatened the owls that were hiding him and insisted that they hand him over so she could kill her brother. Finally, at the owl's coaxing, the boy called out, "Sister, I promise that if you will leave me alone, I will give you the first woman I marry." That pleased the whirlwind, so she departed.

The boy, who was now a young man, traveled west and found his people. His father recognized him and asked about his sister. The young man only said, "She is traveling far away." Then the young man asked to speak with the chief. He told the chief that there were buffalo nearby. Hunters were sent out and found them exactly where the young man had said they would be. Not long afterward enemies attacked the camp. The courageous young man led the warriors out and quickly defeated the enemy. The people were greatly impressed with the young man, and the chief gave him his daughter to marry.

That night the young man called for his sister. When she came to his tipi, he gave her the young woman who was to be his wife. In return, the Whirlwind gave him gifts, including the power of the Whirlwind. She told him that he would have power over his enemy and would not be defeated by them. Then she said that the people should not be afraid of her any longer. They should pray to her and she would hear them. And then she was gone just as quickly as she arrived. In the days to come, the young man became famous as a courageous and powerful warrior and eventually he became a chief of his people.

See also Nihansan

References and further reading:

Curtin, Jeremiah. *Seneca Indian Myths.* Mineola, N.Y.: Dover, 2001. First published 1922 by E. P. Dutton.

Dorsey, George A. *Traditions of the Arikara: Collected under the Auspices of the Carnegie Institution of Washington.* Publication, no. 17. Washington, DC: The Institution, 1904.

Lowie, Robert H., ed. *Crow Texts.* Collected, translated, and edited by Robert H. Lowie. Berkeley: University of California Press, 1960.

WHITE BUFFALO WOMAN

Teton (Lakota), Plains

Also called White Buffalo Cow Woman, White Buffalo Calf Woman, and White Buffalo Calf Maiden, the holy White Buffalo Woman is the principal figure in the

Teton's (Lakota's) most important and enduring legend. According to belief, approximately 2,000 years ago she brought the Teton people of the Black Hills the sacred buffalo calf pipe that is central to their religious practices and foretold several ceremonies in which the pipe was to be used. These ceremonies, known as the Seven Sacred Rites of the Lakota, include the Sweat Lodge Ceremony, the Vision Quest, Ghost Keeping Ceremony, the Sun Dance, Throwing of the Ball Ceremony, the Making of Relatives, and Girls' Puberty Rite.

Various versions of the story have been recorded. This version was told by Teton medicine man John Fire Lame Deer.

One summer the seven sacred council fires of the Teton came together and camped. There was no game and the people were starving, so two young men went out to hunt. Along the way, they met a beautiful young woman dressed in white buckskin. Because she was floating instead of walking, they knew she was holy. One of the men desired her and reached out to touch her. This woman was *lila wakan*, very sacred, and could not be treated with disrespect. Lightning instantly struck the bold young man and burned him up, leaving only a small heap of blackened bones. The White Buffalo Woman spoke to the other man, who had behaved honorably, and told him to announce to his nation her impending arrival.

This young hunter returned to the camp with the White Buffalo Woman's message. As she had instructed, a large tipi was built and the people waited. After four days she approached and entered the tipi, walked in a sunrise (clockwise) direction and stopped before the chief. She opened the wrapped bundle she carried and presented the sacred pipe to the people. The pipe was decorated with twelve eagle feathers, and on one side of the bowl was carved a bison calf, on the other were seven circles of various sizes.

The White Buffalo Woman then gave the people sacred teachings. She explained the meaning of the pipe itself and each of its components. She taught the people how to use it to pray, with the appropriate words and gestures. She explained that the seven circles stood for the seven ceremonies in which the pipe should be used, and for the Ocheti Shakowin, the seven sacred campfires of the Teton nation. She presented the first rite, the Ghost Keeping Ceremony, and explained that the other six would be revealed in time.

Before leaving the tipi, the White Buffalo Woman told the people she would return, walked again in a sunrise direction and left. Going in the same direction from which she had come, she stopped and rolled over four times. The first time, she turned into a black buffalo; the second into a brown one; the third into a red one. Finally, the fourth time she rolled over, she turned into a white female buffalo calf and then disappeared over the horizon. As soon as she had vanished, buffalo in great herds appeared, allowing themselves to be killed so that the people might survive. From that day on, the buffalo furnished the people with everything they needed: meat for their food, skins for their clothes and tipis, bones for their many tools.

Dakota man with calumet kneeling by altar inside tipi, 1907. (Library of Congress)

The prophecy of the White Buffalo Woman's return appeared to be fulfilled by the appearance of a female buffalo calf on August 20, 1994, on a farm near Janesville, Wisconsin. Named Miracle, she was considered to be the first white buffalo calf (she is not albino) born since 1933. Like the buffalo in the story, she has changed color four times. Another sacred white buffalo calf, Wahos'i, was born on August 7, 2001, in Vanderbilt, Michigan. And four white buffalo calves were born on a ranch in Westhope, North Dakota, between August 17 and September 2, 2002.

Miracle's birth focused the world's attention on the story of the White Buffalo Woman and inspired modern interpretations of it. Some Native American elders interpret her color changes as a representation of the four colors of the human race. The White Buffalo Woman promised she would return in time of need, but to whose need does the story refer? Because she was born to owners who are not Native American, Teton elder Floyd Hand believes that Miracle's message of hope, renewal, and harmony applies to all people. Some suggest that the birth of a female white buffalo calf symbolizes the evident resurgence of Native American political, economic, and cultural strength.

See also Culture Hero(es)

References and further reading:

Black Elk. *Black Elk Speaks: Being the Life Story of a Holy Man of the Oglala Sioux.* 21st Century edition. Lincoln: University of Nebraska Press, 2000.

Fire, John, and Richard Erdoes. *Lame Deer, Seeker of Visions.* New York: Simon and Schuster, 1972.

Hirschfelder, Arlene, and Paulette Molin. *Encyclopedia of Native American Religions: An Introduction.* Updated edition. New York: Facts on File, 2000.

Pickering, Robert B. *Seeing the White Buffalo.* Denver, Colo.: Denver Museum of Natural History Press, 1997.

Walker, James R. *Lakota Belief and Ritual.* Lincoln: University of Nebraska Press, 1991. First published 1980.

WHY STORIES

Siksika (Blackfeet), Cheyenne, Kiowa, Plains

Many myths from a variety of areas across North America can be classified as Why Stories because they explain the reason for an event or for a geographical or physical feature.

Frank B. Linderman collected numerous Why Stories during his years in Montana with the Siksika people. Why Stories contained in Linderman's publications include: "Why Our Sight Fails with Age," "Why Children Lose Their Teeth," "How the Skunk Helped the Coyote," "Why the Dogs Howl at Night," "Why the Kingfisher Always Wears a War-Bonnet," and "Why the Birch-Tree Wears the Slashes in Its Bark."

A Kiowa story explains "Why Dogs Do Not Speak." One day the trickster Saynday was traveling along and came to the dogs' village. They were all making a lot of noise with each of them talking at the same time. Saynday asked them to be quiet as he wanted to talk with them. But the father and mother dogs and even their puppies just continued to talk. Again Saynday asked them to be quiet, but to no avail. He began to get very annoyed with them, but that just made the dogs talk even more.

Finally, Saynday gave them an ultimatum: "All of you be quiet or something bad will happen." Still the dogs kept on talking. This was more than Saynday could take. He said, "You've had your warning. From this moment on you will not be able to speak; you'll only be able to growl and bark and yap. Nobody will be able to understand what you are trying to say. You'll only be able to communicate with your eyes and your tails." And so it has been ever since that day.

The Cheyenne's "Why the Turtle's Shell Is Checked" is another example of a Why Story.

The animals decided to go to war, so Turtle, Skunk, Porcupine, Grasshopper, Snake, Cricket, and Willow all started off. They made camp the first night, and on the following morning, Grasshopper had lost one of his legs and had to return home. The others traveled on and then made camp that night. On the following morning Cricket was singing under a bush and would not join the others when they departed. That night they made camp again and on the following morning, Snake went for a swim but would not come out of the water when the others set out.

The four remaining companions continued on their way. That evening they made camp near a stream. In the morning they found that Willow had waded in and now was stuck fast in the mud. The other three had to leave him there and continue on their way. Finally, Turtle, Skunk, and Porcupine arrived at the enemies' village and waited until everyone was asleep. They crept into camp and found the chief's tipi. While the chief slept, they scalped him and cut off his head.

When the people found out what happened they were distraught. They searched for tracks leading away from the village but could not find any. Then a woman noticed that a large bowl was turned upside down and a wisp of smoke coming from under it. She kicked the bowl over and found the three warriors who were preparing their victory celebration. Everyone in the village came running to see the three culprits, but Porcupine grabbed the chief's scalp and ran off. Skunk raised his tail and sprayed everyone. As the people backed away, Skunk ran to catch up with Porcupine.

Turtle was too slow and was captured by the angry villagers. As they pondered what to do with him, Turtle retreated inside his shell. Occasionally he would stick his head out and snap at the people, but this just made them even angrier. Finally, they decided to burn him. They made a great pile of branches, set it on fire, and then tossed Turtle into the flames. He kicked furiously and got away from the burning branches, but not before his shell became cracked and checked from the heat.

Again the people debated about what to do with Turtle. Eventually it was decided to toss him into the river. Turtle made a great noise with his protests but finally said that he wanted to die like a man. He requested that two of the biggest chiefs take him to the river. That is how it happened. Two large war chiefs dragged him to the river and waded out into it. Suddenly Turtle grabbed the men and drowned them both. The people tried to get to Turtle but they could not. Turtle pulled the two dead chiefs to the opposite bank and scalped them.

Turtle returned to his village just as everyone was celebrating Skunk and Porcupine's return with the one scalp. Turtle quietly went to his sister's tipi. When she saw him, she was thrilled that he was still alive. She ran out to tell everyone that her brother had returned with two enemy scalps, but Turtle angrily called her back in.

Eventually, the word spread around the village that Turtle had returned with two scalps. Skunk and Porcupine came to welcome him back and to let him know that they were holding a victory dance in his honor. This pleased Turtle. He went out to find his sister who was crying because of his harsh words to her. "Cheer up, Sister! I went to war to bring you happiness. When the enemies threw me into the fire, my shell became cracked and checked, but it was all worth it. Now, get ready and go to the dance with these two scalps."

See also Old Man; Skinkuts

References and further reading:

Linderman, Frank B. *Indian Old-Man Stories: More Sparks from War Eagle's Lodge-Fire.* 1920. Authorized ed. Lincoln: University of Nebraska Press, 2001.

———. *Indian Why Stories: Sparks from War Eagle's Lodge-Fire.* 1915. New authorized ed. Lincoln: University of Nebraska Press, 2001.

———. *Kootenai Why Stories.* Authorized ed. Lincoln: University of Nebraska Press, 1997. First published 1926 by Scribner's.

Marriott, Alice, and Carol K. Rachlin. *Plains Indian Mythology.* New York: New American Library, 1985. First published 1975 by Thomas Y. Crowell.

WIND

Dakota (Sioux), Teton (Lakota), Plains

The story of Tate (the Wind) is part of the ancient and complex mythology of the Dakota (Sioux) and Teton (Lakota) people. Inyan (the Rock) had no beginning. Inyan created Maka (the Earth) from a part of himself and gave her part of his spirit. Skan (the Sky) was created from Inyan's blood that was lost when he created Maka. Skan became the foremost god and judge over all. Skan then created Wi (the Sun). In time, these gods created companions for themselves, placed animals and vegetation on the earth and in the waters, and formed humans. Skan created Tate (the Wind) as his companion and messenger.

Eventually, Tate took a beautiful but treacherous woman named Ite as his wife. She bore four sons, Yata, Eya, Yanpa, and Okaga, and was pregnant with another child, Yum, when she schemed against Skan. Her punishment was to live on earth as a Double-Face. Besides her beautiful face, she was given a second, hideous one. People who saw her became insane or ran away in terror.

Tate, however, loved Ite and interceded for himself and his sons. Skan allowed them to remain on earth in order to live near Ite. Tate made his home at the center of the world and instructed his four sons to establish the four directions and to oversee the four seasons. He told them to travel to the edge of the world and place the directions at equal distances from each other. When they had accomplished this task, they would become spirits and messengers for the gods. Tate warned his four sons to be wary of Iktomi, who would attempt to deceive and destroy them.

On their journey, they were helped at times by the wizard Wazi, who was their maternal grandfather. At other times they were tricked by Spider into abandoning their purpose. However, Wakinyan (the Thunderbird) sent his messenger, the swallow, to assist them and to get Tate's sons back on track. With Wazi's help the brothers eventually reached the four points around the edge of the world. At each of the points, one of the brothers set a marker to claim the direction for himself. When their task was completed, the brothers returned to

Tate's lodge. It had been twelve months since they had departed. This is how a year's time was first measured.

See also Spider; Thunderbirds

References and further reading:

Melody, Michael Edward. "Maka's Story: A Study of a Lakota Cosmogony." *Journal of American Folklore* 90, no. 356 (April–June 1977): 149–167

One Feather, Vivian. "The Four Directions." *Parabola* 3, no. 1 (1978): 62–70.

Walker, James R. *Lakota Belief and Ritual.* Lincoln: University of Nebraska Press, 1991. First published 1980.

WINDIGO

Ojibwa, Northeast Woodlands

These giant cannibals roamed the northeastern woods in the dead of winter and devoured any humans they found. The only way to escape was for a person to also turn into a *windigo* and fight the monster.

One day the kettles started moving over the fire. The villagers were all frightened because they knew that a windigo was coming. A young girl who lived with her grandmother asked the old woman why everyone was so nervous. The grandmother explained, "When the ice-hearted giant gets here, we will all die." The girl thought about the problem and then asked someone to bring her some long sticks with the bark removed. Then she went back home and waited.

Before long the air turned very cold. The people could hear the ice and the trees cracking. The girl asked her grandmother to heat a kettle full of tallow. When they looked outside, there was a windigo walking toward the village. He was at least twenty or thirty feet tall, and as he walked the trees cracked and the lake froze over.

Then the girl and her two dogs went out to meet the windigo, and her dogs killed the windigo's dog. As she walked along, she kept getting bigger and bigger. Then she attacked the windigo with her sticks that had turned into copper rods. She hit him hard and knocked him down. Then she hit him again and killed him. Her grandmother gave her the hot tallow and as the girl drank it she returned to normal size. The people from the village came out and hacked the windigo to pieces. Inside they found a normal man. The villagers were so pleased with the girl that they promised to give her anything she desired.

Another story tells of a man who was very gluttonous. He had four wives and was a good hunter. But to get enough food for himself and all of his wives, he had to go long distances in search of game. One day when he returned, he told his wives that a man was coming to see him, but that he would be ready. His wives understood him to mean that the visitor could turn himself into a windigo. When they saw the visitor approach, the man went outside. The one approaching yelled eight times and each time he yelled, he was bigger than the last. Finally he was as tall as the trees. But the gluttonous man yelled ten times and became bigger than the windigo. The two fought and beat each other with trees that they ripped out of the ground. But finally the windigo was defeated. When the man returned home, his wives gave him tallow they had melted and he returned to normal size.

References and further reading:

Barnouw, Victor. *Wisconsin Chippewa Myths & Tales and Their Relation to Chippewa Life: Based on Folktales Collected by Victor Barnouw, Joseph B. Casagrande, Ernestine Friedl, and Robert E. Ritzenthaler.* Madison: University of Wisconsin Press, 1977.

Largent, Floyd. "Windigo: A Native American Archetype." *Parabola* 23 (1998): 22–25.

Miller, Jay. *Earthmaker: Tribal Stories from Native North America.* New York: Perigee Books, 1992.

WISAKA

Fox, Sauk, Northeast Woodlands

Known by various names among people of the western Northeast Woodlands region, this culture-hero taught the people how to live in harmony with his grandmother, the Earth.

Long ago the orphan Wisaka was raised by his grandmother. At that time there were giants on the earth (some say they were *manitous*, mighty spirits) who became jealous and warred against Wisaka and his brother because the boys had become so powerful. Only by deceit were their enemies able to get an upper hand and kill the brother. During the four days of mourning, his brother's ghost came to the lodge. Wisaka refused to let him in, and instead told the ghost that he must travel to the west and there he would find their mother. From that time on, the brother was the guardian of the land of the dead. Eventually Wisaka was victorious over his enemy, and while still a young man, he began preparing the earth for the people he created. He brought fire to the people to keep them warm. He discovered tobacco and shared its spiritual mysteries with them. He taught the people and the animals many things he had learned from his father, the Great Manitou, and his grandmother, the Earth, including many sacred ceremonies.

One time Wisaka was traveling and saw a buck with large antlers running at him. Wisaka asked, "Where are you going?" The buck replied that he was hungry and was hunting humans. So Wisaka told him to go on about his business. Wisaka continued on his way until he saw a grove of crabapple trees. He filled his bag full of the fruit and slung it over his back. Then he stepped out of the woods. Not long afterward, the buck saw what he thought was a big, fat, tasty human and ran after Wisaka. He bit into the bag and ended up with a mouth full of the sour apples. The buck decided that he no longer cared for the taste of humans. From that time on humans have hunted and enjoyed the taste of deer.

Some time later, Wisaka was resting from his journey and all sorts of animals came up to him. They wanted to know how they were supposed to live. To the eagle, Wisaka said, "Little brother, you will eat birds and small animals, but your feathers will be prized by men." Wisaka continued to name the remaining creatures and decide their natures. He told the fox that he would be very quick and cunning but man would prize fox hides and tails for clothing and ornaments. Wisaka told the turkey that men would seek him for his tasty meat and use his feathers for decoration. The raccoon wanted to know if he would have enemies. "Yes, the dog," said Wisaka. So the raccoon attacked the dog, but the dog struck back and sent the raccoon running up a tree. Wisaka told the squirrel that he would make a tasty soup. The animals all wondered why humans would want to eat them. At Wisaka's command a nearby lake turned into tallow. Then he dipped each animal into the tallow, but the mink jumped into the lake before its turn, so Wisaka pulled him out and shook off all of the tallow. That is why mink are never fat.

When Wisaka was finished fattening up the animals, he returned home and told his grandmother what he had done. She was very pleased with his work.

Finally, Wisaka was very old. He had taught the people many things and had been involved in many adventures. So he went into the north where he now sits and keeps watch over men and animals. It is said that he will return some day and make things as they were before.

See also Culture Hero(es); Transformer

References and further reading:
Briggs, John E. "Wisaka." *Palimpsest* 7, no. 4 (1926): 97–112.
Jones, William. "Episodes in the Culture-Hero Myth of the Sauks and Foxes." *Journal of American Folklore* 14, no. 55 (October–December 1901): 225–239.
———. *Fox Texts.* New York: AMS Press, 1974. First published 1907 by E. J. Brill.
Skinner, Alanson. "Sauk Tales." *Journal of American Folklore* 41, no. 159 (January–March 1928): 147–171.

WOMAN WHO FELL FROM THE SKY
Northeast Woodlands
There are various versions of this myth among the people of the Northeast Woodlands. Among the Wyandot (Huron), the woman who fell from the sky was called Ataensic (or Ataensie), and the Seneca called her Iagen'tci.

Long ago the world was covered by water and there were people living in the heavens. The chief's daughter became ill, but the healers were unable to cure her. One night a friend and adviser of the chief had a dream. He related his dream to the chief when he awoke and the chief decided to follow the dream's instructions. So the people laid the young woman next to the great tree that was the source of all of the corn the people ate. However, a stipulation in the dream was that the tree had to be dug up and destroyed.

When they had finished digging the tree up, a young man came along and said angrily, "It was wrong to destroy this tree that supplied us with food." Then the young man gave the girl a shove with his foot and she fell through the hole in the ground where the tree used to stand. Two great birds saw her falling through the air. They flew close together, swooped underneath her, and caught her on their backs.

Eventually the birds became tired of carrying the young woman, so they asked, "Who will care for her?" Turtle volunteered, but eventually he tired of the task. Turtle asked for another volunteer. However, the animals and birds who lived on and in the water decided that a permanent place was needed for the woman. The plan called for mud to be brought up from the bottom of the sea and spread out on Turtle's back. As the mud was placed on Turtle's back, it began to expand in area until it was large enough to sustain the woman, vegetation, and all creatures that were created soon afterward.

Eventually, the young woman's condition improved and she built a shelter. Some time later, she gave birth to a daughter and the child grew quickly. The mother warned her daughter to always face the west when she dug for roots. But in time the daughter showed signs of being pregnant. Her mother scolded her for disobeying. The West Wind had blown up under the girl's skirt while she was digging with her face to the east and had caused her to conceive. The girl was pregnant with twins, and before they were born, her sons argued about which one of them should be born first and what was the best way to do it.

One twin wanted to be born in the manner that babies are born today. But his twin had a rebellious nature and tore through his mother's body and exited under her armpit. She died soon after and her mother buried her. From the daughter's body grew the first food. Corn stalks grew from her breasts, beans from her arms and legs, and squash vines grew out from her belly. Their grandmother, the Woman Who Fell from the Sky, raised the boys and called one Sapling and the other Flint. Right from the beginning she favored Sapling and despised Flint because he had caused their mother's death.

One day the grandmother had enough of Flint's mischief and took him out into the woods and left him in the hollow tree trunk. She doted on Sapling and taught him how to hunt and fish. Often Sapling came home from hunting without his bow and arrows and his grandmother would have to make him new ones. Finally, she asked him about it and he told her that the boy who lived in the woods would steal them from him. The grandmother asked Sapling to take her to the boy. When they found Flint, they brought him back to their home.

Sapling grew to be a good man who went about creating streams and lakes, fish and game animals, and making the whole earth habitable for humans. Flint, however, had a destructive nature. He was responsible for causing cold and icy conditions, creating weeds, snakes, and insects. The brothers eventually argued about each other's creations. In the ensuing fight, Flint was killed. But it was too late for Sapling to undo the evil his brother had created in the world.

See also Corn; Earth Diver

References and further reading:

Hazen-Hammond, Susan. *Spider Woman's Web: Traditional Native American Tales About Women's Power.* New York: Berkley, 1999.

Leach, Maria. *The Beginning: Creation Myths Around the World.* New York: Funk & Wagnalls, 1956.

Parker, Arthur Caswell. *Seneca Myths and Folk Tales.* 1923. Lincoln: University of Nebraska Press, 1989.

Thompson, Stith. *Tales of the North American Indians.* 1929. Bloomington: Indiana University Press, 1971.

WOODWORM

Haida, Northwest Coast

Hereditary family crests or emblems have been used in many cultures around the world. In the Pacific Northwest region, crests often decorated household items and clothing and were featured on great poles outside the houses of the clan chiefs.

It was the custom for girls entering puberty to be kept in seclusion for a time while they were being prepared for marriage. The only people they could come in contact with were a few of their female family members. During this time they were thought to possess great powers that could bring bad luck to hunters and fishermen. This story about a young girl in seclusion who exhibits great motherly love explains how a clan got its crest.

The daughter of a great chief began her period of seclusion and lived in the far back corner of the house behind a wall. The girl could hear her friends playing outside and she knew she could no longer join in their childhood games. She became very lonely.

One day while tending to her fire, a woodworm fell out of the wood. She wrapped it in a blanket and it became her pet. The woodworm would not eat anything she offered until finally she offered her breast and it drank heartily. Her pet grew rapidly and she rocked it in her arms and sang it lullabies.

However, when any of her attendants were near, she kept it hidden behind boxes. Finally the woodworm grew to be so large that she had trouble keeping it a secret. It no longer nursed, but raided the food storage pits under the chief's house. Then it tunneled from house to house, raiding food that had been stored for the winter.

The people complained that some monster was stealing their food, but no one ever saw it. One day, however, as the girl was singing a lullaby, her mother peeked around the wall and saw her daughter rocking a huge worm. The mother went out and told her husband. Then the chief and the girl's uncle went in and looked into her living quarters. There they saw the huge monster. Later the chief called the people together to explain what was stealing all of their food. Even though it was his daughter's pet and companion, it had to be killed or it would cause all of the people to starve.

The girl was invited to visit her uncle's house. Her mother told her that her time of seclusion was over and she could leave the house. She suspected that her secret had been found out and feared for the pet that she now called her son. But after much coaxing, the girl finally left the house. While she was gone, the men of the village came with long, sharp spears and killed the woodworm.

When she saw that the woodworm was dead, she wept and accused the people of killing her child. She was inconsolable and continually sang about her child. The people were moved by her despair and her devotion to her son, and honored him by burning his body on a huge fire, just as the girl had asked. She continued to sing her sad songs and refused to eat or sleep. After a while the girl died and her people moved from that place. However, because of her devotion to her son and the special powers she must have had to be able to raise a small woodworm into a giant monster, the people took the Woodworm as their crest.

References and further reading:

Beck, Mary Giraudo. *Heroes & Heroines: Tlingit-Haida Legend.* Anchorage: Alaska Northwest Books, 1989.

Bierhorst, John. *The Mythology of North America: With a New Afterword.* New York: Oxford University Press, 2002. First published 1985 by William Morrow.

Webber, William L. *The Thunderbird "Tootooch" Legends: Folk Tales of the Indian Tribes of the Pacific Northwest Coast Indians.* Seattle: Ace, 1936.

4

ANNOTATED PRINT AND NONPRINT RESOURCES

BOOKS AND ARTICLES

Beckwith, Martha Warren. **"Mythology of the Oglala Dakota."** *Journal of American Folklore* 43, no. 170 (October–December 1930): 339–442.

This massive article contains myths collected by the author in 1926 on the Pine Ridge Reservation. The introduction provides background regarding the collection and selection of these narratives. Following the introduction is a section entitled "Contents" listing the various entries and a summary or explanatory note for each one. Footnotes supply additional background and source information. A list of references is also included in this article.

Bierhorst, John. *The Mythology of North America: With a New Afterword.* New York: Oxford University Press, 2002. First published 1985 by William Morrow.

This updated guide presents an overview by region of major North American Indian gods, heroes, and myths. The author provides thoughtful commentary on the background, history, and connections between the various myths and stories, as well as their current significance and impact on contemporary American Indian affairs. The text is complemented by illustrations of Native American artwork and detailed maps showing tribal locations and the distribution of primary stories. This essential work includes a bibliography and index.

———. *The Red Swan: Myths and Tales of the American Indians.* Albuquerque: University of New Mexico Press, 1992. First published 1976 by Farrar, Straus, and Giroux.

Sixty-four myths are arranged into topical groupings that include From the Body of Our Mother; Tales of War; Winter and Spring; Birth of the Hero;

Hero as Provider; Hero as Deliverer; Comedy of Horrors; Ghosts; Tales of the White Man; Myths of Returning Life; and Death and Beyond. This title also includes notes, references, and a glossary of tribes, cultures, and languages. Also published under title: *Myths and Tales of the American Indians* (New York: Indian Head Books, 1992).

Blue Cloud, Peter. *Elderberry Flute Song: Contemporary Coyote Tales.* 4th ed. Buffalo, N.Y.: White Pine Press, 2002.

This classic work, with delightful illustrations by the author, contains fifty-six of Blue Cloud's poems, prose poems, and tales featuring the colorful, enduring, and multidimensional character Coyote. The prolific Blue Cloud is a Mohawk of the Turtle Clan and recipient of an American Book Award from the Before Columbus Foundation.

Boas, Franz. **"Mythology and Folk-Tales of the North American Indians."** *Journal of American Folklore* 27, no. 106 (October–December 1914): 374–410.

In this 1914 publication, Boas, called by some the "father of American anthropology," gave an overview of the state of contemporary anthropological research and the body of knowledge of Native American myths and folktales. Boas also discussed topics such as what constitutes a myth, what sets myths apart from folk-tales, and how they are disseminated among cultures and regions. Various recurring themes are summarized, such as origin, trickster, and human society/tribal life. Among other points, Boas discussed personification within myths and folktales (the attributing of human characteristics to animals and natural phenomena). In his conclusion, Boas suggested that much work was still needed in the study of mythology and folklore.

Bruchac, Joseph. *Our Stories Remember: American Indian History, Culture, and Values Through Storytelling.* Golden, Colo.: Fulcrum Publishing, 2003.

Prolific award-winning Native American author and storyteller Bruchac offers the reader a fascinating mix of information about Native origins and lifeways with his retelling of stories by such diverse groups as the Abenaki, Cherokee, Cree, Navajo, Dakota (Sioux), Tlingit, and others. Each chapter opens with a Native epigraph and features a story or stories—sometimes separate from and other times woven into—a main text that includes historical, cultural, or autobiographical details and commentary by the author. Chapters are devoted to such topics as art, ceremony, contact with Europeans, origins, the spirit world, and plants and animals. This illuminating work is enhanced with source notes for the stories and epigraphs and brief annotated lists of recommended works, most by Native authors. An index is included.

Bullchild, Percy. *The Sun Came Down.* San Francisco: Harper & Row, 1990.

Bullchild, a Siksika (Blackfeet) Indian artist and musician, has made available in this work, subtitled *The History of the World as My Blackfeet Elders Told It,* a most rich and fascinating collection of Native American oral tradition. He gathered these Siksika legends and stories over a period of eleven years, and he tells them with refreshing dignity, grace, and vigor in the personal, authentic, and compelling language of an Indian storyteller. Bullchild also reveals much about sacred ceremonies of the Siksika.

Champagne, Duane, ed. *The Native North American Almanac: A Reference Work on Native North Americans in the United States and Canada.* 2nd ed. Detroit: Gale Group, 2001.

This valuable serial publication, edited by the director of UCLA's American Indian Studies Center, is more accurately described as a combination encyclopedia/handbook/directory than an almanac. Over seventy authors and specialist editors contributed to eighteen chapters covering such topics as arts, culture areas, law and legislation, education, economy, women and gender relations, languages, activism, and more, including a chronology from 11,000 B.C. through 2000. The resource concludes with a chapter containing brief biographies of prominent Native North Americans, followed by its own index by occupation. This work distinguishes itself from other recent similar publications through its coverage of Canadian aboriginals in the latter part of each chapter, and its focus on the twentieth century. Close to 350 photos, maps, charts, and drawings complement the text. Chapters include subject bibliographies and listings by state; a general bibliography, dictionary index, and glossary round out this comprehensive, easy-to-use, authoritative volume.

Clark, Ella E. *Indian Legends from the Northern Rockies.* The Civilization of the American Indian Series, vol. 82. Norman: University of Oklahoma Press, 1966.

An anthology of tales primarily from the area that is now Idaho, Montana, and Wyoming. Clark states in her introduction that she purposely left out many of the myths about culture heroes, transformers, and tricksters that are usually cited. She included instead a variety of tales that had never been published before. Some of these were told to Clark by elderly storytellers; the rest were gleaned from private collections or archived manuscripts from early explorers or settlers in the area.

Clements, William M., and Frances M. Malpezzi. *Native American Folklore, 1879–1979: An Annotated Bibliography.* Athens, Ohio: Swallow Press, 1984.

Focusing on the oral arts of Native Americans north of Mexico, this extensive bibliography of over 5,000 entries needs updating, but it is nevertheless an important addition to any Native American studies collection. Covering the century after the founding of the Smithsonian Institution's Bureau of Ethnology, during which time there was a remarkable increase in the amount of available published material, much of the literature identified in this guide appears in diverse serial publications that are often difficult to locate. Descriptive but brief annotations for works in English and Native American languages are arranged by culture areas subdivided by tribe. An index of authors, editors, translators, and subjects is included.

Curtin, Jeremiah. *Creation Myths of Primitive America.* Edited by Karl Kroeber. ABC-CLIO Classic Folk and Fairy Tales. Santa Barbara, Calif.: ABC-CLIO, 2002. First published 1898 by Little, Brown, and Company with title: *Creation Myths of Primitive America in Relation to the Religious History and Mental Development of Mankind.*

This anthology features a set of animal myths of the Wintu and Yana of California, collected and translated by Curtin, one of the foremost figures in nineteenth-century American linguistics and ethnography. The stories offer contemporary readers great insight into how Native Americans perceived and interpreted their natural world and its elements. Karl Kroeber, Mellon Professor of the Humanities at Columbia University, has provided an informative introduction. Curtin's willingness to detail and condemn mistreatment of Native Americans by white settlers and government officials was unparalleled among other anthropologists and linguists of his time, which contributed in part to his successful relations with Indians and his ability to collect their stories.

Deloria, Ella C., comp. *Dakota Texts.* 1932. Freeman: University of South Dakota Press, 1992.

Deloria, who was raised on the Yankton Sioux Reservation in South Dakota, included sixty-four tales in this collection. The eight beginning entries feature Iktomi, the trickster, while the remaining entries cover a wide variety of mythological and legendary figures. A useful section is the *Synopses of Tales* that includes summaries of each myth.

Deloria, Philip J., and Neal Salisbury, eds. *A Companion to American Indian History.* Malden, Mass.: Blackwell, 2002.

A collection of twenty-five essays written by leading Native American and non-Native authors that brings an exciting and fresh perspective to the study of Indian history and culture. Aimed at scholars, students, and general readers, this volume covers a wide range of topics related to the Native American experience and their practices, including art, religion, literature, language, law, economics, politics and government, family, gender, education, and contacts with non-Indians. Each chapter contains a bibliography of selected works, and an index is included. This is a timely contribution to Native American research and scholarship and the ideal guide to issues, concepts and literatures that have emerged within the field.

Deloria, Vine, Jr. *Red Earth, White Lies: Native Americans and the Myth of Scientific Fact.* Golden, Colo.: Fulcrum, 1997. First published 1995 by Scribner.

A thought-provoking, sometimes bitingly humorous critique of modern scientific theories about evolution, creation, natural history, and population movements in the Western Hemisphere as they relate to Native oral traditions. Deloria, a preeminent Native American activist and author, challenges the idea that these theories are more valid and truthful than facts preserved in the centuries-old traditional knowledge and lore of tribal peoples.

Dooling, D. M., ed. *The Sons of the Wind: The Sacred Stories of the Lakota.* Edited by D. M. Dooling from the James R. Walker Collection, with an introduction by Vivian Arviso One Feather. Norman: University of Oklahoma Press, 2000. First published 1984 by Parabola Books.

This updated edition contains a new afterword by Elaine A. Jahner. In less than 150 pages, Dooling summarizes the mythology of the Teton (Lakota) based on information recorded by James R. Walker. Included in this brief volume are stories about the formation of the world by the eternal Inyan; the creation of his companions, the Sacred Spirits; the organization of the earth into its current form and function; the struggles between forces of good and forces of evil; and the creation of animals and humans. Includes a glossary and Teton pronunciation guide.

Dorsey, George A. *The Pawnee Mythology.* 1906. Sources of American Indian Oral Literature. Lincoln: University of Nebraska Press, 1997.

These myths and legends were collected by Dorsey and his assistant, James R. Murie, a member of a Pawnee band, in the early 1900s. There are

148 stories and their abstracts, divided into sections that include True
Stories of the Heavenly Beings and Coyote Tales. Douglas Parks's introduction gives a brief overview of Pawnee history, society, and religion.

————. *Traditions of the Skidi Pawnee.* 1904. New York: Kraus Reprint Co., 1969.
Dorsey began collecting these 300 myths in 1899 while associated with
the Field Columbian Museum. The introduction includes a description of
Pawnee culture, social organization, and cosmology. Each myth narrative
is preceded by a brief summary. Also included are notes, some detailed,
giving the source, additional background, or an explanation for each myth.
This is the companion volume to *The Pawnee Mythology.*

Dorsey, George A., and Alfred L. Kroeber. *Traditions of the Arapaho.* 1903.
Sources of American Indian Oral Literature. Lincoln: University of Nebraska
Press, 1997.
This work, originally published in 1903, consists of 146 myths and traditional stories gathered independently by Dorsey and Kroeber between 1899
and 1902. Abstracts of each myth are included, along with a list of contributors, and translations of passages the authors wrote in Latin (a common
practice of the time where the actual text may have been viewed as being
too sexually explicit). The introduction gives a brief history of the Arapaho
people and describes some of their traditional beliefs and culture.

Edmonds, Margot, and Ella E. Clark. *Voices of the Winds: Native American
Legends.* New York: Facts on File, 1989.
An anthology of over 100 myths from across North America. Myths are organized into six geographic regions. Gives brief introductions for each region as well as for most of the myths. Includes numerous illustrations.

Erdoes, Richard, and Alfonso Ortiz, eds. *American Indian Myths and Legends.*
New York: Pantheon Books, 1984.
This excellent collection of over 160 tales representing eighty North
American tribal groups combines classic myths and legends, some captured in nineteenth century documents, with those voiced by contemporary storytellers and collected by the authors in their extensive field research. The book is organized, for convenience, into ten general chapters
of tales and stories of human creation, the sun, moon, and stars, war and
the warrior code, love and lust, and trickster tales, to highlight a few. Each
chapter opens with introductory commentary provided by the editors, but
their objective is to preserve the stories and make them available to new

audiences, not to provide analysis. They have chosen to retell those stories from older sources in an attempt to remove embellishments and restore their authenticity. A note at the end of each tale details its origin. A bibliography and index of tales is included, as well as an appendix of tribes, with a short description of each. Another collection edited by Erdoes with a more narrow focus is *The Sound of Flutes and Other Indian Legends,* which includes stories from the Great Plains.

———, eds. ***American Indian Trickster Tales.*** New York: Viking Books, 1998.
The editors have compiled over 100 trickster tales from across North America. The tales are organized by trickster type: Coyote, Iktomi, Veeho, Nixant and Sitconski, Master Rabbit, Nanabozho and Whiskey Jack, Old Man Napi, Glooskap, Skeleton Man, and Raven. The introduction provides a lucid overview of the various Native North American tricksters with comparisons to figures from classical mythology. An appendix provides information about various tribes whose myths are included in the volume. A list of sources is provided.

Fenton, William N. **"This Island, the World on Turtle's Back."** *Journal of American Folklore* 75, no. 298 (October–December 1962): 283–300.
This article describes three myths found among the tribes of the Northeast Woodlands, particularly the Iroquois and Wyandot (Huron). These myths include the Earth-grasper (also known as The Woman Who Fell from the Sky); the Deganawidah epic regarding the founding of the Longhouse League; and Kai'wi'yo, the revelation of the prophet Handsome Lake. A summary of the main themes of Iroquoian life as based on their cosmology is included at the end of the article. The notes include references cited by the author.

Gill, Sam D., and Irene F. Sullivan. ***Dictionary of Native American Mythology.*** Santa Barbara, Calif.: ABC-CLIO, 1992.
This broad, well-researched guide contains over 1,000 cross-referenced, A–Z entries of varying length representing myths, tales, rituals, characters, themes, symbols, and motifs of over 100 different Native American cultures from northern Mexico to the Arctic Circle. An excellent tribal index is keyed to both the entries and the bibliography of primary resources and secondary works representing well-known scholarly research in the field (most by non-Native ethnographers and folklorists). Captioned illustrations and maps of culture areas enhance this important work, which greatly facilitates further investigation of the topic.

Grantham, Bill. *Creation Myths and Legends of the Creek Indians.* Gainesville: University Press of Florida, 2002.

> Part I, "Beliefs and Rituals," contains chapters including The Role of Mythology, Cosmogony, Creek Cosmology, Souls, Sacred Plants or Medicines, Sacred Time and Space, and Ceremony and Ritual. Part II, "Myths and Legends," includes numerous myths on themes such as Earth Diver, Emergence, Migration, Relationships Between Tribes, Journeys into the Sky World, Snake Man, and Tobacco and Corn. Also included in this volume are an appendix of sources, phonetic guides, glossary of Creek words, list of geographical locations, a bibliography, and a list of stories by culture group.

Grinnell, George Bird. *Pawnee Hero Stories and Folk-Tales: With Notes on the Origin, Customs and Character of the Pawnee People.* 1889. Lincoln: University of Nebraska Press, 1990.

> In the late 1880s, Grinnell, concerned that these oral traditions were being lost, set out to transcribe the history and tales of the Pawnee people. Included in this collection are stories about historical heroes and mythical figures. The last half of the book contains "Notes on the Pawnee," which describe the people, customs, and beliefs. The final chapters give a brief account of their removal from Nebraska to "Indian Territory," in what is now Oklahoma.

Hazen-Hammond, Susan. *Spider Woman's Web: Traditional Native American Tales about Women's Power.* New York: Berkley, 1999.

> This collection of twenty-five traditional oral stories from various Native peoples focuses not only on women's experiences, but also on how women have influenced their families and the societies in which they lived. After each tale, Hazen-Hammond has included brief background information and a section called "Connecting the Story to Your Life" in which she lists discussion questions and activities. These can be used by an individual to delve into the deeper meanings of the tales, or they can be used in a group setting to facilitate dialog and understanding.

———. *Timelines of Native American History: Through the Centuries with Mother Earth and Father Sky.* New York: Berkley, 1997.

> Authored by a descendant of the Abenaki, this valuable and attractively formatted reference work documents 22,000 years of Native American history and culture in chronological form. Covering what is now the United States, minus Hawaii, this outstanding volume includes 1,500 carefully re-

searched entries, complemented by informative sidebars featuring profiles of individuals and tribes, quotations, folklore, extracts of speeches and writings, and interesting facts. Attention is given to less prominent Native American groups. A bibliography and index are included. Another excellent chronology of Native peoples and cultures of North America is Francis Lee's *Native Time: A Historical Time Line of Native America* (New York: St. Martin's Press, 1996).

Hirschfelder, Arlene, and Paulette Molin. ***Encyclopedia of Native American Religions.*** Updated ed. New York: Facts on File, 2000.

Featuring more than 1,200 cross-referenced entries, this encyclopedia provides a broad introduction to the sacred beliefs, spiritual traditions, and practices of Native Americans in the United States and Canada. Included are such topics as beliefs about the afterlife, symbolism, creation myths, and vision quests; consequences of European contact; important ceremonies and dances; and events, legislation, and court cases involving Native American religious practices, reclamation of tribal lands, sacred objects and sites, etc. Biographies of prominent American Indian religious figures and Christian missionaries are included as well. An extensive bibliography, general index, and subject index arranged by categories is included. This volume is the first available reference tool devoted solely to Native American religions.

Leeming, David, and Jake Page. ***The Mythology of Native North America.*** Norman: University of Oklahoma Press, 1998.

This introductory volume includes commentary on seventy-two significant myths of Native North America. The myths included, selected for their "literary" appeal, are presented in one of three parts into which the book is divided: pantheons, cosmos, or heroes and heroines. Stories are honored as cultural expressions and also placed in the broad context of world mythology and human experience, with similarities to other mythic traditions highlighted. A bibliography and index are included.

Linderman, Frank B. ***Indian Old-Man Stories: More Sparks from War Eagle's Lodge-Fire.*** 1920. Authorized ed. Lincoln: University of Nebraska Press, 2001.

———. ***Indian Why Stories: Sparks from War Eagle's Lodge-Fire.*** 1915. New authorized ed. Lincoln: University of Nebraska Press, 2001.

These two titles contain myths and legends from the Siksika (Blackfeet), Ojibwa, and Cree tribes who lived in what is now Montana. In 1885, Linderman moved to the region as a sixteen-year-old trapper and developed lifelong friendships with many of the people he met. From the tribes' elders he learned the oral history and cultural traditions that were passed down through the generations. The *Why Stories* volume includes "Why the Chipmunk's Back is Striped," "How the Ducks Got their Fine Feathers," and twenty other explanatory tales. The second Linderman title contains thirteen myths featuring Old-Man (also known as Napa or Napi), who was described by Linderman as a creator god, but not the supreme deity. Besides Old-Man's extraordinary powers, he also exhibited many human characteristics.

Miller, Dorcas S. *Stars of the First People: Native American Star Myths and Constellations.* Boulder, Colo.: Pruett, 1997.

This extraordinary volume is a unique survey of Native American constellations such as Bringer of Daylight, Celestial Bear, and Harpooner-of-Heaven, and the cultures that gave rise to stories of their origin. Organized by culture area, each chapter includes drawings of the constellations and related myths about creation, hunting, tricksters and culture heroes, ritual, power, and others. An introduction to the constellations from the Ancient Greek perspective is included, together with star maps illustrating major features. An appendix identifies the Native constellations and their classical equivalents. A bibliography and index are included.

Miller, Jay. *Earthmaker: Tribal Stories from Native North America.* New York: Perigee Books, 1992.

This is a brief collection with just twenty-four mythological tales. However, the introduction gives an overview of the major culture areas and the environmental forces that helped shape the way the people in each region saw and related to the world around them. An appendix briefly discusses scholarship relating to Native American mythology from nineteenth century anthropologists such as Boas to contemporary Native authors such as Bruchac.

Momaday, N. Scott. *The Way to Rainy Mountain.* Tucson: University of Arizona Press, 1996. First published 1969 by University of New Mexico Press.

Momaday, also known as Tsoai-talee ("Rock Tree Boy"), is professor of English at the University of Arizona and widely regarded as one of the most successful of contemporary Native American writers. In this attractive, moving, and beautifully written autobiographical work, he retells

Kiowa myths he learned from his grandmother, each of which is accompanied by historical commentary and Momaday's reminiscences of his life as a Native American youth. Spanning 300 years of Kiowa history, the book's three sections—*The Setting Out, The Going On,* and *The Closing In*—contain information on tribal customs, the Kiowas' golden age, and the white settlers' intrusion onto Kiowa lands in the 1800s. Momaday is the first Native American recipient of the Pulitzer Prize, earned in 1969 for his novel *House Made of Dawn.*

Mourning Dove. *Coyote Stories.* 1933. Lincoln: University of Nebraska Press, 1990.

This collection of twenty-eight delightful stories is the result of Mourning Dove's tireless efforts to record the tales of her Okanagan people. Most feature Coyote in his common roles as culture hero or bungling fool, but other Animal People are the focus of the stories as well. Some explain why mosquitoes bite people, why the marten's face is wrinkled, how the turtle got his tail, and more. It should be noted that Mourning Dove and her primary editor, Heister Dean Guie, had divergent intentions for this book. She wanted to emphasize Native American themes and issues, but Guie's desire to produce bedtime stories for children won out. Despite their diluted authenticity, Mourning Dove's tales as presented here represent an important contribution to the preservation of Okanagan culture, and an effort to convey aspects of that culture to a Euroamerican audience. Mourning Dove is thought to have produced the first novel published by an American Indian woman, *Cogewea, the Halfblood* (1927), the work for which she is best known. Her final volume was her autobiography, *Mourning Dove: A Salishan Autobiography.* Published posthumously in 1990, it has received much attention from scholars.

Parker, Arthur Caswell. *Seneca Myths and Folk Tales.* 1923. Lincoln: University of Nebraska Press, 1989.

A collection of over seventy myths and legends covering topics and characters such as origins, heroes, love and marriage, talking animals, cannibals, giants, and other monsters. This work includes introductory material regarding the collection of the narratives and how such oral (or written) literature fits into the study of a given culture and particularly the study of the Seneca and other Iroquoian people. Parker also included chapters on literary themes and the discussion of how and when mythological stories and legends were told and retold among the Seneca themselves.

Penn, W. S., ed. *The Telling of the World: Native American Stories and Art.* New York: Stewart, Tabori & Chang, 1996.

>An anthology of inspirational Native American legends and stories that follow the path of life, collected from both traditional and contemporary sources. Beautiful drawings, paintings, and sculpture by Native American artists, plus significant artifacts and antiquities, enhance the texts. Among the artists included are Fred Kabotie, George Longfish, Jaune Quick-To-See Smith, Pablita Velarde, and Emmi Whitehorse.

Pijoan, Teresa. *White Wolf Woman: Native American Transformation Myths.* Collected and retold by Teresa Pijoan. Little Rock, Ark: August House, 1992.

>The thirty-seven myths in this collection feature both human and animal characters that possess the spirit power to transform themselves into another form. This is not an alien concept for many Native Americans who understand that the demarcation between the spirit world and the physical world is not clearly defined. Indeed, many humans and animals have the capability to transform from their natural state into that of the other and back again if they so chose.

Ramsey, Jarold, ed. *Coyote Was Going There: Indian Literature of the Oregon Country.* Compiled and edited by Jarold Ramsey. Seattle: University of Washington Press, 1977.

>The once prodigious body of ancient myths and stories of Native Americans from Oregon, like the oral literature of other Indians of North America, is now represented largely as remnants, at one time preserved only in academic journals and monographs and scattered among library collections of colleges and universities. Largely recorded by anthropologists and linguists who dedicated themselves to transcribing this mythological heritage as accurately as possible before it vanished without a trace, it would remain less available to the public at large if not published in anthologies such as this one. The editor's intent with this valuable and careful compilation, minimally edited and arranged by geographical area within the state, is "to make a representative selection of accurately rendered Oregon Indian myths accessible to the general public as literature." He encourages the reader to delve into the original texts identified in the notes and bibliography, to more clearly see how rich the stories are despite great difficulties faced by translators in collecting them, and by editors of Indian myth-literature in presenting them to a modern audience.

Shoemaker, Nancy, ed. ***American Indians.*** Blackwell Readers in American Social and Cultural History 2. Malden, Mass.; Oxford: Blackwell, 2001.

> This collection of essays selectively combines primary sources with the best of contemporary scholarship to introduce the reader to the history of Native Americans from a socio-cultural perspective. Arranged chronologically, coverage is over a 500-year period; each chapter presents a main essay paired with a set of related historical documents, which examined together reveal the complex and dynamic changes that occurred within American Indian societies. Each essay and document is prefaced by provocative introductory material. Titles for further reading are identified at the end of each chapter, and an index is included. Ms. Shoemaker, the editor and an Associate Professor of History at the University of Connecticut, has included an excellent historiographical introduction to the volume. A valuable resource for students, scholars, and instructors. See also Pulitzer Prize-winning historian Alan Taylor's engaging *American Colonies* (New York: Viking, 2001), a defining reassessment of sixteenth-through eighteenth-century Indian-European relations that demonstrates how the histories of early America and the American Indian are inextricably linked, and how important it is that those histories be understood in tandem.

Sturtevant, William, general editor. ***Handbook of North American Indians.*** Washington, DC: Smithsonian Institution, 1978–2001.

> An important, multivolume overview. The set has not been published in numerical order and is incomplete. Volumes 4–13, 15, and 17 are currently available. Volume 4 deals with Indian-white relations, volume 17 covers languages, and volumes 5–13, plus volume 15, address culture areas and peoples. Maps, history, languages, customs, and religion are discussed for nearly every North American native group. Forthcoming are volumes on the following topics: Indians in contemporary society; environment, origins, and population; Southeast; technology and visual arts; a two-volume biographical dictionary; an index; and the introduction.

Swann, Brian, ed. ***Coming to Light: Contemporary Translations of the Native Literatures of North America.*** New York: Vintage Books, 1996. First published 1994 by Random House.

> In this colossal, sweeping volume, organized by geographical region, Swann has assembled a rich collection of texts from Native American storytellers, orators, and singers from the Arctic to the American Southeast. New and

reliable translations of more than fifty ancient stories are included, by both Native Americans (Larry Evers, Calvin W. Fast Wolf, Darryl Babe Wilson) and non-native experts in the field (William Bright, William Shipley, Dennis Tedlock). Swann's extensive introduction discusses the oral tradition and places the translations as a whole in historical context. A feature that distinguishes this anthology from many others is the inclusion of introductory and explanatory material, provided by the translators themselves, which places each translation within its own cultural and historical context. This invaluable volume, recommended for both general readers and specialists, is a solid entrée to Native American mythology and oral tradition. A bibliography and index are included.

Tate, Henry W. *The Porcupine Hunter and Other Stories: The Original Tsimshian Texts of Henry W. Tate.* Vancouver: Talonbooks, 1993.

Editor Ralph Maud has included selections from Tsimshian Henry Tate's original stories, written in English, found in the manuscripts that were heavily revised by Franz Boas and published in his ethnological classic *Tsimshian Mythology* (1916). Impressed by the vibrancy and engaging quality of the unedited texts he found during research at Columbia University Library, Maud's objective in publishing this work is to make available to the interested reader the best of Tate's stories as they were initially written. Categorized into appropriate genre types, each story is supplemented by an introduction and annotations.

Thompson, Stith. *Tales of the North American Indians.* 1929. Bloomington: Indiana University Press, 1971.

Thompson has conveniently compiled in one volume an impressive collection of myths and tales first issued separately in various government reports, journals, and publications of learned societies. Stories included are from points as distant from each other as southern California and Labrador; some are common to tribes of a particular culture area, others from a region, and some are known over practically the entire continent. While stories from the various tribes are different, they exhibit striking similarities. Arrangement is by type of tale, not culture area, and they may be grouped into three general categories: creation myths, trickster tales, and stories of ordinary human beings entangled in the marvelous or supernatural. A chapter entitled *Comparative Notes* presents distribution of each tale and motif. A bibliography and list of motifs are also included. Thompson, a Distinguished Professor Emeritus of English and Folklore at Indiana University, was one of the world's leading authorities on folklore and compiler of the landmark *Motif-Index of Folk Literature* (1932–1937).

Velarde, Pablita. ***Old Father the Story Teller.*** Santa Fe, N.M.: Clear Light Publishers, 1989. First published 1960 by D. S. King.

Acclaimed artist Velarde has translated and presented six of the most memorable stories told to her and her sisters as children by their father, a respected Tewa-speaking storyteller of Santa Clara Pueblo, New Mexico. Illustrated with some of her beautiful paintings, this book is the first ever to be published by a Pueblo Indian woman. Born in 1918, Velarde says in her preface, "I was one of the fortunate children of my generation who were probably the last to hear stories firsthand from Great-grandfather or Grandfather. I treasure that memory, and I have tried to preserve it in this book so that my children as well as other people may have a glimpse of what used to be."

Williamson, Ray A., and Claire R. Farrer, eds. ***Earth & Sky: Visions of the Cosmos in Native American Folklore***. Albuquerque: University of New Mexico Press, 1994. First published 1992.

A collection of essays describing various mythologies related to the sun, moon, and stars from across Native North America. Included are myths from the Seneca, Alabama, Mescalero Apache, Zuni, Navajo, Tsimshian, Lakota, Ojibwa and other tribes. The essays explore topics such as an explanation of the seasons and the rituals connected with them, the cycle of life and death, and deities that reside among (or as) the stars.

NONPRINT RESOURCES

DVDs

In the Land of the War Canoes: A Drama of Kwakiutl Indian Life on the Northwest Coast. New York: Milestone Film & Video. Distributed by Image Entertainment, 2000.

In the summer of 1914, as part of his monumental undertaking to capture and record as much of traditional Native American life as possible, renowned still photographer Edward S. Curtis filmed this motion picture documentary, originally titled *In the Land of the Head-Hunters*, at Kwakiutl villages on Vancouver Island. Presenting an epic saga of love, war, revenge, and death based on Kwakiutl legend and rituals, the story features a wicked sorcerer, a hero, and their respective factions as they battle for a woman. As part of Curtis's effort to painstakingly reconstruct a setting that reflects pre-contact authenticity, the film features not only the magnificent painted war canoes of the title, but genuine native costumes, ceremonial dancing, and religious ritual. Lost for many years, the film was rediscovered, edited, restored, and enhanced by the addition of an authentic soundtrack of Kwakiutl chants and music recorded in 1972. Added to the National Film Registry in 1999, the short (forty-three minutes) film is accompanied by a brief documentary on Curtis, *The Image Maker and the Indians.* Also available on videocassette.

The Way of the Pow-Wow. Stockton, Utah: Sundance Media Group/Indian Summer, 2002.

Shot at powwows from Canada to California, this DVD features every popular powwow dance style in slow motion, with close-ups, and describes and explains clothing and regalia, plus foot and body movements. Details about the dances are complemented by interviews with traditional dancers, fancy dancers, arena directors, dance judges, drum groups, and powwow people. Primary footage from Indian Summer's world famous September gathering, plus music from "Tha' Bucks" as well as Douglas Spotted Eagle, Brule, Blackstone Singers, and other great drum groups is featured. Produced by Indian Summer, Indigenous Pictures, and Douglas Spotted Eagle, this program is aimed at a wide audience, including powwow people, educators, enthusiasts of Native American culture, and anyone interested in learning more about Native American dance. Running time is seventy-five minutes; available also on videocassette.

The West. Alexandria, Va.: PBS DVD Gold; Burbank, Calif.: Warner Home Video, 2003.

Produced by acclaimed filmmaker Ken Burns, this ambitious, epic documentary series represents a crowning achievement in an effort to redefine American's collective understanding of the West. Spanning the history of the American West over several centuries, it focuses on the period from 1800 to 1915, when westward expansion had its greatest impact on both the country and its people. Writers Geoffrey C. Ward and Dayton Duncan have balanced, with success and sensitivity, the turbulent and triumphant move west of white settlers, adventurers, and exploiters with the tragic loss and suffering of Native Americans who were steadily dispossessed of the lands they had inhabited for thousands of years. Interviews with more than seventy-five historians and experts provide depth and accuracy and lend credibility to the series. Foremost among them is N. Scott Momaday, scholar, historian, and Kiowa Indian. Other experts include historians Stephen Ambrose, Patricia Nelson Limerick, and Richard White; writers Michael Dorris and Maxine Hong Kingston; Teton (Lakota) descendant Charlotte Black Elk; and many others. Includes discussion of the peoples, the wagon trains, the Gold Rush, the Civil War, the building of the transcontinental railroad and destruction of the buffalo, wars against the Indians, the tragedies at Little Big Horn and Wounded Knee, and beginnings of the New West. Episode titles on five DVDs include: *The People, Empire Upon the Trails, The Speck of the Future, Death Runs Riot, The Grandest Enterprise Under God, Fight No More Forever, The Geography of Hope, Ghost Dance,* and *One Sky Above Us.* Also available on videocassette.

Videos

Alcatraz Is Not an Island. Berkeley: University of California Extension Center for Media and Independent Learning, 2002.

More than thirty years afterwards, this remarkable, award-winning, hour-long documentary combines archival footage and modern-day interviews to provide an in-depth look at the historic and daring Indian occupation of Alcatraz Island that lasted for nineteen months between 1969 and 1971. Initiated by a small group of Native Americans to draw attention to the issues, concerns, and problems of the Bay Area Indian community, particularly those resulting from the government's disastrous Relocation/Termination Programs of the 1950s, this retaking of "Indian land" inspired thousands of others to participate and soon escalated into a movement that rippled throughout the United States and Canada. In retrospect, scholars, important leaders (both Indian and non-Indian), and the occupiers themselves view this important political event as one that altered forever the relationship between the American government and Indian Nations, marked a renaissance in Native American culture and identity, and inspired great pride and hope. Executive producer Millie Ketcheshawno, a longtime Bay Area Indian community advocate, participated in the Alcatraz occupation. Produced by Jon Plutte and directed by James Fortier (Métis-Ojibwa), in association with the Independent Television Service and KQED Television, and broadcast on PBS, *Alcatraz Is Not an Island* was awarded Best Documentary Feature at the American Indian Film Festival in 1999.

The American Indian Collection. Alexandria, Va.: PBS Home Video; Beverly Hills, Calif.: Manufactured and Distributed by Pacific Arts Video, 1991.

Not a true series, but a collection of five one-hour documentaries first shown on PBS between 1981 and 1990 and produced for PBS itself (e.g., as a segment of the program *Odyssey* or *The American Experience* series), or in conjunction with individual public television stations. In *Geronimo and the Apache Resistance*, modern-day Chiricahua break a tradition of silence among members of the tribe and reveal their views of the long struggle in the Southwest between the Apache, settlers, and the Army during the nineteenth century. In *Myths and Moundbuilders*, archaeologists explore the contents of the huge earthworks and mounds of the eastern half of the United States in an attempt to better understand the ancient Hopewell and Mississippian cultures. *Seasons of the Navajo* presents a year in the life of an extended family on a Southwestern reservation. *The Spirit of Crazy Horse* surveys the current situation of the Oglala on the reservation and documents their struggle to preserve their culture and heritage and reclaim ownership of the Black Hills. *Winds of Change: A Matter of Promises*, presented by Native American author N. Scott Momaday, investigates the struggle of the Onondaga, Navajo, and Lummi to maintain their cultural identity and national sovereignty in the United States.

The American Indian Series. Berkeley: Distributed by the University of California Extension/Center for Media and Independent Learning, 1983.

Originally produced from 1961–1965, this series of instructional films was executed in the classic anthropological tradition that features careful, detailed documentation accompanied by explanatory narration. Despite their age and dated style, they represent a significant contribution to the understanding of, appreciation for, and preservation of the culture, practices, skills, and art of several Indian tribes, primarily from California and the Northwest Pacific coast. Titles include: *Acorns: Staple Food of California Indians; Basketry of the Pomo: Introductory Film; Basketry of the Pomo: Forms and Ornamentation; Basketry of the Pomo: Techniques; Beautiful Tree: Chishkale; Buckeyes: Food of California Indians; Calumet: Pipe of Peace; Dream Dances of the Kashia Pomo; Game of Staves; Kashia Men's Dances: Southwestern Pomo Indians; Obsidian Point Making; Pine Nuts; Sinew Backed Bow and its Arrows; Totem Pole; Wooden Box: Made by Steaming and Bending.* Running times vary from ten to thirty-three minutes. Also distributed by PBS Video, Alexandria, Virginia.

Ancient Spirit, Living Word: The Oral Tradition. Directed by Daniel Salazar. Denver, Colo.: Front Range Educational Media, 1984.

> This fifty-seven-minute program provides a portrait of Native American oral tradition as a bridge between the past and the future. Native Americans are featured discussing the importance of a vital oral tradition in passing cultural values and identity from generation to generation.

Clash of Cultures. Directed by Scott Nielsen and Dick Blofson. Great Plains Experience, no. 3. Lincoln, Neb.: University of Mid-America, 1978.

> Interviews with four Teton (Lakota) elders, who draw upon their oral tradition, are used in conjunction with historical documents, photographs, and paintings to examine the clash of cultural attitudes of Indians and white settlers, missionaries, and teachers on the Great Plains in the nineteenth century. The history of battles that occurred and treaties that were made between 1851 and 1890 is traced. Running time is twenty-eight minutes.

Coming to Light: Edward S. Curtis and the North American Indians. Oley, Pa.: Bullfrog Films, 2000.

> This video tells the dramatic story of the life and work of Edward Sheriff Curtis (1868–1952), a noted ethnologist and pioneer in visual anthropology who produced, during the first third of the twentieth century, *The North American Indian*, one of the most significant yet controversial works to portray traditional Native American culture. Featuring over eighty tribes, this twenty-volume publication, which contains over 1,500 sepia-toned photogravure plates and narrative, each accompanied by over 700 portfolio plates, continues to influence greatly the image of Indians in popular culture. Curtis's enormous body of work includes a total of 40,000 photographs, 10,000 recordings, and a full-length ethnographic motion picture, *In the Land of the War Canoes*. Native Americans who are descended from Curtis's subjects or who are currently using his photographs for purposes of cultural preservation react to his pictures, tell stories about the people who appear in them, and discuss the meaning of the images. Originally produced as part of the PBS television program *American Masters*, this 56-minute video is also issued in a longer version (85 minutes). Another excellent film profile of Curtis is *The Shadow Catcher* (1975), directed by Teri McLuhan (New York: Mystic Fire Video, 1993).

Corn Is Life. Directed by Donald Coughlan. Berkeley: University of California Extension Media Center, 1984.

> A nineteen-minute documentary that depicts and explains the importance of corn to the Hopi as a food, holy substance essential to nearly all aspects of religious life, and major cultural symbol. Traditional activities shown include preparing and planting corn seed, and cultivating and harvesting the crop. Also available is *Mother Corn,* which explores the significance of corn among Hopi and Pueblo cultures (Lincoln, Neb.: Native American Public Broadcasting Consortium, 1978).

Distant Voices, Thunder Words. Directed by Luis Peon Casanova. Lincoln, Neb.: Great Plains National Instructional Television Library, [2001?].

> Originally produced in 1990, this documentary on Native American storytelling traditions examines the influence of oral tradition on contemporary Native American literature. Oral storytelling is compared and contrasted with authorship of poetry and novels. Featuring interviews with Native American storytellers, poets, and writers, the running time of this program is sixty minutes.

Emergence: A Creation Myth Derived from Navajo Chants. Produced and directed by Barbara Wilk. Boulder, Colo.: Centre Communications, 1981.

> This fifteen-minute animated version of a Navajo creation myth features characters from sand and cave paintings that journey through three underworlds to the surface of the earth. Versions of traditional chants sung in the original Navajo creation stories are heard. A discussion of the sacred mountains, sacred colors, the four sacred plants, and cardinal directions is included.

Images of Indians. Written, produced, and directed by Phil Lucas and Robert Hagoplan. Seattle: KCTS-TV; Lincoln, Neb.: Distributed by Native American Public Broadcasting Consortium, 1979.

> A series of five videocassettes (thirty minutes each) that explores the superficial and demeaning stereotypes of Native Americans created and perpetuated by Hollywood movies, their passing into popular American culture, and their acceptance the world over. Also examined is the impact these stereotypes have had on the self-image of Native Americans, particularly on their youth. Titles include *The Great Movie Massacre; How Hollywood Wins the West; Warpaint and Wigs; Heathen Injuns and the Hollywood Gospel; The Movie Reel Indians.* A co-production of KCTS-9 Seattle and United Indians of All Tribes Foundation.

Little Filth and the Tláchees. Taos, N. Mex.: Distributed by Mixtech Productions, 1990.

This seventeen-minute cassette by Native American videomakers features a tale known as a *tlache'na,* a story in Tiwa culture that is used to teach one how to live a life in harmony with all. Claymation, live action, and video effects are interwoven with the words of a grandfather to vividly retell an ancient story called *Little Filth and the Tlachees.* In this tale, the evil Tláchees are jealous of Little Filth's luck at hunting deer. With the help of his grandmother's advice and her special medicine, Little Filth overcomes his enemies and frees the world of almost all its bad people. A brief, stark, untitled claymation tale of a coyote that babysits beaver children with tragic results follows.

Live and Remember (Wo Kiksuye). Directed by Henry Smith. Lincoln, Nebraska: Distributed by Native American Public Broadcasting Consortium, 1987.

Teton (Lakota) elders, medicine men, and traditional dancers discuss efforts to preserve their culture and heritage despite the adverse effects of poverty, acculturation, and the generation gap in this thirty-minute documentary produced by the Solaris Dance Theater in association with South Dakota Public TV. Topics include oral tradition, the spirit world, medicine, song and dance, the role of women in native society, the Peace Pipe ceremony, bicultural lifestyles, and evolving relationships between the reservations and the outside world.

The Loon's Necklace. Chicago: Distributed by Encyclopedia Britannica Educational Corporation, 1981.

This classic short (eleven minutes) dramatizes the Tsimshian legend that explains how the elegant, mystical loon acquired its distinctive necklace of white feathers. In this tribe's version of the story, an elderly medicine man's failing eyesight is restored by a loon. To thank the bird, the old man gives it his magic white shell necklace that turns into a feather collar around its neck. Told by silent actors wearing authentic wooden masks carved by Indians from British Columbia, this film was originally produced in 1949 by Crawley Films.

More Than Bows and Arrows. Seattle: Camera One, 2000.

First issued as a motion picture in 1978 and narrated by Pulitzer Prize winning author N. Scott Momaday, this is one of the most popular films about Native Americans ever produced. It examines the impact of technological innovations and other native contributions on various aspects of the development of the United States and Canada. Examples include early mines and mining, medicine men, net fishing off cliffs in the Northwest, prehistoric mounds that rival the pyramids of Egypt, and an ancient irrigation canal system in Arizona. Wonders such as the Mesa Verde cliff dwellings, the re-created colony at Jamestown, and the frozen lands of the Inuit are featured. A winner of eleven major film awards, the running time of this video is fifty-five minutes.

The Real People. Lincoln, Neb.: Distributed by Native American Public Broadcasting Consortium, 1990.

This nine-part series was the first made about Native Americans by Native Americans for television in 1976. Produced by KSPS (Spokane), in consultation with a largely Native American advisory board, the historical events and current lifestyles and customs of seven tribes are highlighted: The Skitswish (Coeur d'Alene), Colville, Salish (Flathead), Kalispel, Kootenai, Nez Percé, and Spokane. The following programs (thirty minutes each) comprise the series: *A Season of Grandmothers; Hn-shil-ki-um (Circle of Song, two parts); Mainstream; Awakening; Spirit of the Wind; Buffalo, Blood, Salmon, and Roots; Legend of the Stick Game; Words of Life: People of Rivers.* George Burdeau, Larry Littlebird, and Maria Medina are included among its producers/directors.

Ritual Clowns. Produced and directed by Victor Masayesva. Hotevila, Ariz.: IS Productions; New York: Distributed by Electronic Arts Intermix, 1988.

According to the Hopi, the mischievous clown, a ritual figure that instructs, admonishes, and disciplines, assisted humankind in its emergence into the "fourth world" and became one with the people. In this eighteen-minute documentary, which combines ancient oral tradition, computer-generated animation, and live action, Hopi videomaker Victor Masayesva examines the clown's evolving role in Southwest tribal cultures and rescues this mythic figure from its trivialization in popular culture and reduction by some anthropologists. Contemporary and archival film and photographs of native peoples' ritual ceremonies, as well as footage of clowns in other contexts, is incorporated.

Spirit Bay Series. Norwood, Mass.: Beacon Films; Evanston, Ill.: Distributed by the Altschul Group, 1983–1987.

Produced by Spirit Bay Productions in cooperation with the Canadian Broadcasting Company and TVOntario, this series of short dramas (twenty-eight minutes each) features young Native Americans in situations in which they bridge the gap between their traditional life and the modern world. Set in a Native American community in northern Ontario, this series is aimed at children and young teenagers, but appeals to audiences of all ages. All actors in these productions, as well as the technical staff and camera crew, are Native American: *A Time to Be Brave; Rabbit Goes Fishing; A Real Kid; The Blueberry Bicycle; Words on a Page; The Circle of Life; Hack's Choice; Rabbit Pulls His Weight; Hot News; Big Save; Dancing Feathers; The Pride of Spirit Bay; Water Magic.*

Tales of Wesakechak. Directed by Burton Smokey Day. Kelowna, BC; Carson City, Nev.: Distributed by Filmwest Associates, 1984.

A thirteen-part series of short programs (fourteen minutes each) in which a storyteller uses shadow puppets to dramatize Canadian Cree legends featuring the trickster Wesakechak. Presents lessons and values that endure the test of time. Program titles include *The Creation of the World; The First Spring Flood; Why the Crow Is Black; Wapoose the Rabbit; Ayekis the Frog; How the Fox Earned His Name; Wesakechak and the Medicine; The Stone and the Mouse; Why Bees Have Stingers; Wesakechak and the First Indian People; Wesakechak and the Whiskey Jack; The Creation of the Moon.*

Tales of Wonder: Traditional Native American Fireside Stories. Directed by Chip Richie. Dallas: Rich-Heape Films, Inc., 1998.

Suitable for adults as well as children, this award-winning video features nine enchanting stories and legends narrated by acclaimed storyteller and linguist Gregg Howard. Titles include: *Rabbit and the Bear; Rabbit's Short Tail; Why Possum's Tail Is Bare; The Ruby Necklace; Pleiades and the Pine Tree; Little Grey Bat; Little Turtle; Origin of Fire; How Deer Got Antlers.* Flutist Nash Hernandez and sketch artist Kathleen Raymond Roan accompany Howard as he uses his traditional storytelling style to bring the tales to life. Also available is *Tales of Wonder II*, issued in 2000. In this video, Howard is accompanied by flutist William P. Gutierrez and sketch artist Haley Burke as he tells the following stories: *Flying Squirrel; Hawk and the Hunter; Strawberries; Daughter of the Sun; Sky People; Democracy; Dream Catcher; The Ball Game; Origin of Bluebonnets.* Both videos are suitable for adults as well as children; running time for each is sixty minutes. The stories from the earlier video are also available on a CD.

Words & Place: Native Literature from the American Southwest. Tucson: University of Arizona Radio-TV-Film Bureau; New York: Distributor, Norman Ross Publishing, 1981–[1989?].

This series of programs, ranging from eighteen to fifty-one minutes in length, familiarizes the viewer with the beautiful oral traditions of five tribes of the American Southwest. A Native American storyteller, author, or singer performing a selection from his or her works in a natural setting is featured on each videocassette. Program titles include *By This Song I Walk: Navajo Song; Seyewailo: The Flower World: Yaqui Deer Songs; The Origin of the Crown Dance: An Apache Narrative, and Baí Tsí oosee: An Apache Trickster Cycle; Iisaw: Hope Coyote Stories; Natwaniwa: A Hopi Philosophical Statement; Running on the Edge of the Rainbow: Laguna Stories & Poems; Songs of My Hunter Heart: Laguna Songs & Poems; A Conversation with Vine Deloria, Jr.* Each is accompanied by a printed guide that contains valuable cultural and historical background information. Originally produced in 1978 under the direction of Larry Evers of the University of Arizona English Department.

Websites

Alaska Native Heritage Center, **"Alaska Native Heritage Center,"** *http://www.alaskanative.net/* (accessed September 12, 2004)

A wealth of information for and about the Native people of Alaska. Especially worth viewing are the links accessed via the Learn button, including the "Information about Alaska Native Cultures" pages. Five regions are identified and each area's history, culture, and people are discussed.

Arctic Circle, **"Arctic Circle,"** *http://arcticcircle.uconn.edu/HistoryCulture/* (accessed September 12, 2004)

For background information on the history and culture of the Arctic people, see the section "Ethnographic Portraits." Site also includes links to resources for the Northwest Pacific Coast region.

Blackfeet Nation, **"Welcome to the Blackfeet Nation,"** *http://www.blackfeetnation.com/* (accessed September 12, 2004)

Site includes Siksika (Blackfeet) tribal government information plus pages on culture and history. The Creation Story as told to Ella E. Clark by a Siksika elder named Chewing Black Bones is also included.

Carnegie Museum of the Natural World, **"American Indians and the Natural World: North, South, East, West,"** *http://www.carnegiemnh.org/exhibits/ north-south-east-west/index.html* (accessed September 12, 2004)

    This site contains resources that give overviews of four major tribes: The Tlingit from the Northwest Coast, the Hopi from the Southwest, the Iroquois from the Northeast, and the Teton (Lakota) from the Plains. The site discusses how the various peoples interacted with the natural world.

Cubbins, Elaine, **"Techniques for Evaluating American Indian Web Sites,"** *http://www.u.arizona.edu/~ecubbins/webcrit.html* (accessed September 12, 2004)

    Besides the general guidelines for evaluating Web sites, the sections on this page regarding authority and content guidelines are especially noteworthy.

Foster, Lance M., **"Baxoje, the Ioway Nation: Ioway Cultural Institute,"** *http://ioway.nativeweb.org/home.htm* (accessed September 12, 2004)

    Impressive Web site that includes pages on Iowa myths and legends within the link for Culture. Information on student resources, genealogy, and Iowa language and history are also included.

Government of Canada, **"Aboriginal Canada Portal,"** *http://www.aboriginalcanada. gc.ca/* (accessed September 12, 2004)

    With English and French versions, the site is a gateway to numerous pages organized by topical areas such as National Aboriginal Organizations; Environment and Natural Resources; and Language, Heritage, and Culture. Subcategories under the latter include Canadian Council of the Arts, Canadian Heritage, Canadian Museum of Civilization Corporation, Indian and Northern Affairs Canada, and National Archives of Canada. Each of these subcategories has links to suggested Web sites.

Library of Congress, **"Edward S. Curtis's The North American Indian: Photographic Images,"** http://memory.loc.gov/ammem/award98/ienhtml/ curthome.html (accessed September 12, 2004)

    All of Curtis's published photogravure images portraying the traditional customs and lifeways of over eighty Native American tribes are part of the American Memory Project historical collections of primary source materials relating to the history and culture of the United States. Over 1,500 illustrations and over 700 portfolio plates can be accessed here.

Library of Congress, "History of the American West, 1860–1920," *http:// memory.loc.gov/ammem/award97/codhtml/hawphome.html* (accessed September 12, 2004)

> Also part of the American Memory historical collections, this site features over 30,000 photographs that document the history of the American West and are held by the Western History and Genealogy Department at the Denver Public Library. Included are photographs that portray the lives of more than forty Indian tribes living west of the Mississippi River.

Mitten, Lisa A., "Native American Sites," *http://www.nativeculture.com/ lisamitten/indians.html* (accessed September 12, 2004)

> This site contains links to a large variety of Web sites maintained by, or with content about, Native American and Canadian Aboriginal people. Links are grouped by categories such as: information on Native nations, Native media, and Native music and arts. Brief annotations are given for many of the Web site links. Site also links to the American Indian Library Association.

Strom, Karen M., "Index of Native American Resources on the Internet," *http://www.hanksville.org/NAresources/* (accessed September 12, 2004)

> Site is part of the WWW Virtual Library (vlib.org) Regional Studies Indigenous Studies site. Numerous links are organized in a wide variety of categories, all relating to Native Americans. Categories include: culture, history, education, language, indigenous knowledge, artists, museums, archaeology, electronic texts, books, movies, music, and bibliographies, plus other indices.

University of Virginia Electronic Text Center, "Harry Hoijer's Chiricahua and Mescalero Apache Texts," *http://etext.lib.virginia.edu/apache/* (accessed September 12, 2004)

> This online version of the 1938 publication includes narratives and notes in both Apache and English. Site includes a bibliography of other print and online Apachean texts.

University of Washington Libraries, "American Indians of the Pacific Northwest Digital Collection," *http://content.lib.washington.edu/aipnw/ index.html* (accessed September 12, 2004)

> Hundreds of photographic images from the Pacific Northwest are included on this site from the University of Washington Libraries. There are over

160 documents, including *Coos Myth Texts, Kalapuya Texts,* and *Nez Perce Coyote Tales: The Myth Cycle.*

Woodward, Pauline, and Abby Nelson, **"Halle Library/Endicott College. Guide to Internet Resources in: Native American Literature and Culture,"** *http://www.endicott.edu/production/academic/library/am_indian.htm#2* **(accessed September 12, 2004)**

An index containing brief annotations for links covering a wide range of topics such as history; culture, rituals, religion, etc.; Native American literature; media; and meta sites. A few of the links lead to subscription-based online journals.

5

REFERENCE LIST

Angulo, Jaime de. *Coyote Man & Old Doctor Loon.* San Francisco: Turtle Island Foundation, 1973.

Angulo, Jaime de, and L. S. Freeland. "Miwok and Pomo Myths." *Journal of American Folklore* 41, no. 160 (April-June 1928): 232–252.

Barbeau, Marius. *Huron and Wyandot Mythology, with an Appendix Containing Earlier Published Records.* Memoir 80, Anthropological Series, no. 11. Ottawa: Government Printing Bureau, 1915.

Barbeau, Marius, and William Beynon, collectors. *Tsimshian Narratives.* Vol. 1, *Tricksters, Shamans, and Heroes.* Mercury Series. Ottawa: Directorate, Canadian Museum of Civilization, 1987.

Barnouw, Victor. *Wisconsin Chippewa Myths & Tales and Their Relation to Chippewa Life: Based on Folktales Collected by Victor Barnouw, Joseph B. Casagrande, Ernestine Friedl, and Robert E. Ritzenthaler.* Madison: University of Wisconsin Press, 1977.

Beauchamp, William M. "Indian Corn Stories and Customs." *Journal of American Folklore* 11, no. 42 (July-September 1898): 195–202.

———. *Iroquois Folk Lore Gathered from the Six Nations of New York.* 1922. Empire State Historical Publication 31. Port Washington, N.Y.: Kennikat Press, [1978?].

Beck, Mary Giraudo. *Heroes & Heroines: Tlingit-Haida Legend.* Anchorage: Alaska Northwest Books, 1989.

———. *Shamans and Kushtakas: North Coast Tales of the Supernatural.* Anchorage: Alaska Northwest Books, 1991.

Beckwith, Martha Warren. "Mythology of the Oglala Dakota." *Journal of American Folklore* 43, no. 170 (October–December 1930): 339–442.

———. "Myths and Hunting Stories of the Mandan and Hidatsa Sioux." *Publications of the Folk-lore Foundation* 10 (1930): 1–116.

Benedict, Ruth. *Zuni Mythology.* 1935. 2 vols. Columbia University Contributions to Anthropology, vol. 21. New York: AMS Press, 1969.

Bierhorst, John. *The Mythology of North America: With a New Afterword.* New York: Oxford University Press, 2001. First published 1985 by William Morrow.

Bierhorst, John, ed. *The Red Swan: Myths and Tales of the American Indians.* Albuquerque: University of New Mexico Press, 1992. First published 1976 by Farrar, Straus, and Giroux.

Black Elk. *Black Elk Speaks: Being the Life Story of a Holy Man of the Oglala Sioux.* 21st century ed. Lincoln: University of Nebraska Press, 2000.

Bloomfield, Leonard. *Menomini Texts.* 1928. New York: AMS Press, 1974.

Blue Cloud, Peter. *Elderberry Flute Song: Contemporary Coyote Tales.* 4th ed. Buffalo, N.Y.: White Pine Press, 2002.

Boas, Franz. *Bella Bella Tales.* 1932. Memoirs of the American Folklore Society, vol. 25. Millwood, N.Y.: Kraus Reprint Co., 1973.

———. *The Central Eskimo.* Lincoln: University of Nebraska Press, 1964.

———. *Chinook Texts.* 1894. Temecula, Calif.: Reprint Services Corp., 1995.

———. "The Eskimo of Baffin Land and Hudson Bay, from Notes Collected by Captain George Comer, Captain James S. Mutch, and Rev. E. J. Peck." *Bulletin of the American Museum of Natural History* 15 (1907): 4–570.

———, ed. *Folk-Tales of Salishan and Sahaptin Tribes.* 1917. New York: Kraus Reprint, 1969.

———, ed. *Indian Myths & Legends from the North Pacific Coast of America: A Translation of Franz Boas' 1895 Edition of "Indianische Sagen von der Nord-Pacifischen Küste Amerikas."* Vancouver: Talonbooks, 2002.

———. "Mythology and Folk-Tales of the North American Indians." *Journal of American Folklore* 27, no. 106 (October–December 1914): 374–410.

———. *Tsimshian Mythology.* 1916. Landmarks in Anthropology. New York: Johnson Reprint Corp., 1970.

Boas, Franz, and George Hunt. *Kwakiutl Texts.* 1905. New York: AMS Press, 1975.

Borgoras, Waldemar. "The Folklore of Northeast Asia, as Compared with That of Northwestern America." *American Anthropologist,* n.s., 4, no. 4 (October–December 1902): 577–683.

Bowers, Alfred W. *Mandan Social and Ceremonial Organization.* 1950. Moscow: University of Idaho Press, 1991.

Briggs, John E. "Wisaka." *Palimpsest* 7, no. 4 (1926): 97–112.

Bringhurst, Robert. *The Black Canoe: Bill Reid and the Spirit of Haida Gwaii.* Vancouver, B.C.: Douglas & McIntyre, 1995. First published 1991 by University of Washington Press.

Brinton, Daniel G. *American Hero-Myths: A Study in the Native Religions of the Western Continent.* 1882. Series in American Studies. New York: Johnson Reprint Corp., 1970.

Bruchac, Joseph. *Native Plant Stories.* Golden, Colo.: Fulcrum Publishing, 1995.

———. *Our Stories Remember: American Indian History, Culture, and Values Through Storytelling.* Golden, Colo.: Fulcrum Publishing, 2003.

Bruchac, Joseph, and Diana Landau, eds. *Singing of Earth: A Native American Anthology*. Florence, Ky.: The Nature Company, 1993.

Bullchild, Percy. *The Sun Came Down*. San Francisco: Harper & Row, 1990.

Bunzel, Ruth Leah. *Zuni Ceremonialism*. Albuquerque: University of New Mexico Press, 1992.

Bushotter, George, and J. Owen Dorsey. "A Teton Dakota Ghost Story." *Journal of American Folklore* 1, no. 1 (April–June 1888): 68–72.

Carmody, Denise Lardner, and John Tully Carmody. *Native American Religions: An Introduction*. New York: Paulist Press, 1993.

Carroll, Michael P. "The Trickster as Selfish-Buffoon and Culture Hero." *Ethos* 12, no. 2 (Summer 1984): 105–131.

Chamberlain, A. F. "Tales of the Mississaguas I." *Journal of American Folklore* 2, no. 5 (April–June 1889): 141–147.

Champagne, Duane, ed. *The Native North American Almanac: A Reference Work on Native North Americans in the United States and Canada*. 2nd ed. Detroit: Gale Group, 2001.

Clark, Ella E. *Indian Legends from the Northern Rockies*. The Civilization of the American Indian Series, vol. 82. Norman: University of Oklahoma Press, 1966.

———. *Indians Legends of the Pacific Northwest*. 50th anniversary ed. Berkeley; London: University of California Press, 2003. First published 1953.

———. "The Mythology of the Indians in the Pacific Northwest." *Oregon Historical Quarterly* 54, no. 3 (September 1953): 163–189.

Clements, William M., and Frances M. Malpezzi. *Native American Folklore, 1879–1979: An Annotated Bibliography*. Athens, Ohio: Swallow Press, 1984.

Clifton, James. *Star Woman and Other Shawnee Tales*. Lanham, Md.: University Press of America, 1984.

Coffin, Tristam P., ed. *Indian Tales of North America: An Anthology for the Adult Reader*. Publications of the American Folklore Society, Bibliographical and Special Series, vol. 13. Philadelphia: The Society, 1961.

Cuevas, Lou. *Apache Legends: Songs of the Wind Dancer*. Happy Camp, Calif.: Naturegraph, 1991.

Culin, Stewart. *Games of the North American Indians*. 2 vols. 1907. Lincoln: University of Nebraska Press, 1992.

Curtin, Jeremiah. "Achomawi Myths." *Journal of American Folklore* 22, no. 85 (July–September 1909): 283–287.

———. *Creation Myths of Primitive America*. Edited by Karl Kroeber. ABC-CLIO Classic Folk and Fairy Tales. Santa Barbara, Calif.: ABC-CLIO, 2002.

First published 1898 by Little, Brown, and Company with title: *Creation Myths of Primitive America in Relation to the Religious History and Mental Development of Mankind.*

———. *Seneca Indian Myths.* Mineola, N.Y.: Dover, 2001. First published 1922 by E. P. Dutton.

Curtin, Jeremiah, and J. N. B. Hewitt. *Seneca Fiction, Legends, and Myths.* Thirty-Second Annual Report of the Bureau of American Ethnology to the Secretary of the Smithsonian Institution, 1910–1911. Washington, DC: Government Printing Office, 1918.

Deans, James. "The Raven in the Mythology of Northwest America." *American Antiquarian and Oriental Journal* 10 (1888): 109–114.

Deloria, Ella C., comp. *Dakota Texts.* 1932. Freeman: University of South Dakota Press, 1992.

Deloria, Philip J., and Neal Salisbury, eds. *A Companion to American Indian History.* Malden, Mass.: Blackwell, 2002.

Deloria, Vine, Jr. *God Is Red: A Native View of Religion.* Golden, CO: North American Press, 1992.

———. *Red Earth, White Lies: Native Americans and the Myth of Scientific Fact.* Golden, Colo.: Fulcrum, 1997. First published 1995 by Scribner.

Demetracopoulou, D. "The Loon Woman Myth." *Journal of American Folklore* 46, no. 180 (April–June 1933): 101–128.

Dooling, D. M., ed. *The Sons of the Wind: The Sacred Stories of the Lakota.* Edited by D. M. Dooling from the James R. Walker Collection, with an introduction by Vivian Arviso One Feather. Norman: University of Oklahoma Press, 2000. First published 1984 by Parabola Books.

Dorsey, George A. *The Cheyenne.* 1905. Fieldiana, Anthropology, vol. 9, no. 1–2. Glorieta, N. Mex.: Rio Grande Press, 1971.

———. *The Pawnee Mythology.* 1906. Sources of American Indian Oral Literature. Lincoln: University of Nebraska Press, 1997.

———. *Traditions of the Arikara: Collected Under the Auspices of the Carnegie Institution of Washington.* Publication, no. 17. Washington, DC: The Institution, 1904.

———. *Traditions of the Skidi Pawnee.* 1904. New York: Kraus Reprint Co., 1969.

———. "Wichita Tales I, Origin." *Journal of American Folklore* 15, no. 59 (October–December 1902): 215–239.

Dorsey, George A., and Alfred L. Kroeber. *Traditions of the Arapaho.* 1903. Sources of American Indian Oral Literature. Lincoln: University of Nebraska Press, 1997.

Dorsey, J. Owen. "Teton Folk-Lore." *American Anthropologist* 2, no. 2 (April 1889): 143–158.

Edmonds, Margot, and Ella E. Clark. *Voices of the Winds: Native American Legends.* New York: Facts on File, 1989.

Erdoes, Richard, ed. *The Sound of Flutes and Other Indian Legends.* Transcribed and edited by Richard Erdoes. New York: Pantheon Books, 1976.

Erdoes, Richard, and Alfonso Ortiz, eds. *American Indian Myths and Legends.* New York: Pantheon Books, 1984.

———. *American Indian Trickster Tales.* New York: Viking, 1998.

Espinosa, Carmen Gertrudis. *The Freeing of the Deer, and Other New Mexico Indian Myths.* Albuquerque: University of New Mexico Press, 1999. First published 1985.

Farrand, Livingston. *Traditions of the Chilcotin Indians.* 1900. Memoirs of the American Museum of Natural History, vol. 4, Anthropology, vol. 3, pt. 1. Publications of the Jesup North Pacific Expedition, vol. 2, pt. 1. New York: AMS Press, 1975.

Farrand, Livingston, and Leo J. Frachtenburg. "Shasta and Athapascan Myths from Oregon." *Journal of American Folklore* 28, no. 109 (July–September 1915): 207–242.

Feldmann, Susan, ed. *The Storytelling Stone: Traditional Native American Myths and Tales.* New York: Laurel, 1991. First published 1965 by Dell.

Fenton, William N. "This Island, the World on Turtle's Back." *Journal of American Folklore* 75, no. 298 (October–December 1962): 283–300.

Fewkes, J. Walter. "The Butterfly in Hopi Myth and Ritual." *American Anthropologist,* n.s., 12, no. 4 (October–December 1910): 576–594.

———. "A Contribution to Passamaquoddy Folk-Lore." *Journal of American Folklore* 3, no. 11 (October–December 1890): 257–280.

Fire, John, and Richard Erdoes. *Lame Deer, Seeker of Visions.* New York: Simon and Schuster, 1972.

Fisher, John F. "An Analysis of the Central Eskimo Sedna Myth." *Temenos* 11 (1995): 27–42.

Fletcher, Alice C. "Pawnee Star Lore." *Journal of American Folklore* 16, no. 60 (January–March 1903): 10–15.

Frachtenberg, Leo J. *Alsea Texts and Myths.* 1920. Temecula, Calif.: Reprint Services Corp., 1995.

Gabriel, Kathryn. *Gambler Way: Indian Gaming in Mythology, History, and Archaeology in North America.* Boulder, Colo.: Johnson Books, 1996.

Ghezzi, Ridie Wilson. "Nanabush Stories from the Ojibwe." In *Coming to Light: Contemporary Translations of the Native Literatures of North America,* edited by Brian Swann, 443–463. New York: Vintage Books, 1996.

Gill, Sam D., and Irene F. Sullivan. *Dictionary of Native American Mythology.* Santa Barbara, Calif.: ABC-CLIO, 1992.

Goodwin, Grenville, comp. *Myths and Tales of the White Mountain Apache.* Tucson: University of Arizona Press, 1994. First published 1939 by American Folklore Society.

Grantham, Bill. *Creation Myths and Legends of the Creek Indians.* Gainesville: University Press of Florida, 2002.

Griffin-Pierce, Trudy. *Earth Is My Mother, Sky Is My Father: Space, Time, and Astronomy in Navaho Sandpainting.* Albuquerque: University of New Mexico Press, 1992.

Grinnell, George Bird. *Blackfoot Lodge Tales: The Story of a Prairie People.* Lincoln: University of Nebraska Press, 2003. First published 1892 by Scribner.

———. *Pawnee, Blackfoot and Cheyenne: History and Folklore of the Plains.* New York: Charles Scribner's Sons, 1961.

———. *Pawnee Hero Stories and Folk-Tales: With Notes on the Origin, Customs and Character of the Pawnee People.* 1889. Lincoln: University of Nebraska Press, 1990.

———. "A Pawnee Star Myth." *Journal of American Folklore* 7, no. 26 (July–September 1894): 197–200.

———. 1901. *The Punishment of the Stingy and Other Indian Stories.* Lincoln: University of Nebraska Press, 1982.

Gunther, Erna. "An Analysis of the First Salmon Ceremony." *American Anthropologist,* n.s., 28, no. 4 (October–December 1926): 605–617.

Hagar, Stansbury. "The Celestial Bear." *Journal of American Folklore* 13, no. 49 (April–June 1900): 92–103.

Haile, Berard. *Starlore Among the Navaho.* 1947. Santa Fe, N. Mex.: William Gannon, 1977.

———, comp. *Love-Magic and Butterfly People: The Slim Curly Version of the Ajilee and Mothway Myths.* American Tribal Religions, vol. 2. Flagstaff: Museum of Northern Arizona Press, 1978.

Hale, Horatio. "Huron Folk-Lore. III, The Legend of the Thunderers." *Journal of American Folklore* 4, no. 15 (October–December 1891): 289–294.

Hays, H. R. *Children of the Raven: The Seven Indian Nations of the Northwest Coast.* New York: McGraw-Hill, 1975.

Hazen-Hammond, Susan. *Spider Woman's Web: Traditional Native American Tales about Women's Power.* New York: Berkley, 1999.

———. *Timelines of Native American History: Through the Centuries with Mother Earth and Father Sky.* New York: Berkley, 1997.

Helbig, Aletha. "Manabozho: Trickster, Guide, Alter Ego." *Michigan Academician* 7 (1975): 357–371.

Hemmeon, Ethel. "Glooscap: A Synopsis of His Life; The Marked Stones He Left." *Canadian Forum* 12 (1932): 180–181.

Hertzberg, Hazel W. "The World on the Turtle's Back: An Iroquois Creation Myth." In *The Indian Peoples of Eastern America: A Documentary History of the Sexes,* J. Axtell, ed., 173–79. New York: Oxford University Press, 1981.

Hill, Stephen W. *Kokopelli Ceremonies.* Santa Fe: Kiva, 1995.

Hirschfelder, Arlene, and Paulette Molin. *Encyclopedia of Native American Religions.* Updated ed. New York: Facts on File, 2000.

Howard, James H., in collaboration with Willie Lena. *Oklahoma Seminoles: Medicines, Magic, and Religion.* The Civilization of the American Indian Series, vol. 166. Norman: University of Oklahoma Press, 1990. First published 1984.

Hudson, Charles. *The Southeastern Indians.* Knoxville: University of Tennessee Press, 1992. First published 1976.

Hultkrantz, Åke. *The North American Indian Orpheus Tradition: A Contribution to Comparative Religion.* Monograph Series, Publication no. 2. Stockholm: Ethnographical Museum of Sweden, 1957.

Ives, Edward D. "Malecite and Passamaquoddy Tales." *Northeast Folklore* 6 (1964): 1–81.

Jenness, Diamond. "Myths of the Carrier Indians of British Columbia." *Journal of American Folklore* 47, no. 184/185 (April–September 1934): 248–249.

Jones, William. "Episodes in the Culture-Hero Myth of the Sauks and Foxes." *Journal of American Folklore* 14, no. 55 (October–December 1901): 225–239.

———. *Fox Texts.* New York: AMS Press, 1974. First published 1907 by E. J. Brill.

Judson, Katharine Berry. *Myths and Legends of California and the Old Southwest.* Lincoln: University of Nebraska Press, 1994. First published 1912 by A. C. McClurg.

Kirk, G. S. *Myth: Its Meaning and Functions in Ancient and Other Cultures.* Cambridge: Cambridge University Press; Berkeley: University of California Press, 1970.

Kroeber, A. L. "Indian Myths of South Central California." *University of California Publications in American Archaeology and Ethnology* 4, no. 4 (1906–07): 167–250.

———. "Tales of the Smith Sound Eskimo." *Journal of American Folklore* 12, no. 44 (January-March 1899): 166–182.

Lankford, George E. *Native American Legends: Southeastern Legends: Tales from the Natchez, Caddo, Biloxi, Chickasaw, and Other Nations.* Little Rock: August House, 1987.

LaPointe, James. *Legends of the Lakota.* San Francisco: Indian Historian Press, 1976.

Largent, Floyd. "Windigo: A Native American Archetype." *Parabola* 23 (1998): 22–25.

Leach, Maria. *The Beginning: Creation Myths Around the World.* New York: Funk & Wagnalls, 1956.

Leeming, David, and Jake Page. *The Mythology of Native North America.* Norman: University of Oklahoma Press, 1998.

Linderman, Frank Bird. *Indian Old-Man Stories: More Sparks from War Eagle's Lodge-Fire.* 1920. Authorized ed. Lincoln: University of Nebraska Press, 2001.

———. *Indian Why Stories: Sparks from War Eagle's Lodge-Fire.* 1915. New authorized ed. Lincoln: University of Nebraska Press, 2001.

———. *Kootenai Why Stories.* Authorized ed. Lincoln: University of Nebraska Press, 1997. First published 1926 by Scribner.

———. *Old Man Coyote (Crow).* Authorized ed. Lincoln: University of Nebraska Press, 1996. First published 1931 by John Day.

Lopez, Barry. *Giving Birth to Thunder, Sleeping with His Daughter: Coyote Builds North America.* New York: Avon Books, 1990. First published 1997 by Sheed Andrews and McMeel.

Lowie, Robert H., ed. *Crow Texts.* Collected, translated, and edited by Robert H. Lowie. Berkeley: University of California Press, 1960.

———. *Myths and Traditions of the Crow Indians.* Sources of American Indian Oral Literature. Lincoln: University of Nebraska Press, 1993. First published 1918 by American Museum of Natural History.

———. "Shoshonean Tales." *Journal of American Folkore* 37, no. 143–144 (January-June 1924): 1–242.

Lyon, William S. *Encyclopedia of Native American Shamanism: Sacred Ceremonies of North America.* Santa Barbara, Calif: ABC-CLIO, 1998.

Makarius, Laura. "The Crime of Manabozho." *American Anthropologist,* n.s., 79, no. 2 (June 1973): 663–675.

Malotki, Ekkehart, ed. *Hopi Tales of Destruction.* Collected, translated, and edited by Ekkehart Malotki. Lincoln: University of Nebraska Press, 2002.

———. *Kokopelli: The Making of an Icon.* Lincoln: University of Nebraska Press, 2000.

Marriot, Alice, and Carol K. Rachlin. *American Indian Mythology.* New York: New American Library, 1986. First published 1968 by Crowell.

———. *Plains Indian Mythology.* New York: New American Library, 1985. First published 1975 by Thomas Crowell.

Matthews, Washington. *The Mountain Chant: A Navajo Ceremony.* Salt Lake City: University of Utah Press, 1997. First published 1887 by Bureau of American Ethnology.

———. "Naqoìlpi, the Gambler: A Navajo Myth." *Journal of American Folklore* 2, no. 5 (April–June 1889): 89–94.

Mayo, Gretchen Will. *Star Tales: North American Indian Stories about the Stars.* New York: Walker, 1987.

McLaughlin, Marie. *Myths and Legends of the Sioux.* 1916. Lincoln: University of Nebraska Press, 1990.

McNamee, Gregory, ed. *The Bearskin Quiver: A Collection of Southwestern American Indian Folktales.* Einsiedeln, Switzerland: Daimon Verlag, 2002.

Mechling, W. H. *Malecite Tales.* Memoir 49, Anthropological Series, no. 4. Ottawa: Government Printing Bureau, 1914.

Melody, Michael Edward. "Maka's Story: A Study of a Lakota Cosmogony." *Journal of American Folklore* 90, no. 356 (April–June 1977): 149–167.

Miller, Dorcas S. *Stars of the First People: Native American Star Myths and Constellations.* Boulder, Colo.: Pruett, 1997.

Miller, Jay. *Earthmaker: Tribal Stories from Native North America.* New York: Perigee Books, 1992.

Millman, Lawrence. *A Kayak Full of Ghosts: Eskimo Folk Tales.* 1987. Northampton, Mass.: Interlink Press, 2004.

Momaday, N. Scott. *The Way to Rainy Mountain.* Tucson: University of Arizona Press, 1996. First published 1969 by University of New Mexico Press.

Mooney, James. *James Mooney's History, Myths, and Sacred Formulas of the Cherokees: Containing the Full Texts of "Myths of the Cherokee" (1900) and "The Sacred Formulas of the Cherokees" (1891) as published by the Bureau of American Ethnology; With a New Biographical Introduction, "James Mooney and the Eastern Cherokees."* Asheville, N.C.: Historical Images, 1992.

———. "Myths of the Cherokees." *Journal of American Folklore* 1, no. 2 (July–September 1888): 97–108.

Mourning Dove. *Coyote Stories.* 1933. Lincoln: University of Nebraska Press, 1990.

Nabokov, Peter. *A Forest of Time: American Indian Ways of History.* New York: Cambridge University Press, 2002.

Nagle, Geraldine. "The Nightmare's Mask." *Parabola* 23 (Fall 1998): 64–67.

Newcomb, Franc Johnson. *Navaho Folk Tales.* 2nd ed. Albuquerque: University of New Mexico Press, 2000.

Newcomb, Franc J., and Gladys A. Reichard. *Sandpaintings of the Navajo Shooting Chant.* 1937. New York: Dover Publications, 1975.

Norman, Howard, ed. *Northern Tales: Stories from the Native Peoples of the Arctic and Subarctic Regions.* Selected, edited, and retold by Howard Norman. Pantheon Fairy Tale & Folklore Library. New York: Pantheon Books, 1998. Originally published as *Northern Tales: Traditional Stories of Eskimo and Indian Peoples* (1990).

Nungak, Zebedee, and Eugene Arima. *Inuit Stories: Povungnituk.* Hull, Quebec: Canadian Museum of Civilization, National Museums of Canada, 1988.

One Feather, Vivian. "The Four Directions." *Parabola* 3, no. 1 (1978): 62–70.

Opler, Morris Edward. *Myths and Tales of the Jicarilla Apache Indians.* Sources of American Indian Oral Literature. Lincoln: University of Nebraska Press, 1994. First published 1938 by American Folklore Society.

Parker, Arthur Caswell. *Seneca Myths and Folk Tales.* 1923. Lincoln: University of Nebraska Press, 1989.

Parsons, Elsie Clews. "Pueblo-Indian Folk-Tales, Probably of Spanish Provenience." *Journal of American Folklore* 31, no. 120 (April–June 1918): 216–255.

Pasquaretta, Paul. "Contesting the Evil Gambler: Gambling, Choice, and Survival in American Indian Texts." In *Indian Gaming: Who Wins?*, Angela Mullis and David Kamper, eds., 131–151. Contemporary American Indian Issues Series, no. 9. Los Angeles: UCLA American Indian Studies Center, 2000.

Penn, W. S., ed. *The Telling of the World: Native American Stories and Art.* New York: Stewart, Tabori & Chang, 1996.

Peters, Virginia Bergman. *Women of the Earth Lodges: Tribal Life on the Plains.* Norman: University of Oklahoma Press, 2000. First published 1995 by Archon Books.

Pickering, Robert B. *Seeing the White Buffalo.* Denver: Denver Museum of Natural History Press, 1997.

Pijoan, Teresa. *White Wolf Woman: Native American Transformation Myths.* Collected and retold by Teresa Pijoan. Little Rock, Ark.: August House, 1992.

Prince, John Dyneley. "Passamaquoddy Texts." *Publications of the American Ethnological Society* 10 (1921): 1–55.

Radin, Paul. *The Trickster: A Study in American Indian Mythology.* New York: Schocken Books, 1976. First published 1955 by Routledge and Paul.

Radin, Paul, and A. B. Reagan. "Ojibwa Myths and Tales: The Manabozho Cycle." *Journal of American Folklore* 41, no. 159 (January–March 1928): 61–146.

Ramsey, Jarold, ed. *Coyote Was Going There: Indian Literature of the Oregon Country.* Compiled and edited by Jarold Ramsey. Seattle: University of Washington Press, 1977.

Rasmussen, Knud. *The Alaskan Eskimos, as Described in the Posthumous Notes of Dr. Knud Rasmussen.* 1952. Report of the Fifth Thule Expedition, vol. 10, no. 3. New York: AMS Press, 1976.

———. *Iglulik and Caribou Eskimo Texts.* 1930. Report of the Fifth Thule Expedition, vol. 7, no. 3. New York: AMS Press, 1976.

———. *Observations on the Intellectual Culture of the Caribou Eskimos.* 1930. Report of the Fifth Thule Expedition, vol. 7, no. 2. New York: AMS Press, 1976.

Reid, Bill. *The Raven Steals the Light: Native American Tales.* Boston: Shambhala, 1996. First published 1984 by University of Washington Press.

Ricketts, MacLinscott. "The North American Indian Trickster." *History of Religions* 5 (1966): 327–350.

Rides At The Door, Darnell Davis. *Napi Stories.* Browning, Mont.: Blackfeet Heritage Program, 1979.

Rink, Hinrich. *Tales and Traditions of the Eskimo, with a Sketch of Their Habits, Religion, Language, and Other Peculiarities.* 1875. Reprint, New York: AMS Press, 1975.

Rockwell, David B. *Giving Voice to Bear: North American Indian Myths, Rituals, and Images of the Bear.* Rev. ed. Lanham, Md.: Roberts Rinehart, 2003. First published 1991.

Rooth, Anna Birgitta. "The Creation Myths of the North American Indians." *Anthropos* 52 (1957): 497–508.

Russell, Frank. "Myths of the Jicarilla Apaches." *Journal of American Folklore* 11, no. 43 (October–December 1898): 253–271.

Salvador, Ricardo J., "The Maize Page," http://maize.agron.iastate.edu/maizearticle.html (accessed 12 September 2003).

Schaeffer, Claude E. *Bear Ceremonialism of the Kutenai Indians.* Studies in Plains Anthropology and History, no. 4. Washington, D.C.: U.S. Dept. of the Interior, Indian Arts and Crafts Board, Museum of the Plains Indian, 1966.

Seidelman, Harold, and James Turner. *The Inuit Imagination: Arctic Myth and Sculpture.* Vancouver: Douglas and McIntyre; Seattle: University of Washington Press, 2001. First published 1994 by Thames and Hudson.

Shearar, Cheryl. *Understanding Northwest Coast Art: A Guide to Crests, Beings, and Symbols.* Vancouver, B.C.: Douglas and McIntyre; Seattle: University of Washington Press, 2000.

Shoemaker, Nancy, ed. *American Indians.* Blackwell Readers in American Social and Cultural History 2. Malden, Mass.; Oxford: Blackwell, 2001.

Skinner, Alanson. "European Folk-Tales Collected Among the Menominee Indians." *Journal of American Folklore* 26, no. 99 (January–March, 1913): 64–80.

———. "Sauk Tales." *Journal of American Folklore* 41, no. 159 (January–March 1928): 147–171.

Slifer, Dennis, and James Duffield. *Kokopelli: Fluteplayer Images in Rock Art.* Santa Fe, N. Mex.: Ancient City Press, 1994.

Spence, Lewis. *The Myths of the North American Indians.* New York: Gramercy Books, 1994. First published 1914 by G.G. Harrap.

Spencer, Robert F. *The North Alaskan Eskimo: A Study in Ecology and Society.* 1959. Bulletin, Smithsonian Institution, Bureau of American Ethnology, 171. New York: Dover Publications, 1976.

Sproul, Barbara C. *Primal Myths: Creating the World.* 1st Harper Collins ed. San Francisco: HarperCollins, 1991. First published 1979 by Harper & Row.

Stands In Timber, John, and Margot Liberty. *Cheyenne Memories.* 2nd ed. New Haven, Conn.: Yale University Press, 1998.

Stevenson, Matilda Coxe. *The Zuni Indians: Their Mythology, Esoteric Fraternities, and Ceremonies.* 1905. Landmarks in Anthropology. New York: Johnson Reprint Corp., 1970.

Sturtevant, William C., gen. ed. *Handbook of North American Indians.* Washington, DC: Smithsonian Institution, 1978–2001.

Sturtevant, William C., ed. *Seminole Source Book.* New York: Garland, 1987.

Swann, Brian, ed. *Coming to Light: Contemporary Translations of the Native Literatures of North America.* New York: Vintage Books, 1996. First published 1994 by Random House.

Swanton, John R. "Animal Stories from the Indians of the Muskhogean Stock." *Journal of American Folklore* 26, no. 101 (July–September 1913): 193–218.

———. *Haida Texts and Myths: Skidegate Dialect.* 1905. Bulletin, Smithsonian Institution, Bureau of American Ethnology 29. Brighton, Mich.: Native American Book Publishers, 1991.

———. *Tlingit Myths and Texts.* 1909. Brighton, Mich.: Native American Book Publishers, 1990.

Tall Bull, Henry. *The Turtle Went to War: Northern Cheyenne Folk Tales.* Indian Culture Series, Stories of the Northern Cheyenne, BB-12. Billings, Mont.: Montana Reading Publications, 1971.

Tate, Henry W. *The Porcupine Hunter and Other Stories: The Original Tsimshian Texts of Henry W. Tate.* Vancouver: Talonbooks, 1993.

Taylor, Alan. *American Colonies.* The Penguin History of the United States 1. New York: Viking, 2001.

Taylor, Colin F. *Catlin's O-kee-pa: Mandan Culture and Ceremonial, The George Catlin O-kee-pa Manuscript in the British Museum.* Wyk auf Foehr, Germany: Verlag für Amerikanistik, 1996.

Tedlock, Dennis. "Zuni Religion and World View." In *Handbook of North American Indians.* Vol. 9, *Southwest,* Alfonso Ortiz, ed., 499–508. Washington: Smithsonian Institution Press, 1979.

Teit, James. "Traditions of the Lillooet Indians of British Columbia." *Journal of American Folklore* 25, no. 98 (October–December 1912): 342.

Thompson, Stith. *The Folktale.* 1946. New York: AMS Press, 1979.

———. *Tales of the North American Indians.* 1929. Bloomington: Indiana University Press, 1971.

Ticasuk. *Tales of Ticasuk: Eskimo Legends and Stories.* Fairbanks: University of Alaska Press, 1987.

Titiev, Mischa. "The Story of Kokopele." *American Anthropologist,* n.s., 41, no. 1 (January–March 1939): 91–98.

Trafzer, Clifford E., ed. *Grandmother, Grandfather, and Old Wolf: Tamánwit Ku Súkat and Traditional Native American Narratives from the Columbian Plateau.* East Lansing: Michigan State University Press, 1998.

Ugvwiyuhi. *Journey to Sunrise: Myths and Legends of the Cherokee.* Claremore, Okla.: Egi Press, 1977.

Vancouver Art Gallery. *People of the Potlatch: Native Arts and Culture of the Pacific Northwest Coast.* Vancouver: Vancouver Art Gallery, 1956.

Velarde, Pablita. *Old Father the Story Teller.* Santa Fe, N.M.: Clear Light Publishers, 1989. First published 1960 by D. S. King.

Versluis, Arthur. *Sacred Earth: The Spiritual Landscape of Native America.* Rochester, Vt.: Inner Traditions, 1992.

Walker, Deward E. *Nez Perce Coyote Tales: The Myth Cycle.* Norman: University of Oklahoma Press, 1998. First published 1994 as *Blood of the Monster: The Nez Perce Coyote Cycle* (Worland, Wyo.: High Plains, 1994).

Walker, James R. *Lakota Belief and Ritual.* Lincoln: University of Nebraska Press, 1991. First published 1980.

Wallis, Wilson D. "Beliefs and Tales of the Canadian Dakota." *Journal of American Folklore* 36, no. 139 (January–March 1923): 36–101.

Weaver, Jace, ed. *Native American Religious Identity: Unforgotten Gods.* Maryknoll, N.Y.: Orbis Books, 1998.

Webber, William L. *The Thunderbird "Tootooch" Legends: Folk Tales of the Indian Tribes of the Pacific Northwest Coast Indians.* Seattle: Ace, 1936.

Weltfish, Gene. *Caddoan Texts: Pawnee, South Band Dialect.* New York: AMS Press, 1974. First published 1937 by G.E. Stechert.

Weyer, Edward Moffat. *The Eskimos: Their Environment and Folkways.* Hamden, Conn.: Archon Books, 1962. First published 1932 by Yale University Press.

Williamson, Ray A., and Claire R. Farrer, eds. *Earth & Sky: Visions of the Cosmos in Native American Folklore.* Albuquerque: University of New Mexico Press, 1994. First published 1992.

Wilson, Eddie W. "The Owl and the American Indian." *Journal of American Folklore* 63, no. 249 (July–September 1950): 336–344.

Wissler, Clark, and D. C. Duvall. *Mythology of the Blackfoot Indians.* Sources of American Indian Oral Literature. Lincoln: University of Nebraska Press, 1995. First published 1908 by American Museum of Natural History.

Wright, Barton. *Kachinas: A Hopi Artist's Documentary.* Revised ed. Flagstaff, Ariz.: Northland Publishing with the Heard Museum, [1998?]. First published 1973 by Northland Press.

Zigmond, Maurice L. *Kawaiisu Mythology: An Oral Tradition of South-Central California.* Socorro, N. Mex.: Ballena Press, 1980.

GLOSSARY

Baffin Island   An island off the northeast coast of Canada, north of the Hudson Strait and part of the Baffin region of Northwest Territories.

Big Dipper   A dipper-shaped group of seven stars within the constellation known as Great Bear (Ursa Major).

Charter Myth   A myth used to justify an institution or custom.

Chinook   The warm, dry wind that blows intermittently down the east side of the Rocky Mountains during the winter and early spring, causing a rapid thawing of snow.

Clan(s)   A social unit, smaller than the tribe but larger than the family, that traces descent from a common real, totemic, or mythological ancestor through either the female (matrilineal) or male (patrilineal) line. Clan numbers vary from tribe to tribe. Members of a clan may observe their own special rituals, and often possess traditional stories in common. Clan members do not necessarily reside in the same place, but have strong bonds and are obliged to assist each other in times of crisis and on various occasions both happy and sad. Generally, clan members are not allowed to marry within their own clan.

Columbia River   The Columbia rises in southeast British Columbia and flows south and west 1,210 miles through Washington State, along the Washington/Oregon border, and into the Pacific Ocean. It was named after the first ship to enter it in 1792.

Crest(s)   A decorative emblem, badge, device, or other object, such as a totem pole, regularly used as a symbol of a family, clan, tribe, or nation.

Dentalia   Any of various tooth shells of the genus *Dentalium*. Small, slender, and horn-like, they were once used and traded as beads and wealth-items.

El Capitan   A magnificent cliff of unbroken granite that rises vertically over 3,600 feet at the lower end of the seven-mile-long, glacially-gouged Yosemite Valley, outstanding feature of California's Yosemite National Park. Native Americans have inhabited the region, rich in plant and animal resources and more mild in climate than the surrounding high country, for as long as 8,000 years. When non-Natives first entered the Valley in 1851, about twenty-two villages of the Miwok were found here.

Etiological Myths   Myths that explain the cause or origin of something, such as a custom, natural feature, or state of affairs.

Frederick Island   A small island located off the western coast of Graham Island, one of the main islands of British Columbia's Queen Charlotte Islands archipelago.

Gaspe Peninsula   A peninsula in southern Quebec, Canada, extending into the Gulf of Saint Lawrence, about 150 miles long and from 60 to 90 miles wide. Exquisite landscapes, seascapes, boreal forests, pristine mountain streams and lakes, abundant wildlife, and some of North America's oldest fossils can be found here. The first documented Native Americans of the area to make contact with Europeans were the Micmac, sometimes called The Indians of the Sea, who were noted for their fishing skills and birch bark canoes that could traverse open water.

Ghost Keeping Ceremony (*Wanagi Yuhapi*)   One of seven ceremonies, the Seven Sacred Rites of the Lakota, brought to the Teton (Lakota) people of the Black Hills by the White Buffalo Woman. Also known as the Keeping of the Soul, this rite ensures that a person's soul is returned to Wakan-Tanka, the Creator, and does not wander about the earth. It also serves as a reminder of death to the living.

Girls' Puberty Rite (*Ishna Ta Awi Cha Lowan*)   One of the Seven Sacred Rites of the Lakota, promised to them by the White Buffalo Woman. Performed after a young woman's first menstrual period, this rite marked her transition to womanhood and included instruction in the importance of fulfilling her duties as a woman, mother, and wife.

Helldiver   An aquatic bird of the grebe family. Known for their swimming and diving abilities.

Kachina   In Southwest cultures, powerful spirits of the dead in the form of plants, birds, animals, and humans whose function is to bring rain and good crops, and ensure the continuity of life. Kachinas also affect curing, fertility, and growth. Kachinas are represented by either masked dancers who personify these spirits or elaborately carved and decorated dolls.

Kiva   The sacred ceremonial chambers of the Pueblo Indians, either circular or rectangular in shape and sometimes built below ground or partly underground. Used mostly by men, the kiva symbolizes the womb of Mother Earth from which people are born and the underworld from which they first emerged.

Klamath River   A river flowing from southern Oregon southwest across northwest California into the Pacific Ocean, about 250 miles.

Lehal   A type of "guessing game" played principally by men and utilizing two short bones, one of which had a sinew thread wrapped around the middle. Players knelt in two rows, facing one another; each side had a set of the bones. Each side took turns passing their bones through their hands and singing a *lehal* song; the other side was required to guess the hand of the player that held the plain bone. The game was sometimes accompanied by drums and/or the beating of sticks.

Making of Relatives, the (*Hunkapi*) Another of the Seven Sacred Rites of the Lakota, foretold by the White Buffalo Woman. This rite established a binding relationship among fellow human beings. Two people could become brothers, sisters, brother and sister, mother and child, or father and child. The ceremony lasted several days and included songs, prayers, purification, offerings, and a feast.

Medicine Bundle A sacred object or collection of objects wrapped in a bundle or contained in a bag of skin or cloth. The bundle may be owned by an individual, group, or tribe, and contain such items as animal and bird parts, stones, herbs, feathers, and pipes. Each bundle has associations that are significant to the owner's heritage, identity, or power, including rituals, stories, songs, responsibilities, taboos, and/or specific powers.

Medicine Man/Woman An English term applied since the seventeenth century to many Native American religious leaders and healers. It is also used to designate shamans, wise elders, priests, ritualists, and storytellers. Each tribe has its own name for their medicine people and their role varies from group to group. Much of their knowledge, which they are trained and empowered to use, is considered sacred, remains secret, and is thought to be a danger to others if they make contact with it.

Milky Way An assemblage of stars, dust, and interstellar gas that appears from Earth as a broad, faintly luminous, milky band arching across the night sky. The Milky Way moves through the sky just as the constellations do.

Motif A main element, idea, theme, or feature in a myth. A simple myth will have several motifs; complex ones will have many. The clever trickster, the transformation of an animal into a person, a flood or deluge, the origin of death, and marriage to a star are all examples of motifs.

Narwhal A rarely-seen whale of the Arctic, known for the long, spiraling tusk (actually a tooth) protruding from its mouth and possessed by the male, which can grow to a length of ten feet. During the seventeenth century, this tusk was thought to be the horn of the legendary unicorn, a belief reinforced by the Vikings when they brought it to Europe. Its name means "corpse whale" in Old Norse, a possible reference to its mottled grey color.

Northern Crown The Northern Hemisphere constellation Corona Borealis, which lies between Hercules and the Herdsman (Boötes). The constellation is a small arc of bright stars, and reaches its highest point in the evening sky in early July.

Okanogan Highlands   The Okanogan Highlands, divided into two geographic regions by the Columbia River, are located in the northeastern part of Washington State, bordered by the Cascade Range on the west, and the Columbia Basin in the south. The highlands extend into northern Idaho to the east, and north into southern British Columbia. They are characterized by rounded mountains with elevations up to 8,000 feet above sea level and deep, narrow valleys.

Okipa   A complex and elaborate ceremony of the Mandan of the Upper Missouri region. Conducted annually and lasting four days, this sacred ritual enacted the creation of the world and the history of the Mandan people. The Okipa was held to pray for plentiful buffalo, to prevent a repetition of a catastrophic deluge, and to obtain other spiritual blessings. In 1832 artist George Caitlin, highly esteemed for his drawings and paintings of Native Americans, became one of the few white men ever permitted to observe the Okipa almost in its entirety.

Palo Verde   A spiny, multi-trunked deciduous tree common to the Southwest and Mexico. The name—Spanish for "green wood" or "green stick"—refers to its greenish branches and trunk. The two species found have either yellow or blue flowers.

Pleiades   Also known as "The Seven Sisters," a cluster of seven stars in the constellation Taurus, six of which are readily visible to the eye. The rising and setting of the Pleiades was associated with planting seasons and the beginning of summer and winter among native cultures.

Point Barrow   The northernmost point of Alaska, on the Arctic Ocean. Point Barrow was named for Sir John Barrow, a promoter of Arctic exploration.

Saguaro cactus   A very slow-growing giant cactus with a thick, spiny stem and creamy-white flowers, native to the Southwest and Mexico. It is noted for its capacity to store vast amounts of water. The flesh, seeds, and juice of its green fruit was an important food source for Native Americans of the region.

Shaman(s)   Men or women who act as intermediaries to the spirit world in order to diagnose and cure illnesses, foretell the future, seek lost objects, perform rituals related to agriculture and hunting, or conduct the dead to the other world. Shamans are particularly respected for their power to heal, though they have often been suspected of being witches because of their control of many powerful forces. Practices of a shaman can vary among tribal groups.

Snake River   A river in the northwestern U.S., flowing from Yellowstone National Park into the Columbia River in Washington, 1,038 miles long.

Soup Dance   The final event, an all-night dance, in the ceremonial year of the Seminole, which begins in May and ends in September. The Soup Dance follows three other ceremonies in the annual cycle. The men hunt while two women ritually prepare soup from wild game for the dance. Both are served to participants after the men return, and the Soup Dance continues throughout the night. It concludes with the performance of a Morning, or Drunken, Dance, which refers to the excitement of the dancers, not inebriation.

Sun Dance   A well-known and spectacular religious ceremony of Native North America, conducted among the buffalo-hunters of the Great Plains region. Variations exist in name, origin, purpose, and ritual elements among tribal groups. Generally, the Sun Dance includes preparation of male pledgers by instructors, prolonged fasting, sweat lodge purification, and dancing before a sacred pole or tree. It is held annually to pray for fertility, plenty, and renewal, to give thanks, to fulfill a vow, to protect from danger or illness, or other religious purposes. Among the Teton (Lakota), a Sun Dance ceremony (*Wiwanyag Wachipi*) is one of the Seven Sacred Rites of the Lakota foretold by the White Buffalo Woman.

Sweat Lodge Ceremony   A sacred rite, sometimes part of a larger religious ceremony, by which purification is achieved with a sweat bath. The sweat lodge itself is typically a small, dome-shaped structure constructed of saplings and covered with hides, canvas, or blankets, between six and twelve feet in diameter, that encloses heated stones on which water is poured to generate steam. In addition to purifying the body, the ceremony may be conducted as a medical treatment to cure or prevent illness by influencing the spirits. As a social function, the ceremony serves as a medium for the elderly to teach youth about culture, traditions, and knowledge of the tribe. Today, it is central to the religious beliefs and rites of many groups of Native Americans across the continent. A Sweat Lodge Ceremony, or Rite of Purification (*Inipi*) is one of the Seven Sacred Rites of the Lakota foretold by the White Buffalo Woman.

Taboo   A social prohibition or restriction resulting from convention or tradition.

Thlakalunka   Another type of "guessing game" played using four square pieces of deer hide placed upon a bear-skin laid down with the hair side up. Participants formed two sides and one player moved a small pebble about in his hands, pretending to put it under one of the pieces of deer hide. When he thought he was able to hide the stone without observation, he placed it beneath one of the pieces of hide. An opponent was given three chances to guess where the pebble had been hidden; if correct, his side took possession of the pebble. If he did not successfully guess where the pebble was after three tries, another of his party tried his skill.

Throwing of the Ball, the (*Tapa Wanka Yap*)   One of the Seven Sacred Rites of the Lakota, foretold to the Teton (Lakota) people of the Black Hills by the

White Buffalo Woman. During the ceremony, a young girl tossed a ball made of buffalo hair and hide, painted to represent the universe, to four teams assembled at the north, south, east, and west. Whoever caught the ball offered it to the earth, sky, and four directions before returning it to the girl. After the ball was thrown and caught in all directions, the girl tossed it into the air for anyone to attempt to catch. The sacred rite itself was believed to represent the stages of a person's life; the ball, the universe of knowledge. Attempts to catch the ball symbolized the struggle to break free of ignorance.

Vision Quest   The solitary, ritual seeking of wisdom and power from the spirit world in the form of a vision. The rites vary from one tribal culture to another; differences include age, gender, length of time, and ritual elements. Generally, one or more medicine people guide the individual in preparing for the ritual. A vision quest may be undertaken in preparation for war or to become a healer or shaman, to seek spiritual guidance, and/or to participate in other ceremonies, such as a puberty rite. A Vision Quest ceremony, or Crying for a Vision (*Hanblecheyapi*), is one of the Seven Sacred Rites of the Lakota foretold by the White Buffalo Woman.

Wolverine   A stocky, ferocious member of a large family of fur-bearing carnivores that also includes the weasel, marten, polecat, and mink. The wolverine is found in the northern U.S., Canada, and northern Eurasia.

Zuni Salt Lake   An inland salt lake located 60 miles south of the Zuni Pueblo in New Mexico and home of the Zuni's Salt Mother deity. The layer of salt left on the lake bottom in the summer by evaporating water is harvested by pilgrims, including medicine men coming from Zuni and other neighboring tribes. The sacred Zuni Salt Lake sat at the heart of a swirling controversy until very recently, and its future was in peril. Salt River Project (SRP), an Arizona-based electric power company, had made plans to operate a massive strip mine in New Mexico that would have extracted over 80 million tons of coal from 18,000 acres of federal, state, and private lands over a period of forty years. In addition to negatively impacting the immediate and surrounding environment, the mining would have severely disturbed or destroyed sacred shrines, archaeological and human burial sites, and places of worship actively used by seven Native American tribes, including the Zuni Salt Lake. A proposed railroad that would carry coal from the mine to the Coronado Generating Station in St. John's, Arizona, would have destroyed many sections of pilgrimage trails and prevented access over those trails. Hydrological studies conducted, except SRP's own, revealed that SRP's plans to pump 85 gallons of groundwater per minute for forty years from the same aquifer that feeds the Zuni Salt Lake might greatly decrease the amount of both water and salt available to it. After nearly two decades of opposition from the Zuni Tribe, environmentalists, and concerned citizens, the SRP relinquished their permits in August 2003.

INDEX

ABOUT THE EDITORS

Dawn E. Bastian is coordinator for Bibliographic Control and Electronic Resource Services at Colorado State University, Fort Collins. Her published works include the *Zaire* and *Mali* volumes in ABC-CLIO's World Bibliographical Series.

Judy K. Mitchell is reference and instruction librarian at Hawkeye Community College, Waterloo, IA.

Ex-cavating Modernism

Distributed by Art Books International Ltd, 1 Stewart's Court, 220 Stewart's Road, London SW8 4UD, UK.
Tel: 0171 720 1530   Fax: 0171 720 3158

Published by BACKless Books in association with Black Dog Publishing
de-, dis-, ex-. © 1996

ISBN 1 901033 05 8

Set in Caecilia and Frutiger

de-, dis-, ex-.

de-, dis-, ex

Volume One

Ex-cavating Modernism

texts:

Contributors:

Andrew Brighton   is a critic and occasional curator and head of Public Events, Tate Gallery. He curated *Blasphemies, Ecstasies, Cries*, Serpentine Gallery, London, 1989 and has most recently authored *Picasso For Beginners* (1995).

Nic Clear   is an architect who lives and works in London and runs his own architectural practice—Clear Space. He teaches a Post-Graduate unit at the Bartlett.

Alex Coles   is a freelance critic and lecturer and is currently undertaking P.h.D research at Goldsmiths' College, University of London.

Peter Halley   is an artist and writer who has written extensively on art and contemporary culture. He is the publisher of *Index* magazine.

Brian Hatton   teaches at the Architectural Association and at John Moores Liverpool. He has recently curated an exhibition for Milan Triennale.

Nicky Hirst   has collaborated with her father on images for this publication.

Susan Kandel   teaches in the Graduate Program in Theory and Criticism at the Art Center College of Design, writes a regular review column for the *Los Angeles Times*, and is the U.S. Editor of *Art + Text*. She has recently published essays on 90's feminism and L.A. anti-architecture.

Fred Orton   is reader in Art History and Theory at the University of Leeds. He is the author of *Figuring Jasper Johns* (Reaktion Books, 1994), and *Jasper Johns: The Sculptures* (The Henry Moore Institute, Leeds,

1996). His most recent book, co-authored with Griselda Pollock, is *Avante Gardes and Partisans Reviewed: A Social History of Art* (Manchester University Press, 1996).

Nikos Papastergiadis is a lecturer at the University of Manchester and the author of *Modernity as Exile* (Manchester University Press) and a collection of essays and interviews *Dialogue in the Diaspora* to be published in 1996. He is also co-editor of *Random Access*—also published by Rivers Oram Press (Two Volumes).

Katerina Ruedi is an architect and Diploma course director at Kingston University School of Architecture, and co-founder of *Desiring Practices*. She has published essays in *AA Files*, *Austrian Architecture*, *Daidalos* and *Diversa*.

Juliet Steyn is Commissioning Editor of ACT, (The Journal of Art Criticism and Theory), co-curator of the exhibition *Pretext: Heteronyms*, London 1995 and touring. Editor and contributor to *Other Than Identity: The Subject, Politics and Art*, Manchester University Press (forth-coming). She is Course Leader of the MA in Art, Criticism and Theory, KIAD Canterbury.

Jon Thompson after leaving the position as Head of Fine Art at Goldsmiths' College has taken up the post as Head of Fine Art at the Van Eyck Academy, Maastricht. He was jointly responsible with Barry Barker for the seminal exhibition *Falls the Shadow*, at the Hayward Gallery in London, and most recently curated *Gravity and Grace—The Changing Condition of Sculpture 1965-75* at the same venue.

Christopher Want is Deputy Course Leader of the M.A. in Art Criticism and Theory at Kent Institute of Art and Design, and lecturer in Critical Theory in the Department of Visual Arts, Goldsmiths' College. He is author of *Kant for Beginners* (Icon Books Ltd.) to be published this autumn.

This volume is dedicated to the life and work of the great interdisciplinary critic and historian Meyer Schapiro, 1904-1996.

When I got to Paris (this was the summer of 1939 before the war started, a very tense moment), I phoned him [Schapiro had been sent by the exiled Frankfurt Institute to persuade Benjamin to come and join them in New York]. He suggested we could meet at the Deux Magots cafe. I asked, "How will we know each other?" and he said "You'll see." So Lillian and I were sitting in the cafe, waiting to hear from him, when I saw a man walking up and down the sidewalk, looking at all the people and holding up a little copy of the Zeitschrift für Sozialforschung, the social research volume. So I called out to him. I said, "Benjamin?," and he said, "Schapiro?"

Taken from an interview with Meyer Schapiro conducted by James Thompson and published in the *Oxford Art Journal* 17:1, 1994.

Introduction

Ex-cavating Modernism

Within a series of volumes *de-, dis-, ex-.* seeks to engage with/evolve a 'critical interdisciplinarity', both through inviting specific contributions and on the level of editorial practice.

The title of this, the first volume, 'Ex-cavating Modernism', is intended to be slightly provocative, as a number of the practitioners discussed here are precisely those that the word 'postmodern' was first used by or in connection to. The answer to what exactly is being ex-cavated, and in the name of what, is, of course, always plural (and as often as not is set up through one text or project only to be questioned by another); thus resulting in a porous volume of debate. Nevertheless, *de-, dis-, ex-.* seeks to invest in the project that is the continual shifting and expanding ground of the exploration, and argumentation, of the constitution of modernism. And linked to this project are the uses of modernism—its practitioners and theoreticians—for the contemporary; after being repressed by the early postmodern project that too quickly schematised and simplified what modernism was. Surely one of the tasks of postmodern criticism has been to re-map modernism, and surface its breaks and discontinuities. Jean François Lyotard's 'What is Postmodernism?', in taking issue with Jürgen Habermas' 'Modernity—An Incomplete Project', and the latter's equation of postmodernism with anti-modernism, sees the postmodern and the modern as being continually bound in a dialectical relationship, so that "the postmodern supersedes the modern only in order itself to become the modern." But of course, what postmodernism is depends largely on what modernism is—how it is named, how it is defined. "In any case, postmodernism, articulated in relation to modernism, tends to reduce it. Is there a modernism that can be so delimited?" (Hal Foster)

Many of the texts presented here can be seen, partly, as a response to this question, albeit within the limited space available. Juliet Steyn's centres attention on the modernist critic who is seen as largely being responsible for the vehement negation of modernism—particularly in its late stage in America. Where postmod-

ernists have finished Greenberg off—on account of certain texts—
Juliet Steyn seeks those texts that have been banished to the margins of Greenberg's practice, those that articulate the Other
Greenberg; the one that wrote 'Kafka's Jewishness' and 'Self-hatred
and Jewish Chauvinism'—revealing his concerns with his Jewish
identity. Steyn *dis*-locates us from the Greenberg we thought we
knew. In the case of Christopher Want, however, he does exactly the
opposite and goes to the centre of Greenberg's practice—to his reading of Kant—in an attempt to propose a way forward in this area, as
opposed to simply attempting to construct the weakness of
Greenberg's reading of Kant, as others have done. Creating a dialectic with these, within the volume, is Jon Thompson's text on the figure practicing within the modernist period that is seen as radically
undermining the assumptions, and schematisation, of modernism
by critics like Greenberg. Indeed it was Duchamp that would be the
motivating vehicle of the first reactions against such schematisa-
tions in America: Joseph Kosuth, claiming the Other history of modernism via Duchamp in 'Art After Philosophy', and Rosalind Krauss'
texts 'Notes on the Index', claiming the validity of certain tropes
utilised by Duchamp for a theoretisation of the postmodern. But
while Duchamp has been the subject of volumous publication and
debate (especially) recently, Jon Thompson's text 'In the Groves of
Philadelphia—A Female Hanging' pushes the reading of certain
aspects of Duchamp's oeuvre to a new, erotic, *ex*-treme.

Dis-location, *de*-familarisation, and *dis*-mantlement are then, common tendencies throughout this volume, whether it be from a certain dominant understanding of a particular practitioner like
Duchamp in Thompson's text, Jasper Johns and Robert
Rauschenberg in Fred Orton's 'Figuring Jasper Johns, Supplement
One: The Object After Theory', or on the level of practice of a practitioner. An example of the latter being Nicky Hirst, who's appropriations of cartoons originally drawn and published by her father in
the 60s adjust and readjust their details through erasure; in a
process not dissimilar to Rauschenberg's in *Erasure of a de Kooning
Drawing*, and Sherrie Levine's erasures, as appropriations of works
from the modernist canon. Yet here, the 'erasure of the father' takes
form in the domain of a familial wrestle. Herein Hirst's 'erasures'
take on a different relationship heretofore known to them, as that
which has been erased—the pun line etc.—is supplemented by a
very particular textual context.

Peter Halley's 'Against Postmodernism: Reconsidering Ortega' has been included in this volume not only to establish a further trajectory of debate with the texts on Greenberg, Duchamp and Johns, but also because since its publication in 1981, it has been virtually excluded from the postmodern (re-reading of the modern) debate. If one considers the collections of (post)modern essays from this time that were going to print, Halley's text seems far more radical—and sensitive—in its consideration, and extension, of modernism. Halley wishes to see the writings of Ortega as being relevant for the art from the beginning of the century onwards. (His problem with Greenberg, and those reacting against him, being that Greenberg wrote a theory of modernism that started in the 1860s, and any reaction against this, taken on Greenberg's grounds, is a falsehood, as it simply inherets the paradox of his chronological genealogy; i.e., it doesn't go to what for Halley is its key problematic: taking into account the ramifications of industrialisation from the turn of the century, and thus ignores one of the main differences of nineteenth and twentieth century art. The importance of the text that follows Halley's in this volume—Susan Kandel's 'Theory as Phantom Text: Plundering Smithson's Non-Sites'—can only really be understood in relation to the fate of Halley's text in the 80s. For it extends the fate of his practice—and artists giving a similar precedence to theory in their work, such as Sherrie Levine's—to what Kandel terms the 'retreat' from theory by practitioners in the 90s. (So, as Halley wishes to dislocate us from the terms of the debate of Greenbergian modernism—and in turn its negation through what we can term an anti-Greenbergian postmodernism—Kandel seeks to give reason as to why Halley has been dis-located from the aforementioned debate altogether.)

Further overlaps in theme come from Nikos Papastergiadis' 'The Home in Modernity' and in Nic Clear's 'Refurbishments to Alteration to a Suburban House'. In Papastergiadis' text the de- and dis-, as such, are felt through notions of exile, in Nic Clear's project we have an ex-tension of a very particular Dan Graham project—as realised within the contingencies of his own country, England. (In relation to Clear's project, Brian Hatton's text on Dan Graham suffices as a point of orientation; of the Dan Graham we know.) So, as 'the subject', is narrated in its de-familiarised state in Papastergiadis' text, the subject of Dan Graham's Alteration project—an America suburban tract house—is itself (while as a strategy recuperated and relocated) dis-mantled, de-familiarised, and dis-located from its primary site.

The text here that directly deals with Interdisciplinarity itself—
Andrew Brighton's 'Flogging Dead Horses'—does so in a way that
charts its current predicament, so as to intimate a possible way forward. (A second would possibly be Katerina Ruedi's text: whereby
the architect, in many cases today, is coerced towards the 'interdisciplinary', because of the economic predicament s/he finds themselves in.) The former, through its disgust with the recent attempts
at defining an interdisciplinary site, calls for both art and architecture to "*de*-define the other" through a "visual practice that *de*-
habituates." A practice that the texts and projects share then, is an
impulse to not define difference according to over simplified terms
of debate, and view movements and tendencies as simply supersed-
ing and over-writing others. That is to say:

> Ex-centric, dis-integrated, dis-located, dis-juncted,
> deconstructed, dismantled, disassociated, discontinu-
> ous, deregulated...de-, dis-, ex-. These are the prefixes
> of today. Not post-, neo-, or pre-.
>
> Bernard Tschumi

Alex Coles &
Richard Bentley,

London, Autumn 1996

Flogging Dead Horses
Andrew Brighton

Much of what is discussed under the rubric 'art and architecture' offers the almost obscene spectacle of an attempt to create siamese twins out of two corpses. The cadavers are the professional ideologies of art and architecture.

Both need to confer special status upon the mysteries of their practices. An artist is supposed to be more than just a maker of decoration and an architect more than just an organiser of building. Past practice, more grandly known as the history of art and architecture, is pressed into service. The notion of great artists or architects serves to bolster the status of current practitioners: they are descendants of gods. In practice, both groups tend towards a craft conception of their activities; just look at the bulk of art and architecture education: much of it is concerned with handing on technical knowledge and unquestioned professional beliefs.

Looking at some of the publications and remembering the public forums around the issue 'art and architecture', the abiding motive for them seems to be nostalgia: the desire for a return to secure, homogenous culture. Contributors look back to a time when art and architecture were in some kind of union, and look forward to some coming synthesis when the artist and the architect will again share a common language. The implication is that the diverse and contradictory practice of art and architecture in the twentieth century was a mistake, an arbitrary neglect of the true and the beautiful, a wilful aberration by immature men and women. A new union would be possible if sensible folk could get together.

The first refutation of this argument is provided by the kind of work which it singled out for attention as produced under the rubric of 'art and architecture'. They are predominantly banal buildings with decorative kitsch. One senses behind art and architecture club-able and complacent architects and confusedly eclectic artists and craftspersons, clever with their hands and conceptually innocent. Nice enough people, but what they desire is authoritarian. A shared symbolic order is only possible in a totalitarian culture.

What is productive about bringing art and architecture together is the mutual destruction they bring to each other's professional ideology. To take two simple examples: the specialness of artists is expressed in the uniqueness of their artefacts; their most highly priced objects are one-offs. Artists' drawings, for instance, are valued as intimate prints of their unique minds. So for artists to make drawings from which others can construct something, a drawing devoid of the rhetoric of self-expression, is for some a radical act. Such drawings are, of course, the bread and butter of architecture. Similarly, it is troubling to most architects to work on the assumption that a judgement of what is functional and what serves utility is as ideologically contingent as is an aesthetic judgement. The technological authority of architecture and its supposedly value-free codes are put into question.

What this suggests is not art and architecture brought into synthesis, in an attempt to construct an apparently homogenous culture, but rather both serving to de-define the other: a fracturing of boundaries. This opens up the possibilities of a critical visual practice: a visual practice that de-habituates, that can, with humour and seriousness, explore culture across professional ideologies.

Marcel Duchamp, *Fresh Widow*, 1920, Miniature French window, painted wood frame, and eight panes of glass covered with black leather, 77.5 x 44.8 cm. The Museum of Modern Art, New York, Katherine S. Dreier Bequest. Photo: © 1996 The Museum of Modern Art, New York.

In the Groves of Philadelphia—A Female Hanging:
Jon Thompson

Fresh Widow points to the separation by death from a subject of affection, and in Duchamp's case this would seem to imply the death, or temporary submersion, of the male aspect of the self. The taboo this work represents thus goes beyond that which operates against incest to reach into the more troubling depths of necrophilia.

When Marcel Duchamp arranged for the clandestine submission of the work *Fountain*—the now notorious gentleman's urinal, signed 'R. Mutt, 1917'—to the first exhibition of the newly formed American Society of Independent Artists, he set in motion a controversy which is still alive today. More than any of Duchamp's works, it is *Fountain* that has maintained the capacity to intrigue, to confound, even to shock. And despite an extensive and erudite literature—an endless stream of learned articles and a number of books—despite all of this written material, the artist's intentions remain obscure and the question of Duchamp's authorship a matter for continued speculation. Even though he admitted responsibility for the *Fountain* fairly soon after its rejection from the exhibition of the 'Independents', this did little to dispose of the questions raised but left unanswered by his previous explanations, not least in respect of the "woman artist friend from Philadelphia," Duchamp's earliest and most enigmatic contribution.

As a founder-member of the American Society of Independent Artists, intimately involved in drawing up the rules governing the first, major 'open' exhibition and elected head of the hanging committee too, Duchamp was no doubt admirably well placed, first of all to engineer the scandal which attended the submission and rejection of *Fountain*, and thereafter to exploit the discomfiture of all concerned to the absolute maximum. In this respect, it would appear to be a classic surrealist stratagem. With the intention, presumably, of eliciting a knee-jerk reaction from the rest of the committee—a response that was out in the open before reflection could temper it and one that could not easily be revoked without further increasing the embarrassment quotient—Duchamp, with character-istic precision, succeeded in locating a point of bourgeois suscepti-bility around which there cohered a treacherous accretion of barely conscious social taboos. His chosen weapon—the men's urinal—this curiously fashioned, functional object, abstracted from an exclu-sively male domain and subject—in normal circumstances—to an exclusively male address; this gaping creature of the gentleman's room, so alluringly female in its form, carried with it an array of provocative associations and references likely to ensnare even the most liberal members of the so-called enlightened middle class. In as far as it focused attention on personal hygiene—the private uri-nals, gender division, transgressive curiosities and desires which situate themselves around human acts of secretion—it was of a character perfectly fitted to insinuate itself into the psychological fabric of middle class propriety, and to demolish it from within. Duchamp's circle were confronted, then, with a precisely coded invitation to enter into a speculative relationship with an object, the identity of which was not in doubt, and yet the proffered engage-ment was aggressively ambivalent. Is it really a vessel in which to urinate, or is it a drinking fountain, a watering hole, a place from which to take refreshment? Is it mouth or vagina, or is it, as Duchamp himself would perhaps have it, the 'Infra-thin' impression of their opposites; that which snugly fits within, male into female, positive into negative, like the cast adhering to the mould?

Is it not possible, then, that this urinal is as much a mould—some-thing which determines form—as it is a thing cast? And if this is so, what of its blank interior space, what image might we inscribe upon that: a dematerialised pouch of genitalia, perhaps, or a mound of Venus turned in upon itself, geometric perforations indicating front and back passages—a sort of gynaecologist's eye view but from the inside looking out? And why has Duchamp chosen to rotate the object thus and present it to us laid on its back?

Much later on in his life, when asked precisely this question in an interview with Pierre Cabanne, Duchamp proffered the explanation that this kind of inversion and rotation around a double axis of symmetry effectively transported the object—in this case the uri-nal—out of the third dimension and into the fourth. In the 'Notes to the Glass', just such a 'passage' of transformation—I use the word 'passage' in the strictly Duchampian sense—is referred to as a 'demi-tour', in other words as a journey which, according to the pre-fix used, has been halved, shortened, or curtailed. A slight stretch-ing of the meaning would perhaps permit the use of the word to which Duchamp gave such prominence in the sub-title to the *Large Glass*: the word 'delay'. This 'switch', as Duchamp called it, into the fourth dimension, by its very nature is never completed, always it is shortened, truncated, its climax always and forever 'delayed'.

But there is also a deeply hidden and erotic aspect to this notion of a geometric 'passage'. About the time that Duchamp was conceiv-ing the work *Fountain*, he was greatly intrigued, even influenced by the ideas of the French mathematician Esprit Pascal Jouffret. Jouffret argued—prophetically as it later transpired—that a simulta-neous rotation of the kind advanced by Duchamp in his interview with Cabanne—a three dimensional object 'switched', taken on a 'demi-tour' through the fourth dimension—would necessarily involve a 'flip-flop', the effect of which would be to return the object mirror-reversed and inside-out. Furthermore, the mathematician exampled this phenomenon by reference to one of Duchamp's favourite play-things: a pair of gloves. The left-hand glove, Jouffret observed, rotated about an axis drawn along its length and simulta-neously turned inside-out, is made coincident in every respect to the right-hand glove. Thus, as Duchamp was quick to appreciate—the difference between the left and right might just as easily be cat-egorised as temporal, as physical. Rather than its being attributable to a difference in material form, it could be more interestingly explained, perhaps, as a 'more-or-less minuscule difference in time'. Given this conceptual framework, the difference in time between inside and outside, too, would no longer enjoy a depend-able status—unless it was as an unbound region of erotic interac-tion, in which two absolutely contiguous surfaces continuously massage each other.

There are echoes here of the poet Paul Valéry's obsession with the 'finger-stall', and of his fictional hero Mons. Teste's fixation upon the 'cucumber'—a creature which Valéry describes as having 'no obvious fixed dimensions'. It can appear as a floating flat disc in one instant and as a tube with a closed end the next. In this form too, it can travel at great speed by drawing water into its interior and then forcefully expelling it by means of muscular contraction. It reverses instaneously simply by turning itself inside-out. This capacity to inflate 'inside' and 'outside' experiences, or at least to exchange one for the other seemingly at will, brings us close to the sort of intimate exchange suggested by Duchamp's several definitions of the concept that he labelled the 'Infra-thin': the difference between the mould and the cast; that which distinguishes two casts taken from the same mould; the sound of velvet trouser legs brushing against one another in the act of walking; the warmth that remains behind when a seat is vacated, and so on. All of these examples speak initially of a close coincidence of some kind, and then an exchange of properties, even a transmission. But this transmission, this exchange, at the point at which it is 'stopped', ostensibly so that it might become visible, paradoxically—by dint of the very fact that it has been arrested, curtailed, 'delayed'—is rendered invisible. It is, for instance, of the very essence of our experience of the *Large Glass*, that none of the processes to which it refers can be seen. We are given the apparatus that impels the exchange but nothing of the fluid substance in motion. We are provided with a diagram of its trajectory, but have no means of testing its efficiency. The imaging of 'delay' which the *Large Glass* provides, then, is not that of a coitus interruptus but an ejaculation endlessly postponed. The bridal cloud is permanently congealed, the tubes, the condensers, the love-filters are unused, barren. The possibility of the 'demi-tour'—a fruitful exchange between the two halves (top and bottom) and the two sides of the 'Glass'—is revealed as little more than a cruel parody of the 'demi-urge': the creative force all dried up.

Craig Adcock, in his fascinating essay, 'Duchamp's Eroticism—A Mathematical Analysis', develops the argument further by suggesting that it was this idea of the 'demi-tour'—the switch through the fourth dimension—which, in the manner of H.G. Wells' hero, Mr. Plattner, provided Duchamp with the rationale for his adoption of the female alter ego, Rrose Sélavy. In short, that it was this key concept which grounded the puzzling and provocative gender-inversion which surfaced in Duchamp's work some three years after the submission of the 'urinal', in the attribution of the 'assisted readymade'—*Fresh Widow*: "R[r]ose Sélavy, New York, 1920."

The implications of Adcock's proposition are worthy of more extended analysis in two important respects. Firstly, it would seem to suggest that Duchamp intended to shift the distinction between 'male' and 'female' out of the static, biophysical domain and into the temporal, and secondly, that he wanted the gender difference itself to be considered as nothing more significant than a particular example in the category of the 'Infra-thin'. The argument is best

de-, dis-, ex-.

understood by reference to the mechanisms of conceptual translation exampled by Jouffret's inversion of the 'left-hand glove', whereby concavities are made into convexities; outside becomes inside; conspicuous promontories—things which stick out—are transformed into ingressive passageways; and in the course of which, at a very particular stage in the process—just like Mons. Teste's 'sea-cucumber', drifting in its relaxed, disc-like flattened form—the 'sphincteral' contradiction between 'opening as entrance' and 'opening as exit' is completely neutralised. If we are able to take Adcock's suggestion seriously, then Duchamp is positing an instant of absolute inter-penetration of inside and outside, such as that which obtains between mould and cast, before separation is attempted. Locked in such a close embrace it appears, from the outside at least, as if neither party is dominant, but inside—in the 'Infra-thin' interval between the two—there rages a continuous, essentially sub-visible struggle to establish specificity of gender. Arguably, it is this seemingly closed state, this impenetrable condition of coexistence which constitutes the 'delay' to which Duchamp refers in the subtitle to the *Large Glass*. In other words, the 'delay', as well as being a sucking resistance to withdrawal, a denial of separation and therefore of the possibility of an excited 'transmission', as we have already remarked, it is also a 'delay' in the mutual recognition and reinforcement of specific gender difference.

Significantly, after the initial controversy which attended the submission of *Fountain* and Duchamp's resignation from the Society of Independent Artists, as the scandal was beginning to die down, Duchamp—by deploying friends as more-or-less unwitting intermediaries—began, cautiously, to insinuate into the minds of the so-called radical, middle-class, New York cultural set and the press too, the idea that the 'urinal' had been submitted on legitimate aesthetic grounds; that far from being 'obscene' or 'dirty' as the accusation ran, it in fact represented the beautiful in everyday things. And he took his provocation even further: firstly by accepting publicly Katherine Dreier's somewhat giddy assertion that the "chaste simplicity" of the 'urinal' was "like a lovely Buddha," and then by the artist himself suggesting that its elegant curvilinear exterior shape was quintessentially 'feminine'. Suddenly the notion was abroad that *Fountain*—this functional object, mass-produced for the exclusive use of men, intimately connected with their private functions and therefore deemed to be deeply offensive to women—in fact partook of the archetypal form of the Christian 'Madonna'. Here, then, we no longer have an object suitable for vilification, but one that verged upon the venerable. It reflected the most mysterious and enigmatic of Judaeo-Christian desires, the dualistic desire for two bodies—the corruptible and the incorruptible—in the sublime concatenation of fecund mother and Virgin Queen.

In retrospect, there seems little doubt that Duchamp deliberately unleashed this deeply subversive second reading of Fountain with deliberate intention of thoroughly confusing those members of the Society who had been instrumental in ensuring that the work be rejected from the exhibition. It should be remembered that Fountain had been temporarily mislaid—deliberately lost, it had been suggested, for the period of the opening of the exhibition—and that it was Duchamp accompanied by his close friend, Walter Arensberg, who went in search of it, eventually discovering it packed out of sight behind the exhibition screens. Together they transported it to the studio of the photographer Alfred Stieglitz, where Duchamp had arranged for it to be photographed for inclusion in the next issue of his magazine, Blind Man. Stieglitz later gave testimony to the close attention paid by Duchamp himself to the taking of this particular photograph. He recalled that they discussed the project at great length, paying close attention to the positioning of the camera and the placing of the image of the urinal within the frame. Duchamp's declared intention was to enhance the 'voluptuous' feminine characteristics of the object. As the art historian William Camfield puts it in his excellent essay on the subject, Duchamp was intent on producing "an image which exuded sexuality."

Duchamp published the resulting photograph as planned in Blind Man, no.2, in the late spring of 1917. More interestingly though, he gave a second version of the photograph—taken from the same negative, but this time cropped so that the forward reaching lip of the urinal is just within the bottom edge of the frame—as a present to Walter Arensberg, some time during the following year. The timing of this gift is sufficiently close to the dating of the 'rectified' reproduction of the Mona Lisa, L.H.O.O.Q., to justify speculation about the close connection between the two. Certainly, it would seem to show that the artist continued to experiment with the Steiglitz photograph after it appeared as the leading page in Blind Man, and with the apparent intention of bringing the image even closer to that of a seated, Madonna-like woman, with long hair or head covered by a shawl. In this respect, L.H.O.O.Q. offers some striking similarities with the earlier work. Visually speaking, there is a clear dual resemblance to its sweeping curvilinear form; firstly, out of the way in

de-, dis-, ex-.

which the face and the neck down to the top of the breasts, where they are cut by the braided edge of the dress, are framed by the downward sweep of the woman's hair; and then again by the way in which her arms and hands are linked in front and the feeling of enclosure that this linkage generates.

But the most important common thread linking these two works is to be found in the phonetic punning of the title in the later work: L.H.O.O.Q.—"Elle a chaud au cul"—"She has a hot bottom." This title, replete with its subversive erotic meanings, together with the drawn addition of masculine facial hair, serves to complete a complex, cyclical process of double-inversion, from female into male and back into female once again. In linguistic terms the title turns the whole arrangements into the very model of 'demi-tour'. Starting from the original image of the enigmatic courtesan, face animated by a post-coital smile, Duchamp first switches the reading to that of a somewhat fastidious, perhaps even a slightly effeminate man-about-town—waxed moustache erect and beard like a young girl's pudenda—and then, by means of the title, he returns it to a full-blooded representation of female sexuality: "She has a hot bottom"; she is a woman who itches to have sex. The phrase presents us with two alternative readings: as a description of type—she has a tendency towards promiscuity, she is the sort of women who is characterised as having a 'hot bottom'—or as a description of a present condition—she desires sexual satisfaction, her present state is that of having a 'hot bottom'. Either way, the implied trajectory of transformation moves from first to last, out of the past into the future: from the expression of an appetite recently satisfied, through a state of nominal neutrality and towards the expression of a sexual desire in urgent need of satisfaction. Thus desire is passed in time and space, through itself in order to renew itself, in the endless alterity that exists between satiety and hunger.

But what of the gender transformation worked by the drawing on of the beard and moustache. Here, surely, we are given the very opposite case to that represented by Fountain. There Duchamp was overlaying the feminine upon the masculine, whereas in the case of L.H.O.O.Q., it would seem that the opposite is true: the male identity is superimposed on to the female. However, this apparent difference soon dissolves when the argument is taken to a deeper level.

Both works, it should be remembered, were what Duchamp himself described as 'rectified' readymades. They were altered by an action of the hand; in both cases by means of inscription. As we have already remarked, in the case of *Fountain* this took the form of a false signature—'R. Mutt, 1917'—which inscription, as the artist later acknowledged, was a complex amalgam of references and multilingual puns. The urinal itself was selected by Duchamp from the New York showrooms of the Philadelphia based firm of 'J. L. Mott, Iron-founders and Sanity Engineers'. Even before he altered it, then—with the intention as he told Cabanne of making the subterfuge less obvious—the name resonated with alternative meanings linked with his native French tongue: "mot," the answer to a riddle; "bon mot," a witticism, a double entendre, a practical joke; "motte," a clod of turf, in Parisian slang a woman's pubic bush. Changing the 'O' for 'U' produced further layers of meaning. Apart from the well documented reference to the short, fat character "Mut" in the popular strip cartoon *Mutt and Jeff*, it suggests additional truncated, translingual puns: "Mutt(er)," or the more affectionate "Mutt(i)," mother in German; or in English "mutt(er)," to speak inaudibly; and in Italian, the several declensions of the verb "mutt(are)," to change. The inscription was also intended to act as a bridge to other works, the most notable of which was the last of Duchamp's 'painted' works commissioned and already planned for the Katherine Dreier library and bearing the deliberately nonsensical title, *Tu'm*—to which it was possible to respond by attaching "any (French) verb as long as it begins with a vowel"—a purposeful inversion of the inscribed surname 'Mutt'. Mystery still surrounds the addition of the fictitious 'Mutt's' christian name, 'Richard.' Viewed in retrospect, it was certainly a part of Duchamp's original intention; he admitted as much in an interview with Otto Hahn: "...I added Richard, French slang for money-bags. That's not a bad name for a pissotière. Get it? The opposite of poverty ('Armut' is German for poverty). But not even that much, just 'R. Mutt'."

Nevertheless, the first press reports referred to the unknown artist as 'J.C. Mutt'—a confusion, no doubt, with the manufacturer's name of 'J. L. Mott'—and thereafter as plain 'Mr. Mutt'. And Duchamp himself, when approached during the heat of the controversy, unhesitatingly attributed the work to an "unknown woman artist friend of mine from Philadelphia," only to change his mind later, referring to it in the editorial board of *Blind Man* as the work of "Mr Richard Mutt of Philadelphia."

It would seem that there is ample evidence, then, to support the view that Duchamp—despite its having originated in the gentleman's room—saw the urinal as essentially feminine in character, even as the very essence of womanhood. And this impression is reinforced by reference to the anonymous photograph of his studio at 33 West 67th Street, in which the urinal is clearly visible hanging from the ceiling. This photograph, cryptically annotated in Duchamp's hand with the title phrase, *Le Pendu Femelle* (the female hanging), taken in concert with the earlier notes included in the *Box of 1914*, where Duchamp writes, "one only has for public the female urinal—and one lives by it," bears ample witness to his persistent, almost obsessive conflation of the idea of the feminine with the male urinal. Further more given the evidence overall, it would seem reasonable to suppose that his original attribution was a fully worked out part of the game plan. In other words, that his reference to the "woman from Philadelphia" was intended as a tautological description of the urinal itself: that the work that Duchamp called *Fountain* was none other than the "woman from Philadelphia" in person.

At this time, the artist was still working to define and refine his concept of the 'readymade', of which, eventually, there were three quite distinct categories: the 'readymade' pure and simple—a pre-factured object of some kind (the Bottlerack would be one example) brought within the arena of art by an enactment of placement; the 'assisted readymade'—pre-factured object (the bird cage in *Why Not Sneeze*, for example) transformed into a work of art by the addition of new and unexpected elements; and the 'rectified readymade'—a pre-factured object, re-contexted by an act of inscription. This last category, which includes both *Fountain* and *L.H.O.O.Q.*, would seem to imply some form of correction, or a restoration of the object to a previously more total, less deviant condition. In both of the works in question the act of inscription serves to overlay a male identity upon a female one. But this is no gesture towards a crudely sexual or bestial coupling. In as far as it is intended to restore or 'rectify', to return the object to its original identity in some way, it is a motion towards the neutral, towards, if you like, the primal state of the mythic androgyne. The process is reminiscent of that which Freud points to in *Beyond the Pleasure Principle*, when he speaks of a property, observable as a general tendency in organic life, "impelling it towards the reinstatement of an earlier condition...that of the inorganic. The sexual act, the combining of male and female, remains the place where Eros measures up to Thanatos; but the victories of life are never more than respites in the journey towards death. Life's provisional equilibrium always, unfailingly ends by disintegrating into the definitive equilibrium of death." At the very centre of Duchamp's notion of 'rectification', then, is a movement towards a state of absolute stasis—a kind of death—in which difference is permitted no observable visual dimensionality; in which difference, in other words—if it is allowed a place at all—is confined to the conceptual (non-retinal) domain of the 'Infra-thin'. For Duchamp, as we have already remarked, the co-existence of mould and cast represents a state of absolute, mutual pathicity and the type of circularity—in material form—that we associate with the great metaphysical systems: the eternal return to a pre-existent state of unity. Here though, in Duchamp's case, this unity is highly eroticised. The uncomposing of the original, androgynous condition of oneness its potential for splitting into male and female parts—has as its necessary sequel the pathology of a species divided according to gender: an unrelenting and ultimately unassuageable attraction between the sexes. In this respect, the condition of androgynous unity between mould and cast can also stand for a version of absolute creativity: a self-completing coincidence of masculine and feminine principles in which duality is held in check (delayed) just long enough to allow for something approaching autonomous incarnation. It holds out the tantalising possibility of a thing that can make and remake itself ad infinitum.

Fountain, the urinal, the "woman from Philadelphia"—author as well as the thing authored—in as far as it might, quite legitimately, be said to have made itself, presents us then with a very special case within the overall category within the 'readymade'. Perhaps it even sheds important new light on Duchamp's thinking with regard to 'readymades' in general. It is one thing to pay lip-service to the prefacture and pre-existence of a chosen object by designating it 'readymade' and emphasising selection and placement over any aesthetic qualities it may possess. It is quite another matter to suggest that this same object might, in some strange way, have made or 'authorised' itself. Such a notion would, however, serve to explain why Duchamp repeatedly and so vehemently denied the play of his own taste in relation to the appearance of the 'readymade' A miraculous autonomy of the kind suggested would argue some sort of radical disjunction between the world of art and the world of everyday things, a disjunction which would demand of an object passing from one into the other, that it re-make itself. In other words, wrested from the visual conditioning placed upon it by its mundane function, it would be forced to take responsibility for its own appearance.

To example this by reference to a similar kind of self-generating translation, we might usefully turn to a later work by the artist, *Door, 11 rue Larrey, 1927*: two doorways set side by side at right-angles to one another—one leads to the bedroom the other to the bathroom—sharing a single door hinged between the two, capable of closing off one or the other of the rooms but never both at the same time. According to Man Ray, Duchamp was fond of asking visitors to the apartment whether the door 'was always the same door'; "a rhetorical question which seemed to cause him some considerable amusement." If one stays within the realm of common sense, of course the answer to such a question can only be both 'yes' and 'no'. But in the realm of Duchampian language games and spatio-temporal 'switches', it becomes a more complicated matter. Certainly, with each successive swing of the door it changes, nominally speaking, from being the 'bedroom door' to being the 'bathroom door', but it also undergoes an implied dimensional change too, not dissimilar in kind to Jouffret's example of the glove: the inside becomes the outside, and the 'left-handed door' becomes a 'right-handed' one, or vice versa. But this is no simple one for one swapping of identity. In fact, within the space of one swing of the door, its identity changes twice. There is a neutral mid-point at which the door is neither one thing nor the other: it is neither bedroom nor bathroom door, neither right-handed nor left-handed, its surface neither inside nor outside. At this moment, stripped of both identities—with its functional identity delayed—it is simply what it is: a door. More significantly it is a door which denies retinal confirmation. In this proposition, it must be approached from its leading edge so as not to privilege one possible reading over another, and suddenly the door is tucked away out of sight, submerged within itself, rendered invisible. It is collapsed into another telling example of the 'Infra-thin', the invisible line which dissects a right-angle; the conceptual and schematic representation of a regression to infinity. And out of this fleeting moment of invisibility, the door re-emerges dressed in its other guise. Once again, as with *Fountain* and *L.H.O.O.Q.*, we find Duchamp passing the object through its own hybrid, androgynous self, to return it to us as its seeming opposite.

But this point of neutrality, as well as a location for transformation, is also a locus of reconciliation. Francis Naumann, in his essay 'Marcel Duchamp—a Reconciliation of Opposites', makes a direct and convincing connection between *Door, 11 rue Larrey* and the theme of the book on chess which Duchamp co-authored with the German master, Halberstadt: 'L'Opposition et les Cases Conjugées sont Reconciliées'—'Opposition and Sister Squares are Reconciled'. Naumann points out that the main purpose of what otherwise is a highly arcane, and as far as the game of chess is concerned, a relatively useless book, is to show that in the 'endgame', 'oppositional' and 'sister' squares, far from being the functional antithesis of each other, can be seen as having a common identity and a common purpose. Similarly, that *Door, 11 rue Larry* is intended to disprove the French adage: "Il faut qu'une porte soit ouverte ou fermée"—a door must be either open or closed. Duchamp's door, when in its median position, is cunningly disconnected from both of the available apertures in equal degrees. In this respect it might be said to be neither open nor closed: the either/or is simply not applicable. In this instant the door is oddly free-standing, independent, responsible for its own identity. Neither is it like a discarded door. In no sense is it bereft of its function or denied an appropriate context. As Jean François Lyotard has indicated in his remarkable book *TRANS/formation*, it is the 'hinge' that, for Duchamp, determines the sum total of relationships. All the 'analagisms' of the passage from three to four dimensions, with that from the second to the third: a rectangle turning like a hinge engenders a cylinder; imagine the hinge-plane of a volume (three-dimensional) engendering by rotation a four-dimensional figure. The two transversals of glass that separate the Bachelor region and the Brides region are also generators of this sort. "Make a hinged picture." (M.D.) The door, hinged between bathroom and bedroom, would seem to represent precisely this case, as indeed does the 'reconciliation' of 'sister' squares, demonstrated by Duchamp's poster for the French Chess Congress of 1927 and one of his last etchings, *King and Queen*, of 1968. Here the chessboard has been broken up and turned into three-dimensional segments, three hinged squares at a time, one black and two whites, or vice versa. Thus the oppositional square is placed in an equal, but at the same time highly ambiguous relationship with the diagonally related 'sister' squares of the opposing colour by a process of double hinging. In the course of this dimensional translation, the field of combat— which in the case of the 'endgame' is given over to one purpose and one purpose only: that of manoeuvring the opposite King into a 'mating position', usually after a Pawn (the Page-boy, the young male servant reminiscent of the Malic Moulds resplendent in their liveries) has been converted into a Queen—is rendering in-operable and no longer amenable to reconstruction. The tumbling cascade of half-cubes, like the 'stripping', diagrammatised in the iconography of the *Large Glass*, represents a frozen and ultimately unrealisable enterprise. The King's direct progress along his own file is denied.

de-, dis-, ex-.

His potency is thus blunted by an alliance of feminine forces. We might almost say that the King has suffered castration at the hands of a doubled representation of dissimulating hand-maidens: the Queen's household. In this scheme of things, the attacking oppositional square is not available to him; instead he must make common cause with the Queen's interests. He cannot avoid what Jaques Derrida has called the inversion that comes with negation.

What is at stake here—it might even be the central thread that connects all of Duchamp's work—is an elaborate theory of opposition, chiefly exampled by a strangely ambivalent reconstruction of the male/female relationship. Looked at through one end of the telescope Duchamp's attitude here might appear to be an utterly reactionary one. The male is cast in the active role and the female in the passive. The man—the Post-Freudian man that is replent with his overweening sexual drive—is seen as a kind of Honest-John figure; the woman, as a deceiver and a seducer. The masculine principle represented as a transparency—the *Large Glass,* for example—while the feminine principle is represented by an opacity. However, as we have already demonstrated, Duchamp was possessed of a much more complex turn of mind than would permit such an inelegant and one-sided formulation. The view from the other end of the Duchamp telescope provides for a very different topography of gender and sexual difference. To begin with, things are much closer together: far more difficult to separate and to hold apart. Qualities are never intrinsic either. They can easily up and migrate to and fro across the gender divide. The principle of opposition then, in a Duchampian sense, is only realisable as a fluid, ongoing engagement. Difference is a form of transaction: it is the very essence of the 'Infra-thin' that difference exists not in things but in the space between them. The idea of observable, fixed, masculine and feminine characteristics is thus the product of a curtailment of exchange out of which there arises an illusion of difference. Jacques Derrida, in the footnotes to his *Spurs/Eperons,* makes the following telling observation with regard to oppositional formulations of sexual difference in general. At the moment that the sexual difference is determined as an opposition, the image of each term is inverted into the other. Thus the machinery of contradiction is a proposition whose two Xs are once subject and predicate and whose copula is a mirror. Under this rubric, the game of gender difference is perhaps best understood as a kind of filial square-dance in which brother and sister images exchange with each other qualities drawn from a predetermined catalogue of familial resemblances. The difference discernible between members of the filial foursome is determined from within the over-arching edifice of a larger, common identity. Seen in this light, the oscillation that we have observed elsewhere, between male and female parts in his works such as *Fountain* and *L.H.O.O.Q.*, and in the proposition of an intimate coupling and exchange in the *Large Glass*, might be accurately compared with a situation in which an image of a 'sister' faces the mirror and receives back the familiar image of a 'brother', which in turn causes its opposite and so on, thus inaugurating a recurrent pattern of mutual confirmation in which the recognition of difference is endlessly delayed.

Viewed in this light too, *Fountain*—the gentleman's urinal turned female hanging; the "mysterious woman from Philadelphia"; a self-made woman, author as well as thing authored—assumes a pre-eminent position in the progress of Duchamp's work overall.

The clue to this pre-eminence is to be found in Duchamp's choice of Philadelphia as domicile for his fictitious artist. Literally translated, Philadelphia means 'city of brotherly love', after the teachings of the Greek philosopher Ptolemy Philadelphus. Philadelphia Pennsylvania, took its name from the 'Philadelphians', a highly secretive, non-conformist religious sect, not unlike the Quakers, which flourished in England at the time of the Pilgrim Fathers; and no doubt it found its echo in Duchamp because of the late eighteenth-century neo-classical brotherhood of an almost Masonic kind which bore the same name. The name Philadelphia, then, represents an esoteric site, which allows under the cloak of secrecy for certain transformations to be set in motion. Most importantly, it allows for the kind of 'reflexive' quadrille between paired brothers and sisters, touched upon by Derrida, with its undercurrents of transexuality, narcissism and incest, to be danced to its icy conclusion in an eroticism without fulfilment; in an altogether de-sexualised amour. The consummation of this amour occurs, paradoxically, with the narcissistic splitting of male and female identities within the same persona, allowing each to become the subject of the other's gaze. That such a relationship is necessarily governed by filial resemblances—it is dependent, in other words, on recognising the self in the other—needs no further elaboration. That it is governed, in the psychological sense, by filial taboos of a similar order to those that intended inhibit sexual activity between brother and sister is perhaps worth more extended consideration, especially in the light of Duchamp's later invention of a female alter ego in the person of 'Rrose Sélavy'.

The title of the first work signed by 'R[r]ose Sélavy', *Fresh Widow* (1920), would seem to be highly significant in this respect. In one of the interviews that Duchamp gave to Cabanne, he speaks of the idea of 'being freshly widowed' as representing a crucial change of state, but ventures no more than this. How then are we to construe this change, unless it be in terms of splitting, a breaking apart of something which hitherto had appeared as an indissoluble unity. To be 'freshly widowed' is to be separated by death from a subject of affection, and in Duchamp's case this would seem to imply the death, or temporary submersion, of the male aspect of the self. For this reason the windows of *Fresh Widow* are dressed in black leather to prevent their offering back any confirmative reflection. The taboo this work represents thus goes beyond that which operates against incest to reach into the more troubling depths of necrophilia.

*   *   *

(This essay was written after a visit to the Duchamp exhibition at Ronny Van de Velde and after reading an excellent collection of essays, *Marcel Duchamp, Artist of the Century*, from which I have drawn.)

Dan Graham, *Pavilion for Schloss Buchberg*, Austria. Completed 1996.
Photo: Courtesy of Brian Hatton.

Dan Graham
Brian Hatton

Dan Graham once described himself as a 'photojournalist'. That is, one who provides a documentary mirror with its current actuality, one who is continually present in order to make diverse parts of the present continuous with each other. Such work involves a time-delay place-shift, although in live coverage and real-time video the delay and distance are reduced. But Graham does not document events; his work over the last thirty years has been a rendition of available forms of engagement with the actual, the ongoing, the vernacular.

It has involved a sort of paradox: to enable, on the one hand, new exchanges and encounters, and on the other, a perspicacious beholding of moments of actuality. These are framed within screens, windows and mirrors that resemble sculpture but which in fact function as architecture, insofar as they house and facilitate real social interactions. These inter-subjective phenomena—our behaviour for ourselves and for others—are brought, without losing their personal (and political) 'aliveness' to a condition of para-aesthetic 'objecthood' that is co-present and co-incident with the formal status of the 'artwork' be it sculpture, gallery performance, video piece, or architectural pavilion. Across all Graham's work there has prevailed this common theme of live rendition: to see ourselves being and to be ourselves seeing.

This involves something very concrete and yet at the same time quite abstract. In this, Graham reminds me of Gertrude Stein, for instance Stein on Picasso said: "This one was one and always there was something coming out of this one..." But imagine Stein's diffractive, reitaritive style enacted in continuous description, meditation, in performance, video, and mirrors, and the "one" from which "always there was something coming out of" as us—we the public and private subject—viewing ourselves as our object. Graham's photo journalism bridges the most intimate distances, the most discrete distances of delay, to restitute them as 'own signs' yet in a social milieu—the 'primitive' pavilion in the 'natural city' that is not just a monad of ideal form relations, like Mies' pavilions, but a facili-ty-for fun, amongst other things.

Let us consider some passages in this work, starting with the piece from 1964 that prompted the self-epithet 'photo journalist': *Homes for America*. It was a magazine article about suburban 'tract' housing, serial-produced in a limited number of shapes and colours. Permuted, their configurations became analogues of the 'specific objects' of minimal sculpture. *Homes for America* proposed this ver-nacular isomorph as a 'found' stratagem for recasting the site of art through the social milieu. Throughout Graham's diverse activity, the chief experiment has been to reinsert the art-work among the lived pragmatics of the contemporary life world.

It is possible now to see the recent pavilions of reflective/transparent glass as restitutions of those suburban balloon-frames to their arca-dian premise: prismatic fragments of a utopia that would be both individually liberal and collectively affirmative. Visually and spatially opening to shift balances of present and virtual image, they perme-ate the actual passages of that ambiguous latitude that modernism has made into a symbolic realm of freedom, the myth-space post-romantic imagination. Into daily urban-suburban no-place, the pavil-ions insert specific devices that refract social encounter into new forms of recognition and engagement, paradoxically, by discrete acts of variation, separation, and displacement that induce disorientated delight in self-estrangement, and sudden unexpected familiarities. It is as if the romantic models of picturesque and sublime have been rendered both precise and intimate in a social lens.

It cannot be over emphasised that Graham's pavilions are psycho-socially functional. They are not so much to be looked at, as to be looked with. It is in the presence of others, and in continuously changing sky-light, that they are themselves most fully present. There is time in them, the suspended time of contemplation, and real-time interaction, so that although they may be a 'time-capsule' in the manner of total environments such as Lissitzky's PROUN rooms, or Brancusi's studio, or Rothko's chapel, they are not hermet-ic, and their space is defined less by formal dimensions than by the alterities of what and whom we encounter through them. Not cap-sules, but passages in time. As for the rate of that time, that depends upon the variables of site and useage: a skateboard canopy or a child's pavilion will differ from a bower of contemplation or an altered suburban house.

In understanding Graham's pavilions then, it is important to recall all the work he did during the seventies with temporal media-like film (*Body Press*, 1970-72, recorded helical camera paths around two subjects in a mirror-clad cylinder), real-time feedback forms of performance and video (*Local Cable TV Project for Two Polemical Interlocutors*, 1977; *Performance Audience Mirror*, 1977, in which a performer continuously relates his/her description of the audience, alternating with self-description through the distance of a mirror), and delayed-time feedback installations, both in gallery chambers and in real-life spaces. Since *Two Adjacent Pavilions*, 1978, Graham has turned from video codes to an architectural code of unitary simultaneous presentness, in which literal time-tags are replaced by naturally triggered shifts of internal time (sky-light alters inside and out, self and other) and by historical awareness of the pavilion in relation to the park, museum, and the city.

Jasper Johns, *Flag*, 1954-5, encaustic and collage on fabric mounted on plywood, 107.3 x 153.8 cm. The Museum of Modern Art, New York, Gift of Philip Johnson in honour of Alfred H. Barr, Jr. Photo: © 1996 The Museum of Modern Art, New York.

The Object After Theory
(Figuring Jasper Johns—Supplement 1: *Flag*)
Fred Orton

'The Object after Theory'.[1] There's a kind of familiar ambiguity and uncertainty that is part of the point of this session's title with which we speakers are expected to play. It would be churlish not to. Let's start with that 'after'.

This could mean: 'the object following, behind, in view of, in pursuit of and next in importance to theory'. And it could also mean: 'the object concerning, according to, in spite of, in allusion to or in imitation of theory'. It gets complicated as to what is meant in each case. Much depends on the meaning of 'object', on what kind of 'object' comes into focus: whether it is a material entity or an aim. Purpose or intention. 'The material entity *after* theory', not so much behind it or in pursuit of it but perhaps *following* it in time, next in importance to it, concerning it, alluding to it, or in imitation of it. Or 'the aim, purpose or end in view *concerning* theory, or according to it, or in spite, of it or in allusion to it, or in imitation of it'. And, finally: what of 'theory'? What are we to make of it? Current usage has it that 'theory' is a supposition or system of ideas explaining something, especially one based on general principles independent of the particular things to be explained; a bit of (or sphere of) abstract knowledge or speculative thought; or the exposition of the principles of a practice—'theory' as the opposition of 'practice'. There is, however, something lacking in current usage—and that is the spectator or beholder. This definition, taken from the *Shorter Oxford English Dictionary*, returns him or her to 'theory': "A scheme or system of ideas or statements held as an explanation or account of a group of facts or phenomena; a hypothesis that has been confirmed or established by observation or experiment, and is propounded or accepted as accounting for known facts; a statement of what are held to be the general laws, principles, or causes of something known or observed." 'Theory' comes from the Greek verb 'theoria', to look at, to contemplate, to survey, from 'theoros' or spectator, and from 'theoria' a group of spectators.[2] But this is not only looking and the spectators are not just any spectators. In Greece the 'theoria' were individuals of probity and status in the polity who were summoned to attest to the occurrence of some event, to witness it and to verbally certify that it had taken place. Their function was to see-and-tell. The 'theoria' undertook certified seeing-and-telling. Other persons could see-and-tell but only that which the 'theoria' saw-and-told had any social standing. Only the theoretically attested to could be treated as fact. The 'theoria' saw, and how it told what it had seen affected an object of knowledge. Theories don't just find their objects, they constitute them which is to say that the individual agents—working collectively—do the constituting. 'Theory' is certainly not independent of what it has previously constituted as knowledge nor is it interest free. How could it be? But I value this view of 'theory' because it holds that the phenomenal—the material object—is the basis of perception, consciousness, cognition and that understanding is constructed in and by language. I value it precisely because it moves our understanding away from 'theory' as speculative knowledge to an emphasis on theory as a relation between seeing—and seeing material objects, events and so on—and the representation in speech and/or writing of what has been seen. 'Theory' holds within it phenomenalism and reference. As with Marx's and Engels' base-superstructure model, there is determining, mediating and interfering reciprocity here—and, also, language intervening between material existence and consciousness. (Mistaking the certifying statement for the material object is ideology.)[3] In a sense, there is no 'before' or 'after' with 'object' and 'theory' relation, the 'object' becomes an object of knowledge only when and because it becomes an effect of 'theory', and there is only 'theory' because of the 'object' that the 'theoria' come together to certify. It is here that the so-called resistance to theory can be located: in the materiality of the object to be looked at (which if it is a manufactured object will include its willed figuration); and in the way the object has been seen and told which "is a resistance to language itself or to the possibility that language contains factors or functions that cannot be reduced to intuition."[4] Theory is always in need of more theory.

What I want to do in this paper is to re-engage with a bit of my own theory of a particular object and the problem that object posed and poses to theory. You'll have gathered from the title of my paper that I'm going to re-engage with how in my book *Figuring Jasper Johns* I theorised Johns' *Flag*.[5] Here I'm concerned to place *Flag* in relation to a determining moment of production that I'd previously overlooked and then to consider what the implications of its effects might be when seen and understood in relation to that moment.

I'll begin, as I began writing about *Flag* in the book, with the Stars and Stripes, the flag of the United States of America with its legally fixed component parts, colours and proportions. In 1954, towards the end of the year, Johns began work on his own version of the Stars and Stripes. It was the very security of the Stars' and Stripes' established visual appearance that made me take it as the beginning for what I wrote about *Flag*.

Flag is not in the proportional ratio of 1:1.9 that is mandatory for flags displayed by government departments. But that doesn't matter. Not with regard to its effect. The number, size and placement of the stars and stripes were—are—as they should have been in 1954. Whatever *Flag* was *of*, there was an aspect of it that visually and conceptually was—is—the Stars and Stripes as defined in the U.S. Statutes at Large where little or no distinction is between the Stars and Stripes as it might be painted, printed or otherwise made on any surface and as it might be made to be attached to a flag-pole.

To those potential explainers who have asked him why he made *Flag* or how he came to make it, Johns has always replied with the same answer that he had a dream in which he saw himself painting a "large flag" or "a large American flag" and soon after began painting one.

In order to make a painting you must be able to conceive of what it is that you intend to make as a painting. Though artists do not always do or make what they intend, it is the fact, to only slightly rephrase what one contemporary philosopher of art has pointed out, that in doing painting or making a painting a concept enters into, and plays a crucial role in, the determination of what is done and made.[6] That is to say, when we make a painting, we make it under a certain description. Or, we make it after or according to a theory of painting. In the modern epoch the 'dominant theory' at work in "the mainstream of modern art"—Modernism—restricted to painting 'Modernist Painting'—insisted on the surface of the painting and its possession by the artist, who regarded the manipulation of paint—the medium of painting—not as preparatory to making art, realising or representing subject matter, but as the making of art. The dominant theory, then, insisted on the possession of the subject over the surface over the subject. But not only that. The artist had not only to insist and possess the surface, he or she also had to use it to expressive effect—the use of the surface was to produce and preserve a formal counterpart for the expressive quality of painting.

It can be said outright that Johns was not interested in using the surface to expressive effect. He was not interested in expressing himself. But he was interested in possessing and using the surface to effect, and he was interested in painting. He went along with the dominant theory in quite conventional terms. At least to start with. He began work on *Flag* with what would have been regarded as respectable, even conventional, avant-garde materials: enamel paints on a bed sheet. But he could not make the paint do what he wanted it to do and so changed to a process that involved dipping collage elements (mainly pieces of newsprint) into hot coloured wax—red, white and blue—and fixing them to the sheet before the wax cooled and solidified. In other words, he insisted on and possessed the surface by building it up from collage matter stuck in place by hot coloured wax. Some areas also include the use of paint and brush. The two ways of applying paint—with material dipped into hot coloured wax and with brushes—have equal value and follow no particular sequence. The surface of *Flag*, then, is made of something which is quite like painting but can not accurately be referred to as painting and quite like collage but can not accurately be referred to as collage. It's something that is neither painting nor collage but both painting and collage.

Flag begins in the story of a dream. When Johns dreamt he saw himself "painting a large flag" did he see himself making a painting of a flag or was he making a flag with paint? To make a painting of a flag is not the same as making one with paint. The former involves the artist in the practice of representing a flag—a flag is the subject-matter which must, according to the dominant theory, give way to surface matter. The latter means dispensing with the insistence on surface over subject-matter according to the theory of painting the better to make the object in and with paint. Awake and in the studio, or wherever, from the moment Johns hit on the idea of having the Stars and Stripes provide the precise structure for the way he used the surface, the idea of making a painting of a flag was compromised. What Johns was doing was more like making a Stars and Stripes than making a painting. A major problem must have been how to ensure that what he painted did not fuse the Stars and Stripes to such an extent that he made a flag of the United States of America. With the change from enamel paints to coloured wax and collage he hit on an admirable way of preventing that from happening. What prevents *Flag* from securely or thoroughly being a flag of the U.S.A. is, more than anything else, its beguiling factitiousness. The surface matter interrupts the flagness. But this hardly secures *Flag*'s identity in art as a painting—'Modernist' or otherwise.

Alan Solomn, in his catalogue essay for the Johns retrospective in 1964, asked, "Is it a flag, or is it a painting?" *Flag* offers us a choice, an 'either' and an 'or'. A year later, when he asked which it was, Johns said that it was a way of beginning, that "the painting of a flag is always about a flag, but it is no more about a flag than it is about a brushstroke or about a colour or about the physicality of paint." The peculiar character of *Flag*, where the Stars and Stripes and the art object are so thoroughly congruent, is such that wherever one looks there is both flag and painting (or something that is neither painting nor collage, but both a painting and a collage). Both are in place, and each works to interrupt the effect of the other to the extent that *Flag* seems neither one nor the other. It is the site where the two categories confront each other and proliferate. Any commentator who privileges its flag-ness over its work of art-ness, or vice versa, tries to make it more comfortable in discourse. But it can never be made thoroughly comfortable there. *Flag* causes problems for the spectator and especially for the art critic and art historian who is concerned to fix or attest to its meaning and value. For theoreticians of *Flag* the problem was, and is, how to tell it like it is when its is-*ness* is so unstable or uncertain.

Flag has something of the qualities and effects of one of Jacques Derrida's 'undecidables'.[7] It is always 'neither/nor' and 'both/and'. It is neither content nor form but both content and form; neither subject nor surface but both subject and surface; neither subject nor picture but both subject and picture; neither flag nor painting (or something that is neither painting nor collage but both painting and collage) but both flag and painting.

What hasn't been considered in the literature of art and what I overlooked in my previous work on *Flag* was the degree to which in the early to mid-1950s amongst certain persons in New York's avant-garde artistic community, the dominant theory of art was held to be either moribund or irrelevant, there in place to be denied, negated or sublimated.

Two examples. The first is taken from the art criticism of Harold Rosenberg because it specifically concerns painting but something similar without the overt politics was, at about the same time, being thought about dance, music and theatre.

Rosenberg's essay 'The American Action Painters' was published in December 1952.[8] Most of the artists Rosenberg had in mind were over forty years old before they became 'action painters'. We would more usually refer to them now as Abstract Expressionists. Before then, he says, many of these painters had been "Marxists (WPA unions, artists' congresses)...trying to paint society. Others had been trying to paint Art (Cubism, Post-impressionism)." For Rosenberg, it amounted to the same thing. They had been trying to paint the 'Modern'. There were two Moderns, the Society and the Art of the Modern, and, as far as he was concerned, by 1940 both were dead. It is in this double demise that Rosenberg locates the beginnings of 'action painting'. It was at this moment of 'grand crisis' when the two Moderns of Art and Society were recognised as having failed that it became necessary to make an Art of the Modern again. But what kind of painting was possible if the once dominant theories of Art and Society no longer applied? In coming to nothing, the two Moderns provided artists with a major resource for any vanguard practice—nothingness. With the idea of nothingness the action painter decided "to paint...just TO PAINT." Action painting is, in Rosenberg's account of it, painting at the point of formation when everything had to be redone; it is Ur-painting at the moment of thematisation; but it is not yet, and, as far as he is concerned in 1952, painting as an art. This is Rosenberg's theory in part on what he had seen mainly in the studios of Barnett Newman and Bill de Kooning between 1948 and 1952. However, when it comes to giving an example of the kind of painting he has in mind he chooses work by neither Newman or de Kooning. This is as close as he comes to giving an example of 'action painting'. "The new American Painting," he writes, "is not 'pure' art, since the extrusion of the object was not for the sake of the esthetic. The apples weren't brushed off the table in order to make room for perfect relations of space and colour. They had to go so that nothing would get in the way of painting. In this gesturing with materials the esthetic too, has been subordinated. Form, colour, composition, drawing are auxiliaries, any one of which—or practically all, as has been attempted logically, with, unpainted canvases—can be dispensed with." "Unpainted canvases," it seems to me—I'm convinced of it—that what Rosenberg has in mind here are paintings that were "untouched by any instrument," the so-called White Paintings, that Rauschenberg made in 1951 and exhibited two years later at the Stable Gallery.[9] So that is

de-, dis-, ex-.

my second example: Rauschenberg's *White Paintings*. According to Rosenberg in the 'American Action Painters', these "unpainted canvases," understood as 'action paintings', were the results of actions that had "broken down every distinction between art and life." Read one way, for all Rosenberg's talk of a complete break with the Art and Society of the Modern, this statement seems no more than a rephrasing of the paradigmatic avant-gardist desire for art to dissolve into or fuse with social life. Another version of Morris' utopian dreaming and Mayakovsky's poetry readings in the factory yard. Read another way it is less about the desire to integrate art and life—the moment of integration occurs in the act of painting—than it is about the concern to keep to the distinction *between art and life.* The possibility of a revolution in life had been closed down. The distinction between art and life, he is writing, had to be broken down by and in the act of painting—that's the moment (the inevitable moment) of integration and synthesis—but with the 'revolutionary' aim of redefining the identity of the artist and art. That was the only revolutionary act possible at that particular historically and culturally specific moment.

No matter how mediated Rauschenberg's use of it was, he surely had Rosenberg's ideas on action painting, art and life in mind when, in 1959, he stated about his own practice that "Painting relates both too art and life. Neither can be made. (I try to in that gap between the two.)"[10] In so far as this can be made sense of—and no-one, not even Rauschenberg, has explained it sensibly—this statement holds to painting and a problematised distinction *between art and life.* It is not a statement that should lead us to think that Rauschenberg was concerned with the dissolution of the one into the other. Both are insisted upon (in a neither/nor-ish kind of way) and so is the 'gap' *between* them. If Rosenberg's and Rauschenberg's statements are anything to go by, the avant-garde project with regard to art and life has changed. Their difference was to be insisted on and problematised by acknowledging the 'gap' between them.[11] The point I want to make now, of course, is that Johns' *Flag* is also made out of a concern to insist upon and problematise the distinction between art and life—for that must be the last of the falling binaries: form and content; surface and subject; picture and subject; painting and referent; art and life.

In so far as Rosenberg's account of the development of Abstract Expressionism is catastrophic, it is wrong but it is correct in locating the beginnings of Abstract Expressionism in the art and politics of the avant-garde's redescription and relocation in New York during 1939-1940.[12] However, the *White Paintings* cannot be understood in terms of that moment. Regardless of how they might be claimed to relate to its deep archaeology, they must be seen and understood as of being a moment more immediate to their production and consumption than 1939-40. Whatever moment they are of, it will also be the moment of Rosenberg's writing 'The American Action Painters'. The paintings of the Abstract Expressionists on the one hand and *White Paintings* on the other are utterly distinct in meaning, effect, and social function, a distinction that can be accounted for by their different determined positions in relation to capital.

It is *as if* Rosenberg confused or compacted the moment who's history he was determined to write with the moment of his writing that history. Abstract Expressionism was determined by the political and ideological circumstances concomitant on the demise of monopoly capitalism and its metropolitan nuclei in Europe. In a sense it was the last flowering of High Modernist painting. What Rosenberg wrote about 'action painting', 'art' and 'life', and what Rauschenberg made when he insisted on but didn't use the surface of the *White Paintings* according to the dominant (we should perhaps refer to it more accurately as 'residual') theory of art was determined by the burgeoning of another mode—multi-national capital.[13] Seen and understood like this, Rauschenberg's *White Paintings* wiped the slate clean or set a *tabula rasa* for art and visual culture at the beginning of multi-national capitalism and, most immediately, for the avant-garde artists at its metropolitan centre in New York. Shortly afterwards, within three or four years, Johns gave that mode its premier canonical object—*Flag*.

To my mind, *Flag*'s value rests on its identity as an 'undecidable'. Making *Flag* Johns identified a whole range of conceptual or binary oppositions at work in the theory and practice of Modernist painting, dismantled them, accounted for their differential function and situated his own practice between them and prevented them from getting re-established by making sure what he made could not be securely included within them. For the moment, *Flag* is an object that is always neither/nor and simultaneously either/or, always effecting deferral and always one step ahead of its telling inscription by and in theory. As an object *Flag* is not beyond the resources of Modernism. It is not 'Post-Modernist'.[14] But it tests those resources—of the art and life of the Modern, of making and explanation—to and at their limits. The focal concern of the avant-garde's concern with fine art is painting conceived in the most ambitious terms available. *Flag* is painting pushed to its limits where, still painting or painting problematised, it is also that painting's problematised referent. It is something which for the sake of speed we can refer to as a 'painting' but it was not done by 'painting'. It is a flag, but in art it is also not a flag. Still *of* the dominant theory of art, its meaning and value (as 'art') is interrupted by its meaning and value as 'life' (as an aspect of multi-national capital at its triumphant beginnings); and *of* life its meaning and value (as 'life') is interrupted by its meaning and value as 'art'. In the 'gap' between is a way beyond both 'art' and 'life' and what both are of. In 'theory'.

*   *   *

1. This paper is a slightly amended version of a paper presented at the College Art Association 84th Annual Conference, 21-24 February 1996, Boston, Massachusetts, in the session, chaired by Ann Rosenthal and Richard Shiff, concerned with 'The Object after Theory'.
2. These remarks on 'theory' come out of my reading Wlad Godzich's 'Foreword. The Tiger on the Paper Mat', in Paul de Man, *The Resistance to Theory*, Manchester University Press, 1986, reprinted in Wlad Godzich, *The Culture of Literacy*, Harvard University Press, Cambridge and London, 1994.
3. See Paul de Man, op. cit., p. 11. It would be unfortunate, for example, to confuse the materiality of the signifier with the materiality of what it signifies. This may seem obvious enough on the level of light and sound, but it is less so with regard to the more general phenomenality of space, time or especially of the self; no-one in his right mind will try to grow grapes by the luminosity of the word 'day', but it is very difficult not to conceive the pattern of one's past and future existence in accordance with temporal and spatial schemes that belong to fictional narratives and not to the world. This does not mean that fictional narratives are not part of the world and reality; their impact on the world may well be all too strong for comfort. What we call ideology is precisely the confusion of linguistic with natural reality, of reference with phenomalism. It follows that, more than any other mode of inquiry, the linguistics of literiness is a powerful and indispensable tool in the unmasking of ideological aberrations, as well as a determining factor in accounting for their occurrence. Those who reproach literary theory for being oblivious to social and historical (that is to say ideological) reality are merely stating their fear at having their own ideological mystifications exposed by the tool they are trying to discredit. They are, in short, very poor readers of Marx's German Ideology
4. Op. cit., pp. 12-3.
5. Fred Orton, Chapter 2: 'A Different Kind of Beginning', *Figuring Jasper Johns*, Reaktion Books, 1994.
6. What follows here is for the most part taken from Richard Wollheim's 'The Work of Art as Object', first published in *Studio International*, vol. 180, no. 928, December 1970; a later version is to be found in Wollheim's *On Art and Mind*, Harvard University Press, Cambridge and London, 1973, reprinted in Charles Harrison and Fred Orton eds., *Modernism, Criticism, Realism: Alternative Contexts for Art*, Harper & Row, London, 1984, pp. 9-17.

7. See, for example, Jacques Derrida, *Positions*, trans. and annotated by Alan Bass, Athlone Press, London, pp. 42-3.: "Henceforth, in order to mark this interval ('between inversion, which brings low what was high, and the irruptive emergence of a new "concept," a concept that can no longer be, and never could be, included in the previous regime')...it has been necessary to analyse, to set to work, within the test of the history of philosophy, as well as within the so-called literary text...certain marks...that by analogy...I have called undecidables, that is, unities of simulacrum, 'false' verbal properties (nominal or semantic) that can no longer be included within philosophical (binary) opposition, but which, however, inhabit philosophical opposition, resisting and disorganising it, without ever constituting a third term, without ever leaving room for a solution in the form of speculative dialectics..."

8. Harold Rosenberg, 'The American Action Painters', *Art News*, vol. 51, no. 8, December 1952, pp. 22-3 and 48-50, reprinted in *The Tradition of the New* (New York, Horizon Press, 1959), The University of Chicago Press, Chicago, 1982, pp. 23-39. For a lengthy discussion of the art and politics of 'The American Action Painters', see Fred Orton, 'Action Revolution and Painting', *Oxford Art Journal*, vol. 14, no. 2, 1991, pp. 3-17.

9. The phase "untouched by any instrument" comes form Dore Ashton's review of the Rauschenberg and Twombly show at the Stable Gallery, New York, Sep. 15-Oct. 3, 1953, see *Art Digest*, September 1953, pp. 21 and 25.
Note also Hubert Crehan's discussion of the *White Paintings* under the title 'The See Change. Raw Duck', op. cit., p. 2: "Until the exhibition now at the Stable Gallery, one would hardly have believed that painters could get along all together without the benefit of pigment. Nevertheless, at the stable we have seen the wan spectacle of two albinos out of white canvas by Bob Rauschenberg. His Duck is sized, but otherwise unsullied by even a freckle of paint. To have any kind of exciting of visual experience while beholding these two pallid pictures, we obviously ought to be under hypnosis. A blank canvas provides a blank look, and we like our duck wild."
Crehan informs us that Rauschenberg exhibited two *White Paintings*: "one...made up of seven tall panels, the other of two wider panels."
In 1969 Rosenberg told this story against the *White Paintings*, see 'Icon Maker Barnet Newman', *The De-definition of Art*, (1972), Collier Books, New York, 1973, p. 91: "The late Barnett Newman worked with emptiness as if it were a substance. He measured it, divided it, shaped it, coloured it, He might even be said to have had a proprietary interest in it; when Rauschenberg, some years after Newman's first exhibition at the outset of the fifties, showed four [sic] unpainted canvases joined together, the older artist commented, "Humph! Thinks it's easy. The point is to do it with paint.""

10. (Statement), *Sixteen Americans*, 16 December 1959-14 February 1960, The Museum of Modern Art, New York.

11. Note that Alan Kaprow's programme in the manifesto essay, published in the same year as Johns' and Rauschenberg's first single artist exhibitions at the Castelli Gallery, New York, 'The Legacy of Jackson Pollock', *Art News*, October 1957, pp. 24-6 and 55-7, was thoroughly traditional in the way it insisted on the idea of the 'artist' and on blurring the distinction between 'art' and 'life'.

12. On the redefinition and redescription of the avant-garde in New York, 1939-1940, see Fred Orton and Griselda Pollock, 'Avant-Gardes and Partisans Reviewed', *Art History*, vol. 4, no. 3, 1981, pp. 305-27, reprinted in Francis Frascina, ed., *Pollock and After: The Critical Debate*, Harper & Row, London, pp. 167-83.

13. For a discussion of Abstract Expressionism (and the 'Cold War') in relation to monopoly capitalism and international multi-national capitalism, see Fred Orton, 'Footnote One: The Idea of the Cold War' in David Thistlewood, ed., *American Abstract Expressionism*, Liverpool University Press and Tate Gallery Liverpool, pp. 179-92.

14. For an account of 'Postmodernism' understood as a form of consciousness deter-

mined by a break in the cultural development and character of capitalism, see Fredric Jameson, 'Postmodernism, or The Cultural Logic of Late Capitalism', *New Left Review*, 146, July-August 1984, pp. 53-92. While there was a shift in the development in capitalism after WW2 (the shift was publicly announced on 2 March 1947 in the so-called Truman Doctrine), there was nothing postmodern about it, not in terms of the 'cultural dominant' which merely became more complex and expanded, more thoroughly international in its circumstances of production and consumption.

Nic Clear, *Alteration Number Ten*, 1996.

The Re-furbishment of Alterations to a Suburban House
General Light and Power | Nic Clear

The entire facade of a typical suburban house has been removed and replaced by a full sheet of transparent glass. Midway back and parallel to the front glass facade, a mirror divides the house into two areas. The front section is revealed to the public, the rear section is not disclosed. The mirror as it faces the glass facade and the street, reflects not only the house's interior, but the street and the environment outside the house. The reflected image of the facades of the two houses opposite the cut away 'fill in' the missing facade.

The proposed refurbishment of Dan Graham's *Alteration to a Suburban House* addresses specific themes both in the re-formation of the original work and as a commentary on the practices of contemporary art and architecture.

The importance of Graham's piece as a canonical object of post war art is recognised, but like any other work it can also be seen to signify the inability of conceptual strategies to affect everyday life.

The inability of conceptual art to avoid its own recuperation demonstrates the recursive nature of art and its capacity to only function within the confines of its own discourse. Similarly, the fact that art can never escape its status as a product, even when considered as a conceptual piece, is addressed by reconstructing the work as a series of commodity forms which could equally be seen as art objects or novelty items.

The supposed contextual nature of the project, relating as it does to the American icons of the Tract House, the Glass Skyscraper and the Private Glass House, is replaced with a typical example of British Mass Architecture, the layout for the building is taken from the GLC Good Detailing Guide.

Alt 1.

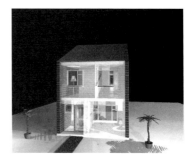

Alt 2.

Alt 5.

Alt 6.

Alt 3.

Alt 4.

Alt 7.

Alt 8.

One and Several Houses

It is suggested by Graham that the project is possibly unrealisable, its abstract nature being addressed by proposing the implementation of his strategy on to a real building. Various details have already been worked out to facilitate the construction of this proposal. The kitchen will be donated by IKEA.

The original status of the work as a gallery project is assumed in the intention to remake the piece as a 1:10 model to be constructed out of sandblasted perspex, with the original mirror wall being replaced with a screen painted in grey, black and white winter camouflage.

This model will be bought by Charles Saatchi, it will never be shown at 98A Boundary Road.

A series of 200 numbered smaller versions of this model will be constructed at a scale of 1:100 as a limited edition multiple. They will make handsome paperweights ideal as Christmas gifts.

T-shirts bearing the legend "Conceptual art was just a good idea" below an image of the House will shortly be availible. Size XL only

The virtual nature of the original is re-inscribed in the proposal to make the house as a complex computer model. This model will become an interactive computer game and as such the project becomes accessible in a number of ways unimaginable from the original proposal. A score of 500,000 will be considered impressive.

As a computer simulation the model will be available as an artist's edition CD ROM and a version will be posted as a site on the internet—it will be accessible to anyone with a computer and a modem. Its address will be http//www.altgraham.com.

A cardboard fold-out of the house will be distibuted by Toys'R'Us, five year-olds will question its intellectual credibility.

Inflatable refurbishments will be used as pool loungers: a drinks compartment will be located in the chimney.

Small plastic refurbishments will given away with special McDonalds' meals these can be exchanged for a small soft drink if the customer prefers.

A solid gold refurbishment brooch encrusted with precious stones will be availible (matching earings are considered too tacky even for us).

A version of the refurbishment as a self-assembly garden shed will be particularly suitable for conceptual artists who are also keen gardeners.

A 'magic eye' poster will be contructed which will reveal the image of the refurbishment if you can do that defocussing thing with your eyes.

A refurbishment shaped picture disc will be released, with the members of General Lighting and Power performing a cover version of 'I'd Like to Teach the World to Sing'.

General Lighting and Power are a London based digital art practice.

The Subliminal Greenberg:
The Americanisation of Aesthetic Identity
Juliet Steyn

What I want to be able to do is accept my Jewishness more implicitly, so implicitly that I can use it to realise myself as a human-being in my own right. I want to be free to what I need to be and delight in being, as a personality without being typed and prescribed to as a Jew or, for that matter as an American.[1]

Greenberg here describes a desire: like all desire it is bound to paradox. Whilst he espouses uncategorisable identity to achieve this end—in itself an impossible desire—the particular must be subsumed by homogeneity. So it was that Greenberg, driven by the logic of assimilation, falls prey to the American dream and perhaps in spite of himself, resolves the paradox.

By considering Greenberg's attitude towards Jewishness, in the postwar period, some further light can be shed on his solution to one of the problems inherent in modernist aesthetics, the conflictual demands of the 'particular' and the 'universal'—which in this case meant Jewish and American.

In the late 1940s and 1950s, questions of Jewish identity and the formation of an American national culture were on the cultural and political agendas. Before the war, as Irving Howe points out in his autobiography, his own and others of his generation felt that their position as Jews was largely subordinated to commitments to cosmopolitan culture and socialist politics on an international scale:

> The fact of Jewishness figured much more strongly than we acknowledged in public. We still didn't identify with a Jewish tradition, yet in practice we grew increasingly concerned with Jewish themes. There was a kind of cultural lag: a recognition behind reality.[2]

Indeed Greenberg's own contributions to the journal *Partisan Review* between 1936 and 1940 show his negotiations with a Marxism distinct from Stalinism in the wake of the Popular front (1935) and the Moscow Trials (1936).[3] It was in 'Avant-Garde and Kitsch' that he developed his most sustained critique of capitalism.[4] In this seminal essay, Greenberg defines high culture (reflexive, critical and demanding) against Kitsch, (ersatz culture, easy enjoyment and passive consumption). The methods of the avant-garde are justified by him as enabling culture to progress. Progress is productive of its own forms of violence. Greenberg's affirmation of modern (abstract) art was a complex cultural/political strategy which entailed boundary-building, precipitating the violence of exclusions. The subsequent de-politicisation of his aesthetic theory has been explained by Serge Guilbault as part of a move towards the de-Marxification of American culture after the Second World War.[5] But this is not the whole story. I would emphasise additionally that the impact of the Jewish Question had on American cultural politics cannot be overlooked at a moment so marked by the Shoah. Excavating Jewish identity in this period was painful, troubling and for some even traumatic and contributed to re-appraisals of the politics of social democracy.

In New York, the focus for intellectual debate on the theme of Jewish identity turned on Jean-Paul Sartre's 'Reflections on the Jewish Question' published in *Commentary* in 1948.[6] Both Greenberg and Harold Rosenberg provided two major and very different responses which were also a reaction to criticism from orthodox Jewry who described them as "uprooted intellectuals."[7]

In 'Self-Hatred and Jewish Chauvinism: Some Reflections on Positive Jewishness', Greenberg expanded Sartre's definition of the 'inauthentic Jew' as one who regards his Jewishness as a 'psychological handicap' in seeking acceptance in the Gentile world:

> The ultra-assimilationist Jew does violence to himself as a human being pure and simple, as well as Jew because he tries to make himself more typically English, French or German than any Anglo-Saxon, Gaul or Teuton ever is. He over-defines himself.... The nationalist Jew, too, always acts with reference to his Jewishness. But even though it is an ostensibly political reference, by the too great strenuousness of his effort to assert his Jewishness he likewise over-defines himself.[8]

To create the 'authentic' Jew, the 'inauthentic' Jew must be first creat-ed and negated. For Greenberg, "the problem has to be focused directly in the individual Jew and discussed in personal, not commu-nal terms."[9] Through a negative move he creates a space in which Jewish identity can be embraced willingly and spontaneously on an individual basis. His determination to salvage the 'authentic' Jew (and by extension 'authentic' art which takes to an extreme the rebuttals that have been the central concern of avant-garde mod-ernist art) led him to embrace the ideology of the democrat, the 'friend' in the sense Sartre had given to the term: "...by individuals he [the democrat] construes everything as a singular incarnation of those universal traits which, according to him, make up human nature."[10] The Jew in this discourse is a free subject of history. Greenberg adopts a position that is similar to his aesthetics in which notions of the artist are predicated upon concepts of freedom. As an effect the erosion of the 'political' in his writing is further legitimated.

Greenberg had earlier elaborated in 'Towards a Newer Laocoon', his defence of 'abstract purism' and 'non-objective art'.[11] He argued that the duty of art in modernity was to test the adequacy of its own resources. Accordingly each form of art must determine the effects special to itself and by so-doing achieve autonomy. Hence Greenberg rejected 'subject matter' which he described as a diversion from the purity and specificity of the medium of art itself. Barnett Newman's work was for him the perfect demonstration of his argument that modern art was inevitably and necessarily engaged with the purifica-tion of its medium.

In *Art Chronicle*, Greenberg championed Newman as a major painter who displays "both nerve and conviction." He continues, "[Newman] keeps within the tacit and evolving limits of the Western tradition of painting."[12] The force of his argument led Greenberg to suppress any notions extrinsic to the work of art itself. The quality of a work is to be measured in terms of its ability to demonstrate what is valuable in its own right and which cannot be attained from any other kind of activity. What Greenberg evaluated as 'good' was that which makes explicit what is unique or irreducible in art in general and also in each particular art.

The question of Jewish identity was directly confronted, if only to be subsumed by his over-arching desire to reinvent the universal, in Greenberg's essay on Franz Kafka published in 1956:

...Jewishness becomes the condition of Kafka's art mainly to the extent that it emerges as its subject, it informs its forms—becomes indwelling form. Through his Dichtung—literally, his imaginings and musings—Kafka wins through to an intuition of the Jewish condition in the Diaspora so vivid as to convert the expression of itself into an integral part of itself: so complete, that is, that the intuition becomes Jewish in style as well as in sense.[13]

Kafka's work achieves its identity through the subject: the subject defines and is itself inscribed in and by its form. There can be no separation between the form and subject of Kafka's art. Jewishness is integral to the content which is itself the result of the effect of a work of art.

By contrast, Jewish identity in the modern era was for Rosenberg a question of will based upon memory—the midrashic idea of remembrance, the recreation of the past for the present, 'a net of memory and expectation'. His critique of *Reflexions on the Jewish Question* focused on Sartre's no-history thesis of the Jew: the Jew always remains an outsider. Rosenberg insisted:

Here in America where Jews are not the only "foreigners", nor the only target of racialism, it should be clear that being singled out by the enemy is not the cause of our difference from others, is not what makes us Jews.[14]

Rosenberg stressed that Jews have their own history and tradition maintained by Talmudic scholarship:

...the continuity of the modern Jew with Jews of the Old Testament is established by those acts which arise from his internal cohesion with his ultimate beginnings, in which his future is contained as possible destiny—the acts of turning towards the Promised Land in his crisis. And these acts, not deducible from his surroundings, make the Jew's situation and reveal who the Jew is.[15]

Rosenberg believed that the work of Newman confronted the problem of Jewish identity in an especially profound and immediate way. Yet, at one and the same time he argues that Newman's work escapes the strictures of identity to create a universal aesthetic filled with meaning for all people of all eras.

The 'Sublime' is the aesthetic category invoked by Barnett Newman to describe the aim of his work which is to reach for the absolute. Moreover he claimed:

> We are freeing ourselves of the impediments of memory, association, nostalgia, legend, myth, or what have you that have been the devices of Western European painting. Instead of making cathedrals out of Christ, man or 'life', we are making it out of ourselves, out of revelation real and concrete, that can be understood by anyone who will look at it without the nostalgic glasses of history.[16]

This quote can be understood perhaps, as the avant-garde artist overthrowing tradition in order to create anew. Or perhaps, as the assertion of difference from the tradition of oil painting, and of humanist man. Or again perhaps, as an assertion of his identity as a second generation Jew in America: a purgative act of regeneration. In this latter sense Newman's work can be seen also as an articulation of particularism in tension with universalism. However, in Newman's own account, as well as in Rosenberg's and Greenberg's such a tension is eradicated. The rhetoric of the sublime with its appeal to the universal, effectively conceals its own contradictions. The eradication of the subject in purified sublime abstraction answers aesthetically to Greenberg's thinking on the question of 'authentic' Jewish identity. Both are reduced to a universalist category of formal adequacy.

Struggle as Greenberg did with criticality, it is perhaps the nature of sublime abstraction to evade criticism: the image impresses its immediate presence but not the meaning of the instance of its appearance. Purity, through a chain of associations is connected to the universal and is the defence of progress and modernity. Through Greenberg's pursuit of the universal, conflict is wiped out. Difficulty turns to certainty. The purification of the medium becomes a way of defending art against its own potential dissolution and of founding a new certainty.

Greenberg ended his article on Kafka with the declaration: "Kafka's Jewish self asks this question and in asking it, tests the limits of art." Perhaps we could reformulate this remark to suggest that "Kafka's Jewish self" yet again tests the limits and ethics of liberal democracy.[17] Sartre described the deception played out in democratic liberalism: on the one hand it advocates the protection of individual rights; whilst on the other, it conceals the limits to those rights. In this discourse the liberal defenders of the Jews claimed that all people are equal but they also claimed that a Jew could only belong to society so long as he ceased being a Jew. Sartre demonstrated the hollowness of democratic liberalism and its blindness to relationships of power, where perforce everything is assimilated to the same.

Greenberg's project was to affirm the universal emancipatory possibilities of modernity but it also violently negated anything which transgressed the rites of purification he considered necessary to preserve it. He sought to complete the project of modernity by ironing out difficulty in favour of purity. His work was a desperate attempt to defend art against the uncertainties of meaning in capitalist society and hence to make culture more secure.

Art criticism must be prepared for surprises precisely because meanings are both structured and changeable. Moreover, it is the very articulation in tension between universalism (homogeneity) and the demands of the particular (heterogeneity) which must be the precondition of a modern liberal and democratic society. In an argument presented by Chantal Mouffe the importance of differentiating between the democratic logic of identity (universalism) and the liberal logic of pluralism (particularism) is stressed. These two logics, she argues, must never be reconciled or resolved for without the tension between them, either totalitarianism or unfettered individualism emerges.[18]

Greenberg participated in formulating an aesthetic in which the tension between the universal and the particular was eradicated. This very tension must be maintained to save democracy from sliding into totalitarianism. It is the abandonment of this tension, if we follow Mouffe's logic, which makes Greenberg's writings open to charges of authoritarianism. The certainty of judgement, for which he strove, subjugates. This is not to suggest that judgement should be eschewed: it is to advocate that its precondition is doubt and uncertainty.

Writing his 'desire', Greenberg creates history as the possible reconciliation of the universal and the particular, between America and Jew. His work can be read as a testimony to and a witness of that desire. To attain the universal, conflict must be suppressed and assimilated to identity: his work is a sacrifice to an ideal. The Americanisation of aesthetic identity is hence paradoxically secured.

*　　*　　*

1. Clement Greenberg, 'Self-Hatred and Jewish Chauvinism: Some Reflections on Positive Jewishness', Commentary, November, 1950, p. 434.
2. Irving Howe, Margins of Hope, Secker and Warberg, 1981.
3. Fred Orton and Griselda Pollock 'Avant-Garde and Partisan Review', Art History vol. 4 no. 3, 1981 pp. 305-27.
4. Clement Greenberg, 'Avant-garde and Kitsch', Partisan Review, vol. vi, no. 5, Fall, 1939, pp. 3-39, in Art and Culture, Boston, Beacons Press, 1961, pp. 3-22.
5. Serge Guilbaut, How New York Stole the Idea of Modern Art: Abstract Expressionism, Freedom and the Cold War, Chicago University Press, 1983.
6. Jean-Paul Sartre, 'Reflections on the Jewish Question', Commentary, April, May and June 1948, trans. from Réflexions sur les Questions Juive, Gallimard, 1946. Later published as Anti-Semite and Jew, Schoken Books, 1949.
7. Clement Greenberg, 'Self-Hatred and Jewish Chauvinism', p. 431. In an acerbic footnote, he castigates Rabbi Silver who in The Day, 16 July 1950, had used the term 'uprooted intellectuals' to criticise secular Jewish intellectuals. Greenberg reminded him that the 'uprooted intellectual' had been and continues to be 'a favourite in the totalitarian (and anti-semitic) lexicon of abuse, from Mussolini and Hitler to Stalin'. Harold Rosenberg in 'Jewish Identity in a Free Society', Commentary, June 1950, p. 510, is also critical of the 'rootless' metaphor and argues against the 'affirmative' stance of those he calls the 20th century Sadducees who desire absolute and exclusive commitment from other Jews.
8. Clement Greenberg, 'Self-Hatred and Jewish Chauvinism', op. cit., p. 432.
9. Ibid., p. 433.
10. Jean-Paul Sartre, Réflexions sur les Questions Juive, p. 66 (my translation).
11. Clement Greenberg, 'Towards a Newer Laocoon', Partisan Review, July/August, 1940, In F. Frascina and C. Harrison (eds.), Pollock and After, London, 1989, pp. 35-46.
12. Clement Greenberg, Partisan Review, 'Art Chronicle: 1952', in Art and Culture, p. 150.
13. Clement Greenberg, 'Kafka's Jewishness', in Art and Culture, p. 266.
14. Harold Rosenberg, 'Jewish Identity and a Free Society', op. cit., p. 18.
15. Ibid, p. 12.
16. Barnett Newman, 'Sublime is Now', Tiger's Eye, Vol. 1, December 1948. Reprinted in Readings in American Art 1900-1975, Barbara Rose (ed.), Praeger, 1975, p. 135.
17. Clement Greenberg, 'Kafka's Jewishness', op. cit., p. 272.
18. Chantal Mouffe, 'Pluralism and Modern Democracy: around Carl Schmitt', New Formations, no. 14, Summer 1991, pp. 1-17.

de-, dis-, ex-.

Form without form: Revaluating Greenberg's Kant
Christopher Want

Writing in 1955 about the critical and theoretical concerns of modernist discourse, the art critic Clement Greenberg declared that Kant's philosophy provided, "the most satisfactory basis for aesthetics we yet have."[1] Five years later in his programmatic article, 'Modernist Painting', Greenberg reiterated the point that Kant was an originary source for modern aesthetics: "the first real Modernist."[2]

These claims indicate a shared historico-conceptual genealogy between the two writers, which is given further credence by Greenberg's writings through recurrent usage of certain key tropes from within Kant's philosophy. Namely, the notion of critique, and the idea of an experience of disinterestedness within aesthetic judgment. How is this purported relationship to be understood, and of what significance is it for assessing Greenberg's position and status within modernism?

Opinions are divided. Some dismiss or ignore this proposed link to Kantian philosophy, substituting instead a concern for Greenberg's relationship with Marxist and modernist formalist theories. (A consequence of the stakes of much art historical debate over the last fifteen years.) Others have attempted to address the complexities of this issue, but with the conclusion either that Kant's ideas are distinct from Greenberg's (in part, implying that Greenberg's claims were made for self-validating reasons) or that they are absorbed in ways which are predetermined by contradictions and inconsistencies within Greenberg's ideas.[3]

These responses to Greenberg's Kantianism seem over-determined by the question of influence. As if Kant's aesthetics might somehow explain, or not explain (as the case may be), Greenberg's theories of art and establish their meaning by means either of a similarity or difference. This denotes a fantasy of stabilising Kant's and Greenberg's ideas into discrete entities, whereby each would be reducible to the question of whether they are mutually informative and self-supporting. In cases where these assumptions have not been made, as in Thierry de Duve's recent work,[4] there have been equally problematic teleological suppositions inferred, whereby Greenberg's use of Kant is seen to engender a conceptual crisis for modernist discourse.

In addressing the question of Greenberg's Kantianism, such that it might avoid the difficulties outlined above, it seems necessary to develop an approach which might not only take into account the historical and conceptual differences between the two writers (for example, the way in which Kant's aesthetics are primarily concerned with nature and not art), but also avoid the problematic of influence and causality. It seems important to direct attention towards issues which are not specific to Kant and Greenberg alone but with which they are mutually concerned. This might be achieved through addressing the question of form as this pertains to an ontological inquiry, to which notions of critique and judgment are appended. The primary issue, therefore, becomes in what ways these writers conceptualised and conceived of processes by which representation might be, or is, obtained and formed. This essay attempts to indicate, within a limited space, some of the principle issues involved in such an analysis of form. Initially via Greenberg's ideas of critique and of judgment and then in relation to Kantian conceptions developed in his 'critical philosophy'.

Greenberg's ideas concerning 'critique' can be divided into two conceptual positions, which are not necessarily distinct but which can be separated as a way of indicating the theoretical concerns at stake. The most well-known account of the notion of critique offered by Greenberg occurs in his article, 'Modernist Painting', in which he outlines the dominant tendency within the arts to focus upon that which is exclusive to their interests. This is identified in terms of the specificity of the medium:

> The essence of Modernism lies, as I see it, in the use
> of the characteristic methods of a discipline to criti-
> cise the discipline itself—not in order to subvert it, but
> to entrench it more firmly in its area of competence.[5]

According to Greenberg, Kant initiated this process of criticality applied to the specificity of the medium. Thus, within philosophy—"which is critical by definition"[6]—"Kant used logic to establish the limits of logic."[7] And this critical self-investigation then provided a model for, "every formal social activity,"[8] even if it was not always taken up and followed (Greenberg cites religion as a case in point).

Another position is investigated by Greenberg over a number of years prior to the writing of 'Modernist Painting', roughly from the late thirties to the sixties. This is explored inconsistently and often merges with the theory posited subsequently in 'Modernist Painting', but it is important for a moment to differentiate the two approaches. This earlier position is taken up in regard to the question of critique (or, more specifically, 'self-criticism') as applied to 'specificity' and is most clearly exemplified by the article, 'Towards A Newer Laocoon' (1940).[9] The reason why Greenberg's ideas in this essay are not entirely of the same order as those expressed later in 'Modernist Painting' may be partly due to the fact that the situation is complicated in 'Towards A Newer Laocoon' by the desire to offer an account which takes in a range of different arts: not only painting, but also music, poetry and sculpture. An emphasis remains in this article upon 'specificity' as related to the individual medium, defined a priori from within its own parameters. But equally there is an idea advanced concerning difference, wherein each art defines itself in relation to literature's perceived competence (according to Greenberg literature is 'a dominant art form'[10] prior to Modernism). In other words, 'specificity' is achieved only in each individual art by defining what it is not (with literature as the yardstick), and it is through this process that the a priori might be conceived.

The consequence of this thesis is that modernist art forms acquire a more complex range of analyses and sense of related histories than subsequently became the case. Over several sections of the essay, Greenberg considers early modernist practice in terms of:

> a common effort in each of the arts to expand the expressive resources of the medium not in order to express ideas and notions, but to express with greater immediacy sensations, the irreduceable elements of experience.[11]

For Greenberg, this is not an opportunity to outline an expressionist theory of art in which art is considered as a transparent sign for quasi-spiritual and metaphysical aspirations. (Greenberg's set intention in 'Towards A Newer Laocoon' is to counter, "The dogmatism and intransigence of the 'non-objective' or 'abstract' purists of painting today who support their position with metaphysical pretentions.")[12] Instead, Greenberg proposes that certain early modernist art forms work upon a difference between form and content as this may pertain to their respective disciplines, "Impressionist painters were trying to get at the structure beneath the colour, Debussy was trying to get at the 'sound underneath the note'."[13]

These formulations may sound neo-Platonic, but when considered in relation to other statements their purpose can be seen in a different light. Greenberg's analysis of Mallarmé is relevant here:

> Poetry subsists no longer in the relations between words as meanings, but in the relations between words as personalities composed of sound, history and possibilities of meaning....The poem still offers possibilities of meaning—but only possibilities. Should any of them be too precisely realised, the poem would lose the greatest part of its efficacy, which is to agitate the consciousness with infinite possibilities by approaching the brink of meaning yet never falling over it.[14]

In other words, in these art forms signification is divested of content, but not in order to isolate the signifier. A process of negation occurs such that content is consistently put under threat, but never disappears—despite appearances to the contrary. Thus, as Greenberg says, pure art is "an impossible ideal."[15]

For Greenberg—as with Kant—a disinterested aesthetic judgment is necessarily universal, to which everyone is obligated and bound. In Greenberg's case judgment occurs within the structure: this is (good/bad) art. It is a generic judgment, attached to a recognition of specificity achieved through an individual art form. The issue of specificity is a historical one, but it ultimately exceeds the question of convention. To use the example of the tradition of modernist painting, Greenberg suggests that the ongoing historical process in this instance has been to stress, "The limitations that constitute the medium of painting—the flat surface, the shape of the support, the properties of pigment."[16] This process has always been formed through a dialectic between two-dimensionality (flatness) and three-dimensionality (illusion), with the former dimension predominating over the latter, unlike in pre-modernist painting where the reverse was true. Aesthetic judgment consists of deciding whether a painting has exceeded the historically constituted tradition in terms of the foregoing dialectic, such that it produces a renewed stress upon two-dimensionality (flatness) at the expense, but not entirely so, of three-dimensionality (illusion). Such a judgment is 'disinterested', which is to say it is not a matter of individual taste or preference, or even of historically produced knowledge: it is universal.

Inconsistencies arise in Greenberg's writings over the bases for judgment. These inconsistencies do not necessarily emanate from the contradiction surrounding the role of knowledge of the history of modernist conventions in making a so-called disinterested judgment, as is often suggested. Nor are they solely produced from the discrepancy of an aesthetic judgment being generic even though it is based upon the identification of progress or advancement in a specific area of competence (a point which Thierry de Duve is concerned to stress).[17]

Greenberg maintained, particularly in the post-war writings, that judgment arose in relation to 'inspiration' and 'vision' ('content').[18] "Technical preoccupations, when searching enough and compelling enough"[19] also played a part in prompting judgment. 'Form' seems to be related to both these factors: "'form' not only opens the way to inspiration; it can also act as means to it."[20] Technique, "can generate or discover 'content'."[21] 'Content' cannot be separated from 'form'. It is apparent from these arguments that Greenberg is uncertain about form's location, whether it lies prior to, or exceeds, inspiration and/or technical discoveries, or whether it is bound up with either or both of them. Such a confusion stems from his earlier theories concerning 'form'—described in relation to 'Towards A Newer Laocoon'—in which form is conceptualised as an unstable and irreducible element capable of divesting representation of its literary function(-alism).

It can be seen from this foregoing account that Greenberg's views about art are fundamentally auratic.[22] Art is not conceived of as a process of representation, rather it presents that which otherwise cannot be presented. Art, and all that which is bound up in its creation, is a medium for form's realisation. This is why Greenberg's ideas in 'Towards A Newer Laocoon' are not ultimately different from those expressed in 'Modernist Painting', since an interest is maintained around the means (i.e. paint on a two-dimensional surface) by which form is given, or produced. It can be argued that Greenberg gradually sought to expunge the auratic conception of art indicated in 'Towards A Newer Laocoon', replacing it with the ideas which received their final form in 'Modernist Painting'. But the more he attempted to do so, the more he was forced to acknowledge, at least subliminally, how his entire project was governed by such a conception. Thus, the 'crisis' in modernist discourse in the sixties, of which Thierry de Duve speaks,[23] may need re-evaluation more in terms of an affirmation. A recognition, perhaps, of a residual Kantianism within modernist aesthetics.

Kant's philosophy, especially the *Critique of Pure Reason*, is oriented around the the problem of the foundations and origins of knowledge (i.e. the question of predication). In this first *Critique*, Kant pinpoints the irreducibility or overlap between the question of predication (upon what is knowledge based; how is it extended?) and speculation, itself. Speculation is not seen as dissimilar from the question that originates its processes. And, together they continually attempt to repeat the idea of an originary process of knowledge. Speculation seems to inaugurate the question of predication by imposing a limit upon, and thus forming, the question, itself.

This analysis by Kant is certainly comparable to Greenberg's ideas about the role of form within signification. In which form is envisaged as the repetition of a discontinuity, with the power to delimit representation. However, Kant's views differ from Greenberg's, in so far as he suggests a critical project for philosophy: to continually guard against the error by which speculation attempts to identify with this process of repetition as origination.

For Kant, form then is not that which separates the question of predication from speculation, only to seem to bring them into being once more. Form can only be a critical project (philosophy), with the power to delimit its own misunderstandings or delusions of power. Whilst Kant holds out the critical possibility of recognising such delusions, he affirms that they can never be overcome: this is why form is irreducible to itself. He maintains similar views in the second *Critique* (*Critique of Practical Reason*) in relation to the problematic of freedom: philosophy must continually guard against the error—without hope of ultimate success—of identifying the desire for freedom with the question of freedom.

That the form of critical philosophy is always dependent upon misidentification and the failure of philosophy is affirmed in the third *Critique* (*Critique of Judgment*). Misunderstanding is seen to possess its own sensuality or beauty: as Kant suggests it is linked to the power to form concepts, and this power is nothing less than the capacity to generate (the failure of) philosophy.

That philosophy's failure is 'pleasurable' is affirmed again, in relation to the sublime. The experience of the sublime is an experience of formlessness. But this is not seen as a lack of form. Rather it is an interruption as well as an excess of sensory data and information. In connection with the sublime, Kant is intent upon illustrating the experience associated with the recognition of misidentification. Inevitably, this leads to a sense of threat and pain as a consequence of the interruption involved, but this can never be entirely overwhelming since, like misidentification itself, it is always part of the matter of knowledge and, indeed, of freedom.

By way of conclusion, it can be said that, unlike Greenberg, Kant does not hold the view that representation is somehow limited or tainted (this is most forcefully expressed by Greenberg in his essay, 'Avant-Garde and Kitsch').[24] Quite the contrary: for Kant, representation is the only means by which a universal project may be achieved, although this is always given by philosophy in the form of a judgment. Such judgment rules over philosophy's realisation, ensuring that it cannot be self-identical; in this way it may succeed in negotiating its own failure. This is quite distinct from Greenberg's views about judgment which seek to assign it a divisive role, not only in its capacity to judge good art from bad art but, more significantly, to occupy the site that lies between form and content, on the one hand, and representation, on the other.

And yet, as indicated earlier, Greenberg's ideas may open out on to those of Kant's, if only because of the nature of their inconsistencies. They were bound to fail in terms of a conceptual programme for modernism, the more the question of form became confused. In Greenberg's writings this was displaced into two contrary tendencies. On the one hand, an attempt to secure an increasingly dogmatic programme for modernism. On the other hand, the development of a theory of 'openness' (in relation, for instance, to the work of Pollock, Newman and Rothko)[25] which was richly suggestive of an impossible ideal or striving in modernist painting's programmatic concerns. This is summarised in Greenberg's analysis in 1948 of contemporary painting as that which, "rejects the easel and yearns for the wall."[26] Such a theory moved Greenberg's criticism towards a a sense of the performative nature of representation, which was at odds with his romantic ideas about 'conception' and originality. As if painting accepted the necessity and strictures of judgment but was not necessarily produced with a view to being judged. In other words, painting was conceived of as an enunciative act made in the absence of rules governing signification. (These ideas draw together similarities in approach with Lyotard's later views of Newman's art.)[27]

A cautionary note, therefore, needs to be borne in mind in the attempt to mount a critique of Greenbergian aesthetics, especially if Kantian ideas about misidentification are to obtain. In Kant's view, writing and, more generally, representation is a parasitical activity: it is always already dependent upon (its own) failure. A 'critique' of Greenberg then can never hope to dominate its object. For it is always in the process of displaying its own finitude: such is the form of its affirmation.

*   *   *

1. *The Collected Essays and Criticism; Affirmations and Refusals, 1950-56, vol. 3*, ed. J. O'Brian, Univ. of Chicago Press, 1986, p. 249.
2. The Collected Essays and Criticism; *Modernism with a Vengeance, 1957-69, vol. 4*, ed. J. O'Brian, Univ. of Chicago Press, 1986, p. 85.
3. See for instance, P. Crowther. 'Greenberg's Kant and the Problem of Modernist Painting', *British Journal of Aesthetics*, vol. 25, 1985, pp. 317-25.
4. 'The Monochrome and the Blank Canvas', *Reconstructing Modernism; Art in New York, Paris and Montreal 1945-1964*, ed. S. Guilbaut, MIT Press, 1990, pp. 244-310.
5. *The Collected Essays and Criticism, vol. 4*, op. cit., p. 85.
6. Ibid.
7. Ibid.
8. Ibid.
9. *The Collected Essays and Criticism, Perceptions and Judgments, 1939-44, vol. 1*, ed. J. O'Brian, Univ. of Chicago Press, 1986, pp. 23-38.
10. Ibid., p. 24.
11. Ibid., p. 30.
12. Ibid., p. 23.
13. Ibid., p. 31.
14. Ibid., p. 33.
15. Ibid., p. 34.
16. 'Modernist Painting', (1960), *The Collected Essays and Criticism, vol. 4*, op. cit., p. 86.

17. Op. cit.

18. 'Necessity of Formalism', *Esthetics Contemporary*, ed. R. Kostelanetz, Prometheus Books, 1978, p. 174.

19. Ibid.

20. Ibid.

21. Ibid.

22. For a discussion of this concept, see W. Benjamin, 'The Work of Art in the Age of Mechanical Reproduction', *Illuminations*, Fontana, 1982, pp. 219-53 and 'A Small History of Photography', *One-Way Street and Other Writings*, New Left Books, 1979, pp. 240-57.

23. Op. cit.

24. *The Collected Essays and Criticism, vol. 1*, op. cit., pp 5-22.

25. For Greenberg's views on Newman and Rothko in this connection, see for instance, 'After Abstract Expressionism', an edited version of which is published in *Art in Theory 1900-1990; An Anthology of Changing Ideas*, eds. C. Harrison and P. Wood, Blackwell, 1992, pp. 766-69.

26. 'Review of Exhibitions of Worden Day, Carl Holty, and Jackson Pollock', *The Collected Essays and Criticism, Arrogant Purpose, 1945-1949, vol. 2*, ed. J. O'Brian, Univ. of Chicago Press, 1986, pp. 200-03.

27. 'Newman: The Instant', *The Lyotard Reader*, ed. A. Benjamin, Blackwell, 1991, pp. 240-49.

Rendezvous: Walter Benjamin and Clement Greenberg—Programme of the Coming Art
Alex Coles

We see once again that by driving a tendency to its furthest extreme...one finds oneself abruptly going in the opposite direction.

Clement Greenberg

The continuing relevance of Greenberg today cannot be questioned. He is still used tactically by theorists of the postmodern—and those of the 'repressed' modern—as signifying modernism, so as to enable them to make their task easier. To date, the most important (and recent) reading of his writings (leaving aside his subliminal return as 'The Father' in Rosalind Krauss' *The Optical Unconsciousness*) has been undertaken by Thierry de Duve in *Clement Greenberg: Between the Lines* and in *Kant After Duchamp* (both 1996). Herewith de Duve undertakes a project of close reading that I wish to pursue in entirely different ways. While I feel de Duve's concerns with Greenberg are distinct in some respects from Krauss' and other critics', they do have certain traits in common: both wish to foreclose his ideas within their historical epoch, and both do not put Greenberg's theories to work other than where he left them.

The complete adverse can be said of the German literary and art critic Walter Benjamin. The darling of postmodernism, he can do no wrong; and his ideas and aphorisms have been imported to areas far from his own—and rightly so. But what if we were to attempt this with Greenberg? Furthermore, what would happen if they met in this rico-chet between their time and "now time"? Once I have remarked upon what are not, but what could be viewed as coincidental meetings in the subjects of, and philosophical influences upon their work, I wish to work them both into each other—against each others 'grain'—towards intimating why there is the necessity for this meeting and what it will constitute.

Benjamin had less than twelve months to live in the winter of 1939—the date of publication of Greenberg's first published writing: 'The

Beggar's Opera—After Marx: Review of A Penny for the Poor by Bertolt Brecht'. Benjamin, as is well known, had been a close confident of Brecht's and had written vastly on him from the early thirties, addressing the Institute of The Study of Fascism with what was to become 'The Author as Producer' in 1934 and also writing 'What is Epic Theatre?' and the rest of the papers that were eventually to constitute the posthumous collection *Understanding Brecht*. However, the overlaps do not stop here. Benjamin and Greenberg were both involved in an ongoing dialogue with their Jewishness. Benjamin's reflections upon his Jewishness haunt much of his writing, and indeed, much of the commentary on him reflects this. However, Greenberg's reflections on his Jewishness, along with his activity as a literary critic which dominated the first five or six years of his activity—most notably in 'The Jewish Joke: Review of Royte Pomerantzen' (1947), 'Autobiographical Fragment' (1955), 'Self Hatred and Jewish Chauvinism: 'Some Reflections on Positive Jewishness" (1950)—have been banished to the margins of his oeuvre. This has occurred so as to ease the schematisation of Greenberg's 'position'—and thus its foreclosure (although admittedly in his later writings he does not help himself here). Benjamin's concern with Kafka, unlike Greenberg's in 'Introduction to 'The Great Wall of China' by Franz Kafka' (1946), 'The Jewishness of Franz Kafka' (1955) and 'The Great Wall of China' (1958), is weighted towards the latter end of his work: 'Franz Kafka' (1934) and 'Max Brood's Book on Kafka and Some of My Own Reflections' (1938). (Greenberg also translated Kafka's 'Josephine, The Songstress: Or, the Mice Nation' [1942] for *Partisan Review* and Kafka's *Parables*, with Willa and Edwin Muir, for Schocken Books in 1947.) One cannot, of course, leave aside their concerns with Marxism which appear at the reverse times in their practices in relation to their concerns with Kafka: Benjamin's being towards the middle and late period (finding full expression in the sprawling *Passagen-Werk*), and Greenberg's being relatively early in 'Avant-garde and Kitsch' (1939) and in the text on Brecht. In different ways they both valued the work of Paul Klee; Benjamin even owned his painting *Angelus Novus*, which he planned to name his projected journal after, and was to meditate on in his 'Thesis on the Philosophy on History' (1940). Last, and certainly not least, is both Greenberg's and Benjamin's ongoing dialogue with the eighteenth century philosopher Immanuel Kant. Greenberg's concerns with Kant—beginning in 1943—are peppered throughout his writings. They are mostly concerned with his third *Critique* (*The Critique of Aesthetic Judgement*).[1] Kant's moral philosophy proved to be the source that "Benjamin [chiefly] drew his inspiration" from in his pre-war writings. While there were earlier published works that are evidence of

Kant's influence upon Benjamin (most notably—according to Richard Wolin—'Die Freie Schulgemeinde') the first major piece is 'The Programme of the Coming Philosophy' (Über das Programm der Kommenden Philosophie') (1918).

If Benjamin had made it to America to join the exiled Frankfurt School, as was the intention, he may have met Greenberg. Given that this was not to be, a quotation from Greenberg's 'Review of an Exhibition of Gustave Courbet' (1949) will have to do to serve to ignite the initial sparks that are to fly here on account of the theoretical meeting between them that I am concerned with:

> One might think that his desire to convey the solidity of nature, and the emphatic modelling that this required, would have induced a strong illusion of three-dimensional form, but his simultaneous desire to make the picture itself solid and palpable worked against this in a subtle way. True, we get a vivid impression of mass and volume from Courbet's art; yet he seems to have wanted to render the palatability of substance and texture even more. Thus in his landscapes and marines he tends to suppress atmospheric recession in order to bring the background forward so that he can make evident the texture—even if it is only the colour texture—of cliffs, mountains, water, or sky. The resulting effect sometimes approaches bas-relief, just as in his figure pieces, but his marines also arrive at a clarity of colour and a sudden flatness that anticipates the impressionists. We see once again that by driving a tendency to its furthest extreme—in this case the illusion of the third dimension—one finds oneself abruptly going in the opposite direction.

Greenberg is obviously cannily twisting this tendency in these particular paintings of Courbet's so as to support his theory of modernism, as initially reflected upon (commonly thought of as prescribed) in 'Avantgarde and Kitsch' (1939), 'Towards a Newer Laocoon' (1940), and later in 'Modernist Painting' (1961). But what if one was to exaggerate this twist, until it became more of a turnabout upon his notion of self-criticism? The question I am implying by this is as follows: what would happen if Greenberg's notion of 'self-criticism' was driven to its "furthest extreme"? Would we abruptly find ourselves "going in the opposite direction"? In any such activity Benjamin will have to do the driving, as Greenberg started to run down, "loose his stuff" (his words regarding any flagging artist), and get sloppy regarding his use of this concept by the late 50s/early 60s (resulting in his support of some of the worst 'modernist painting' of the century: namely Noland and Olitski.) It is here that Benjamin's allegorical concept of the 'ruin'—which finds fruition in his *Origin of German Tragic Drama* (*Urspung des deutschen Trauerspiels*) (1926)—will do the transforming to Greenberg's Kantian concept of self-criticism.[2] Moreover, as we shall see, the Greenbergian concept, will, in turn, contaminate Benjamin's—pushing them both to a point whereby they are almost unrecognisable. Consequently, this meeting finds Greenberg's (again Kantian) 'empirical[art]object' "abruptly going in the opposite direction"—towards its ruin. (I will have to leave the subsequent effects on Kant to one side, to be taken up elsewhere.) But I am already moving ahead of myself; before we can even think of allegory and self-criticism—and their contaminating each other—we must initially work through the reasons why the first has recently been entrenched by myth and see how the latter has been allowed an almost unnoticed fruition in art practice. (The latter being because, as we shall see, it has not gone under the name of self-criticism.) This, in turn, will allow us to approach the questions: is there the necessity for the continuation of this self-critical tendency and if so, how, and under what guise, can it continue?

Myth is Depoliticised Speech

> Every image of the past that is not recognised by the present as one of its own concerns threatens to disappear irretrievably.[3]

It was (and for some still is) a tendency to write the break between the postmodern and the modern on the account of an 'allegorical impulse'.[4] While this was initially with good intention, its consequences on allegory being a mode of speech used to enable the Other (whatever this Other may constitute)[5] to speak have been apocal. Owens' use of the above quotation from Benjamin's 'Thesis on the Philosophy of History' at the start of 'The Allegorical Impulse' has disastrous effects on the work of allegory. While for him the image that threatens to "disappear irretrievably" is that of the work of allegory, he actually facilitates the next step of this disappearance through his

positioning of certain art works, and artists' practices, as being inherently allegorical.[6] But *no* work is inherently allegorical; allegory stays
with the work for a fleeting moment only. The image that threatens to
"disappear irretrievably" through Owens' arrest of allegory (which is
what it is) is that which characterises allegory's relationship to the
temporal: the image of the ruin (the work decays into ruin once the
life allegory breathes into it has passed).

As a consequence of Owens' actions we are faced with something
which is being called allegory, but which is not allegory nor is it actually doing the work of allegory. Moreover 'speaking allegorically' now
becomes a type of myth.[7] These are the disastrous consequences I was
talking about: because the whole notion of Other speaking, of speaking difference (which is what speaking allegorically is) and being audible in doing so is herein endangered through the work of myth. (I am
of course, here thinking of Barthes' famous account of myth in 'Myth
Today' from *Mythologies*.[8]) This is explained by the fact that it will
always be through a first mythological language that the second political language will be heard, and thus muffled, because "myth is a second language in which one speaks about a first." Allegory is also a second language, as such, because it speaks through a second language.
But it will subsequently leave this in ruin[9] (thus indicating its absence
as it has passed on) whereas myth will eternalise it. (Here lies the central danger, because it may seem from the outside that allegory is still
at work when in fact it has fled. This occurs when myth works to conceal the ruin of the palimpsest and arrests and falsely projects the
image of the work of allegory—resulting in the myth-image.) Owens,
despite his intention, has the effect, in time, of an oppressor and
tyrant of the emancipatory work of allegory, he *works* it in opposition
to the redeeming and politicised function that Benjamin assigns it.[10]

Only through a process of thinking self-critically can one discern
whether the art work is speaking politically, mythologically, or is in a
state of ruin.[11] And so only self-criticism can emancipate allegory in
art works. It is to self-criticism then, that we must turn.[12]

Self-Criticism

For Greenberg, self-criticism in the arts was always understood in relation to a discipline—he gave particular precedence to painting. But we
need a broader sense of this history for our use here. In 'What's Neo
about the Neo-Avant-Garde?' (1994) Hal Foster traces the transitive
history of critique in the avant-garde.[13] Foster begins this—"the

becoming-institutional of the historical avant-garde"—with Duchamp, which "prompts in a second neo-avant-garde...a creative analysis of the limitations of both historical and first neo-avant-gardes."[14] What is surfaced through the rest of Foster's tracing of the various moments of the (neo)avant-garde is the self-critical nature of it. But of course Foster does not call it being self-critical. Whether it is Foster's 'post-modernism' or his fear of the connotations of the word self-criticism with American formalism that prevents him from using it, I do not know. (A third reason may, of course, be that he wants this tendency to continue, but feels it can only do so, as it has done for some time: 'under-cover'). But one thing is for sure: Foster recognises the importance of this tendency for the present, and is probably one of the few critics to do so. He goes on to describe this chain as a:

> collective labour that now cuts across entire genera-tions of neo-avant-garde artists—to develop paradigms like the readymade from an object that purports to be transgressive in its very facticity (as in its first neo repe-tition), to a device that addresses the seriality of objects and images in advanced capitalism (as in Minimal and Pop art), to a proposition that explores the linguistic dimension of the work of art (as in Conceptual art), to a marker of physical presence (as in site-specific art of the 1970s), to a form of critical mimicry of various dis-courses (as in allegorical art of the 1980s), and, finally, to a probe of sexual, ethnic, and social differences today (as in the work of such diverse artists as Sherrie Levine, David Hammons, and Robert Gober). In this what the so-called failure of both historical and first neo-avant-gardes to destroy the institution of art has enabled, is the deconstructive testing of this institution by the sec-ond neo-avant-garde—a testing that, again, is now extended to different institutions and discourses in the ambitious art of the present....[15]

Foster avoids the dangers of Owens' positioning of certain work as having some kind of inherent quality (whether this be allegorical or self-critical). While this account of self-criticism differs greatly from Greenberg's—which is the *theory* of the account I am concerned with here—as it gives emphasis to the transitive (and gives precedence to almost entirely different artists), his theory is in fact not that far away from what we have in the Foster tracing.

> The essence of Modernism lies, as I see it, in the use of
> the characteristic methods of a discipline to criticise the
> discipline itself—not in order to subvert it, but to
> entrench it more firmly in its area of competence...
> Modernism criticises from the inside, through the pro-
> cedures themselves of that which is being criticised.[16]

If we replace the word modernism for critique (the paradigm I am concerned with here) and discipline for paradigm, we begin to see how
Greenberg's theory of self-criticism does in fact work in relation to
what essentially is Peter Bürger's tracing of the critical nature of the
avant-garde (with Foster's contemporary additions) from his *Theory of
the Avant-Garde* (1974).[17] Moreover the Greenberg passage helps us to
make sense of how the history of the chain has always been able to
assist the current precedent of the chain to 'Other speak'—because
the ability to 'Other speak' is "entrench[ed] more firmly in its area of
competence"—as it moves along.[18] So, something important has
occurred: at last Greenberg's theory has been cut loose from its time
and artists, so that it can be put to work elsewhere.

Self-criticism and the Ruin

> In the ruin history has physically merged into the set-
> ting. And in this, history does not assume the form of
> the process of an eternal life so much as that of irre-
> sistible decay...so that historical transiency (ruin) is the
> emblem of nature in decay.[19]

Benjamin's concept of the ruin, as I mentioned earlier, comes from his
study of seventeenth-century *Trauerspiel* (*The Origin of German Tragic
Drama*). "The book is divided into two parts. The first deals specifically
with the Trauerspiel, the second with the technique of allegory, intimately related to the drama of the seventeenth century."[20] For
Benjamin, the ruin characterised "processes of decay"; whether this be
of the corpses in the "mourning-play" (Trauerspiel) as they piled upon
one another (Benjamin referred to these plays as "ruins"), or of the
artefacts of capitalism, as found in the arcades of Paris and Berlin (in

the *Passagen-Werk*). Here my central concern with the ruin is its expression of the transitory.

Greenberg himself (i.e. aside from anything I will do to him here that he probably would not agree with) also had, from the late thirties, through to, say, the late fifties, an intuition for "historical transiency" (as practised in his journalism).[21] (By 1961 with 'Modernist Painting' he was no longer practising this on a day-to-day level—he had had a "belly full" of that—but through a kind of process of retrospective description.) It is here then—through their very different ways of expressing the transitory (Benjamin's in the ruin and Greenberg's through self-criticism)—that their theories shall meet. The destruction that the meeting brings to Greenberg's theories is obvious: the ruin of his Kantian empirical object, the interrogation of the "barbarism" of his process of self-criticism, to name just two areas.[22] Yet those on Benjamin, which I shall come to in a moment, are not so obvious.

The biggest squabble in this meeting over the expression of the transitory is the way the two of them ordered historical experience. For Benjamin this means no order at all: the events of history were "one single catastrophe which keeps piling wreckage upon wreckage"[23] in front of "his [the angel of history's] feet." But for Greenberg, this means the piling up of (art)history hierarchically, with fixed notions of importance, origin, and future essence in sight. So the concepts of ruination and self-criticism would appear divided on this point. However, if we look closer at what structurally allegory is we could start to expose a flaw in Benjamin's concept of it, which in turn will have massive ramifications for the concept of ruination and help us to understand its relationship to self-criticism better. The following quotation from Joel Fineman's 'The Structure of Allegorical Desire' (1981) will provide the explanation, if we can take allegory to be understood as that which results from the projection of the metaphoric (the synchronic study of language) on to the metonymic (the diachronic study of language) axis of language: "and so it is always the structure of metaphor that is projected on to the sequence of metonymy, not the other way around, which is why allegory is always a hierarchising mode, indicative of timeless order, however subversively intended its contents may be."[24] In other, words it is the single object (as metaphor) that is projected on to the sequence of objects (the metonymic). I am here understanding the sequence of objects as constituting the single object's precedents which it is mapped on to and which subsequently have to be 'spoken through' by it in order for it to be audible. (Because it is on the basis of our recognition and understanding of this sequence/history of objects that we interpret the present one.) Thus allegory, in this sense, is "always a hierarchising mode" because it demands that the present must first answer to the past.[25] For if it is the past that can ruin a trajectory of politicised speech by entrapping it with myth, it is therefore that which the present must 'work-through' and answer to; in Greenberg's words it is that which "will be brought to bear."[26]

Hereupon lies my central find: self-criticism and allegory both occur at the same point (where "metaphor is projected on to the sequence of metonymy") and are interdependent on one another, that is, one can only occur through the work of the other. I should briefly explain this: allegory only occurs if the art form(s) being motivated as a vehicle for 'speaking' are self-critical. This is to say that the art form is critical regarding where those forms have been used and for what they have been used. (Or, where those techniques, devices, and strategies that are set up through the forms have been used and for what they have been used for). Self-criticism can only occur now through a process of speaking allegorically (Other speaking), because only the Other can constitute a further precedent in the history of critique. (The above quotation from Hal Foster explains this.)

But current 'critical' art practice must do more than just realise this interdependency to maintain a position continually one step ahead of the claws of myth. It must pursue a working model of *perpetual* self-criticism, that is not only reflexive about this whole transitive history of the self-critical avant-garde, but also creates within itself the appearance of that which "threatens to irretrievably disappear"—the readjustment/recuperative inscription of the temporal (i.e. types of transiency)—in the image of the ruin. Why the ruin? Because again, whereas before with the Greenbergian understanding of self-criticism—whereby the tradition (discipline/art form) being handed over would be further "entrenched in its area of competence" (and consequently be all the more stable) by doing so—herewith, that being handed over is destroyed and ruined in the process of handing over itself.[27] This must occur so that the form cannot be re-used and thus, in time, project the myth-image of the work of allegory. (The now historic avant-garde art work can now maintain its 'integrity' while its hollowed out form [the allegorical shell][28] cannot be re-used to 'speak' about the same thing.[29] It can only be used in a self-critical [reflexive] way—that somehow overturns its precedent, or reveals hitherto unknown things about it—as it is in ruin.)

So, we see once again, that by driving two very different tendencies to their furthest extreme, one finds them abruptly going in the same direction. (Self-criticism and ruination have been driven to their "furthest extreme" and have, within themselves, gone in opposite directions, while they have gone in the same direction in relation to each other, or indeed have been revealed as already occurring at the same point. Consequently, we have a ruinous notion of self-criticism and a hierarchising concept of ruination.) Greenberg has helped us then, in at least initiating the project ahead for allegory if it is to be repoliticised, after its depoliticisation by myth. Benjamin's meeting with him has not only informed us about how to extend his concept of self-criticism in the arts beyond where he left it (for Benjamin has ruined Greenberg's 'modernist painting'), but also put it to work where it was most needed.[30] Needless to say, the task remains to find just exactly where (for at least we know how) the next precedents will occur. It is as if there were a "secret agreement" between Greenberg and Benjamin; as one is called upon to assist the other, and so in turn, to assist the present.

(My thanks to Howard Caygill for commenting on an earlier version of this paper.)

*　　*　　*

1. For an insufficient account of Greenberg's problematic relationship with Kant see Paul Crowther's 'Greenberg's Kant and the Problem of Modernist Painting', *British Journal of Aesthetics* 25, no. 4, 1985, pp. 317-25. Also see Ingrid Stadler, 'The Idea of Art and its Criticism: A Rational Reconstruction of a Kantian Doctrine', in *Essays in Kant's Aesthetics*, eds. Ted Cohen and Paul Guyer, University of Chicago Press, 1982, pp. 195-217.
2. Greenberg and Benjamin are both loosely associated with two different types of critique; the first with Kantian 'Critique' and the latter with The Frankfurt School's 'Critical Theory'. Horkheimer makes a distinction between the two in 'Traditional and Critical Theory': "The term ["critical"] is used here less in the sense it has in the idealist critique of pure reason than in the sense it has in the dialectical critique of political economy. It points to an essential aspect of the dialectical theory of society" (reprinted in *Critical Sociology*, ed. by Paul Connerton, Penguin, New York, 1976, p. 217.) However, there are some links between the two types of critique: S.E. Bronner picks up on the passages in Horkheimer's text that are evidence that the latter's "version of [critical] materialism did not reject the moment of critique inherited from idealism" (S.E.Bronner, 'Horkheimer's Road', in *Of Critical Theory and its Theorists*, Blackwell, Oxford and Massachusetts, 1994, p. 76).
New evidence has been brought forward by Francis Frascina, who quotes from a letter that Adorno had written to the managing editor of the University of Chicago Press in 1962 (and conceals its source), "I know Clement Greenberg very well from my American time and I think exceedingly highly of him. His opinion on [Walter] Benjamin, without

any doubt, will not only agree with my own one but will also carry great objective weight," (Francis Frascina, *Art Monthly*, 178, July-August 1994, p. 18).

Benjamin's 'The Programme of the Coming Philosophy' reveals his concern with Kant in his formative years as a thinker, in *The Philosophical Forum*, vol. XV, nos. 1-2, Fall-Winter, 1983-84, pp. 41-51. Regarding this paper, Peter Wolin remarks that, "The degree to which 'The Programme of the Coming Philosophy' anticipates the Kant-critique of Horkheimer and Adorno in Dialectic of Enlightenment is especially striking," (from *Walter Benjamin an Aesthetic of Redemption*, University of California Press, California, p. 280). Part of my task will be to pursue this connection further.

3. Walter Benjamin, 'Thesis on the Philosophy of History', in *Illuminations*, Fontana Press, 1973, p. 247.

4. Craig Owens, 'The Allegorical Impulse', in *Art After Modernism*, eds. Brian Wallis and Marcia Tucker, The New Museum of Contemporary Art, 1984, pp. 203-37. Benjamin Buchloh, 'Allegorical Procedures: Appropriation and Montage in Contemporary Art', in *Art Forum*, September, 1982.

5. Etymologically, *allos* = other, and *agoreuein* = to speak (in publicñ from agora, an assembly). So roughly: speaking allegorically is Other speaking.

6. He is thinking of the Metro Pictures generation of artists, which includes: Cindy Sherman, Robert Longo, Richard Prince, et al.

7. "Allegory and myth [are]...'antithetical'. Indeed allegory [is]...the antidote to myth, and precisely this was to be demonstrated [by Benjamin] in the *Passagen-Werk*," (Susan Buck-Morss, *The Dialectics of Seeing: Walter Benjamin and the Arcades Project*, MIT Press, 1989. p. 164).

8. Roland Barthes, 'Myth Today', in *Mythologies*. While I am using Barthes' account of myth here, its similarity with Benjamin's has been remarked upon by Peter Wolin (*Walter Benjamin: An Aesthetic of Redemption*, op. cit.). University of California Press, 1994. Their disparity has been remarked upon by Winfried Menninhaus ('Walter Benjamin's Theory of Myth', in *On Walter Benjamin: Critical Essays and Reflections*, ed. Gary Smith, MIT Press, 1988. pp. 292-325).

Barthes states (op. cit.): "The oppressed has nothing, he has has only one language, that of his emancipation; the oppressor is everything, his language is rich, multiform, supple...he has an exclusive right to metalanguage. The oppressed makes the world, he has only an active, transitive (political) language; the oppressor conserves it, his language is plenary, intransitive, theatrical: it is myth. The language of the former aims at transforming the latter at eternalising."

Wolin (op. cit., p. 51) remarks that, "Benjamin counterposes now-time, "which is shot through with chips of Messianic time," to the homogenous time of the historical era, which he equates with the notion of eternal repetition or myth. Man stands under the domination of mythical fate when his powers of remembrance fail him: that is, he is condemned to repeat."

Also see Barthes' 'self-critical' reappraisal of his account of myth from Mythologies fifteen years later in 'Change the Object Itself', in *Image-Music-Text*, Hill and Wang, New York, 1977.

9. Benjamin's observations on allegory and the ruin can be found in *The Origin of German Tragic Drama*, (originally pub. 1926), New Left Books, London, 1977. Peter Bürger, a descendent of The Frankfurt School, has used Benjamin's notion of the ruin and allegory in relation to the avant-garde in Chapter 4 of his Theory of the Avant-Garde, (originally pub. 1974), University of Minnesota Press, Minneapolis, 1984.

10. It could be argued that the Benjamin quotation redeems itself by the way it subverts its instrumental positioning by Owens. It is as if the quotation acts as a hinge: seemingly complicit through Owens' positioning at the time (1981) but then, in time, working for allegory, and against Owens' positioning by subverting it, and even collapsing the whole argument that is set up through the quotation.

11. Let me be clear about how artworks are endangered by myth: it can occur through two things (both are, in some accounts, the same problem)—the first is the arrest of allegory through naming an object as being inherently allegorical, the second is attempting to motivate a form (trope, technique, strategy etc.) without being critical (reflexive) regarding where it has been and what it has been used to facilitate (and thus occurs endless repetition; see Benjamin's and Barthes' quotations in footnote no. 8). In the case of the Owens text, he says that the 'allegorical works' "narrate their contingency," and that it is this that separates them from their modern counterparts that "narrate their self-sufficiency." Through this he is also making distinction between the modern work as having its meaning enclosed within it a priori to the viewer's contact with it, and the postmodern work as emphasising the inclusion of the viewer in the 'meaning' of the work. He forgets that his criticism is now part of the contingency of the work itself. Thus, in turn, the works become self-sufficient because they have a priori built-into themselves the 'allegorical' discourse. (Owens speaks of the contingency of the work being partly constituted of where the [often appropriated] images are 'originally' from. Yet this too becomes built into the discourse, and the 'issues' that the work is 'speaking' about become there so as to be read-off as so many stereotypes.)
Hal Foster identifies Owens' inherent contradiction in his splitting between the modern and the postmodern regarding allegory because "as Owens works out his genealogy of the allegorical impulse, he finds it via Benjamin and Baudelaire: 'at the origins of modernism'." (Hal Foster 'Wild Signs: The Break up of the Sign in Seventies Art', in *Universal Abandon*, ed. Andrew Ross, 1987).
12. A wider ramification of my text will be that, in turn, Benjamin's work has, in certain cases, an affinity with aspects of self-criticism. As partially revealed in the following passage: "Simile: one learns to know a young person who is handsome and attractive, yet, who appears to conceal a secret within. It would be indelicate and objectionable to use force to pry it from him. However, it is permissable to inquire whether he has brothers or sisters and whether their character and nature could to some extent explain to us the mysterious nature of the stranger. It is precisely in this way that the true critic inquires after the brothers and sisters of the work of art. And every work of art has its sibling (brother or sister?) in a philosophical domain." Walter Benjamin, 'Theorie der Kunstkritik', GS 1 (3), p. 835. The translation is Richard Wolin's from *Walter Benjamin: An Aesthetic of Redemption*, op. cit., p. 90.
13. Hal Foster, 'What's Neo About the Neo-Avant-Garde?', *October 70*, Autumn 1994, pp. 5-32.
14. The first being Kaprow and Johns, etc., the second being Buren and Asher.
15. Hal Foster, op. cit., pp. 23-4. It is an interesting point to note that within this "ongoing dialectic" the return to traditional notions of studio practice, after Conceptual art's critical examination, remains unquestioned. See Daniel Buren, 'The Function of the Studio', *October 10*, 1979.
16. Clement Greenberg, 'Modernist Painting' (originally published as part of the Forum Lectures, *Voice of America*, Washington D.C., in 1960), in *Clement Greenberg: The Collected Essays and Criticism, vol. 4*, ed. John O'Brian, 1993, p. 85.
17. Peter Bürger, *Theory of the Avant-garde*, op. cit.
18. While the last precedent in the chain must be, to an extent, 'depoliticised' by this passing on of the ability to 'Other speak' through critique, it has not necessarily been lost for ever. This can occur because the palimpsest is never completely overwritten, and traces of what has gone before can always be found again, in different ways, in the future. (Thus we have a situation not dissimilar to a kind of "return of the repressed.") This is one of Owens' chief mistakes: he thinks that complete overwriting can occur.
19. Walter Benjamin, 'Allegory and Trauerspiel', *The Origin of German Tragic Drama*, op. cit., pp. 177-8.
20. Charles Rosen, 'The Ruins of Walter Benjamin', in *On Walter Benjamin*, op. cit., p. 142.

21. "Anything can be art now or in the future—if it works—and there are no hierarchies of styles except on the basis of past performances. And these are powerless to govern the future. What may have been the high style of one period becomes the kitsch of another." This expresses, I think, his awareness of transience; he knows here, that a 'style' has nothing inherent in it and indeed can signify, in time, what was once anti-thetical to it. 'Review of an exhibition of Hans Hofmann and a Reconsideration of Mondrian's Theories', The Nation, April 21, 1945, in Clement Greenberg The Collected Essays and Criticism, Arrogant Purpose, vol. 2, ed. J. O'Brian University of Chicago Press 1986, p. 19, (my emphasis).

22. I think Benjamin would have read many of Greenberg's canonical texts as being a good example of his ethic: "There is no document of civilisation which is not at the same time a document of barbarism." 'Thesis on the Philosophy of History', op. cit. p. 248. Especially in view of Greenberg's banishing of the Surrealists from his canons, and Benjamin's empathy with them.

23. Ibid., p. 249.

24. Joel Fineman, 'The Structure of Allegorical Desire', in October: The First Decade, MIT Press, 1986, p. 377.

25. I do not wish to rule out the possibility of a contamination down the diachronic axis of metonymy, but this must be left aside for the moment for discussion elsewhere.

26. In the introductory paragraphs to 'Elective Affinities', Benjamin speaks about the activity of the critic (he could almost be referring to Greenberg himself): "One may liken him [the critic] to a paleographer in front of a parchment whose faded text is covered by the stronger outlines of a script referring to that text. Just as the paleographer would have to start with reading the script, the critic must start with commentating on the text. And out of this activity there arises immediately an inestimable criterion of critical judgment: only now can the critic ask the basic question of all criticism, namely, whether the work's shining truth content is due to its subject matter or whether the survival of the subject matter is due to the truth content.... In this sense the history of works prepares their critique...." The translation is Hannah Arendt's from the Introduction to Illuminations, op. cit., p. 11. (my emphasis).

27. Here my twist of Greenberg is evident because while I see the ability to critique as being all the more secured by this handing over, painting is not. This is explained by the fact that critique has no essence or goal in sight as painting did have for Greenberg—no "purity." Thus, once modernist painting had reached its "essence"—the flat canvas—in someone like Newman, it could go no further so, from thereon, as it was handed over, it was subsequently ruined as a discipline whose subject matter was the condition of the conventions of the discipline. Interestingly enough, this point actually coincides with the 'post painterly' generation of abstract painters that were in fact by far the worst. For critique, the form being handed over is in ruin while the paradigm of critique is not—as it either turns over the current form or finds a 'new' one.

28. "Allegory consists of an infinite network of meanings and correlations in which everything can become a representation of everything else.... That which is expressed by and in the allegorical sign is in the first instance something which has its own meaning-ful context, but by becoming this something loses its own meaning and becomes the vehicle for something else...what appears in the allegory, in short, is the infinity of meaning which attaches to every representation." Gershom Scholem, Major Trends, New York, Schoken Books, 1946.

29. See the Richard Wolin quotation in footnote no. 8; regarding the notion of myth in connection with being "condemned to repeat."

30. As a consequence of this we have to ask: is self-criticism redemptive? For if it is self-criticism that emancipates the redemptive working of allegory, then, in turn, is its role redemptive?

Against Postmodernism: Reconsidering Ortega
Peter Halley

In the last few years, there has been growing interest on the part of many critics in the idea of post-modernism. These writers define post-modernism in various ways, but they share in common the belief that the age of modernist art is over and that a new set of theories is needed to describe art today.

No writer, however, seems to have entertained the possibility that what is today thought of as modernism is not really outdated, but merely badly formulated in the first place. Critics today seem to universally equate modernism with the formalist ideas developed by Clement Greenberg in the 1950s. But Greenberg's definition of modernism has never been adequate to describe the full range of twentieth-century modernist art. This formalist modernism was no better suited to define the past than it is the present. Another definition of modernism, outlined by the Spanish writer Jose Ortega y Gasset in his 1925 essay, *The Dehumanisation of Art,* is both possible and more useful.

Any attempt to define the extent and character of modernist art is both a descriptive and a prescriptive exercise, since no definition of the characteristics of a society's artistic production can be free of the author's aspirations for that society. Greenberg's modernism sought to provide an artistic equivalent for America's post-war aspirations to leadership of the western and developing nations. Today, with those aspirations in shambles, it is not suprising that the ideas behind the equivalent aesthetic movement seem irrelevant and distant.

Greenberg also sought to provide a theory of modernism for a country that, unlike its European counterparts, was not yet post-industrial, but still completing its initial surge of industrial growth. The art of post-war America, Abstract Expressionism, was transcendentalist, expressionistic and confident, like European art of the nineteenth century, when Europe was still an industrialising culture. Greenberg's modernism provided a positivist, determinist theory to support American art that was tied, ironically, to the values of both nineteenth-century capitalism (with its emphasis on 'taste' and 'quality') and nineteenth-century Marxism.

In order to form such a theory, Greenberg was forced to ignore a great deal of twentieth-century European art. Dada, Surrealism, Duchamp had no place in his system. He was forced to label even Analytic Cubism a "counter-revolution" against modernism and to push back the beginning of the modernist era to the middle of the nineteenth century to include the Impressionists (especially Monet), who were paradigmatic to his theory.[1]

This strategy blurred important distinctions between this century and the last. In Greenberg's formalist modernism, the nineteenth and twentieth centuries are treated as a unified historical epoch. The essential differences between the industrial nineteenth century and the post-industrial twentieth century are ignored. But, in fact, the nineteenth century was the era of industrialisation in the Western world, of mechanism empiricism, and of popular art (both romanticism and realism). It was characteristically confident and passionate.

The twentieth century, on the other hand, is the age of relativity and doubt: Einsteinian physics replaces Newtonian mechanism as Freudian subjectivity succeeds Victorian absolutism. In philosophy, Marxist positivism is replaced by existential and phenomenal doubt. Automation, electronics, and the welfare state halt the ascendancy of the worker in heavy industry.

To create a theory of modernism that bestrides these very different periods, as Greenberg attempted to do, is bound to create difficulties. In Ortega, we find instead a theory of modernism that confines itself to the art of the twentieth century.

Like Greenberg, Ortega has a prescriptive role for modernist art. He sees modernism as the characteristic art of the twentieth century and of the liberal society, which he extols. For Ortega, the primary intellectual force in the twentieth century is relativism. This relativism is produced by individuals with a profound capacity for doubt, and necessitates the invention of a tolerant political system that can encompass such doubt. For Ortega, that political system is liberalism, "the noblest cry that has ever resounded in this planet."[2] In 1930, at a time when fascism was on the rise throughout Europe and the Russian revolution had degenerated into the horrors of Stalinism, he wrote:

> Liberalism is that system of political rights, according to

which the public authority, inspite of being all powerful, limits itself and attempts, even at its own expense, to leave room in the state over which it rules for those to live who neither think nor feel as it does....

At the root of Ortega's liberalism is his belief that the positive technological and political advances in society are caused by the unusual individual who is separated by the "mass" of humanity by his "interior necessity...to appeal from himself to some standard beyond himself, superior to himself, whose service he freely accepts." Such individuals, by force of their unusual effort, bring about the characteristic institutions that define our civilisation, although their work more often than not remains unacknowledged. Advances like municipal water systems, the protection of law, or automobiles are seen by the "mass" as natural rights instead of the result of the struggles of committed individuals.

In contrast to the unusual individual, Ortega defines the "mass man." The mass man is not synonymous with the common man. He is not a member of any particular socio-economic class, but rather is an individual who "regards himself as perfect." The mass man "feels the lack of nothing outside himself." He feels no compulsion to follow principles of legality when they are not in his self-interest. He regards the benefits of civilisation as his natural right rather than as the result of complex chain of social interactions. The mass man believes in "direct action." When he rules (as in Nazi Germany or in Stalinist Russia), "the homogenous mass weighs down on the public authority and crushes down, annihilates every opposing group," because the mass "has a deadly hatred of all that is not itself."

Ortega's liberalism is at odds with the populist aspirations that have shadowed artistic thought in this country throughout the twentieth century. In part, the aspiration to populism is due to the belief in majority opinion which is so much at the basis of the American democratic approach. It is also the result of the humanistic aspirations of American intellectuals of the post-war era. From the Marxist flirtations of Clement Greenberg and Meyer Schapiro to the socialist populism of Gregory Battock and Kim Levin, to such recent rightist enfant terribles as Jed Garet, there has been a recurring discomfort with liberalism by writers on art and a consequent desire to make modernist art somehow conform to the populist mould. Ortega, in contrast, maintains that modernist art is not only by nature unpopular but anti-popular, since the ideals it embodies are antithetical to the opinions of the mass man.

According to Ortega, modernism is essentially art that is premised on doubt. In *The Dehumanisation of Art*, he sets out the characteristics of such an art. The "new style" tends to:

1) dehumanise art
2) avoid living forms
3) see the work of art as nothing but a work of art
4) consider art as play and nothing else
5) be essentially ironic
6) beware of sham and hence to aspire to scrupulous realisation
7) regard art a thing of no transcending consequence

In each of these points, he seeks to differentiate the doubting art of the twentieth century from the passionate, positivist, and confident art that characterised the nineteenth. Fifty years later, the legacy of nineteenth-century art is perhaps no less with us, and it is worthwhile to retrace Ortega's reasoning.

In his first point, Ortega claims that modernist art is "dehumanised." Here he attempts to separate the effect of art, a "seeing pleasure," from the autobiographical emotionalism that dominated nineteenth-century art. By dehumanisation Ortega means to "de-emotionalise." Modernist, doubting art must be aloof from the "contagion" of "personal feelings." Ortega traces this phenomena in music:

> From Beethoven to Wagner music was primarily concerned with expressing personal feelings. The composer erected great structures of sound to accommodate his autobiography... Wagner poured into Tristan and Isolde his adultery with Mathilde Wesendonck, and if we want to enjoy this work we must, for a few hours, turn vaguely adulterous ourselves.

But "lived" realities are too overpowering not to evoke sympathy, which prevents us from perceiving aesthetic relationships in their

de-, dis-, ex-.

"objective purity," and so should be avoided as the content of modernist art.

> Music has to be relieved of private sentiment. This was
> the deed of Debussy. Owing to him, it became possible
> to listen to musical serenely, without swoons and tears.

The contrast between these two attitudes is explicitly evident in the cinema today, where modernist and popular art exist side by side. In the popular cinema, we are wrenched by coercive illusionistic techniques into experiencing fear and joy almost beyond our will. In the modernist cinema of Stan Brackage, Hollis Frampton, or Jean-Luc Goddard, on the other hand, we are treated to an "algebra of metaphors" that allows us to "be surprised, to wonder," those facilities which "lead the intellectual through life in the perpetual ecstasy of the visionary."

Ortega claims that "art ought to be full clarity, high noon of the intellect. Tears and laughter are aesthetically frauds. The gesture of beauty never passes beyond smiles, melancholy or delight." Only in such an atmosphere is doubt and reflection possible. And in Ortegan modernism, such reflection has a high purpose which relates it to the mainstream of twentieth-century of phenomenological thought:

> We use our ideas in a "human" way when we employ
> them for thinking things. Thinking of Napoleon, for
> example, we are normally concerned with the great
> man of that name. A psychologist, on the other hand,
> adopts an unusual "inhuman" attitude when he forgets
> about Napoleon and, prying his own mind, tries to
> analyse his idea of Napoleon as such an idea. His per-
> spective is the opposite of that prevailing in sponta-
> neous life. The idea, instead of functioning as the
> means to think an object with, is itself made the object
> and the aim of thinking.

In this way, Ortega ties his modernism to the attitudes of twentieth-century Husserlian phenomenology rather than to the positivism and determinism of nineteenth-century Marxism. Ortega emphasises the limitations of human ideation: "We possess of reality, strictly speaking, nothing but the ideas we have succeeded in forming about it." But for Ortega this process is unnoticed. "By means of ideas we see the world, but in a natural attitude of mind we do not see the ideas...the spontaneous movement mind goes from concepts to the world." He points out that traditional art was content to accept ideas as synonymous with reality; reality was "idealised, although this was a candid falsification." The modernist, aspiring to "scrupulous realisation," inverts this process:

> ...if turning our back on alleged reality, we take the ideas for what they are—mere subjective patterns—and make them live as such, lean and angular, but pure and transparent; in short, if we deliberately propose to "realise" our ideas—then we have dehumanised and, as it were, derealised them.

The modernist artist reverses the "spontaneous" movement from world to mind. "We give three-dimensional being to mere patterns, we objectify the subjective, we 'worldify' the imminent." Writing in the 1920s, he finds this tendency "in varying degrees" in both Expressionism and Cubism, reconciling approaches that formalists consider antithetical. "From painting things, the painter has turned to painting ideas. He concentrates on the subjective images in his own mind."

From this derealised view of art follow the other characteristics of Ortega's definition. The modernist avoids "the round and soft forms of living bodies" because of their strong associations with both "lived realities" and with traditional Western art and its aspirations to the "salvation of mankind" that had been so strong in the transcendentalist atmosphere of the nineteenth century.

Ortega claims that, steeped in Husserlian doubt, the modernist is "ironic," that "whatever its content, the art itself is jesting. To look for fiction as fiction...is a proposition that cannot be executed except with one's tongue in one's cheek.... Being an artist means ceasing to take seriously that very serious person we are when we are not an artist." Modernist art functions as "a system of mirrors which indefinitely reflect one another [in which] no shape is ultimate, all are eventually ridiculed and revealed as pure images."

Similarly, he views art as a thing of "no transcending consequence," of no pretences. "The kingdom of art commences where the air feels lighter and things, free from formal fetters, begin to cut whimsical capers." Ortega connects the modernist impulse with playfulness and youthfulness. In fact, modernism has been characteristically the stance of young artists who, as they grow older, often lapse into a condition of solemnity reminiscent of the nineteenth-century artist-hero.

In order to establish the value of Ortega's definition of modernism, we must demonstrate its applicability to the past art of the twentieth century as well as to events occurring today. An Ortegian modernist pantheon is very different from that of formalists like Greenberg. In contrast to a Greenbergian selection, the modernists chosen here demonstrate no unity of formal concerns. Instead, a like mechanism of meaning unifies their work.

As Ortegan modernism is a theory of the behaviour of all the arts, it applies equally well to music and writing. Quintessential modernist musicians are figures like Erik Satie and John Cage; modernist writers are playwrights like Pirandello, Samuel Beckett, and Bertolt Brecht, or novelists like James Joyce, Alain Robbe-Grillet, or Thomas Pynchon.

Concentrating on the visual arts, one can point to Picasso (between 1907 and 1914), Duchamp, Jasper Johns (between 1955 and 1960), Ad Reindhart, and Andy Warhol. All are unmistakably committed to creating art based on twentieth-century relativism rather than on the "psychic contagion" of romanticism or the mechanism of nineteenth-century empiricism.

In the visual arts, of course, Picasso initiates modernism. Analytic Cubism is a complete negation of previous assumptions about visual art. In Cubism, we first see the artist concentrating completely on the patterns in his mind and 'realising' them on canvas. It is in Cubism that we first find the artist content to regard his work as a "thing of no transcending consequence," an essentially ironic and playful undertaking. (Note the frequent puns on the letters J-O-U in which the reality of the nineteenth-century *journal* is transformed into pictorial play.)

In Duchamp, this modernist point of view is equally well defined. The ready-made is an attempt at "scrupulous realisation" in which the representation of the object is exactly equated with the (presumed) presence of the object itself. Similarly, *The Large Glass* is, as Duchamp himself describes it, "the apparition of an appearance." Duchamp was, as well, largely occupied with play (note his fascination with games, with roulette and chess). One of his later pieces is a plaster relief with the entirely Ortegan title of *With My Tongue In My Cheek, Torture-Morte* (1959).

In Jasper Johns, we also observe this concern with "scrupulous realisation." In his early work, he abandoned the attempt to represent three-dimensional objects on a two-dimensional plane, preferring either to scrupulously confine his representations on two-dimensional planes to two-dimensional motifs (such as flags, targets, or numbers), or to render three-dimensional objects by making casts of them (in the case of body parts, flashlights, etc.). Overlapping objects are only rendered by overlapping canvases (as in *Three Flags*, 1958). Through all this, Johns maintains his ironic stance (he has even made an imprint with a clothes iron on some of his recent canvases). Play is specifically evoked in his work by the target (equipment in a game of marksmanship), his use of newspaper cartoons (in *Alley Oop*, 1958) and rubber balls in *Painting with Two Balls*, 1960. By making signs the subject of his art, Johns has "given three-dimensional reality to mere patterns" as Ortega suggests. Johns himself states that he painted "things the mind already knows. That gave me room to work on other levels."[3]

In Reindhart, we see represented an Ortegan approach to abstraction. In his "Art-as-Art Dogma," he states, "Art-as-art is a concentration on art's essential nature." Reindhart claimed:

> The next revolution in art will sound the farewell of the old favourite songs of "art and life" that the old favourite artist-ducks love to sing along with the old bower birds and the new, good, rich swallow audiences.[4]

How closely Reindhart's statement reflects Ortega's ideas:

> Not only is grieving and rejoicing at such destinies as a work of art presents or narrates a very different thing from true artistic pleasure, but preoccupation with the human content of the work is in principle incompatible with aesthetic enjoyment proper.

To achieve this end, Reindhart wishes to radically free his art from any subject other than mental patterns and intellectual process. In another diatribe he writes:

> ...no representations, no associations, no distortions, no paint-caricaturing, no cream pictures or drippings, no delirium trippings, no sadism or slashing, no therapy, no kicking-the-effigy...no impasto, no plasticity, no relationships, no experiments....

Instead, he advocates "painting as absolute symmetry, pure reason, rightness...Painting as central, frontal, regular, repetitive.... Colour as black, empty.... Verticality and horizontality, rectilinearity, parallelism, stasis." Reindhart exemplifies Ortega's claim that modernist "art must not proceed by psychic contagion, for psychic contagion is an unconscious phenomenon, and art ought to be full clarity, high noon of the intellect."

We also find that Reindhart's aesthetic was shaped by the decision to take an ironic stance in his work:

> Everything that the [abstract] artists were called that was bad I've picked up and I've made them not bad words. Words like inhuman, sterile, cold—they become cool.... And the others—academic, dogmatic, absolute— I picked them up and said, "Well, why not academic?"

But it is perhaps Andy Warhol who takes the premise of Ortegan modernism to its furthest limit. Warhol applies the "inversion" of modernist dehumanisation not only to his art but to his life. He is not content simply to accomplish the "realisation" of his ideas in art, but, to a greater extent than even Duchamp, he realises his ideas in his day-to-day life as well. He abandons his "human" life not only in his art but also in his daily existence. As Warhol himself states:

> I think that once you see emotions from a certain angle you can never think of them as real again. That's what more or less has happened to me.[5]

With the help of electronic recording devices, Warhol abandons "lived realities" to concentrate on the pane of glass of perception:

> The acquisition of my tape recorder really finished whatever emotional life I might have had, but I was glad to see it go. Nothing was ever a problem again, because a problem just meant a good tape, and when a problem transforms itself into a good tape, it's not a problem anymore.

This echoes Ortega's description of the artist:

> The painter, in fine, completely unconcerned, does nothing but keep his eyes open. What is happening here is none of his business; he is, as it were, a hundred miles removed from it. His attitude is a purely perceptive attitude; indeed, he fails to perceive the event in its entirety. The entire inner meaning escapes his attention which is directed exclusively toward the visual part.... In the painter we find a maximum of distance and a minimum of feeling intervention.

Warhol was fascinated with figures in the media whose lives had been "dehumanised"—movie stars, celebrities, transvestites. To Warhol, the movies provided the most vivid example of this inversion:

> The best atmosphere I can think of is film, because it's three-dimensional physically and two-dimensional emotionally.

At the same time, Warhol shares with Ortega an appreciation of the playfulness of the whole modernist endeavour. Again, Ortega states:

> To the present-day artist the kingdom of art commences where the air feels lighter and things, free from formal fetters, begin to cut whimsical capers.... The

symbol of art is seen again in the Great God Pan which makes the young goats frisk at the edge of the grove.

Warhol echoes this view:

> In some circles where very heavy people think they have very heavy brains, words like "charming" and "clever" and "pretty" are all put-downs, and all the lighter things in life, which are the most important, are put down.

Today, the post-modern critics claim, younger artists are no longer working within the parameters of modernism. This is true—and has been for a long time—if we define modernism as Greenbergian formalist modernism.

However, if we adopt the assumptions of Ortegan modernism, we find that good many younger artists, especially among those supported by post-modernist critics, are working within the assumptions of this fifty year old theory. R.M. Fisher, Steven Keister, Cindy Sherman, and Richard Prince come to mind as artists who aspire to the kind of modernism that Ortega advocates.

On the other hand, a variety of art being produced today truly is something other than modernist. However, to call this art post-modernist is probably a mistake, since it exhibits all the signs of being, in fact, premodernist. The return to perspective techniques, the unique art object, human expression, 'sensibility'—these are simply a retreat into nineteenth-century strategies by retrograde artists, as Benjamin H.D. Buchloh has pointed out in his essay on "new image" painting. [6]

There has always been regressive art in our culture, but the unusual phenomenon today is that such work has gained the status of major art. This is the result of changes in our society that have occurred within the last decade.

From the 1950s to the 1970s, it was the entrepreneurial class, buoyed up by economic prosperity, that supported modernism, in the medium characteristically associated with that class—the visual arts. Today that class has largely retreated from its interest in the mod-

ernist point of view (just as it has retreated from its aspirations to liberalism). Instead, it seeks to reassure itself by withdrawing into his-
toricism, romanticism, and a kind of parodic individualism.

Today, modernism has largely moved to a different arena, where it is
supported by a different class. Modernism is as alive in music as it is
under attack in the visual arts. Groups with such names as the Talking
Heads, the Clash, the Gang of Four, and Public Image limited, have all
moved to an essentially modernist position. David Bryne, of the
Talking Heads, for example, sings that "facts are useless in emergen-
cies," that

> Facts are simple and facts are straight
> Facts are lazy and facts are late
> Facts all come with their own point of view
> Facts don't do what I want them to
> Facts just twist the truth around
> Facts are living turned inside out.... [7]

Here he reflects Ortega's stance on the limits of ideation. The Clash
sing about a cartoon confrontation between "G.I. Joe" and "Ivan," a
"Ruskie Bear," ironically turning jingoistic labels in upon themselves.
The Gang of Four sing:

> The problem of leisure
> What to do for pleasure
> Ideal love a new purchase
> A market of the senses [8]

They are turning the methods of advertising into an "algebra of
metaphors" and neutralising the "contagion" of popular culture.
Similarly, the leader of the band the Dead Kennedy's uses the modernist *nom de plume* of Jello Biafra (running for mayor of San Francisco
on the slogan, "There's always room for Jello").

In their instrumentation, these bands constantly parody the characteristic phrasing of earlier, unconscious pop music. Their playfulness
allows the B-52s to transform the mindless drone of early 60s instrumental music into something else. Many of these musicians have also

adopted a clearly modernist attitude toward their own public personas. John Lyndon of Public Image Limited said in an interview in the Canadian magazine, *MacLean's*: "I'm tired of the past and even the future's beginning to seem repetitive. I don't really know what to say. I'm a liar, a hypocrite, and a bastard. I shouldn't be tolerated...."

The modernism of these musicians is particularly significant because it is assaulting one of the most important strong holds of popular art in the nineteenth-century mould—electronically reproduced music. Because they apply modernist attitudes of irony and doubt to political and social issues, their work comes to serve the very purpose that was advocated by Ortega as the aim of modernism—the preservation of the possibility of liberal democracy. Their willingness to deal with the major events of our culture singles out these musicians as important successors to the daring modernists of the past.

In times of economic adversity and uncertainty, like the present, it is characteristic of the wealthy to retreat into a position of fear and reaction. On the other hand, during these adverse periods, there are likely to be small groups without a large investment in the status quo who will be moved by adversity to a position of intense thought and doubt. These musicians are not supported by a wealthy entrepreneurial class (as have been modernist artists), but by this minority: those thinking, doubting individuals with the few dollars available necessary to purchase a record album.

This market-structure has allowed modernism to flourish today in music. It could provide the necessary impetus for a modernist resurgence in the visual arts.

*   *   *

1. Clement Greenberg, 'Modernist Painting' from *Collected Essays and Criticism, Modernism With Avengeance, vol. 4*, John O'Brian ed., The University of Chicago Press, Chicago, 1993.
2. All quotations from Ortega are from two sources: *The Dehuminisation of Art*, Princeton University Press, Princeton, 1968, and *The Revolt of the Masses*, W.W. Norton and Co., New York, 1932.
3. Leo Steinberg, *Other Criteria*, Oxford University Press, 1972
4. Quotations form Ad Reindhart are from *Art-As-Art: The Selected Writings of Ad Reindhart*, Barbara Rose, ed., Viking Press, New York, 1975.
5. Warhol is quoted from *The Philosophy of Andy Warhol*, Harcourt, Brace, Jovanovich, New York, 1975.
6. Benjamin D. Buchlöh, 'Figures of Authority, Ciphers of Regression', *October 16*, spring 1981.
7. The Talking Heads, 'Cross Eyed and Painless', *Remain in Light*, Sire Records, New York, 1980.
8. Gang of Four, 'Natural's Not in It', *Solid Gold*, Warner Brothers Records, New York, 1981.

Robert Smithson, *Closed Mirror Square*, 1969. Collection: The Estate of Robert Smithson. Courtesy of Jon Weber Gallery, New York.

Theory as Phantom Text: Plundering Smithsons Non-Sites
Susan Kandel

Here is the (latest) art world consensus: "In the 80s, theory and practice engaged in mutual masturbation and we wound up with art that was notoriously cold and difficult. In the 90s, art is as fabulous as sex: impassioned, spontaneous, powerful, delicious, delightful, lyrical—and meaningful, too."

Beware. A consensus is always suspect; one this fulsome is particularly so. And yet today, the art world—like the *Artforum* contributor who recently described herself as a "recovering theorist"[1]—is indeed 'recovering' from theory. As Jerry Saltz, in the midst of *Art in America's* 1994 fête in honour of the 'return of painting', gleefully observed, "It appears as if numbers of people are about to abandon their allegiance to theory. You can almost smell it."[2]

These days, the snide post(theory)mortems infiltrate virtually every text about visual culture. Presented in the form of fragments, rejoinders, qualifications, asides, told-you-so's, or outright confutations, such comments are designed to signify the writer's knowingness (however after the fact). A random sample would include historian Martin Jay pontificating on the "increasingly bad odor" theory has lately come into—this, in a recent issue of *October*, the journal which once consecrated itself to making 'theory' a household word.[3] Or, the L.A. *Times* critic Christopher Knight barely concealing his contempt for "theory-driven work that regards with suspicion the pleasurable uselessness of art."[4] Or, even the reviewer Giovanni Intra declaring (with the world-weariness of a self-anointed survivor) that, "in the end it's hard to know what's worse—being drunk on theory or wallowing in the hangover."[5]

What was it that Intra and the others ostensibly survived? In many quarters, the 80s has already been constructed as a decade of stylistic revivalism, an amorphous, indeed vacuous period caught up in all things 'neo' and 'post'. (Neo-expressionism, post-pop appropriation, and post-conceptualism are merely the most familiar of the schools or sobriquets to emerge during this period). According to this scenario, the theoretical practice being abandoned in droves by today's zeitgeist-seeking artists was and remains nothing more than quaintly retro, a retread of 60s and 70s conceptualism bolstered by a different, and decidedly continental reading list.

In 1992, Robert C. Morgan cynically characterised the hyper-presence of theory in 80s art as a "careerist's" gambit: the artist slyly plays the innocent, enmeshed in the day-to-day exigencies of practice, and relies upon the theory-besotted critic to play Svengali or apologist. "One way of succeeding within the context of the game," Morgan wrote, "was to be adopted by a writer or a magazine—preferably both—with the right art-world credentials, who would quote Benjamin, Adorno, and the five famous French post-structuralists, and thus…reify or legitimate one's position in the mainstream."[6]

More recently, Joanna Frueh described the "unloving tongue of schlock theory" (chock full of suspect words like 'sign, code, text, discourse, problematic, privileged male gaze, phallic mother, hegemony, praxis, fetish commodity'), and the tendency of schlock theorists to "make mental masturbation into the Postmodern Mysteries." For her, postmodern theory, as it has been taken up by critics, artists and others, is nothing more than "an amazing gracelessness," gaudy, not to mention pretentious.[7] Yet there are clearly other ways to read the moves particular to the theoretical (end)game.

'Theory', to begin with, was always an imaginary construct: no single entity, but rather a phantasmic hash of miscellaneous specimens (structuralism, post-structuralism, deconstruction, post-modernism, psychoanalytic feminism) which in the 80s indeed masqueraded as the latest thing. All dressed up in little, black *Semiotext(e)* paperbacks—designed to fit into the vest pocket of an artist's leather jacket—theory beckoned to the art world, promising many things. For those seduced by its look and/or linguistic rhythms, the call was answered; for those watching from a distance, this was a dangerous thing. Art was compromised, they lamented; and so, too, were specific discourses, lost in a tumult of buzzwords and catch-phrases which insinuated themselves into artworks in lieu of 'real' content.

Yve-Alain Bois, one of those watching, derided the tendency within 80s art toward what he called "theoreticism"—the desire, or sense of obligation to be "theoretical."[8] Eliding the question of his own theoretical investment, Bois shuddered at the very notion of using theory in and for practice. In this he echoed Baudrillard, who once noted—with

de-, dis-, ex-.

Sherrie Levine, *After Degas*: 4, Black and white photograph, edition of 5, 10 x 8 inches
Courtesy of: Margo Leavin Gallery, Los Angeles.

impressive condescension—that it was particularly American to assume that theory could be utilised, recast as one among many artistic materials and transmuted from a metaphysical state into something as unequivocally physical as the object of art.[9]

Yet both Bois and Baudrillard were short-sighted. What they seemed to imagine was a realm of pure ideas, an impossible space where language—theoretical or otherwise—floats free, untethered to anything material. The theoretical practice of the 80s—and by that I refer to the work of artists as disparate as Barbara Kruger and Richard Prince, Stephen Prina and Mark Tansey, Peter Halley and Sherrie Levine—was more sophisticated than these purists would allow, and than Saltz et al. would ever admit, in their zest to celebrate the new (art) world order.

Despite divergent approaches, these artists all treat words as inherently material, and objects as linguistic entities which are scripted and can be read. In this, their work plays out Robert Smithson's notion of art as a space in which distinct categories, genres and media are frustrated. In this space, language does not so much trespass on art's sacrosanct province as become wholly imbricated within it, blurring old borders forever. As Smithson put it in the title of a 1972 press release, here is "Language to be Looked at and/or Things to be Read."[10] Craig Owens, reading Smithson, characterised this as the defining element of the postmodern: the "eruption of language into the field of the visual."[11] The theoretical practice of the 80s seems to reify Owens' characterisation, though in fact it renders his 'eruption' hyperbolic, as the language with which Halley, Levine, and many of the others were concerned was the meta-language of theory.

From the beginning, art critics of all stripes misunderstood the radical nature of this proposition; they went in for the "emperor's new clothes" routine instead. Halley was a favoured target. His geometric abstractions of the mid-80s were deemed baffling insofar as they appeared to circumnavigate theoretical language only to pay homage to it in the accompanying rhetoric. Or, they simulated high-modernist abstraction as if in critical mode when, in fact, they participated in the system's relentless retooling of the outré. Halley explained things this way: his squares and grids of pure colour were not actually abstractions; they were diagrams of the panoptic structures of late capitalism. They emphasised, along with a whole array of Foucauldian truisms, "the role of the model within the simulacrum [which] Baudrillard states is 'characterised by a precession of the model'."[12]

It may have been a strategic error for Halley to acknowledge his theoretical pre-texts so baldly. Indeed, it set him up for invective like the
following, from *Flash Art* in 1987: "To 'buy' New French Theory is in
essence to commit Theory Suicide, and necessarily places the artist
in the arena of the collaborator, binding him inextricably to the mar-
ket/commodity realism upon which he is attempting to comment."[13]
Yet Halley has never been coy. A scavenger with a refined palate, his
paintings of the 80s used this or that metaphor and this or that visual
cue to fashion an oneiric postmodernity, one both sleekly totalised
and irreducibly fragmentary—a network of 'cells' and 'conduits'. If
Baudrillard figured in all of this, it was as one among many formerly
discrete referents whose lines of demarcation were willfully blurred—
a found object rather than a founding metaphysic.

Yet Hal Foster, too, dismissed Halley's project on the basis of its "dras-
tic Baudrillardian perspective."[14] And Foster's colleague, Rosalind
Krauss, while ever-ready to champion post-structuralist theory, sav-
aged such work as exemplary of "a production that wants to legitimate itself by reference to certain post-structuralist ideas."[15] Indeed,
throughout the 80s, Foster, Krauss and their *October* confrères alternated between a frothing enthusiasm for theory and strident refuta-
tions of its use: the historical avant-garde could be read through post-
structuralist theory, but—with few exceptions —contemporary practice could not claim it. This prickliness betrays a proprietary attitude
which Bois' notion of theoreticism amplifies: theory belongs to those
able to 'master' it, not to those artists who would splinter it at whim.

Indeed, theory was—for many artists working in the 80s—a whimsy,
nothing more: part of the local colour, especially in New York City;
one among a myriad of influences; or better yet, something whose
presence was trumpeted only after the fact by writers, dealers, and
curators likewise caught up in the decade's rarefied atmosphere.
This, however, was not the case for Halley, nor was it for Levine in
particular, for whom theory has always been pivotal. If there is
indeed a theoretical practice particular to the 80s, she is its avatar.
Though her work is ongoing and variant, she is best known for re-
photographing works by famous, male modernist artists. This act is
quite delirious, as intemperate as stalking an ex-lover; or, it is as cool-
ly rational as animal mimicry behaviours, adopted for the purpose of
survival. Levine has commented that she gave the art world the
images of male desire it seemed to want, nodding in the direction of
Lacan.[16] Yet Barthes comes into it, as well; her serial acts of theft
enacted (without precisely saying so) the scenario he described in his

1968 essay, 'The Death of the Author'. For those unsure of the nature of her project, she tipped her hand, tweaking selected portions of that essay as her exhibition statement—'The Death of the Painter'—in 1981.

Evacuating authors and painters, however, was easier said than done. Curator Susan Krane's reluctance showed when she gushed over the "exquisite physicality" of Levine's 'generic abstractions' of the mid-80s—a deadpan suite of stripe and check paintings designed to function as mnemonic triggers rather than a brand new round of late-modern masterpieces. "Levine's paintings have a delicate quality," Krane proclaimed, "and often a very romantic look: it is as if each stroke and decision were cherished."[17] Krane's florid prose insisted upon an author. Ironically, Levine's minimalist prose yearned for one, too: "...I make the pictures that I want to make," Levine said in a 1987 interview with Paul Taylor, "and I look for theory that I think is going to help me in a different kind of language. It's not that the theory precedes the work."[18]

Levine embraced theory; that is quite evident. But equally evident is the fact that she resisted acknowledging its priority ("It's not that the theory precedes the work"), for that would be the death of her. This struggle to embody a philosophical system of her own choosing is what made, and continues to make Levine's work interesting, and not merely illustrational. She stages a dialogue between theory and practice in which neither voice, in fact, has priority. Her art objects do not synthesise, but reconcile two different things—however uneasily. They direct the viewer elsewhere, to the register of theory; but they also fabricate their own reality, one which is ironic, because unverifiable. Levine's work remains profoundly restless. As such, it elides the closure modernism promises, and obscures—if it does not entirely erase—the authorial body modernism necessitates.

So, is there any model which can account for the operations put into place by photographs as deceptively transparent as Levine's, or by paintings as deceptively obfuscatory as Halley's? Sherry Turkle offers one way to begin to fathom this practice. In her treatise on computer hackers, *The Second Self*, she specifies two different styles of man/machine interface, two alternate modes of mastery.[19] "Hard mastery" is the imposition of will over the machine; "soft mastery" is more interactive: "It is more like a conversation than a monologue." "Soft mastery" is a neat metaphor around which to figure the relationship between theory and practice in the 80s (without resorting to

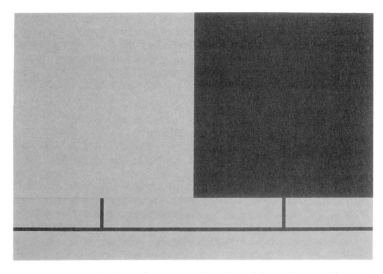

Peter Halley, 1982, *Glowing and Burnt-out Cells with Conduit*, Acrylic, Day-Glo
Acrylic and Roll-a-Tex on canvas, 96" x 64". Photo: Courtesy of the artist.

the by-now predicatable formulae of cannibalism, parasitism, and cynicism), for the qualifier "soft" renders the whole notion of mastery upon which Bois' "theoreticism" is predicated absurd.

I also invoked Smithson, and of specific relevance is his notion of the dialectic of site and non-site. It is here, I think—in Smithson's perpetual relay between here and there, open and closed, edge and centre— that any such model locates its history and derives its particular logic. Smithson made his first non-sites in 1968, transporting rocks, slate fragments or mica from geological sites into the gallery or the museum. Arranging these substances in the sort of rigid, geometric containers made familiar by minimalism, Smithson found a way to muddy up the 'white cube' while playing at accommodation.[20] Like scale-models, these receptacles mimicked the gallery's desire for containment; yet Smithson continually transgressed their borders with photographs and maps which pointed the way out, toward the site from which the rocks or fragments were taken.

The notion of the map is crucial to Smithson's work. Many of his essays are constructed as travelogues, with the map operating as a key component—a specific object in which a particular place is diagrammed, approximated and rendered into symbolic language. If the map is a two-dimensional arrangement of lines and forms which evokes a three-dimensional space, the non-site is, as Smithson has described it, "a three-dimensional map of the site." Like the map, it offers a synthesis between representation and abstraction.[21] It depicts something beyond, intertwining the here with that which is there—or at least elsewhere.

The work of Halley, Levine and their peers recapitulates the logic of Smithson's non-sites. In fact, one can think about these artists' works themselves as non-sites: maps, courses of hazards, and double paths which are here while referring us elsewhere—to the absent work of theory, to the absent register of language. How does the "absent register of language" in the work of these artists correspond with Owens' notion of "the eruption of language into the field of the visual"? The latter's insistence upon language as constitutive of the postmodern moment does not refer to the literal presence of language in the work of art (though this may indeed be the case); rather it refers to a complex interchange between presence and absence, and between the implicit and explicit—a notion of language as always already sited within the work, indeed, a notion of the work as text.

de-, dis-, ex-.

So what these artists produced in the 80s, then—in the mode presaged by Smithson—are phantom texts: complex, heterogeneous, and full of both visual and verbal information. Their art objects are sites where different discourses meet, as well as sites where yet more discourse is produced. At the same moment, they are non-sites, lacunae, haunted by those missing bodies (of theory) which can only be conjured second-hand. Here, theory and practice are—as Smithson predicted of "everything" in 1970—"two things that converge."[22] In the 90s, when the two things that are converging are on either side of the mirror (narcissism is the art world's current addiction), this heady episode is worth bearing in mind.

*   *   *

1. Rhonda Lieberman, 'Small Talk: Rhonda Lieberman on the Divine Host', *Artforum*, December 1994, p. 10.
2. Jerry Saltz, 'A Year in the Life: Tropic of Painting', *Art in America*, October 1994, pp. 90-101.
3. Martin Jay, 'Visual Culture and Its Vicissitudes', *October 77*, Summer 1996, p. 42.
4. Christopher Knight, 'When More is Really More', in *Los Angeles Times*, June 16, 1996, p. 83.
5. Giovanni Intra, 'Hangover', *Art + Text 54*, 1996, p. 92.
6. Robert C. Morgan, 'After the Deluge: The Return of the Inner-Directed Artist', *Arts Magazine*, March 1992, p. 50.
7. Joanna Frueh, *Erotic Faculties*, Berkeley: University of California Press, 1996, p. 47.
8. Yve-Alain Bois, 'Resisting Blackmail', *Painting as Model*, Cambridge and London: MIT Press, 1990, pp. xii-xiii.
9. Isabelle Graw, 'Interview with Jean Baudrillard', *Wolkenkratzer Art Journal*, n.d., p. 104.
10. Reprinted in Robert Smithson, *The Collected Writings of Robert Smithson*, ed. by Nancy Holt, New York: New York University Press, 1979, p. 104.
11. Craig Owens, 'Earthwords', *October 10*, Fall 1979, p. 122.
12. Peter Halley, 'The Crisis in Geometry', *Collected Essays*, Zurich: Bruno Bischofberger Gallery, 1988, p. 102.
13. Shaun Caley, 'Group Show at Sonnabend, New York', *Flash Art*, no. 132, February/March 1987, p. 104.
14. Hal Foster, 'Signs Taken For Wonders', *Art In America*, June 1986, p. 87.
15. Rosalind Krauss, 'Theories of Art After Minimalism and Pop', in, *Discussions in Contemporary Culture*, ed. Hal Foster, no. 1, Seattle: Bay Press, 1987, p. 83.
16. 'Sherrie Levine Plays with Paul Taylor', in *Flash Art*, no. 135, Summer 1987, p. 56.
17. Susan Krane, *Sherrie Levine*, Atlanta: High Museum, 1988, p. 13.
18. 'Sherrie Levine Plays With Paul Taylor', op. cit.
19. Sherry Turkle, *The Second Self: Computers and the Human Spirit*, New York: Simon and Schuster, 1984, pp. 104-5.
20. Brian O'Doherty, *Inside the White Cube: The Ideology of the Gallery Space*, Santa Monica: Lapis Press, 1976.
21. Eugenie Tsai, *Robert Smithson Unearthed: Drawings, Collages, Writings*, New York: Columbia University Press, 1991, p. 36.
22. 'Earth: Symposium at White Museum, Cornell University, 1970', in *Collected Writings of Robert Smithson*, op. cit., p. 166.

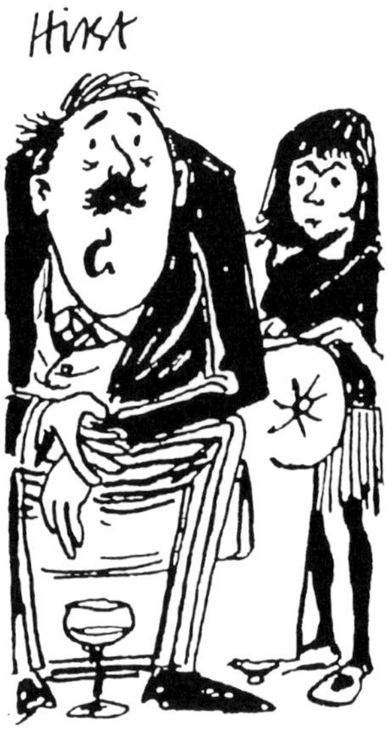
Hick

The Home in Modernity
Nikos Papastergiadis

The ideal of home is always situated uncomfortably on the cleft stick of tradition and modernisation, yet what is lacking in most theories is an understanding of how a home may connect together and ground conflicting worldviews and social processes.

The Promised Land

The context for thinking about where we belong can no longer be defined according to a purely geographic notion of place and historical sense of connection. Our location is now largely influenced by the global processes of a project called modernity. Naming the project is one thing but knowing its trajectory is another. Does modernity still promise to be the home of enlightenment, progress and reason, or is it an exilic state shrouded by techno-mystification, sliding deeper into chaos, committed to inequality, a shabby justification for ecological and cultural upheaval? Modern assumptions are contradictory; on the one hand there is the belief that change makes things better, and on the other we would prefer that things stay as they are. Modernity begins with the belief in both the journey away from and the permanence of the home. For all of us who are travellers on the major highways and multiple backroads of modernity there are some lurking hopes, that,

> No matter how far we go, we can always return home. No matter how crazy the world gets, things will always be the same back home. No matter what they expect you to become out there, you can always be yourself at home. No matter what they do, this is how we do things here, at home.

In these four statements we can hear the promise of return and stability that underwrites the journeys of modernity: home is where the heart lies. These 'maternal' assurances remind us that despite the geographic migrations, social upheavals, personal crises, and cultural differences there is one privileged place where origin and destiny intersect, a place where security and integrity are not compromised. In the opening song to the popular American comedy *Cheers* we hear these very assurances in the most touching way:

> Be glad there's some place in the world
> where everybody knows your name
> and they're always glad you came.
>
> You wanna go where the people know
> people are all the same.
>
> You wanna go where everybody knows your name.

In a society where the domestic space is so filled with trauma and insecurity the idealised image of a 'pub' can appear as a more plausible symbol of home. Irrespective of its location the home is the sacred place from which everything else is mapped. Our outward adventures are measured in relation to the home. Dreams of journeys begin from home and the rest of the world extends outwardly from this radix. Mapping elsewhere is also a homing device. Our inward returns are read as confirmations of an incontrovertible dynamism. The meaning of the home has both a centrifugal and centripetal force, it combines both our inner and outer trajectories. Home is the centre of the world.

This seemingly universal belief is indifferent to any rational argument about the relativity of our particular view of home. Even if we are to admit that not every house is a home, we still have to acknowledge that the ideal of the home is not totally defined by the realities of the house. Such a concept of home is impervious to any criticism that seems to come from outside. The ideal home is not just a house which offers shelter, or a repository that contains material objects. Apart from its physical protection and market value a home is a place where personal and social meaning are grounded. Different parts of a house may serve as the home for different members. The space of the house may be defined by its material structures whereas the home is divided by symbolic boundaries. These boundaries emerge from a matrix of identification and projection and vary according to gender and age. Home is more of a symbolic space than it is a physical place.

The centrality of the home does not seem to be disturbed by drawing our attention to the particularity of all our different notions of what the home is, however a more fundamental challenge may now be coming from within. We can always defend against or even rebuild after the home has been attacked from outside, but how do you deal with that slow but determined process of implosion? What happens when our sense of home is filled with trauma? In contemporary Britain the discussions of home are not usually couched in terms of ontological mapping, but rather framed by the burden of negative equity, the incessant fear of burglary, the unknown pathologies of mass murder and the increasingly stringent policies of asylum from our Home Secretary. Care for the elderly and disabled is administered in institutions which are euphemistically named 'homes'. The home is now a place of ambient fears.

Homes and Their Histories

In folkloric tales the significance of the home is defined by its relation to the outside space. The home may be a clearing within a forest, a camp in the midst of a desert, an island surrounded by the sea. The outside space is usually perceived as dark, hostile and capricious. Beyond the clearing is where the devil lies. Away from the camp there are no signs of life. Out in the sea things can change without notice. This sense of the outside as the place of threat and the unknown heightens the significance of home as the place of safety, order and even divine protection. Home is not only the place which is marked out as your own, but also the specific place in which you will be recognised by others and most importantly by God. To leave home is always a risky enterprise.

Novalis' aphorism that "philosophy is a homesickness of the mind" has found resonance in many great literary works, which often written from the perspective of exile, give us the most clear sighted views of home. The exile misses many things: the loss of familiar signs makes every turn problematic. Disconnected from the place where action was guided by experience the exile is catapulted into social space where nothing can be taken for granted. The smell of the sea, the glare of sunlight, a certain way of greeting people, all these ordinary things once deprived, make the rest of living a drudgery. Exiles always complain about the food and weather.

Dante even found stairs more difficult to climb when he was away from his native Florence. It is narcissism's energy and the momentum drawn from recognition by others that is undermined by exile.

When Ovid was banished to the outposts of the Roman Empire his judges made this punishment on the basis of two calculations. The state would find security by establishing a distance between its capital and this critic, but it would also find some aesthetic pleasure in silencing his "wicked tongue." Ovid's punishment was not just measured by the miles he was sent out of Rome, but by the relationship to language in this antipode. Flung out in this 'bar-bar-ous' outpost where physical subsistence was the imperative Ovid's communication was stripped of the excesses of language. In this case exile is a place where the author is threatened with silence, where one's link to the historical chain of peers, ancestors and successors is cut.

These oppositions between home as the embodiment of culture, order, history and exile as wilderness, chaos, oblivion are repeated in modern literature. Through the representation of the home as the place where it is possible to observe the expression of specific cultural values, the development of unique traditions and the display of certain states of emotion we are also witness to the characteristic forms of modern identity. However, the focal point of identity and historical consciousness shifts as it stresses a relationship between the home and the nation. The symbols and narratives of the nation can only resonate if they are admitted into the chamber of the home. The memory of the nation must also inform the life-narratives of the people. The language that is spoken at home becomes the most intimate medium of a national soul. Language, religion and nationality were envisaged by Stephen Dedalus as a series of constrictive nets, but wasn't Joyce, the exile, aiming to forge in the smithy of his soul 'the uncreated conscience of his race'. The symbolic space of the home in modernity is pressed up against both the traditional values of stability and unspecified desires for transformation.

While Mircea Eliade defined the traditional home as the axis point which secured the unity between the domestic and the spiritual, a link that connected the individual both vertically in time to ancestry and horizontally in space to kin, this process of ontological reconciliation is also echoed in Gaston Bachelard's reading of the metaphors of home in modern poetry.[1] The only difference between the traditional and the modern home is that the former was always

de-, dis-, ex-.

seen as a complete container of memories and a stable site identification, whereas the latter is more a patchwork of silent ambitions and temporary arrangements. John Berger hints at the unstated dreams and unstable ground in modernity when he states that, "Home is no longer a dwelling but the untold story of a life being lived."[2]

When Georg Lukacs developed the concept "transcendental homelessness," he was speaking as much about the modern intellectual condition as he was about any individual's fate.[3] Hannah Arendt was one of the philosophers who escaped Nazism. After surviving the tragic crossing of the Pyrennes where Walter Benjamin took his life, she eventually arrived in New York and stayed for the rest of her life without unpacking her suitcases.[4] This figurative expression of existential homelessness is not a dismissal of the hope of home for there are only three options for an exile; to defer the homecoming to an idealised time in the future, to find a substitute home in the here and now, or else, there is madness. The exile becomes most conscious of both the necessary illusions of integration in the home, and the imaginary boundaries of belonging. In the brilliant and haunting fragments of Minima Moralia Theodor Adorno evoked his own experiences of exile as a precarious balance between the dislocation from the past and the poisonous relations in the present.[5] Adorno becomes his own torturer, always interrogating himself against the losses of language, the betrayal of values and the destruction of an historical consciousness. 'After Auschwitz' exile is paradoxically a permanent condition, even as redemption is not foreclosed but deferred to an indefinite future.

Mapping the World From Home

Let us return to the idea that our mapping of the world starts with the primary marker of the home. The distinctions between self/other; inside/outside; order/chaos revolve around the prior constructions of the home as the position from which these values can be discerned. Home is the place where moral knots are untied and ethical patterns are stitched together. Cosmologies are significant insofar as they can address the local by differentiating it from the beyond. The primacy of the home is however not simply determined in a strict opposition to the space beyond. Between the inner sanctum of homely order and the outer territories of chaos lies a continuum of intermediate spaces. For the Russian semiotician of culture Yuri Lotman a variation of anti-homes are erected between the home and the state of homelessness. These anti-homes confirm the use of the home as the primary mapping mechanism because their identity is defined in relation to the ideal type of the home. The status of silence may serve as the key marker between home and anti-home. Silence signifies tranquillity in the home, whereas in the anti-home silence is filled with a deafening anguish.

Social critics who see modernity only in apocalyptic terms have not missed out on the opportunity to classify the obvious sites of deprivation as the negation of the home. The anti-home has been identified as being located on the peripheries of the city, buried in the underground passages, raised on wheels and traversing the open roads. Brothels for instance, which are wedged between the sites of all male industrial labour, are places which are conventionally seen as inverting the norms of domestic life. Yet, in Lotman's terms the anti-home is not defined by inversion or deprivation, the cardboard homes of 'travellers' which are precariously positioned in the entrance of exclusive department stores may commune with the principles of the ideal home. "What distinguishes a home from an anti-home is not just dilapidation, neglect and lack of cosiness."[6] In Lotman's account the anti-home is always riven with jealousies and rivalries. In contrast the home is where you are above suspicion and reproach. Where belonging is free from the curse of evil or the burden of conflict. Or as an Australian suburbanite once noted, "home is a place where you can sing as you please and not care what your neighbour thinks." In other contexts the closing of curtains does not announce the beginnings of intimacy and freedom but the concealment of shame. The private is always a subject of scrutiny for the public.

The identification of home as a place of personal and familial development is, as David Morgan has observed a phenomenon which is neither a permanent nor universal feature of social life. The value given to home can only be understood in its variations. Morgan's discussion of the home highlights two important relationships, firstly its inscription in a series of strategies of surveillance, and secondly as a gendered space.[7] When the concept of home is confined to domesticity this space is usually identified as maternal or feminine. However, not all of the home belongs to women, the division of labour, say from the kitchen to the garage, constructs gendered boundaries that differentiate the spaces within the home. The performance of banal tasks like who takes out the rubbish may highlight both the contingency and the continuity of boundaries between inside and outside. As the outside world is characterised as dangerous and impersonal the home becomes a privileged space for nurturing intimacy. The Australian suburbanite may harbour the fantasy of freedom in his home, but this freedom is in turn dependent on a broader social stability. In a world where trust has been thoroughly eviscerated and the watchful eye of the neighbourhood not only extends from the maintenance of taste, to protection against crime, but also includes the monitoring of sexual and childhood abuse, then the sanctity of privacy at home is far from assured.

Moving on with Modernity

The concept of home is not safe in modernity. One of the clear objectives of modernism is to move out of the old home but the precise shape and location of the new home of modernity is never specified. The old home needs to be left behind because from the modernist's perspective it is locked into the frozen time of the past; bound to unchangeable customs; restricted to only pure members; ruled by strict authoritarian father figures; stifled by superstitious beliefs. In short the old home represents closed traditions. To stay there is to atrophy. By contrast modernity promises a sense of the present which is open, encourages mobility over stability, promotes difference as the stimulus for novelty, suggests that decision making should be participatory, and recognises that reason bows to no god. The spirit of modernity is defined by the dynamism for change, the significance of place is always secondary in this revolution against the questions of being and belonging.

Modernity sought to sweep away the remnants of tradition, yet it actually displayed a degree of "dialectical hesitancy"[8] when it came up against the home. For if modernity swept away the past it also had to invent a new mode of living in the present. The forms of individualism that are expressive of this new age emphasise that identity is not bound to a specific past or a particular place. The 'self-made man' of modernity needed a new home, yet the modern home could also be read as the greatest oxymoron of our age. For if the home nested in traditions which were by definition incompatible with modernity, then the modern home could only, and at best, be the white cubic spaces divested of any crannies in which traces of the past may lurk, or a crowded museum in which kitsch orders memory. The concept of home haunts modernity. In an age where moving out of home is the first sign of independence, and yet when there is no definite sense of where to go, the prospects of finding the ideal home seem constantly threatened by a looming fear of living in a state of permanent homelessness. Modernity may be fully committed to a process of detraditionalisation but it either bawks at pursuing its central target or only partially achieves its own goal by hollowing out any value in the prize. What many of the modernists, like Baron Hausmann who saw space as either a neutral stage or an impediment to their utopian grids failed to appreciate, was that the semantic richness in the experience of the home was also inextricably linked to an historically elliptical and unconscious process of ontological mapping.

The significance of traditions was found in the extent that they enable individuals to connect their identity within a time-space continuum. Traditions are forms for the articulation of memory and meaning. The technocratic assumption that traditions can be dispensed with, presumes that after a certain change of season they are as superfluous as the snake's winter skin. This analogy overlooks the resilience of traditions, they return like the next layer of skin. Yet this rhetorical oversight is repeated throughout the discourses of modernity. When Marx gave us that insight into the drive of modernity with the iconic phrase: "all that is solid melts into air," this was also a prophecy of the perils of detraditionalisation. This ambivalence towards tradition in modernity is compulsively reiterated by the founding fathers of classical social theory. These great bearers of the enlightenment felt deeply opposed to tradition, they saw it as a source of mystification, an enemy to reason and an obstacle against progress. Yet it is tradition which offered the necessary interpretative framework and safety net for social meaning. The moral deficit that is expressed in Weber's phrase "the iron cage of disenchantment," and Durkheim's account of vertiginous "anomie" is nowhere felt so painfully as it is in the modern home.

Despite the contemporary anxiety over the status of the home, with responses varying from the extreme sterilisation of domesticity in the radiant plans of Le Corbusier,[9] to the bulimic display of homeliness in the 'cyburbian' pastiche of American cities that has been described by Sorkin and others;[10] either way, it is unlikely that the concept of the home will disappear in modernity. The search for home is neither a nostalgic retreat to a familiar past nor a defensive reaction against the brutalities of the present. The meaning of home is now found in the future oriented projects of constructing a sense of belonging in a context of change and displacement.

Lazlo Maholy-Nagy was one of the few artists/critics to understand that the problem of housing was far too important to be left to the specialists. Throughout his writing there is the suggestion that our relationship to space is never neutral but expressive of all the broader contradictions that affect the intensity and clarity of living in a modern context. This aspiration to positively shape the space which we inhabit is, he notes, totally alien to architects and builders. "Yet, beyond the satisfaction of his eliminatory bodily needs, man must also experience space in his home—at least, he must learn to experience it. The home must not be allowed to be an escape from space but a living-in-space, an honest relationship with it."[11]

The question of belonging in modernity requires a fundamental rethinking of our relationship to space. In classical social theory the predominant understanding of this relationship proceeded from a strict polarity which stressed that the traditional home was a place of integration and conformity whereas the modern home is a place of self-expression and freedom. The shift from one position to the other can be heard in every teenager's demand: "I need my own space." It is indicative of the limited frameworks for understanding change in our culture that the space of the past is considered as embedded within a closed territory. This is evident in the classical definitions of community which stressed unity of purpose and the occupation of a given place. The idea that community is formed out of the sharing of not only particular interests by a group of people but a common and universal framework "wide enough and complete enough to include their lives" is looking increasingly remote.[12] Such a view on the question of belonging is now bending to a perspective which stresses that the consequences of industrialisation and global migration have generated looser social affiliations and more hybrid cultural formations. Anthony Giddens has argued that one of the characteristic features of modernity is the destruction of fixed attachments to place. The dynamic of modernity is towards fragmentation and dispersal and therefore all identifications with place are invariably contingent and partial, and inevitably disruptive of the embedded character of traditional social relations. Giddens argues that:

> In traditional societies, the past is honoured and symbols are valued because they contain and perpetuate the experience of generations. Tradition is a means of

handling time and space, which inserts any particular activity or experience within the continuity of past, present and future, these in turn being structured by recurrent social practices.[13]

Modern identity is no longer confirmed by an exclusive and autonomous linkage between time and space. The question 'who am I?' can no longer be answered by identifying our place of origin and the time of living there. Even the most local identities are now influenced by global processes. The disjunctive processes of globalisation and even the defensive strategies of localisation are both defined by a framework of 'time-space distanciation'. Modernity increasingly tears space away from place, and Giddens describes this process of lifting out relationships from local contexts as the disembedding of the social system.[14] Perhaps this ambivalence with the concepts of home and community is expressive of an unresolved yearning for domesticity in an age of excessive mobility.[15]

Modern nostalgia is not a wish to return to the mother's womb. The answer to the dilemmas of the migrant experience is not just to pack up and go home. Few who have left their native village and headed to the foreign city retain the illusion of a triumphal return. It is not just the chilling thought that their place of origin will have changed, leaving them with the sense that they are still out of place, but there is also the wish to claim something for themselves within the new city. Having grown up in the migrant neighbourhoods of Melbourne I've become conscious of how the home is the archetypal test-tube of modernity. Greek migrants were obsessed with home ownership. Not only were loans repaid with record speed and at great personal sacrifice, but the structures of these homes became symbols of their journey. The space for the suburban garden was redrawn into a mini vegetable patch. Neo-classical columns were knocked down and replaced with 'Roman' arches. The sweeping concrete driveway became an expression of cleanliness and order. Whenever I read Homi Bhabha's discussion of the "double frame"[16] of the diasporic aesthetic I think of one of my neighbours who had painted images from his Aegean island within the six inset panels of his front door. Whenever he returned home he would re-see the scenes that were visible from the porch of his father's house: small boats in the harbour and a lighthouse on the cliffs. These 'hand painted postcards' which are like windows on this old Victorian door evoke another world which exists simultaneously in the mind's eye of this householder. This world keeps moving and the current occupants, a family of refugees from Vietnam, when returning home to this door face at least three worlds. Migration is best described as a series of waves. The migrant desires repetition and difference. The migrant home always combines the sensual experience of novelty and familiarity.

A sense of the 'great transformation' ushered in by modernity has been often mapped out in terms of the shift from the 'knowable community' to 'imagined communities'. Traditional communities were considered 'knowable' because most social relations were conducted on a face-to-face basis. Knowledge of others was often determined on the basis of physical and proximate relations or through oral forms of storytelling. By contrast modern societies, as Benedict Anderson pointed out, construct a sense of community out of a much broader social space. The characteristic form of unity in the modern nation is not defined by the 'vertical' development of a local and intimate relation but is an imaginary horizontal association with other members.

> It is imagined because the members of even the smallest nations will never know most of their fellow members, meet them, or even hear of them, yet in the minds of each lives the image of their communion.[17]

How this sense of communion is transmitted in order to consolidate these abstract forms of social bonding is a key question in contemporary thought. Anderson has stressed the importance of the print media and the utilisation of symbols and traditions in the origins of nationalism. Few social theorists have extended this idea to the importance of camera-based media in reconstructing identity in modern society. John Thompson has recently theorised the practice of conducting significant relationships through mediatised technologies as part of the 'remooring of tradition'. "With the development of the media...individuals were able to experience events, observe others and, in general, learn about worlds—both real and imaginary—that extended well beyond the sphere of day-to-day encounters."[18] Mediatised encounters which have scant regard to distance are the ascendant forms of social interaction. The symbolic content in these new forms of communication is in itself expressive of a new relationship to place. Paul Virilio has gone one step further and noted that the impact of new camera-based technologies has fundamentally altered our relationship between perception and agency:

> Everything I see is in principle within my reach, at least within reach of my sight, is marked on the map of the 'I can'. In this important formulation Merleau-Ponty pinpoints precisely what will eventually find itself ruined by the banalization of a certain teletopology. The bulk of what I see is, in fact and in principle, no longer within my reach. And even if it lies within reach of my sight, it is no longer necessarily inscribed on the maps of the 'I can'. The logistics of perception in fact destroys what earlier modes of representation preserved of this original, ideally human happiness, the 'I can' of sight, which kept art from being obscene.[19]

From Virilio's insight into the transformation of the connection between vision and intervention we gain an understanding of both the prevailing blasé attitude in everyday life towards the televisual display of other people's pain, suffering and drama, as well as a hint of the cost of privileging sight as the dominant medium for the linkages of power and knowledge. The enlightenment's elevation of the sense of sight as the ultimate beholder of authority had its limits, and modernity unceasingly pushed itself toward these boundaries. The eye of the enlightenment, with its forward looking fixation, was not entirely detached from the consumerist body of modern culture that both devoured and scorned all signs of backwardness.[20] The presumption that the past was a closed space or that tradition could be reduced to either a manipulable commodity or a reified spectacle that could be inserted within the consumption industry, was symptomatic of the enlightenment view of history as the linear march of progress. Traditions have to be seen as the principles with which a society interprets its place in the world. The construction of tradition as the antonym of modernity was an all too convenient marker for the grand narratives of progress through change. Traditions have become disembedded, or rather the gaps between belief and practice, and the fluidity in the formation of traditions have now become all the more accentuated.

Leaving Home

You won't find a new country, won't find another
shore.
This city will always pursue you.
You'll walk the same streets, grow old
in the same neighbourhoods, turn grey in the same
houses.
You'll always end in this city...

Cavafy

I would like to end by considering the question; 'can we ever leave home?', from the perspective of another question; "what kind of commitments should we give to the home?" Cavafy's poem is a caustic slap against the modern myth that one can escape the past by leaving home. A haunting sense of repetition pumps through the body of the man, who thought that he could leave his old self behind. The dread of eternal return freezes him as if his veins were filled with cold blood. It is a poem that castigates the man who thought he would resolve things by drifting away from the source as it reminds him that that source is always carried within himself. The home is never left behind.

Yet the dream of escaping is a powerful one in our age. From the promiscuous view "wherever I lay my hat that's my home," to the categorical declaration "that you will never see me back home," there is the conviction that one can break with the past and develop new attachments elsewhere. Let me consider these beliefs through a photographic installation of Roger Palmer's in which he explicitly set out to investigate how one responds to a city in which you live but do not belong. The work involved[20] close-up photographs which show castings of Glasgow's coat of arms. The choice of symbol is far from accidental. With a degree of both fondness and sadness Palmer successively stages the decaying spirit of civic pride. Originally each casting had an identical sense of fortitude, but now each is in a different state of blistered, corroded or over-painted transmutation. The signature of the city ages variously according to the strength of local economies. Yet each of these images gives no indication of their location. Place is totally bracketed out from these signs.

Why should these images speak for an artist who has lived for over a decade in Glasgow and who states that "I can be as happy living here as I can be in Capetown, and feel as strange in both these places as I do when I return to the place where I grew up." To feel like this Palmer must position himself like a *flaneur* whose sense of attachment to place is perhaps confined to a form of vision that lightly passes over the surfaces of a city without aiming to disrupt the space. This is neither a boastful cosmopolitanism nor an expression of alienation, nevertheless the haunting air of detachment is unmistakable. Palmer does not give us any insight into what sort of space and time frame he engages with in this city. There is just a slow but abstract display of anonymity in the very signage of place. Does the city mirror back this sense of growing old, being forgotten and leaving without any trace of recognition? Sartre said "Hell is other people," but while they continue to speak of you death and oblivion will have not quite engulfed you. The only way we can break with the past is to pretend that we live in an absolute present. To confine movement to the present is one way of bypassing commitments to space. But as my mother always complained, "your home is not a hotel."

*   *   *

1. Gaston Bachelard, *The Poetics of Space*, trans. by M. Jolas, Beacon Press, Boston.
2. John Berger, ' And our faces, my heart, brief as photos', in *Writers and Readers*, London, 1984, p. 64.
3. Georg Lukacs, *The Theory of the Novel*, trans. A. Bostock, Merlin, London, 1971.
4. This account of Hannah Arendt's life proposed by Richard Sennett clearly exaggerates the asceticism of exile and while it is contradicted by her biographer, it is still revealing of the image of a spiritual homelessness.
5. Theodor Adorno, *Minima Moralia*, trans. by E. Jephcott, Verso, London, 1974.
6. Yuri Lotman, *The Universe of the Mind*, trans. A. Shukman, Tauris, London, 1991.
7. David Morgan, *Family Connections*, Polity Press, Cambridge, 1996, p. 179.
8. To use Steiner's phrase from *Extraterritorial*, London, Faber & Faber, 1972.
9. Le Corbusier, *The Radiant City*, Faber & Faber, London, 1967.
10, Michael Sorkin, ed., *Variations on a Theme Park*, Hill & Wang, New York, 1992.
11. Lazlo Maholy-Nagy, *Man and his House*, Maholy-Nagy, K. Passuth, trans E. Grunz, Thames & Hudson, London, 1985, p. 309.
12. MacIver, 'Society: Its Structure and Changes', quoted in Margaret Wood, *The Stranger: A Study in Social Relationships*, Columbia University Press, New York, 1934, p. 53.
13. Anthony Giddens, *The Consequences of Modernity*, Polity Press, Cambridge, 1990, p. 37.
14. In a parallel vein but with different tones, Nestor Garcia Canclini argues that the traditions which shape contemporary communities are not only no longer bound to specif-

ic locales, but that social theorists overemphasised the way tradition was fixed to a specific place, mired in atavistic rituals and enclosed within specific kinship networks.

15. See "What we suffer most from these days is an excess of domesticity and a nostalgia from mobility." Guillermo Santamarina, 'Recodifying a Non-Existant Field', in *Global Visions*, ed. J. Fisher, Kala Press, London, 1995, p. 23.

16. See Homi Bhabha, *The Location of Culture*, Routledge, London, 1995.

17. Benedict Anderson, *Imagined Communities*, Verso, London, 1983, p. 15.

18. John B. Thompson, *The Media and Modernity*, Polity, Cambridge, 1995, p. 180.

19. Paul Virilio, *The Vision Machine*, Indiana University Press, Bloomington, 1994, p. 7.

20. For a remarkable study of the ubiquity of visual technologies and their effects in the displacements of modernity, see Scott McQuire, *Vision and Modernity*, Sage, London, forthcoming.

The Architect in The Age of Her Mechanical Reproduction
Katerina Ruedi

For a secure market to arise, the superiority of one kind of ser-vices had to be clearly established with regards to competing "products." The various professional services, therefore, had to be standardised in order to clearly differentiate their identity and connect them, in the minds of consumers, with stable criteria of evaluation. A tendency to monopoly by elimination of competing "products" was inherent in the process of standardisation.

Magali Larson

That buildings in the late twentieth century have become commodi-ties to be consumed is difficult to dispute, although many architects and the occasional prince would very much like this not to be true. That architects themselves have become commodities is perhaps more difficult to swallow because it suggests that the identity of architects is beyond the control of the individual architects them-selves. It implies that the architect is not only produced (or repro-duced) but also consumed; that 'he' occupies both sides of the binary divide; that he may be male or female; producer and seller in one.

In the nineteenth and twentieth centuries, the parallel between the professionalisation of occupations and the containment of desire lay in their absorption into discourses of control designed to ensure docile bodies and codifiable practices. With the rise of cheap printing and photography, knowledge, like objects, had become freely avail-able. This posed a threat to the status of architects. New occupational groups tried to claim the right to previously elite knowledge; the pro-fessional institutes came into being to protect their expertise, dis-course of ethics, aesthetics and technical skills. The reproducibility of the professional is not a new idea. Larson explains why and how this process takes place:

for a professional market to exist in a modern sense, a distinctive 'commodity' had to be produced. Now professional work, like any other form of labour, is only a fictitious commodity; "it cannot be detached from the rest of life, be stored or mobilised...it follows therefore that the producers themselves have to be produced if their products or commodities are to be given a distinctive form."

In the nineteenth century, the professions sought to control their own reproducibility through an alliance with the state and its legitimisation of formal education. Education became the assembly-line of architects as commodities.

Under Fordism, product quality was ensured by conformity to a (relatively) standard specification: the possession of planning and constructional knowledge formed the usefulness of the commodity; ethics and aesthetics formed its simulated exclusivity, but were subservient. The body of the stereotypical architect was attached, during this period of education, to a finite range of abilities defined by social need. Ideally, through this long immersion within professionally approved standard educational curriculum and practical training, he was to carry a professional warranty.

From the end of the nineteenth century onwards, entry in to professional practice was therefore only through state education; the professional entered the 'serial form'. Theory finally separated from practice and apprenticeship gave way to educational institutions. The university formed the ideal counterpart to the factory; the instrument through which homogenous technocratic knowledge was reproduced. The body of knowledge that constitutes the 'proper' focus of the profession is therefore not permitted to become decentered, fluid, desiring. Professionalism does not easily tolerate heterogeneity; it still dwells within the unreconstructed house of Fordism.

Yet the external world is more complex than the profession imagines. Governments and multi-national capital, having nurtured the Victorian childhood and Fordist adulthood of the professions, have found that, in order to be sold in the global market place, the 'old boy' must be fragmented, moulded and reconstructed as a 'montage of attractions' to be deliriously consumed, in other words, as a 'new gift'.

de-, dis-, ex-.

Architects have entered new territories; in the post-Fordist era they are designing film sets, furniture, LP covers; they are acting as management contractors and developers; they are writing, drawing, making installations. They are changing jobs more often and getting paid less and less, becoming casualised part-time workers of post-Fordism. Architecture and architects could be called 'empty vessels to be filled by capital's desire'. The profession's assembly line can no longer save the architect's bacon.

Education, too, has been plunged into the free market. Part-time, badly paid staff are a feature of the hippest, most 'post-modern' schools. Students assemble 'modular' courses and are called customers, implying that the staff are to be consumed; yet are defined in quotas, implying that the staff are producing them. Practising architects 'assemble' teams specifically for a single project; clients assemble management teams. The AJ recently reported that a group of clients (incidentally, female) 'designed and manufactured' their own multi-headed architect from several independent individuals. Yet, in a panic, the profession, losing their role as designers and quality controllers of their 'architectural product', rather than inventing new ones, continue with ever greater determination to protect the 'old boy' through its manufacturing process: education. Education that does not fit the picture labelled 'not-architecture'. Architectural knowledge is as defensively policed as in the nineteenth century, when the profession came into being.

Architecture is conventionally seen to reside in a material object which it seems cannot be reduced simply to its mechanical reproduction. The reapropriation of the activities of the architect ought, therefore, to be far harder than, say, those of the lawyer and the accountant. Why then is the architect's traditional territory shrinking? Why do architects in the UK, as in the USA, continue to work on only 20% of building commissions? Have they, like their buildings, become commodities—reproducible, codifiable, exchangeable, consumable, yet of little interest to the consuming public? And, when 90% of practising architects are male, where would that leave the identity and the future of architecture?

The Oxford Art Journal has an international
reputation for publishing innovative critical work
in art history, and has played a major role in
recent rethinking of the discipline.
It is committed to the political analysis of visual
art and material culture and to a critical engagement with problems of representation, in the
belief that a radical re-examination of the visual
has a broad cultural significance.
It represents a diversity of theoretical and political concerns, probing in-depth the real difficulties involved in analysing art and culture.

Following on the heels of the Africa '95' celebrations in London the Oxford Art
Journal has brought out an issue concentrating on post-colonial issues in art history
- Volume 19, Issue 1

ARTICLES TO COME IN VOLUME 19 ISSUE 2
WILLIAM VAUGHAN Constable's England
STANLEY MITCHELL On Mikhail Lifshitz

Subscription Rates, VOL 19 (2 issues))
Institutions £44/US$80
Individuals £25/US$48
Special Offer for new subscribers:
£20/US$38

OXFORD
ART
JOURNAL

Contact Oxford University Press on:
telephone: +44 (0) 1865 267907 fax: +44 (0) 1865 267485
or visit our website at: http://www.oup.co.uk/oxartj/

Goldsmiths
UNIVERSITY
OF LONDON

STUDY ART HISTORY
AT
GOLDSMITHS
UNIVERSITY OF LONDON

We offer art history studies at both
undergraduate and postgraduate levels:

MA ART HISTORY AND THEORY IN THE MODERN PERIOD
POSTGRADUATE DIPLOMA IN ART HISTORY
BA (HONS) ART HISTORY
BA (HONS) ART HISTORY WITH ART PRACTICE
BA (HONS) ART HISTORY WITH ENGLISH
BA (HONS) ART HISTORY WITH HISTORY

For prospectus and application form, contact the Admissions Office,
Goldsmiths, University of London, New Cross, London, SE14 6NW

tel. 0171 919 7171

Take a new look at the contemporary world of film in **Screen**. From pop videos to art films, film noir to third world cinema, **Screen** keeps pace with the changing world of film. Discover the latest developments in film television, and cultural theory in the lively and provocative articles of **Screen**.

Screen is acclaimed as a contemporary media studies journal. Founded nearly forty years ago by the Society for Education in Film and Television (SEFT), **Screen** established itself as the leading international journal dedicated to the advanced study of film and television. Since 1990 the journal has been edited by the John Logie Baird Centre (Glasgow) and published by **Oxford University Press**. It includes an expanded reviews section and forthcoming events, and debates on the latest issues in the world of film.

Recent Articles

Erich Smoodin This Business of America: Fan Mail, Film Reception, and *Meet John Doe*
John Gabriel What Do You Do When Minority Means You? *Falling Down* and the Construction of Whiteness
Sue Harper and Vincent Porter Moved to Tears: Weeping in the Cinema in Postwar Britain
Ben Gove Framing Gay Youth
Shelley Stamp Lindsey Is Any Girl Safe? Female Spectators and White Slave Films

frieze

AVOID
ALL CONTACT

Subscribe and never go out

Individuals £22.50 Institutions £27

Please send a cheque made payable to frieze, together with your order, to
21 Denmark Street, London WC2H 8NA, UK

Acknowledgments

For financial assistance, without which this publication would not have been possible, we would like to express our gratitude to the Department of Historical and Cultural Studies at Goldsmiths' College, University of London.

Our deepest thanks go to those who have generously contributed texts and projects to this first volume. We regret, due to space constraints, that work by the following could not appear in this volume but will appear in the future: Art in Ruins, Graham Marsden, David Reason, Gavin Turk and Artur Zagula.

We acknowledge the following sources where texts have previously appeared: Susan Kandel 'Theory as Phantom Text: Plundering Smithson's Non-Sites' an earlier version of which was published in *frieze* magazine as 'The Non-Site of Theory', Issue 22, May 1995. Peter Halley 'Against Postmodernism: Reconsidering Ortega', was originally published in Peter Halley, *Collected Essays 1981-1987*. A substantially abridged version of Nikos Papastergiadis' 'The Home in Modernity', is to appear in the *INIVA Review*, vol. 1, issue no. 1, 1996. Jon Thompson, 'In the Groves of Philadelphia—A Female Hanging', was originally published in *Terme Celeste*, Summer 1992, no. 36.

We would also like to thank the following: Claire Alexander, Howard Caygill, Mr J.R & Mrs N.G Coles, Robert Gober, Duncan McCorquodale, Lisa Robertson, Sherrie Levine, Clifton Steinberg, Wendy Dimond, Margo Leavin Gallery, Los Angeles, Jon Weber Gallery, New York, and MoMA, New York.

Design and Layout: Simon Goodwin at **workspace** (tel/fax: +44 171 241 2725)
Design Consultant: Paul Khera
Copy Editing: Maria Wilson
Printed by: **Graphite Inc Ltd** (tel: +44 181 289 5555)

de-, dis-, ex-.